The World of Rome is an introduction to the history and culture of Rome for students at university and at school as well as for anyone seriously interested in the ancient world. It covers all aspects of the city – its rise to power, what made it great and why it still engages and challenges us today.

The first two chapters outline the history and changing identity of Rome from 100 BC to AD 476. Subsequent chapters examine the mechanisms of government (from Republic to Empire), the economic and social life of Rome (the city of Rome, production and consumption, the family) and Roman ways of looking at and reflecting the world (ideology, literature, art and architecture). An epilogue discusses continuing Roman influence in language, culture, architecture.

Drawing on the latest scholarship, the book has been edited to make a coherent whole, and cross-referencing between sections allows the reader to make connections between history, institutions, values and environment. All this, in addition to frequent quotations from ancient writers and numerous illustrations, makes this a stimulating, up-to-date and accessible introduction to ancient Rome.

The World of Rome (a companion to *The World of Athens* published by Cambridge University Press in 1984) is particularly designed to serve as a background book to *Reading Latin* by the same authors (Cambridge University Press 1986).

The World of Rome

Statue of Augustus from Prima Porta

The World of Rome

AN INTRODUCTION TO ROMAN CULTURE

Edited by

Peter Jones
Senior Lecturer in Classics at the
University of Newcastle upon Tyne

and

Keith Sidwell
Senior Lecturer in Classics at
St Patrick's College, Maynooth

CAMBRIDGE
UNIVERSITY PRESS

PUBLISHED BY THE PRESS SYNDICATE OF THE UNIVERSITY OF CAMBRIDGE
The Pitt Building, Trumpington Street, Cambridge CB2 1RP, United Kingdom

CAMBRIDGE UNIVERSITY PRESS
The Edinburgh Building, Cambridge CB2 2RU, United Kingdom
40 West 20th Street, New York, NY 10011–4211, USA
10 Stamford Road, Oakleigh, Melbourne 3166, Australia

First published 1997

Printed in the United Kingdom at the University Press, Cambridge

Typeset in Monotype Sabon 10/12 pt

A *catalogue record for this book is available from the British Library*

Library of Congress cataloguing in publication data

The world of Rome : an introduction to Roman culture / edited by Peter
    Jones and Keith Sidwell.
        p.   cm.
    Includes indexes.
    ISBN 0 521 38421 4 (hardback) – ISBN 0 521 38600 4 (paperback)
    1. Rome–Civilization.   I. Jones, P. V. (Peter V.)   II. Sidwell,
    Keith C.
    DG77.W73   1997
    937dc20   96–23376
                                                                    CIP

ISBN 0 521 38421 4 hardback
ISBN 0 521 38600 4 paperback

SE

CONTENTS

PREFACE

This volume was conceived during the preparation of *Reading Latin* (Cambridge University Press 1986). It was intended that it should fulfil the same role as does *The World of Athens* (Cambridge University Press 1984) for *Reading Greek* (Cambridge University Press 1978) – that is, that it should be both a 'background book' for a Latin language course and an introduction to Roman history, society and culture. The project began to take firm shape, however, only after *Reading Latin* had been published. In 1989 we began to invite contributions and in 1990 work began on the book in the following manner.

The initial proposal was laid before the contributors, who met with the editors to discuss the project. This process continued over a period of three years, and resulted in large-scale changes to the original plan as well as smaller changes to individual contributions as they came in. In this way, we hoped to avoid that tendency to intellectual incoherence which is often the hallmark of collaborative books. It has not been possible to avoid differences of emphasis or of intellectual approach among the contributors: but then that would not have been desirable. The existence of such divergences among those who practise the art of Roman history has to become known to students sooner or later. Sooner is better.

The result is, we hope, still both coherent and accessible. The problems we faced were daunting. To produce a reasonably-sized (and reasonably-priced) introduction to Rome, with its vast chronological spread and geographical diversity, was never going to be easy. In the end, it seemed that the best plan was to attempt to provide a very broad intellectual framework for understanding the Roman world both as it was developing and as it later crystallised (from Republic, then to Empire), and to illustrate and argue from specific evidence, so that the vagueness of generality never overwhelmed the student. A book of this kind cannot hope to say everything which is necessary about Rome. But it does aim to ask the central questions which have to be asked if we are to have an up-to-date model for comprehending an ancient – and alien – culture. And it provides a series of snapshots of crucial moments from that culture which make concrete its dynamics.

We would like to offer here our warmest thanks to the contributors (listed below), who gave unstintingly of their time and energy to make this project possible and to bring it to completion. Professor Roger Ling merits particular mention for his sterling efforts with the pictures, a massive task for a book like this, with magnificent results. The editors also owe a debt of gratitude to Cambridge University Press for undertaking to promote a volume which required a large investment prior to publication. We are grateful to Ciara Kierans for her work on various of the indexes.

Peter Jones   Newcastle upon Tyne
Keith Sidwell   Maynooth
December 1995

CONTRIBUTORS

JEREMY PATERSON (chapters 1, 2 and 6) is Senior Lecturer in Classics at the University of Newcastle on Tyne.

JOHN RICHARDSON (chapters 3 and 4) is Professor of Classics at the University of Edinburgh.

NICHOLAS PURCELL (chapters 1, 2 and 5) is Fellow and Tutor in Ancient History at St John's College, Oxford.

ANDREW WALLACE-HADRILL (chapter 6) is Director of the British School at Rome and Professor of Classics at the University of Reading.

SIMON PRICE (chapter 8) is Fellow and Tutor in Ancient History at Lady Margaret Hall, Oxford.

JOHN BARSBY (chapter 9, Appendix 2) is Professor of Classics at the University of Otago, New Zealand.

ROGER LING (chapter 10, and pictorial consultant) is Professor of Classical Art and Archaeology at the University of Manchester.

KEITH SIDWELL (chapter 9 and Epilogue) is Senior Lecturer in Classics at St Patrick's College, Maynooth.

LIST OF MAPS AND ILLUSTRATIONS

Maps

Note: The purpose of these maps is simply to show the position of places, regions, provinces and buildings mentioned in the text. They do not represent the Roman world at any particular chronological point, and no consistent attempt has been made to include places that are not in the text. For historical maps, see further N. G. L. Hammond, *Atlas of the Greek and Roman World in Antiquity*, Park Ridge, NJ, 1981.

Illustrations

NOTES

1 The following abbreviations are used for epigraphic sources (i.e. inscriptions) both in the text and in the Index of Passages:

CIL	Corpus Inscriptionum Latinarum
E & J	V. Ehrenberg and A.H.M. Jones, *Documents Illustrating the Reigns of Augustus and Tiberius*
ILS	H. Dessau, *Inscriptiones Latinae Selectae*
OGIS	W. Dittenberger, *Orientis Graecae Inscriptiones Selectae*
RIB	*Roman Inscriptions in Britain*
SEG	*Supplementum Epigraphicum Graecum*
SIG	W. Dittenberger, *Sylloge Inscriptionum Graecarum*
Tab. Vindol.	A.K. Bowman and J.D. Thomas, *The Vindolanda Writing-Tablets Tabulae Vindolanenses* II

2 Freeborn Roman citizens had three names. These were (1) the *praenomen* (or forename), which is usually abbreviated (see below); (2) the *nomen* (*gens* 'clan' name); (3) the *cognomen* (name of the *familia* 'household', sometimes derived from some exploit of the person or an ancestor). In this book the full name (or if that is not known, as many names as are known) is usually given upon first appearance, with the normal abbreviation. This is either the *cognomen* (e.g. Caesar, Cicero), or the *nomen* (e.g. Virgil, Ovid). The following are the commonest *praenomina* with their abbreviations:

Aulus = A.   Gaius = C.
Decimus = D.   Gnaeus = Cn.

Lucius = L.   Publius = P.
Marcus = M.   Quintus = Q.
Manius = M'   Sextus = S.

3 The official language of Rome was Latin. Latin and Greek (the senior cultural partner) were used to write major histories of Rome from the earliest period. They are indispensable tools for the budding Roman historian. You can begin to learn Latin from this book's companion textbook, *Reading Latin: Text* and *Grammar, Vocabulary and Exercises*, (2 vols., Cambridge University Press, 1986, by the editors of this volume) and progress to later Latin with *Reading Medieval Latin* (Keith Sidwell, Cambridge University Press, 1995). For Greek, we recommend the JACT Greek Course, *Reading Greek* (Cambridge University Press, 1978) and its companion volumes.

4 We have included many Latin (and a few Greek) terms, some Latin phrases and sentences, and one complete poem in Latin. All are translated where they occur. Latin terms can be found, with literal translations and references to their occurrence in the text, in one of the indexes. Since they are used in both singular and plural, you need to be aware of the way Latin nouns form their plurals:

(1) Singulars in *-a* change to *-ae* (e.g. *matrona/matronae*).
(2) Singulars in *-us* change to *-i* (e.g. *amicus/amici*), or to *-us* with long *u* (e.g. *domus/domus*).
(3) Singulars in *-um* change to *-a* (e.g. *plebiscitum/plebiscita*).
(4) Singulars in *-io* change to *-iones* (e.g. *rogatio/rogationes*).
(5) A further group has singulars in a variety of endings (e.g. *-is/-tor/-ns/-ps*), but plurals in *-es* (e.g. *classis/classes, coactor/ coactores, cliens/clientes, princeps/principes*).

5 Latin words are printed in the text with consonantal *-u-* (pronounced *-w-*), not *-v-*. Thus we print *auaritia*, not *avaritia* (English 'avarice').

6 Cross-references are made to JACT, *The World of Athens: An Introduction to Classical Athenian Culture* (Cambridge University Press, 1984), by the abbreviation *WoA*.

7 The book is arranged for reference purposes by paragraphs numbered 1–505 through the book. Cross-references in square brackets in the text are to these paragraph numbers. Paragraph numbers are also referred to in the Indexes and Appendices.

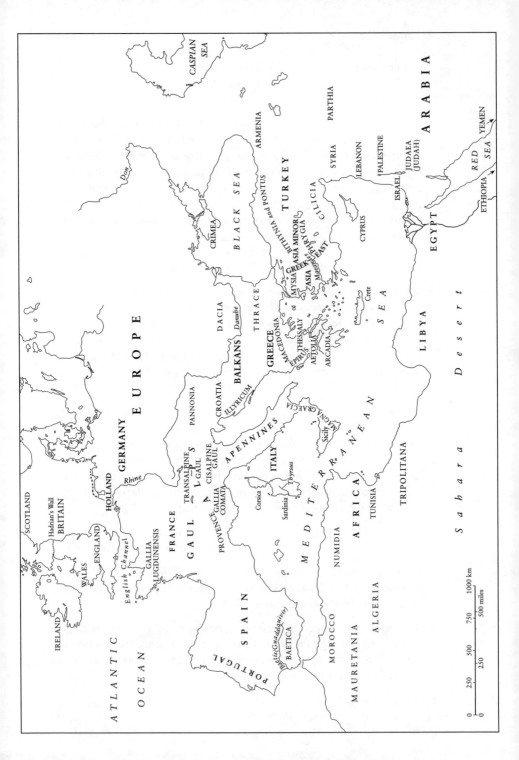

Map 1 The world of Rome

Map 2 The West

Map 3 Greece and the Near East

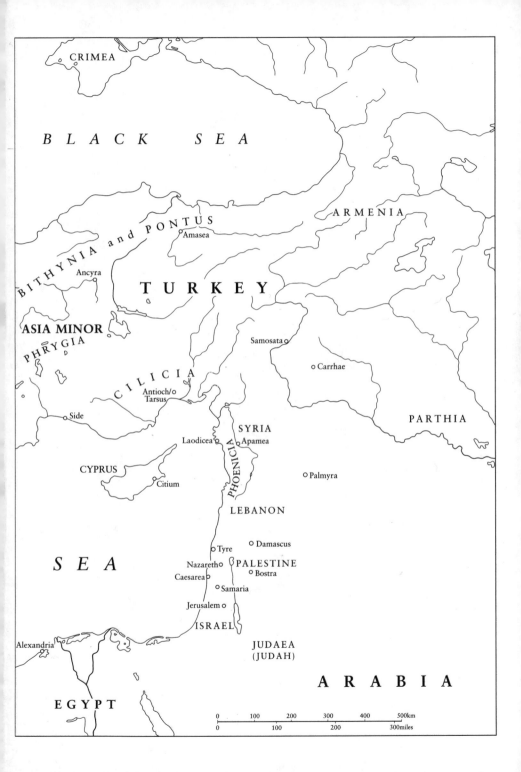

CRIMEA

BLACK SEA

ARMENIA

BITHYNIA and PONTUS

Amasea

Ancyra

TURKEY

ASIA MINOR

PHRYGIA

Samosata

Carrhae

CILICIA

PARTHIA

Side

Antioch/
Tarsus

SYRIA

Laodicea Apamea

PHOENICIA

CYPRUS

Palmyra

Citium

LEBANON

SEA

Damascus

Tyre

Nazareth PALESTINE

Caesarea Bostra

Samaria

Jerusalem

ISRAEL

Alexandria

JUDAEA
(JUDAH)

ARABIA

EGYPT

| 0 | 100 | 200 | 300 | 400 | 500km |
| 0 | | 100 | | 200 | 300miles |

Map 4 Italy

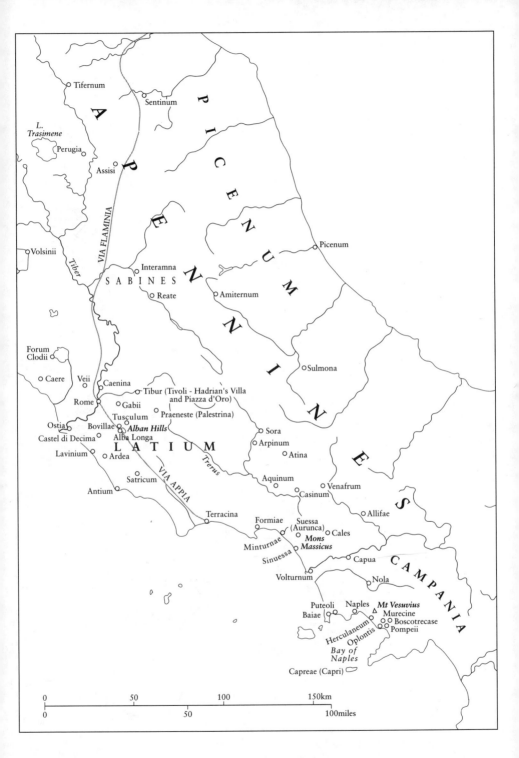

Map 5 Central Italy

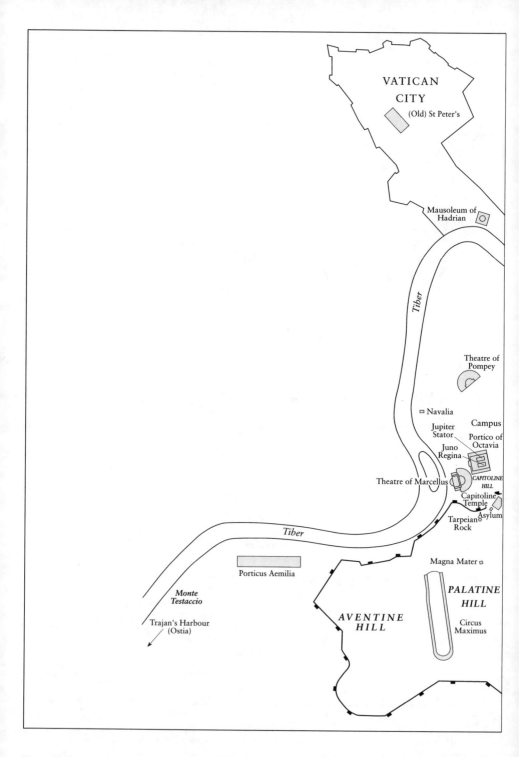

Map 6 The city of Rome

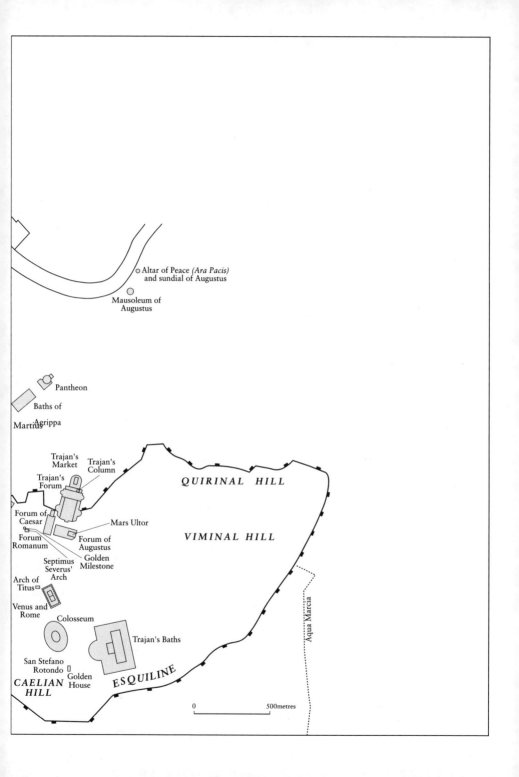

Altar of Peace *(Ara Pacis)*
and sundial of Augustus

Mausoleum of
Augustus

Pantheon

Baths of
Agrippa
Martius

Trajan's
Market
Trajan's
Column

Trajan's
Forum

QUIRINAL HILL

Forum of
Caesar

Mars Ultor

VIMINAL HILL

Forum
Romanum
Forum of
Augustus

Septimus
Severus'
Arch
Golden
Milestone

Arch of
Titus

Venus and
Rome

Colosseum

Aqua Marcia

Trajan's Baths

San Stefano
Rotondo
Golden
House

CAELIAN
HILL

ESQUILINE

0   500metres

1

The idea of Rome (753–31 BC)

1. To begin with a famous story. Paul, the early Christian missionary, was arrested by the Roman authorities in Jerusalem in, perhaps, AD 58 because his presence had caused his opponents to riot against him. The commander of the Roman garrison ordered Paul to be detained and flogged:

> But when they tied him up for the lash, Paul said to the centurion who was standing there, 'Can you legally flog a man who is a Roman citizen, and moreover has not been found guilty?' When the centurion heard this, he went and reported it to the commandant. 'What do you mean to do?' he said. 'This man is a Roman citizen.' The commandant came to Paul. 'Tell me, are you a Roman citizen?' he asked. 'Yes', said he. The commandant rejoined, 'It cost me a large sum to acquire this citizenship.' Paul said, 'But it was mine by birth.' (Acts of the Apostles 22.25ff.)

2. Paul was a Greek-speaking Jew from Tarsus, an important city in southern Cilicia (in south-east Turkey), which had been incorporated in the Roman empire over a century earlier. From his father he had inherited his status as a citizen of Rome, a city which at this time he had never been near. Claudius Lysias, the commander of the garrison, was also a Roman citizen. He was probably a Greek from the eastern Mediterranean who had been a slave in the service of the emperor Claudius. He had bought his freedom and had thus become a Roman citizen by taking on the status of his master, as was normal in such cases. The pointed exchange between these two citizens of Rome raises the question about just what we mean by the term 'Roman'. In what sense was Paul a Roman? Was his feeling of 'Romanness' different from that of Claudius Lysias? Was their idea of Rome very different from that held by, for example, a senator from the city two centuries earlier? If this were a book about ancient Athens, there would be no great difficulty in pinning down the essential features of what was distinctive about being an Athenian. But there is no simple way to explain the idea of Rome, to define what was Roman about what we

1

call Roman. In the process of winning its empire, Rome itself was fundamentally transformed. The stages of that transformation are recorded in the chapters which follow. The rich complexity of the changing and evolving idea of Rome is, perhaps, the most distinctive aspect of 'Romanness'.

In the beginning

3. At the height of Rome's power at the end of the first century BC, scholars sought explanations for Rome's astonishing success. Vitruvius, the writer on architecture, saw it as the inevitable outcome of Rome's geographical position:

> The fact is that the peoples of Italy have the optimum constitution in both respects – both in physique and in the mental intelligence that is a match for their valour . . . It was, therefore, a divine intelligence that placed the city of the Roman people in an excellent and temperate country, so that she might acquire the right to rule over the whole world. (*On Architecture* 6.1.11)

4. This explanation, however, has little to commend it. As the history of the late Empire showed, Rome was very inconveniently sited as a centre for a large empire. By the fourth century AD Rome had become a backwater, rarely visited by emperors, who spent their time in the palaces and cities, such as Milan, Aquileia, Constantinople, and Nicaea, strung out along the great east–west road which formed the vital communication corridor across Europe. All roads did not lead to Rome. But at another level its geographical position can explain the early prominence and exceptional growth of the site of Rome in central Italy. At the point where the Tiber valley opens up to the coastal plain, the Palatine and Capitoline Hills provided easily defensible sites, overlooking the lowest convenient crossing-point on the river. From as early as the ninth century BC routes ran from here down to the saltpans at the mouth of the Tiber, up the river, into Sabine territory, past important Etruscan centres, such as Veii, and on into the interior of Umbria. The inland route to the south ran past the centres of Gabii and Praeneste, down into the valley of the Trerus, while yet another swung round the base of the Alban Hills to connect the line of early communities there, Castel di Decima, Lavinium, Ardea and Satricum and then on down into south Latium. Rome was the key to this network.

5. It is likely that such a strategic site will have attracted human occupation from the earliest of times. However, it is from the very end of the Bronze Age and the beginning of the Iron Age, that is from about 1000 BC, that we have clear evidence of continuous occupation of the central region of Rome, the Forum and the Palatine, and the Quirinal. By the end of the seventh century BC these small villages of huts (figs. 1.1 and 1.2) had joined together to form

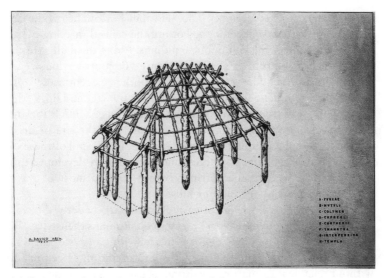

1.1 Reconstruction drawing of a hut in the early Iron Age village on the Palatine in Rome.

1.2 Etruscan hut-urn from Veii; such ash-urns were modelled on the contemporary houses of the living.

the first true urban community. The wet valley bottom below the Capitol was drained and paved to become the Forum, the central meeting-place. Around this were to appear the first public buildings. Along the main street out of the Forum the principal citizens resided in houses of considerable size which were to provide the best addresses in Rome for another six centuries [325ff.]. Down by the Tiber temples rose above the merchant quarter and dock which linked Rome to the seaborne commerce of the Mediterranean. High above the Forum the Capitol became an acropolis for the city and the site of an enormous temple to the cult of Jupiter Best and Greatest. By the end of the sixth century Rome was already by far the largest, most elaborately developed urban site in the region, with a sizeable territory which covered most of the plain and extended up into the surrounding hills.

6. Our modern knowledge of early Rome is largely derived from archaeology. Little of this can have been known to the Romans themselves. They came late to the writing of their history (the first Roman historian was Quintus Fabius Pictor, a Roman senator of the end of the third century BC). Even without reliable information, the Romans had to explain their origins. In the ancient Greek world cities often had a 'city-protecting god' and a myth which told of the beginnings of the city, emphasising features which were thought to be really important. The Roman foundation myth was a very complex one. It was also different from the Greek ones in the way in which it did not point up positive elements like good order or natural advantages. Far from it. It focused instead on things which were agreed to be bad – wildness, exile, rootlessness, brutality and killing. Romulus and Remus were the miraculous sons of Mars, the god associated with the pointless fury of war. Turned out of their household, they were exposed to the savagery of nature, only to be rescued and suckled by a she-wolf, the animal that in the ancient countryside most commonly embodied ferocity (fig. 1.3). Wolves were a terrible and common threat, with none of the grand dignity attributed, alongside violence, to the lion. Later the twins were reared by shepherds, who of all people were considered to be outsiders and uncivilised. When they grew up they decided to found a city in the region where they had been exposed; but in a quarrel over who should have the right to found the city, Romulus killed his brother. He went on to establish Rome by encouraging the homeless and vagabonds of Italy to come to the city and take refuge at the Asylum. The son of his father, he added to these resources by pillaging his neighbours, and abducting from the neighbouring Sabines the womenfolk that his community needed. That the Romans said all this about their early days tells us much about their view of the world in the late Republic and early Empire.

7. Another common thing to say about your beginnings in antiquity was

1.3 Shepherds discovering the wolf suckling Romulus and Remus.

that your ancestors had made a long journey from elsewhere to found your community. In Italy, ancient connections with the Greek world were often given a background in the myth of Herakles (=Hercules) and his wanderings, or of the stories of the wanderings of heroes and their followers which followed the Trojan war – tales made famous in the epics of Homer. The Romulus story did not fit easily into this type of myth. Hercules made an appearance in the original stories, and was worshipped at a Great Altar, appropriately in the part of Rome where the river-harbour on the Tiber encouraged the settlement of people from overseas. But the Romans found a way of tying themselves into the world of Greece and its history in the story of Aeneas, the Trojan hero (fig. 7.1; cf. [301, 475]), who wandered the world after the sack of Troy, before settling in central Italy to found the community into which Romulus and Remus were later to be born (*WoA*, H.I.1–3). By the fourth century BC there was a cult to Aeneas at the sacred centre of Lavinium, in which Roman magistrates were involved. It is likely that the Aeneas myth became popular at the very time when Rome started to be of significance in the wider world of the Mediterranean, and it took its definitive form in the epic, the *Aeneid*, which Virgil wrote to glorify the Rome of the first emperor, Augustus.

Founding fathers

8. The historians of Rome had the city ruled for two and a half centuries by Etruscan kings. Romulus was succeeded by Numa Pompilius, Tullus Hostilius, Ancus Marcius, Tarquinius Priscus, Servius Tullius, Tarquinius Superbus. Little of certainty can be said about them. Indeed, only seven kings seems improbably few for such a long period of time. But there is no need to doubt the existence of the institution or the historical reality of, at least, the last three kings. Indeed, the first Tarquinius is associated with major building works in Rome, and his reign belongs to the end of the seventh century, precisely the time that archaeology reveals the first large civic buildings in the centre of the city.

9. Tradition ascribed to the kings the creation of many of the fundamental institutions and social structures that were characteristic of Rome later. In writing about them, historians borrowed models from the Greek world for this as well. So Numa, who established many aspects of Roman religion, has more than a hint of the Spartan founder-hero, Lycurgus, or the Athenian reformer Solon (*WoA*, H.I.8). Servius, who reorganised the citizen body, has close similarities to Cleisthenes of Athens (*WoA*, H.I.11). The picture of the Tarquins was elaborated from the stories told of Periander and Peisistratos, the archetypal tyrants of sixth-century Greece (*WoA*, H.I.9–10).

10. The society of Rome and Italy in the sixth century BC has been illuminated by an ever-increasing number of inscriptions, particularly from the cities of Etruria. They reveal a world in which men of influence moved easily from community to community with their families and retainers. The *gens* (clan) was an important institution. It consisted of a group of families who claimed descent from a common ancestor and in the sixth century the practice grew up of individuals identifying themselves by adding the name of a *gens* to a personal name (e.g. Publius (personal name: *praenomen*) Valerius (*nomen* of the *gens* Valerii). This is a world where loyalty to family and clan is greater than any identification with a civic community. An inscription from Satricum (*Lapis Satricanus*: fig. 1.4), an important community to the south of Rome, reveals the existence of a group of *sodales* ('retainers', 'friends', 'companions') of Publius Valerius about 500 BC. It is not unreasonable to identify Valerius as the aristocrat who played an important role in the early years of the Roman Republic. The historical tradition, too, preserves memories of this world of clan-leaders. Titus Tatius, king of the Sabines, was supposedly

1.4 Inscription of P. Valerius from Satricum (*Lapis Satricanus*).

invited by Romulus to share in his rule in Rome. More historical is the story that the king, Tarquinius Priscus, was an émigré from the Etruscan city of Tarquinii. In the early years of the Republic Attus Clausus, the ancestor of the great Roman *gens* the Claudii, migrated to Rome 'accompanied by a large company of clients' and was granted land and citizenship. One of the most abiding features of Roman history is the continued importance of aristocratic individuals, whose primary loyalties were at all times to their families and followers, and who only reluctantly, and never completely, subordinated their own interests to those of the broader state [144, 207]. The early history of Rome is littered with the stories of their heroic activities. Look, for example, at the story of how, in the middle of the fifth century BC, the whole *gens* of the Fabii marched out on behalf of Rome to fight Veii (they were defeated and were all killed, except for one survivor from the 306 who set out. He was to keep the family line going).

11. The kings can be viewed simply as clan-chiefs who gained a recognition for their leadership from the community. In Roman terms they were invested with *imperium*, a key concept, which designated the acknowledged right to give orders to those of lower status and expect them to be obeyed (see also chapter 3 *passim*). This power was at all times ill-defined, wide-ranging, and arbitrary. From the start a vital way in which this *imperium* could be expressed was in imposing by war the holder's authority and that of Rome on neighbouring communities who were thought to have challenged it. Conquest was an integral part of the Roman view of themselves. They believed that from the very start Rome's generals and soldiers almost every year marched out, fought and humbled an enemy and returned in triumph. The great Register of Triumphs (*Fasti triumphales*: fig. 1.5; cf. [128] and fig. 3.2) which the emperor Augustus built into his own victory monument in the Forum started with Romulus' victory over the village of Caenina [128]. The early foes may have been puny, but they were the first steps on the path that led to confrontation with Hannibal and the kings of the East. *Imperium* was the word which the

1.5 Detail of the *Fasti Triumphales*, inscribed on Augustus' Parthian Arch in the Roman Forum. This section covers the break-up of the Latin League and the wars against the Samnites. Cf. [85, 150].

Romans came to use for their domination in the world. For them the Roman empire began with Romulus.

No kings please, we're Roman

12. It is a curiosity of early Roman history that at some key turning-points we find stories about women. Perhaps the most famous of these was of Lucretia, whose cynical rape by a son of the king, Tarquininus Superbus, and subsequent suicide enraged a noble, Lucius Junius Brutus, and drove him to expel the king and his family from Rome about 510/509 BC. The romantic stories of the expulsion of the Tarquins were greatly elaborated in the literary tradition. But there is no need to doubt that a revolution took place and that its leaders came from within the Roman aristocracy. Similar tussles between powerful aristocrats and hereditary one-man rule were taking place at much this time in South Italy, Sicily and Greece. What is important is the way in which later Roman historians characterised the political change which came about in 510/509 BC. For centuries to come hatred of the idea of domination by one man was central to the way in which the institutions of the Republic developed. When the monarchy was overthrown, the question became: who now was to exercise the *imperium* which the kings had had? For Livy (2.1) 'you could reckon the origins of freedom as lying more in the fact that the *imperium* held by the consuls lasted only a year than in any diminution of the powers which the kings once held' [120].

13. The key features of the consulship, the office or 'magistracy' which replaced the kingship, were:

(1) Appointment by election by an assembly of the Roman people.
(2) Tenure of the post limited to one year. In normal circumstances a consul could not be immediately re-elected to office.
(3) Collegiality: there were to be two magistrates with equal *imperium*. Never again, in normal circumstances, would a single individual be invested with supreme *imperium*.
(4) Accountability: at some point, perhaps quite early on, the principle was established that a magistrate could be called to account for his actions after the end of his period of office (see chapters 3 and 4).

14. The first two centuries of the Republic were a time of continuous experimentation and change. Indeed, the reality is that the Republican system was at all stages of its existence in a state of change. It was only the writers of the revolutionary period of the last century BC who looked back wistfully to an idealised period of stability at some point in the past [157]. The Republic had what Marxist historians would call inherent contradictions right from the start. The seeds of its downfall were sown at its beginning.

15. As Rome's horizons and obligations broadened, so there was a need for more and new offices. Quite early on, perhaps about 501 BC, it was realised that in times of emergency it might be essential for there to be one person in control. So the dictatorship was created, despite the fact that it offended against the principle of collegiality [134]. The *dictator* was invested with supreme power for a very limited period of time. Tradition has it that in the middle of the fifth century the normal political system was suspended to enable the creation of a board of ten men (*decemuiri*) to carry out the creation and publication of Rome's first law code. Soon after, from 444 BC, in most years no consuls were appointed. Instead, a number of officials with the title of 'Military Tribune with the Power of a Consul' are found in most years down to 366 BC, when the consulship became regular again. It is likely that these magistrates were a reflection of the large number of military activities in which Rome was involved in this period. The public duties of the consuls grew to such an extent that a whole range of other magistrates was created gradually and in piecemeal fashion to take on parts of the administration [130–1]. The origin of the quaestors, for example, who exercised control of public

finances, is unclear, but it lay in the early Republic, became an elective office in 447 BC, and was increased to four holders per year in 421 BC [136]. There were two colleges of aediles, who looked after the markets; the so-called plebeian aediles were created in 494 BC, while the curule aediles were first elected in 366 BC [138]. The appointment of two censors to draw up the lists of citizens was made for the first time in 443 BC [139]. The praetorship, an important judicial post, was created in 366 BC [132].

Conflict of the orders

16. So the administrative machinery of the Roman Republic emerged as a body of annual magistrates, advised by a 'Senate' (group of *senes,* 'old men') which consisted [166], at least in part, of men who had already held some of these posts. Adult male citizens were called together in assembly (*comitia*) to elect the magistrates and to vote on proposals put to them by a presiding magistrate. Right from the start the key question was who was entitled to hold the magistracies. At the very beginning of the Republic a group of *gentes* ('clans'), describing themselves as patricians (*patricii*), claimed the exclusive right to hold the major posts. The basis of their claim is not now recoverable, because even in antiquity there was no agreement over the origins of the term 'patrician'. Clearly it was connected with the term *patres,* used for the senate which existed when kings ruled Rome. It may have been argued that, since they alone held the major priesthoods under the kings, they were the only people who had the necessary religious knowledge to carry out the duties of the magistrates of the new Republic in a way to ensure the favour of the gods towards Rome. In 450 BC they managed to get passed a short-lived law which forbade marriage between patricians and non-patricians. This was an attempt to turn the patricians into an exclusive priestly caste.

17. Those who were not members of the patrician *gentes* were plebeians, members of the *plebs.* In the late Republic the term *plebs* frequently carried with it an implication of low status; but in the earlier period it simply meant all those who were not patricians. These non-patricians would include at one end rich and influential families, who did not qualify as patricians, down to the poorest peasant. There was little or no identity of interest between such people. This was the mistake the Roman historian Livy made. He represented the conflict of the orders, which dominated the political development of Rome, as a simple struggle for equality between two identifiable interest-groups, the patricians and the plebeians.

18. In fact, it must have been much more complicated and less coherent. At least three strands can be identified:

(1) The campaign by rich landowning non-patricians to wrest from the patricians' grasp their exclusive right to hold the high magistracies and control of the state.

(2) Agitation by the mass of people for relief from the problems which perennially afflict peasant societies: poverty, famine, the lack of land, and chronic indebtedness.

(3) The struggle by plebeians in a broad sense for protection from the arbitrary exercise of power by the magistrates and for some measure of recognition for the basic rights of the ordinary citizen.

19. The demand by rich plebeians for admission to the magistracies is recorded as early as 445 BC and culminated in a long campaign associated with the tribunes C. Licinius Stolo and L. Sextius Lateranus in the decade down to 367 BC, which led to a law which opened the consulship to plebeians. L. Sextius became the first plebeian consul in 366 BC. If the law was that it was permissible for a plebeian to stand for the consulship, then from 342 BC it was further tightened up so that one of the consulships had to be held by a plebeian each year. It was only in 172 BC that for the first time both consuls were from plebeian families. From then on the distinction between patrician and plebeian became much less important; by the last century BC it was only some priesthoods which remained exclusively patrician. The opening-up of the magistracies should not be exaggerated. Although Cicero in the last century BC could claim that the path to high office was open to any man of talent, in reality the candidates for the magistracies were drawn from only the richest 2% of the population. After 366 BC a new patrician/plebeian nobility emerged [146]. What Sextius' consulship did do was to pave the way eventually for the local aristocracies of Italy, once they had obtained Roman citizenship, to seek careers in Rome, and at a later date the same was to be true of the élites of the Roman provinces.

20. Rome was an agrarian peasant society. Life was very uncertain for the vast majority of citizens, who struggled to survive on small plots of land. If in good years they could produce enough for their families, in the bad ones they could only turn to the wealthy landowners to provide them with the essentials and thus to enter a cycle of debt-bondage (*nexum*), in which the peasant sought, frequently in vain, to work off his debt for his creditor. The figures given in the tradition for the size of peasant holdings are very small. If they were sufficient to keep a peasant family going, they would certainly not provide for the adult children of the peasants and their families. They needed to find land of their own. So, as the population rose, there was bound to be a continuous demand for new land to be farmed. The remarkable fact is that the

Roman aristocracy, albeit at times reluctantly and under pressure, responded and recognised an obligation on the part of the state to alleviate the distress of its citizens. A whole sequence of laws in the fourth century sought to deal with the debt problem, culminating in the *Lex Poetelia* ('Law of Poetelius') of 326 BC which banned loans on the security of the person of the borrower and brought the system of *nexum* to an end. Livy saw this as a development as important for ordinary citizens as the overthrow of the monarchy had been for the aristocracy. Throughout the fifth and fourth centuries there was agitation for agrarian reform. Again the state responded by annexing territory of defeated enemies as state-owned land (*ager publicus*), which then could be used to establish colonies of Roman citizens or be divided up into parcels of land for grants to individuals, as most notably was done after the annexation of the territory of Veii in 396 BC. The need for such land was a powerful impulse to the early stages of Roman imperialism.

21. The élite did not have it all their own way in public life in Rome. The people of Rome – and there was an ever-increasing number of them – could not be ignored. From the period of the kings, according to the tradition, the people had been called to meet in assembly, and the theory of the ultimate sovereignty of the people assembled is central to understanding Rome at any period. The concentration of power in the hands of the exclusive group of patrician families led to an astonishing response from those outside the élite: the virtual creation of their own parallel state. In 494 BC, at a time of external pressure, the plebeians refused to enlist for the army to defend Rome and withdrew to either the Sacred Mount or to the Aventine (both appear in the sources). Here the plebeians created their own magistrates, the *tribuni plebis* ('tribunes of the plebs'). These tribunes were created 'to counter the *imperium* of the consuls' (Cicero, *On the Republic* 2.58). They gained the right to intervene to bring help (*auxilium*) to any individual who was oppressed unreasonably by a magistrate using his *imperium*. The tribunes' power was reinforced by *sacrosanctitas*, the result of an oath sworn by the plebeians that anyone who forcibly prevented a tribune from exercising his rights would be declared *sacer* ('accursed') and hence could be killed without incurring blood-guilt. The revolt was brought to an end by a formal recognition of the tribunes by the patricians. From the initial meetings emerged a plebeian assembly based on the tribes. This was the origin of the last of the Roman assemblies, the *comitia tributa* [137]. In theory, this assembly was somewhat more democratic than the earlier assemblies, because votes were grouped in tribes, which would include rich and poor alike. Initially the decisions of the *plebs* (*plebiscita*) were not considered binding on the whole population [159–65].

22. In 451 and 450 BC came the publication of the Twelve Tables, the

Roman law code. It is difficult to see how the law code was of any great assistance to the ordinary citizen. Nevertheless, it represents an important development, because the interpretation of the law was taken out of the hands of an exclusive group, who could make arbitrary decisions based on tradition, and instead provided a clear and unambiguous series of remedies.

23. About 287 BC the *Lex Hortensia* ('Law of Hortensius') at last made the decisions of the *plebs* binding on the whole population, and gave them the validity of laws. The conflict of the orders is often considered to close with this decision, which fully incorporated the 'alternative' plebeian state into the mainstream of Roman politics. But in reality the Republic never stopped developing. The magistrates with *imperium*, the Senate, the tribunes, and the assemblies of the people, remained in a state of tension, each jockeying for the position of being the ultimate arbiters of Roman public life.

The most remarkable fact about this complex development of the Roman Republic is that major change was achieved without revolution or serious bloodshed. This contrasts sharply with the politics of the classical Greek world, where bloody civil strife, coups and instability were the norm (*WoA*, H.I.85).

Rome and Italy

24. The Romans, of course, did not speak Roman. Their language was that of their powerful neighbours to the south, the Latins, whose complex civilisation has been revealed by archaeologists over the last twenty-five years. To the north was a second distinctive culture, the Etruscans. Sandwiched between the two, Rome was formed out of both. The Etruscan influence could be seen in Rome's religious practices, customs, symbols of power, and architecture. The family of the Tarquinii had been of Etruscan origin. In the fourth century Rome came to terms with Etruscan cities, such as Caere, or defeated them in war, as most notably in the case of Veii, whose territory was annexed by Rome in 396 BC. The Romans believed that they had had close links with the Latins to the south from early times. All these peoples participated in ancient religious cults at common shrines in recognition of their common identity. Many of them, but not Rome, formed themselves into a political association, the Latin League. Relations between Rome and the League were settled after a war by a treaty in 493 BC. What kept these communities, including Rome, together for the next century was the need to defend themselves against the increasing incursions from the hill tribes of central Italy, the Sabines, the Aequi and the Volsci, which were spurred by lack of land and resources to find new homes in the lowlands of Latium. In the almost yearly fighting Rome played, or claimed to have played, a predominant role; and, when more settled conditions came in the fourth century, Rome's increasing arrogance inspired a war against her by many of the Latins and other peoples in 340 BC. It was all over by 338 BC. Rome had won a decisive victory and dismantled the Latin League.

25. There were still other enemies in this period. In 390 BC a war-band of Gauls from beyond the Apennines in northern Italy captured Rome for a brief time. The incident was elaborated in legend and the scale of the damage to the city may well have been exaggerated. But from this event came the *metus Gallicus* ('the Gallic Fear'), the terror of invasion by the northern barbarians, which was a very real factor in Roman thinking at least down to the time of Augustus. The threat never entirely disappeared and became very real again in the third and fourth centuries AD.

26. Rome's domination of the peninsula of Italy was ensured as the result of the fierce and difficult wars she fought against the Samnites of central southern Italy in the second half of the fourth century BC. These culminated in 295 BC with the hard-won victory at Sentinum against a combined force of Samnites and Gauls.

27. It should not be supposed that Rome's success was either easy or inevitable. The history of almost continuous warfare on an increasingly grand scale in this period can best be summed up in the comment of the emperor Tiberius about another war: *satis iam euentuum, satis casuum* ('win some, lose some'). It was in this period that the Roman aristocratic ideology of war was developed. The Roman histories of this time abound in stories of the single-minded search for glory, of noble self-sacrifice for the fatherland, of adversity endured, and of a succession of ever more formidable and worthy opponents to be triumphed over. Also remarkable was the way in which Rome used her victories. The ideology of war was enriched with the ideology of conquest. Often the territory of defeated states was annexed by Rome to meet the demands of their own land-hungry citizens. It became *ager Romanus* ('Roman land'), was surveyed and parcelled out into plots to be given to citizens, and in some cases, in addition, a *colonia* ('colony'), a community of Roman citizens, was created to provide a focus for the settlers. In other cases the communities of Italy were left autonomous, bound to Rome by an alliance, which promised both parties assistance in time of war. Some people were granted the special status of 'Latins', a bundle of privileges and obligations, which was no longer confined to those of Latin ethnic origin. The most remarkable development of all was the way in which Rome simply absorbed whole communities into itself, by granting Roman citizenship (in many cases this was a restricted citizenship, *ciuitas sine suffragio*, 'citizenship without the right to vote', but others became full Roman citizens). This gave rise to the unique Roman institution, the *municipium*, the community whose members had a sort of dual citizenship.

On the one hand they had their obligations to their own locality, on the other they were citizens of Rome. This was an innovation which would have astonished the Greeks of the classical period. With them citizenship was a jealously guarded privilege, granted to outsiders only rarely as a special honour (*WoA*, 4.6). But Rome's actions should not be interpreted as altruistic and generous. The granting of citizenship was above all part of a system of control. The local gentry of the towns of Italy now had the prospect that the reward for loyalty to Rome might be the opportunity to become magistrates and senators at Rome. But above all citizenship brought with it the obligation of service in the Roman army. Rome's settlement of Italy provided an almost inexhaustible supply of troops for its armies. The Hellenistic king of Macedon, Philip V, at the end of the third century BC, noticed just this in a letter: 'the Romans receive into the citizen body even slaves, when they have freed them, giving them a share in the magistracies, and in such a way not only have they increased their homeland, they have also sent out colonies' (*SIG*³ 543). Being defeated by Rome did not simply mean that your name was listed in the Register of Triumphs and that your valuables were removed. Roman conquest came to bind: your services were required, your land was at risk. Roman victory brought obligations, not just humiliation and transient loss. In this way the Roman concept of *imperium* spawned the reality of empire.

The winning of an empire

28. In 280 BC Tarentum, one of the leading Greek settlements in South Italy (*WoA*, H.I.4, 6), faced with war with Rome, called in King Pyrrhus from Epirus in north-west Greece to help them. Pyrrhus was one of those of the generation after Alexander the Great who sought to carve out kingdoms for themselves from what had been Alexander's empire. The invitation from Tarentum was tempting to Pyrrhus, who had visions of building a great new empire of his own in the West. Initially he had success, defeating Rome in two bloody battles, but with such losses on his own side that he was supposed to have exclaimed that with victories like these, who needed defeats! For a time he diverted his attention to Sicily, but on his return to the mainland was defeated in 275 BC by Rome and decided to retire home, leaving Tarentum to struggle on unsuccessfully. Rome had had intermittent and informal contacts with the Greek world for centuries; but her victory brought her to the notice of other Mediterranean powers as a force to be reckoned with. Rome was now starting to strut on a larger, international stage.

29. The most important power in the West, the Phoenician city of Carthage in North Africa, had established treaty relations with Rome at the beginning

of the Republic and had renewed them intermittently thereafter. On the whole, both sides were warily friendly as long as Rome did not pose any threat to Carthage's trading empire in the West. So it may be that few Romans recognised how momentous their decision was in 264 BC to respond to a call for assistance from a group of Campanian mercenaries, the Mamertini ('Sons of Mars'), who had seized the town of Messana on the north-east tip of Sicily. Certainly the presiding consul, Appius Claudius Caudex, held out as a main objective, a traditional one, the winning of substantial booty. But when he arrived to help the Mamertines, he found them under siege from a joint force from Syracuse and from the Carthaginians, who controlled much of the island of Sicily. Syracuse soon decided to make her peace with the Romans. Gradually Rome made headway against the Carthaginians. After the capture of the Carthaginian base at Agrigentum, the Roman commanders may have set themselves a much larger-scale objective, that of driving the Carthaginians out of Sicily. To do this Carthaginian domination of the seas had to be challenged. So Rome created her first ever large fleet of warships, with which the consul of 260 BC, Gaius Duillius, at Mylae 'was the first Roman to carry out a successful naval action; he was the first to equip and train crews and fleets of fighting ships; and with these ships he defeated in battle on the high seas the Punic [=Carthaginian, since Carthage was a colony of Phoenicia, whose people the Romans called *Punici*] fleets', as an inscription in his honour records (*ILS* 65). The war was to drag on for many years. There was to be a disastrous invasion of North Africa by the Romans, but most of the war centred on and around Sicily. It was another naval victory at the Aegates Islands in 241 BC which decided the First Punic War in Rome's favour. Carthage was forced to accept terms which included the evacuation of Sicily. In the years after 238 BC Rome took advantage of Carthage's internal weakness to expel the Carthaginians from the islands of Sardinia and Corsica, an act of cynical imperialism.

30. Rome was not only determined to exclude the Carthaginians from Sicily, Sardinia and Corsica. She wanted to exploit directly the resources of these islands for Rome's benefit, most notably the corn. They took some time to devise an appropriate machinery; but from 227 BC they appointed two additional annual magistrates, praetors, who had Sicily and Sardinia–Corsica as their *prouinciae*. A *prouincia* was the sphere in which a magistrate was normally expected to exercise his *imperium*; it was frequently a geographical area, but could also be a specific task, such as to look after the corn-supply [136] or to fight the pirates [64]. It is a mistake to suppose that the Romans at this period equated the extent of their empire simply with the boundaries of these *prouinciae*. Rome expected her *imperium*, particularly as represented by

the consuls, to be respected wherever she chose to exercise it, as Greeks, in the second century in particular, were to find out, sometimes to their considerable cost. Their attempts to insist on their autonomy or the rights enshrined in the fine detail of treaties could all too easily be interpreted by Rome as arrogant defiance of her reasonable demands. In this sense Rome's was truly an *imperium sine fine* ('an empire without limits'). To make an area the *prouincia* of an annually appointed Roman magistrate was only one way of exerting authority, and not necessarily the easiest or most economic one. The fact that they were often slow to adopt this solution should not in any way be taken as evidence that the Romans were reluctant imperialists.

Hannibal

31. The First Punic War with Carthage in some ways settled nothing. Her defeat and Rome's subsequent take-over of Sardinia and Corsica rankled with the Carthaginians and their generals, such as Hamilcar, who had remained personally undefeated in the war. There was a story that Hamilcar had made his young son, Hannibal, swear an oath never to be a friend of Rome. The Romans, for their part, were always suspicious of powerful, independent people, seeing in them rivals and threats to Rome's own *imperium*. So another clash was very likely. When it came in 218 BC, the immediate cause centred on a quarrel over the Spanish town of Saguntum, which Hannibal, now a Carthaginian commander, had captured as he sought to expand Carthaginian influence in Spain. In reality both sides were ready for war. In a famous scene, Fabius Buteo, the Roman envoy to the Carthaginian senate, held out his arm and said that the folds of his toga held both peace and war and that he would shake out whichever they wanted. The Carthaginians left the choice to Fabius and when he said that he let fall war, they cried, 'Done!'

32. What the Romans had not anticipated was what sort of war it was going to be. They expected to fight it in Spain and Africa. But Hannibal pre-empted them and in a remarkable march transferred an army from Spain, through southern France, and over the Alps into Italy. Here he proceeded to inflict a series of increasingly serious defeats on the Romans at the Trebia (218 B.C), Lake Trasimene (217 BC), and with most devastating effect in southern Italy at Cannae (216 BC). Such was the scale of the Roman defeat at Cannae, that everyone must have expected them to negotiate what terms they could. Indeed, in 215 BC Philip, king of Macedon, signed an agreement with Carthage in the hope of gaining a seat at the peace negotiations and picking up some advantage for himself. However, Rome would not give in. She created new armies. Very slowly events swung in Rome's favour. In 205 BC, the Roman general,

Publius Cornelius Scipio (Scipio), was able to invade Africa. With Carthage itself now under threat, Hannibal was at last recalled from Italy in 203 BC and in the following year was defeated by Scipio at the battle of Zama. In the settlement of the war Carthage was permitted to survive, but no longer as an international power, and was forced to pay a huge indemnity. As with Sicily after the First Punic War, so now Rome took over Spain. From 197 BC Spain became two *prouinciae* of two new praetors, although the conquest and pacification of the whole peninsula was to take another two centuries. It is no surprise, however, to find the Romans exploiting the mineral wealth, particularly the silver, from an early date.

33. Whenever Romans wanted to pinpoint their 'finest hour', they could highlight the war against Hannibal, and with some justification. The Roman spirit was remarkable. Even at the moment when Hannibal was at the gates of Rome there was no sign of a peace party. When affairs were at their lowest ebb in Italy, Rome still kept, indeed reinforced, armies in the field in Spain to engage the Carthaginians there. Rome's basically amateurish military command system was adapted to counter the strategic genius of Hannibal. Hannibal came into Italy with the proclaimed aim of freeing the communities of Italy from the yoke of Rome. Although in the south he gained some defections, the vast majority remained loyal. Here lies the more mundane, but most important, reason for Rome's success. Year after year Rome was able to mobilise the resources and manpower of Italy on an enormous scale [173]. From the time of the Hannibalic war onwards Rome maintained large numbers of troops in the field around the Mediterranean and beyond in a way that no other ancient state could have even contemplated. Rome's success in the Second Punic War proved that she was no longer in any sense a conventional city-state.

Rome and the East

34. It might be thought that after such an enormous effort Rome would seek a period of recuperation. Yet within a year or so of Zama, Rome was preparing for a new war, one which was to draw her into the world of the Hellenistic kingdoms of the successors of Alexander in the eastern Mediterranean and was to transform Rome in an even more profound way than the war with Hannibal.

35. The Romans had made incursions into north-west Greece in 229 and 219 BC on a scale to raise concern about their ultimate intentions in the mind of King Philip V of Macedon. So since Rome's apparent weakness after the defeat at Cannae was an obvious opportunity for him, he allied himself with

1.6 Coin (gold *stater*) issued to commemorate Flamininus' 'liberation' of Greece in 196 BC: on the obverse, a portrait of Flamininus; on the reverse, a figure of Victory referring to the defeat of the Macedonians.

Carthage. When the capture of the envoy with the treaty revealed to Rome what was happening, she declared war on Philip. It was a war which proved difficult to prosecute. Such friends and allies as Rome gained in Greece eventually dropped away in frustration at the lack of success, and in 205 BC at Phoenice Rome herself made peace with Philip. That treaty was an act of cynicism. As Livy says, the war was 'laid aside' to be taken up again, when the Romans were free of the threat from Carthage. The nature of the Peace of Phoenice was such that it was easy for Rome to claim to be intervening on behalf of Greek friends oppressed by Philip. The Second Macedonian War was declared in 200 BC and settled with the defeat of Philip at the battle of Cynoscephalae in Thessaly in the summer of 197 BC.

36. By their victory the Romans gained the right to dispose of Philip's kingdom and the cities he controlled as they wished. At the Isthmian Games at Corinth in 196 BC the Roman commander, Titus Quinctius Flamininus (fig. 1.6), theatrically proclaimed that those Greek peoples who had been subjects of Philip were now free. In doing this Flamininus was exploiting one of the most emotive concepts of Hellenistic diplomacy. 'Freedom' meant the right to live by the community's own traditional laws, not to have troops garrisoned on them, and not to have to contribute taxes to another power. This was the greatest gift a city could receive from a ruler. However, it should not be thought that the Roman action lacked self-interest. When Flamininus evacuated Rome's forces in 194 BC, he left behind Greek communities who knew what was expected of them. To this end Flamininus was capable of ruthless-

ness, as for example in conniving at the murder of an anti-Roman politician in Boeotia. Roman magistrates in their dealings with the Greeks emphasised that they had not sought to enrich themselves in the settlement and that the Greeks consequently should show their gratitude for this favour. As one praetor put it: 'As for the honours to the god and privileges to you, we will try to help to increase them, while you carefully maintain in the future your goodwill towards us' (Marcus Valerius Messalla to the city of Teos, 193 BC, *SIG* III. 601). If any Greek was in any doubt as to the obligation they were under to Rome, it became painfully clear a few years later in the treaty which the Romans imposed on the Aetolian League: 'the people of Aetolia shall preserve without fraud the *imperium* and majesty of the Roman people'. That spelt out what the Romans had always assumed. The declaration of freedom in 196 BC bound the Greeks inextricably into the Roman empire.

37. At the very time that Rome was involved with the war with Philip, another Hellenistic monarch was reviving the fortunes of his dynasty. Antiochus III, the Greek king of Syria (the dynasty there was called 'Seleucid'), was busily expanding in Asia Minor and in 196 BC even crossed into Europe to annex part of Thrace. Rome became suspicious of his intentions, but in 196 BC could find no basis for action. When Rome withdrew from Greece, Antiochus assumed that they were accepting the *status quo* and sent envoys in 193 BC to regularise the relationship with Rome. To the envoys' consternation they found the Romans ready to make impossible demands for Antiochus' withdrawal from Europe and threatening to come to the aid of the Greeks of the cities of Asia Minor just as they had freed the mainland Greeks from Philip. The ambassadors came to Rome to establish friendly relations and left with a scarcely veiled threat of war. So, when the Aetolian League, resentful at the way Rome had not rewarded them for their support against Philip, called on Antiochus to come to their aid in 192 BC, he responded in the hope of gaining an advantage in a war with Rome which he saw as inevitable. In 191 BC Roman forces returned to Greece, drove Antiochus back to Asia Minor, eventually forced the Aetolians to come to terms, and in late 190 BC decisively defeated Antiochus at the battle of Magnesia. In the so-called Treaty of Apamea, Antiochus' kingdom was reduced and Rome again parcelled out large areas which he had controlled to her loyal allies in the war. Then, once again, the Roman forces withdrew.

38. The lessons had largely been learnt by the Greeks. In the years after the war with Antiochus, embassies streamed into Rome from the Greek world seeking arbitration and assistance and thus acknowledging where the real power now lay. But in 179 BC Philip V of Macedon died and was succeeded by his charismatic son, Perseus. He proceeded to restore the influence of

1.7 Detail of the frieze from the monument of Aemilius Paullus at Delphi, set up to commemorate the battle of Pydna (168 BC). Cf. [473].

Macedon and won widespread popular support in the Greek world. Here was a new patron ready to help and close at hand. The embassies no longer needed to go to Rome. Such a situation was intolerable to Rome. So once again in 172 BC she concocted a case against Perseus sufficient to justify a war. The later Greek historian, Appian, saw the truth: Rome was determined to destroy a 'virtuous, wise and popular king'. The Romans made hard work of the early stages of the war; but in 168 BC Lucius Aemilius Paullus decisively defeated Perseus at the battle of Pydna (fig. 1.7). The king was taken to Italy to live in exile. Macedon was broken up into four small, powerless independent regions.

39. The Third Macedonian War also marked a stage in the growth of Roman impatience with any city which hesitated in its wholehearted support of Rome. Neutrality, or any attempt to negotiate between the parties, was suspicious in Rome's eyes and their reaction could be blunt. Suspect Greek politicians were removed from their communities to be replaced by those who could demonstrate their subservience to Rome. 1,000 Achaeans, including the historian Polybius, were deported to Italy. A few years later the Greek King Attalus II of the Asian kingdom of Pergamum, a friend and ally of the Roman people, confided in a letter that he could not go to war with the Galatians without consulting Rome first, for fear of how they would react. There could be no clearer demonstration of the long arm of Rome's *imperium*. There was bound to be frustration. In 149 BC there was a revolt in Macedon which was suppressed, and at last Macedon was organised as a province under Rome's direct control. Rome went on to pick a quarrel with the Achaean League in southern Greece and defeated them. At the same time Rome turned once again on Carthage, imagining that its revival threatened them. In 146 BC the cities of

Corinth in Greece and of Carthage in North Africa were razed to the ground in a brutal demonstration of Roman power.

Graecia capta . . . 'Captured Greece . . .' (Horace, *Epistles* 2.1.225)

40. The impact of the Greek world on Rome was just as profound and long-lasting as Rome's was on the East. As the poet Horace put it: *Graecia capta ferum uictorem cepit* ('Captured Greece captured her savage conqueror').

41. Rome's generals strode through the Hellenistic world like kings. It was a heady, intoxicating experience for them. *'Ie, ie paean,* O Titus our Saviour' begins a hymn of gratitude to Flamininus, who had declared Greece to be free in 196 BC. Statues were raised to him. An annual festival was celebrated in his honour for centuries after his death. The Roman magistrates were treated like gods, just as Alexander the Great and his successors had been. This language of praise and honour was the way in which Greek communities had become used to winning the favour of their rulers and they transferred it without difficulty to come to terms with their new masters [65]. When the Roman armies came back to Rome, they came in triumph. They crossed the sacred boundary of Rome, bringing back the spoils to be dedicated to the gods of Rome and, above all, to Jupiter. The procession crossed the walls at the Triumphal Gate and wound through the streets to culminate at the temple of Jupiter on the Capitol. The triumphing general was honoured almost as if he was Jupiter. It was precisely in this period that the Roman triumph took on its famous lavish pomp, modelled on the elaborate ceremonies of the Hellenistic kings. The people shared in the triumph (see [122–126]).

42. Then there was the fabulous wealth of the Hellenistic world. Much was transferred back to Rome by her conquering generals, along with vast numbers of slaves. The ordinary Roman soldier was often rewarded with a share of the booty which he would scarcely have earned in decades of work. His generals enriched themselves; but they also used the wealth to transform the city of Rome itself. This was not new in the second century. The conquests of the fourth century and early third were the occasion for the first major changes in how Rome looked. It was then that the city's layout and architecture began to commemorate Rome's imperial power. The first aqueducts were built at this time. Appius Claudius Caecus built the first of Rome's great roads, the Via Appia (fig. 1.8), to link the city with the newly won territories of the south. Now the suburbs and the areas inside the city gates began to be crowded with triumphal monuments. Romans had seen the exuberant architecture of the Hellenistic kings. The hills of Rome were ideal for similar works: broad terraces, artificial platforms, ascents to lofty temples, stoas and

1.8 The Via Appia.

basilicas, enormous buildings for commercial exchange (cf. fig. 5.6). In the eastern kingdoms such layouts came to be a symbol of the power of great kings over the natural landscape and their functioning a demonstration of well-managed government. The buildings provided the stage set for the festivals and games which kept alive the memory of Rome's victories. They bound all the citizens into the system of imperialism.

43. The Greek world also had a distinctive way of life and a highly refined and rich culture. Some Roman aristocrats were bewitched by it. Scipio, the victor over Hannibal, was accused by his critics of adopting, while staying in Syracuse, the Greek city in Sicily, a dress and bearing 'which were un-Roman, and not even soldierly; he strolled about the gymnasium in a Greek cloak and sandals, and wasted his time over books and physical exercise' (Livy 29.19). Reading was not a suitable occupation for a man of action (see chapter 9). However, by her victories, Rome became a centre of the Mediterranean-wide culture of which Greek was the principal medium. The great philosopher Poseidonius, from Apamea in Syria, found a place in the entourages of Roman generals, and drew his information and some of his preoccupations from them. The Greek historian Polybius, deported to Italy in 167 BC,

worked entirely in a Roman context [118]. This process of Hellenisation of Rome came at just the moment that Rome was developing its own truly Roman literature with the dramatist Plautus, the epic poet Q. Ennius, the first Roman historian Q. Fabius Pictor. The models were Greek (and so was the language used by Pictor), but their interests were distinctively Roman. However, some Romans feared that the values of Greek culture threatened to undermine the essential features of what it was to be Roman. This was the uncertainty which inspired the Elder Cato (Marcus Porcius Cato: [148]). From a family from outside the senate and a town outside Rome, he reached the highest offices of a Roman political career (consul in 195 BC, censor in 184 BC). As a commander he was a match for his noble colleagues; as a decision-maker he chose to emphasise in his oratory the moral principles which were at the centre of the difficult choices which confronted the age: the problems of cultural identity, of integrity in government, the duties of world power, the obligations of the wealthy. Through his speeches and his writings he ensured that preoccupation with these things would remain a part of Roman culture. He and his contemporary writers put morality at the very heart of the Roman literary view of themselves. For Cato the values of the Greek world were a threat [435]. As he wrote to his son, 'I will show you the results of my own experience at Athens: that it is a good idea to dip into their literature but not to learn it thoroughly. I shall convince you that they are a most iniquitous and intractable people, and you may take my word as the word of a prophet: if that people shall ever bestow its literature upon us, it will corrupt everything' (quoted by Pliny, *Natural History* 29.13). Yet Cato himself showed in all his own writings his deep knowledge of Greek literature. This double-edged attitude to all things Greek can also be demonstrated by the career of Scipio Aemilianus, a man from the very heart of the Roman aristocracy. In his youth he devoted himself to Greek literature and culture, but confided to Polybius, whose patron he was: 'I am believed by everyone to be a quiet and lazy fellow with none of the energetic character of a true Roman' (Polybius 31.23; see [147]). Yet he was to go on to have a spectacular military career. He was the general who finally defeated Carthage in 146 BC. As he supervised the destruction of the city, a brutal expression of Rome's power, he quoted Homer: 'A day will come when sacred Troy shall perish, and Priam and his people shall be slain.' Nor was the irony of the quotation lost upon him. The Romans saw themselves as the descendants of the Trojans [7]. Scipio turned to Polybius and said: 'A glorious moment, Polybius; but I have a terrible fear and foreboding that some day someone else will pronounce the same fate for my own country' (Polybius 38.21). The remark also brought out another consequence of this period of change: the deep sense of doubt, guilt, and pessimism which was to be found in most Roman thought for the next two centuries.

The spoils of empire

44. There was a very dark side to Rome's rise to power. The razing of cities like Carthage and the enslavement of their populations were just one expression of it. Roman generals in the field regularly resorted to acts of looting, reprisal, massacres, mass deportations and enslavements. The Romans quickly developed a systematic structure for the exploitation of their empire. The income from the imposition of taxation on the empire enabled direct taxation in Italy to be abolished in 167 BC. The system was regularly abused by those in charge of it for their own personal enrichment [183–4]. The victims complained to Rome. There were those among the aristocracy who were sympathetic. In 171 BC the Senate reacted to protests from Spain about the extortion exercised by the Roman official and ordered a judicial inquiry. One Roman was acquitted, two others retired voluntarily from public life. There is no sign of any compensation for the Spaniards. Later in 149 BC came the first of a series of laws which established a permanent court to deal with cases of extortion. From the start the record of the court was not all that reassuring to the victims. Frequently the senatorial governors were able to exploit their connections in Rome to avoid condemnation. There may have been genuine sympathy for the provincials among those at Rome who advocated action. But there was also simple self-interest. No Roman aristocrat wanted to see one of his rivals in public office enrich himself by the exploitation of a province for his advantage. Further it was more difficult to persuade the provincials to remain quiet and peaceful and enjoy the advantages of Roman rule, when they were clearly suffering. The Roman Republic was never to convince the provincials. As Cicero was to declaim in 66 BC: 'Words cannot express how bitterly we are hated among foreign nations owing to the wanton and outrageous conduct of the men whom we have sent to govern them' (*On The Manilian Law* 65).

Crisis

45. When historians at the end of the Republic and in the early Empire sought to understand the failure in the first century BC of the political system which had brought them such success, they first constructed a myth that there had been a period when everything worked well: 'a golden age, free from vice and crime, while the innocence of the old pastoral life was still untainted and uncorrupted, and the ever present threat of our Carthaginian enemies kept alive our ancestral training', as the late writer Florus put it (*Epitome of Roman History* 1.47). From the late second century BC Roman history was seen as a series of stages in an ever-deepening crisis, leading to collapse and civil war. The monarchy which the first emperor, Augustus, created to replace the Republic could now be represented as a revival of all that was good in Rome's past that had been forgotten in the last hundred years. One-man rule was seen as at least inevitable, at best necessary and beneficial. The stages of the decline were seen in moral terms, along the lines established by the Elder Cato. So increasing wealth bred *auaritia* ('greed'), the gentlemanly pursuit of high office became a corrupt race for personal power and domination.

46. For many observers the moment when the vague discontents of the second century crystallised into a crisis was the year of the tribunate of Tiberius Sempronius Gracchus, 133 BC. Tiberius proposed a bill to use the lands in Italy which the Roman state had taken in the period of expansion in Italy and had confiscated seventy years before from those Italian communities which had supported Hannibal. The land was to be parcelled out to peasant-farmers who needed it (fig. 1.9; [276]). Tiberius took the bill straight to the vote of the assembly of the Roman people [164–5], an assembly packed with the peasants who hoped to benefit from the distribution. There it was vetoed by another tribune, M. Octavius (Octavius). Despite Tiberius' best efforts at pressure and persuasion, Octavius persisted in his veto. Tiberius was left with the choice of dropping a bill which he had demonstrated was popular or of finding some way round the veto. He decided on the unprecedented move of putting a proposal to the assembly that Octavius should be removed from his tribunate on the grounds that he was not fulfilling his duty of acting in the interests of the people. So Octavius was forced out and the agrarian bill passed. When the senate tried to undermine the bill by effectively refusing to finance its enactment, Tiberius had a windfall. News came that Attalus III, king of Pergamum, had died and, fearing that his kingdom would be face internal disruption on his death, had bequeathed it to the Roman people. Once again Tiberius took a bill straight to the assembly to annex the kingdom (which became the province of Asia) and exploit its wealth to provide the finance for his land settlements. Since Attalus had given the kingdom to the Roman people, it was their right, Tiberius argued, to dispose of it as they would wish. Threatened with reprisals and prosecution after he left office, Tiberius declared his intention to stand for the tribunate of 132 BC. This was too much for some senators. At election time a mob of senators led by the Pontifex Maximus, Rome's highest priest, clubbed to death Tiberius and his supporters.

47. In all the years of political conflict in Rome no one had lost their life in

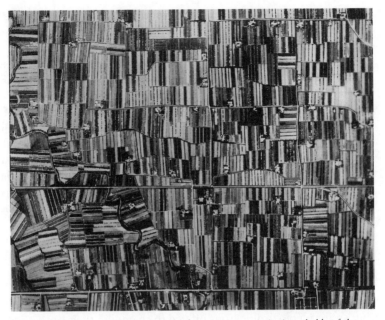

1.9 Land-distribution. Air photograph of Roman 'centuriation', probably of the second century BC, preserved in modern field-patterns near Imola (northern Italy).

this way. Yet most ancient sources blame Tiberius Gracchus, the victim, for inciting the violence which was inflicted on him and his followers. For this to make sense it required Tiberius Gracchus to be represented as a revolutionary, who disrupted a settled political system in which the supremacy of the aristocratic Senate was generally acknowledged. This had never been the case. There were several potential sources of power in the Republic, as the Greek historian Polybius recognised: the magistracies with *imperium*, the Senate, and the tribunate with the assemblies of the Roman people (see chapter 4 *passim*). It was open to any public figure to seek to exploit the potential of any one of these. In seeking to present his agrarian bill to the assembly without putting it first to the Senate, Tiberius could represent himself as acting on unquestionable precedent. The outcome of the Conflict of the Orders had been that it was the assemblies which made law and had the ultimate authority. Plenty of tribunes had presented bills straight to the assembly in the recent past. Some had even faced a veto, but had persuaded or pressurised the opponent into dropping it. As far as precedent went, M. Octavius' stubborn insistence on his veto had no parallel. Indeed, Tiberius could argue that, given the historical tradition and nature of the tribunate, there was something wrong with a tribune using his veto to prevent the people, whose magistrate he was, from getting what they wanted ('the tribunes should always aim to meet the wishes of the people', Polybius (6.16) had written a few years earlier). When it was given the opportunity, the people in assembly agreed with Tiberius by voting Octavius out of office. Furthermore, the land bill itself was hardly revolutionary. Tiberius could point to the long history of Rome using the land which it had confiscated from defeated opponents for the settlement of its own peasantry. The bill was certainly disruptive – those who were presently exploiting that land would lose out – but hardly revolutionary. What was really new about the situation was the attitude of the core of the aristocratic Senate. Whereas in the past the Senate had agreed to, even initiated, land-settlement programmes, a few years before Tiberius Gracchus it had successfully thrown out a land bill brought to it, and it was to oppose nearly all such measures for the rest of the Republic, often with violence. The aristocracy turned in on itself, became absorbed in its own internal battles for wealth, influence and power, stubbornly opposed innovation, and refused to acknowledge the growing social and economic problems of the rest of the population. Little wonder, then, that all the other sectors of society became alienated. They provided a power-base for those members of the élite who either for their own ends or for ideological reasons offered to champion their causes and provide for their needs. So far from being revolutionaries, such popular tribunes could claim that their actions were the only hope of preserving the Republican system by showing that it could alleviate people's problems.

48. A decade after Tiberius, his younger brother Gaius Gracchus became tribune in 123 BC and, by a constitutional freak and to his own surprise, was re-elected for 122 BC. He proposed a much more wide-ranging and diverse programme of bills than his brother; there were various attacks on the senatorial abuse of power: a bill to change the juries of the extortion court and give provincials a better chance of getting justice; a revival of Tiberius' land programme with new colonies in South Italy and, most controversially, an overseas colony on the site of Carthage; a proposal to change the status of Latins and allies to provide them with protection from arbitrary abuses by Roman magistrates. One of his proposals was to use state funds to organise the provision of corn for the city of Rome. Huge granaries were to be built and a quantity of corn was to be offered to each citizen at a fixed price. Opponents saw the scheme as one designed to win popularity and votes for Gaius at the expense of emptying the state treasuries. To counter this charge Gaius reorganised the system of tax-collection in the new province of Asia; the empire was to pay for the needs of the city of Rome. Further, to see the bill as simply a political manoeuvre furthering Gaius' personal ambitions was to fail to recognise that there was a real problem to be solved. The city of Rome had grown to such a size that its basic food needs could not be met from its surrounding territory. If the population (and this was not just a matter of concern to the poor) was to survive, a system of supply was required with funding and organisation which could be provided only by the state.

49. Gaius failed to be elected tribune for 121 BC and those who opposed him began to propose bills to reverse much of what he had done. In the tense atmosphere a servant of the consul Opimius was killed. Opimius went to the Senate demanding support for action. The Senate passed a decree that 'the consul should see to it that the republic comes to no harm', a decree which later became known as the *senatus consultum ultimum* ('the ultimate decree of the Senate'). Armed with this Opimius organised a violent suppression of Gaius and his followers. Some, including Gaius, were killed in the fighting. Others were arrested and summarily executed. In the next year Opimius was prosecuted for his actions. His defence was that the decree of the Senate sanctioned his action. He was acquitted.

Popular politics

50. In the *senatus consultum ultimum* the core of the Senate had devised a quasi-legal cover for the use of naked violence to suppress popular politicians. The followers of the Gracchi found new ways of counter-attacking and reinforcing the claim that the people were the ultimate source of power.

51. In the North African kingdom of Numidia, which bordered on the Roman province of Africa (the old territory of Carthage), a fierce dynastic struggle broke out about 116 BC. Rome was appealed to and tried to negotiate a settlement. When one of the claimants to the throne, Jugurtha, broke the agreement, killed his rival and also some Roman citizens, the Senate was forced to declare war. A brief campaign brought Jugurtha to the negotiating table. In the eyes of some Romans he was treated very leniently and Jugurtha soon demonstrated his lack of good faith. The war was renewed and a Roman army was defeated as a result of alleged incompetence by its commanders. In many ways this was a side-show for Rome. There were more serious threats to the north. Various Germanic and Celtic tribes were on the move. Rome feared that they would enter Italy. They inflicted a series of defeats on the Roman generals sent against them, culminating in a terrible defeat at Arausio in southern Gaul in 105 BC, the greatest loss of Roman forces since Cannae. The men who negotiated with Jugurtha, who commanded the armies in Africa and against the German tribes with such notable lack of success, came from the inner aristocracy which had suppressed the Gracchi. Their failures enabled the supporters of the Gracchan tradition to take their revenge. The accusation was not just incompetence, it centred on corruption: alleged bribes from Jugurtha ('anything can be bought at Rome', he is supposed to have boasted), the disappearance of rich booty taken from the German tribes. In 109 BC a special court set up by vote of the people convicted several leading senators. In the next few years others were brought to trial or driven from public life. The popular tribune Saturninus (Lucius Appuleius Saturninus) proposed a court to deal with the remarkably vague charge of 'diminishing the majesty of the Roman people;' [cf. 91]. This could be taken to cover incompetent leadership in battle, making war without sanction from Rome, or violent action against popular politicians in Rome. It was also probably Saturninus who devised another remarkable expression of popular politics. In a law, or laws, passed by the people in probably 101 BC, which laid down detailed orders for the actions and behaviour of Roman magistrates in the Greek East, a clause was inserted that once the law had been passed by the assembly all the senators had to swear an oath to abide by its terms and see that they were carried out. Senators could hardly do anything except obey. The arrogant way in which senators had taken action against the Gracchi and had undermined their legislation, forced popular politicians to give legal expression to the undeniable principle that it was the assemblies which were the ultimate decision-makers in Rome.

52. The allegations of corruption and incompetence on the part of the aristocracy were exploited in another way by Gaius Marius. Like the Elder Cato, he was an outsider, from a non-senatorial family. Through the patronage of Roman nobles, he had made a fairly successful career for himself and had risen as far as the praetorship. For some years it looked as though he would not make the final step into the consulship. In 108 BC he neatly exploited the popular mood of the time. According to Marius, Rome's failures were explicable because being a member of one of the traditional aristocratic families of Rome greatly helped a man in his campaign to hold the consulship, but it did not ensure his competence in the office; on the other hand outsiders, like Marius, had risen as far as they had only by demonstrating their abilities. He was elected to the consulship of 107 BC, and a tribune then proposed that the war against Jugurtha should be transferred to him. He immediately increased the forces available to him by calling for volunteers from men in the lowest groups in the census, who were not normally conscripted for military service. Within two years Marius had brought the war to a successful conclusion. In the aftermath of the defeat at Arausio it was no surprise to find Marius elected to another consulship for 104 BC, to fight the German tribes. He was to be elected to an unprecedented series of consulships for each of the subsequent years down to 100 BC and, in 101 BC, finally defeated the tribes as well. This

succession of consulships was offensive to the idea of limited tenure of any office. It was yet another piece of popular politics. Marius could have had his command continued after his consulship of 104 BC as a proconsul. But that would have been a decision of the Senate and would have meant that he would have remained in that office only as long as the Senate chose. By re-electing him consul year after year the people in assembly were asserting that Marius was the man they wanted in command and that he should stay there as long as they wanted. Marius exploited popular politics to construct his unprecedented career; but he was not at heart a popular politician. When, in 100 BC, Saturninus and his supporters were causing trouble, Marius, again under the *senatus consultum ultimum*, had them suppressed and killed. In many ways Marius' career was to provide a model for the great war-lords of the last century BC. But significantly the high point in 100 BC, when Marius could claim himself to have been the protector of the Republic, was also the moment of failure. He was never to be accepted by the inner aristocracy and his killing of Saturninus was seen as a betrayal of his popular support.

Italy becomes Rome

53. Marius' spectacular career, with his unprecedented six consulships down to 100 BC, provided one of the catalysts for the next fundamental change to Rome. Marius came from the local gentry of the small Italian town of Arpinum, which had received Roman citizenship only in 188 BC. Within three generations of that grant, the local aristocratic families were contemplating public careers at Rome. The great orator, Cicero, whose family also came from Arpinum, was proud that his grandfather, a contemporary of Marius, had come to the attention of Roman aristocrats. Marius demonstrated what could be achieved. So many of the notable families of Latin and allied cities came to see in the grant of citizenship the possibilities of fame and riches on the much larger stage of Rome. The allies could also claim that they provided a large proportion of Rome's fighting forces, yet saw few of the rewards which came with success. Many were also aggravated by the high-handed and arbitrary treatment they received from Roman magistrates. Citizenship would provide them with some protection. There were from time to time those at Rome who recognised the justice of the allies' demands and proposed concessions; but the Roman aristocracy remained largely opposed to change. They saw in the rich families from the allied communities potential competitors for the leading magistracies and in the allied peoples, if granted citizenship, a huge, volatile, and unpredictable new electorate, which could disrupt existing networks of patronage.

54. The frustration of the leaders of the allied communities grew steadily through the last decades of the second century BC and into the 90s. When in 91 BC the tribune M. Livius Drusus, the latest Roman politician to champion the allies' cause for his own ends, was mysteriously murdered, the allied communities of central and southern Italy went to war (the so-called Social War – *socius* means 'ally' in Latin). 90 BC saw the mobilisation of huge numbers of troops on both sides. The fighting was bloody and far from one-sided. The shock of war on this scale so close to Rome brought concessions from her. By the end of the year citizenship had been granted to Latin and allied communities, which had remained loyal. In 89 BC the war turned in favour of Rome. Having conceded the principle, within a few years she extended citizenship even to those who had resisted. By the end of the decade all the communities of Italy south of the river Po had citizenship of Rome.

55. The integration of Italy into Rome was a complex process which began long before the Social War, but accelerated after it. That process was predominantly one-way, what historians call 'Romanisation'. Within a few generations the local languages of Italy, Umbrian, Etruscan, Oscan etc., had virtually become of interest only to antiquarians. Latin was pre-eminent. Rome devised a fairly standard system of local government for the communities. The local gentry aped Roman aristocrats in their dress, habits, buildings. Only the Greek cities of South Italy retained something of their language and distinctive culture. Yet, in another way, just what the conservative Roman aristocracy feared might happen came to pass. The vast new electorate showed that they had power and influence. Local aristocrats stood for the magistracies at Rome and entered the Senate in ever-increasing numbers. Cicero in his defence of his client, Gnaeus Plancius (from the town of Atina in the same region as Cicero's own homeland of Arpinum), vividly illustrates the enthusiastic sense of local pride which swept such men into office in Rome:

There was not a man at Arpinum, at Sora, at Casinum, at Aquinum, who did not support Plancius' candidacy. All the heavily-populated districts of Venafrum and Allifae, and, in short, all that rugged, mountainous countryside of ours, where men are loyal, unsophisticated and staunch supporters of their own kind, all judged themselves to be honoured by Plancius' holding of office, to be complimented by his distinction. (*In Defence of Plancius* 22)

Civil war and Sulla

56. The Social War saw a massive mobilisation of troops by Rome in Italy – at least 15 legions were in the field in 90 BC – for a war which held out few opportunities for large-scale rewards. With much of the fighting over after one or two campaign seasons, the question was what to do with all these troops. At that moment the best opportunity in a generation for glory and booty arose. Rome responded to the expansion of the monarch Mithridates VI Eupator of Pontus, who had built up a kingdom around the Black Sea region and was now involved provocatively in Asia, where Rome's interests were at stake. Here was a war, which held out the prospect of wealth and fame of the sort that came to Flamininus and Aemilius Paullus, the victors over the great Hellenistic monarchs of the second century BC. The war was assigned in the normal way to one of the consuls of 88 BC, Lucius Cornelius Sulla (Sulla), who had distinguished himself in the recent fighting. However, during the year, a tribune, P. Sulpicius, acting in the tradition of the popular politics of the past fifty years, proposed to the assembly to transfer the command against Mithridates to the ageing Marius, Rome's conqueror of Jugurtha and the German tribes. When a tribune had done something similar in 107 BC, taking the command against Jugurtha from Q. Metellus and giving it to Marius, Metellus had acquiesced in the decision of the people, whatever sense of outrage he may have felt. Sulla's response was totally different and revolutionary. He went to his army and held out the threat that they would not be the soldiers Marius would enlist and take east to enrich themselves. With his troops behind him, Sulla marched on Rome and carried out a coup.

57. To some in Antiquity and to many modern commentators Sulla was able to achieve what he did because of changes in the nature of the army, which, so it is argued, consisted increasingly of professional volunteers with a primary loyalty to their commander. But in reality the Roman forces were made up, as they always had been, of peasants conscripted from the countryside [173]. They wished to get back to their land as soon as possible. Many would hope that service in the army would bring rewards in the shape of booty and grants of better land on discharge, things which would alleviate the grinding poverty of their normal lives. So the army can, in some sense, be seen as representative of the attitudes of ordinary citizens. They would fight loyally in defence of Rome, when it was under threat, and were bound by oath to follow their appointed commanders; but they had no commitment to the *res publica*, the political system which governed them, but did little for them. What had changed was not the attitude of the army, but that of their leader. Sulla dared to do what others scarcely dared to dream. Contrast the support of his soldiers with the story that all but one of his officers, members of the ruling class, refused to march with Sulla. It was they who were appalled at the blow to the principles of the *res publica*. In the civil wars to come the Roman peasants under arms found that they had bargaining power, when their leaders needed their fighting muscle:

When anyone seeks power his greatest help is the man in direst poverty, because he is restrained by no attachment to his property, having none, and considers anything honourable for which he receives pay. (Sallust, *War with Jugurtha* 86)

Despite widespread outrage in the senate, Sulla had Marius, Sulpicius, and a few followers outlawed and their legislation rescinded. He withdrew his army almost immediately, made attempts to restore normality, and allowed free elections. Then, in 87 BC, he set off on his campaign against Mithridates' forces, a campaign which was hard, difficult, but ultimately successful in forcing Mithridates to a settlement which gave up all that he had recently gained.

58. Disruption continued in Rome in Sulla's absence. Before the end of 87 BC Marius had returned from exile and joined up with L. Cornelius Cinna (Cinna) to carry out their own bloody coup, taking vengeance on their political enemies with a violence that disgusted even some of their own followers. Marius died early in 86 BC, soon after entering an unprecedented seventh consulship. Cinna continued to dominate Rome for two years along with his colleague, Gnaeus Papirius Carbo. The regime never made much claim to legitimacy. Not only were there all the aristocrats serving with Sulla, there were also the relatives and friends of the victims of Cinna's and Marius' purge; even the men who had no reason to leave Rome did not associate themselves closely with Cinna. So, when Sulla returned in force from the East in 83 BC, a vast, if disparate, group of members of the nobility flocked to support him, seeing in him the hope of reviving their political careers. Sulla captured Rome in November 82 BC. There followed the long-remembered massacre of opponents, for which Cinna and Marius had set the precedent. Hundreds of people were proscribed: their names published, their lives forfeit, their property confiscated to be sold and distributed to loyal Sullan officers. Whole communities in Italy, which had not chosen the right side, had their land confiscated to provide settlements for Sulla's veterans.

59. The political system now had to be restored. Sulla was appointed to the exceptional position of 'dictator for the making of laws and the establishment of the *res publica*'. He knew what was expected of him: to create a settled political system in which those aristocrats who had returned with him could hold office and exercise influence. Many of them had tasted the bitterness of exile in the past decade. They were the top dogs now and they intended to see to it that they stayed there. It is significant that one of the longest-lasting of Sulla's laws was a ban on the sons of the proscribed from holding public office. They were not to be allowed to disrupt the system he set up nor to haunt the minds of the victors, many of whom were now in possession of the property of

these families. It was only in 49 BC that the ban was lifted. Sulla doubled the size of the Senate to about 600. The holders of the quaestorship were now automatically recruited into the Senate to provide a continuous stream of new blood; but also, since there were now to be 20 quaestors elected every year, he increased the competition there would be for the more restricted numbers of higher posts. He re-established the order and minimum ages at which men could be appointed to the various magistracies. He reformed and expanded the courts, making the senators the jurors. He sought to cripple what he considered to be the main threat to stability: the tribunate in the hands of popular politicians. No holder of the tribunate could go on to any higher office; it became a dead end unlikely to attract the ambitious. Tribunes lost the right to bring forward legislation without the prior approval of the senate. In all this he sought to assert the ultimate authority of the senate in public life – a novel position, one which had never been unequivocally accepted before in the republic's mixed constitution, and one which was doomed to fail because Sulla relied on the reformer's least effective weapon, the law. To prevent repeats of careers like Marius or Saturninus, Sulla simply sought to ban them by law, without seeking to understand or come to terms with the factors which had given such men popular followings and influence.

60. Having completed his settlement, Sulla proceeded to dismantle his own unprecedented position. At the end of 81 BC he ceased to be dictator; then, after a year as consul, in 80 BC he retired from public life, and died a year later. History has comparatively few examples of persons who voluntarily give up their pre-eminent position, and later Julius Caesar, who showed no inclination to follow Sulla's example, accused him of political illiteracy. But the event should occasion no surprise. Sulla realised that the coalition of support which had gathered around him expected him to create a *res publica* in which they could compete for the highest offices and influence; there would be no room in such a system for someone whose authority might transcend theirs. Sulla gave them what they wanted. In the following two decades those who had come over to his side queued up to reach the consulship. The decade of the 80s left another more significant legacy. The men who were to form the last generation of the Republic had in their youth seen armies marching in Italy, and terrible punishments meted out to the losers, had experienced the loss of influence and the frustrations of exile. Such a crisis must never occur again. So there was no compromise they would not make, no threat they would stand up to, no line they were prepared to draw, for fear of provoking another such crisis. This made these aristocrats fodder for men of greater ambition and ruthlessness.

Pompey the Great – too big for Rome

61. Problems and challenges to the regime established by Sulla came thick and fast. At home the courts, manned by Sulla's senators, were rocked by a succession of scandals and allegations of bribery. Year after year came the demand for the restoration of the rights of tribunes. Abroad, Q. Sertorius, who had fought against Sulla, had established himself in Spain as a focus of anti-Sullan forces. Indeed, by the mid-70s he was able to establish a senate in exile and by brilliant use of guerrilla tactics to hold out against the succession of forces sent against him until he was assassinated by his own entourage in 73 BC. In Italy the rural disruption and discontent, exacerbated by Sulla's confiscations of land and enforced settlements of his own veteran soldiers, erupted in rioting in Etruria in 78 BC. The cause of the dispossessed was championed by one of the consuls for the year, M. Aemilius Lepidus. The Senate originally reacted with characteristic indecision and timidity and then in 77 BC with equally characteristic violent suppression after the declaration of a *senatus consultum ultimum*. It was in the same region that there was to be another rising, championed by a senior senator, Catiline, fourteen years later. Military force could re-establish order, but did nothing to eradicate the poverty and discontent which had driven people to revolt in the first place. Then, late in the 70s, came the last of the series of major slave uprisings which had troubled southern Italy from the second century. From 73 to 71 BC the slaves, led by Spartacus, defeated the forces sent to deal with them until crushed bloodily by M. Licinius Crassus.

62. These troubles provide the background to the rapid and remarkable rise of Gnaeus Pompeius (fig. 1.10). Pompey, born in 106 BC, inherited in his youth some of the suspicion which all sides felt for his father, the consul of 89 BC, who played an ambiguous and self-serving role in the civil wars of 87 BC. During the Cinnan regime, Pompey retired to his family estates in Picenum in north-east Italy and from there he hurried with a privately raised force to aid Sulla after his landing in Italy in 83 BC. His savage and highly efficient suppression of opposition forces in Sicily and North Africa won him a reputation for ruthlessness. From Africa he returned to demand and be granted, however reluctantly, a triumph, an unprecedented honour for someone who was not yet a senator. In 77 BC he was called on again to help in putting down the Lepidus rising [61]. Then the Senate voted to send him to co-operate with Q. Caecilius Metellus Pius in fighting Sertorius [61]. Although Pompey was to suffer defeats at the hands of Sertorius, he and Metellus were well on their way to winning the war even before Sertorius was murdered in 73 BC. Pompey returned to Italy just in time to help to mop up the remnants of the Spartacus

1.10 Portrait of Pompey. Cf. [152, 467].

revolt. He then claimed and was granted a triumph for his achievements in Spain, although he and others chose diplomatically to ignore the fact that the victory had been essentially over Roman citizens.

63. The Sullan Senate had spawned a potential monster. In exploiting Pompey's undoubted military talents, they had granted him command after command and conceded two triumphs – all this to a man who was not a senator and had held none of the magistracies. At the end of the decade they could hardly now demand that he start his senatorial career at the bottom of the ladder. So they granted him permission to stand for the consulship of 70 BC, to which he was elected along with a resentful and jealous M. Licinius Crassus. This was an obvious way of drawing Pompey into the system, of regularising his position. Equally, the changes to the Sullan system which Pompey oversaw during his consulship, notably taking away from senators the exclusive right to sit as jurors in the courts and the full restoration of the rights of the tribunes, should not be seen as revolutionary moves designed to

undermine the system created by Sulla, but as concessions, widely accepted by the Sullan Senate, designed to placate opposition and forestall trouble which might have threatened the peace of the *res publica*. Sulla's ghost would hardly have been happy, however. He could point out that within three years men were exploiting the tribunate in the tradition of the popular politics of the period after the Gracchi. In particular, they were asserting popular control of Rome's foreign policy in a way typical of the age of Marius and Saturninus. The immediate beneficiary of this activity was Pompey himself.

64. The Mediterranean had been troubled for decades by groups of pirates who disrupted trade and the corn supply. Some headway was made in the eastern Mediterranean by Rome's generals in the 70s; but the problem was not eradicated. In 67 BC the tribune A. Gabinius, against fierce senatorial opposition, proposed a bill directly to the people that Pompey should be given *imperium* against them covering the whole Mediterranean. With brilliant organisation and strategy Pompey cleared first the western and then the eastern Mediterranean in a single season of campaigning, ending up in Cilicia, south-east Turkey, where he was conveniently situated to take up a new challenge.

65. In 74 BC Mithridates of Pontus took advantage of Rome's troubles to renew his expansion in Asia Minor. L. Licinius Lucullus was sent out to fight him and initially had enormous success, driving Mithridates from Pontus, but failing to capture him. He found himself sucked further and further east with an increasingly demoralised army and ultimately suffered the humiliation of allowing Mithridates to recover his home kingdom. Through the early 60s Lucullus was the subject of violent criticism by popular tribunes, who gradually dismantled his command. When, in 66 BC, the tribune Manilius proposed that Pompey should now be sent to put an end to Mithridates, there was a body of senators who supported this proposal. Pompey's powers were to be wideranging and he was to use them to the full. Pompey defeated Mithridates in the first campaign in 66 BC. Again, the king escaped and fled to the Crimea on the far side of the Black Sea, where, after abortive plans to make a come-back, he committed suicide in 63 BC. Pompey, meanwhile, embarked on campaigns which changed the face of the East. Tigranes, King of Armenia, wisely negotiated a surrender. Pompey annexed the territory of Syria, the crumbling remnants of the Hellenistic kingdom of the Seleucids [37], and settled matters in Judaea. Local kings flocked to him for recognition. Some, like the unpopular Ptolemy Auletes of Egypt, came with massive bribes; others received huge loans from Pompey. He founded cities. He received extraordinary honours from the communities of the East as 'saviour and benefactor of the People and of all Asia, guardian of land and sea' (*ILS* 9459). There was an obvious precedent for all this; his victories 'equalled in brilliance the exploits of Alexander the Great' (Pliny, *Natural History* 7.95). In his remarkable speech in 66 BC in support of Pompey's appointment to the Mithridatic command Cicero extolled the virtues of Pompey: his bravery, uncorruptibility, trustworthiness, accessibility, and humanity. 'Everybody views Pompey not so much as a magistrate dispatched from Rome as someone who has fallen from heaven' (*On the Command of Pompey* 41). This rhetoric is derived from the conventions developed to praise Hellenistic kings, but it also anticipates the language in which Roman emperors were to be honoured [41, 80–81]. Pompey's activities went well beyond any brief given by Rome. The settlement of the East was his, not the senate's. Pompey's power and influence rested not simply upon the *imperium* given by Rome, but on his personal influence, connections and patronage. In the later civil war the East provided Pompey with his most solid support.

Cicero, Catiline and Rome

66. Pompey's achievements could inspire others. After noting the deeds of the great men of the past and of Pompey, Cicero claimed, 'Amid the achievements of these men there will certainly be some place for my own glory' (*Against Catiline* 4.21). Cicero (Marcus Tullius Cicero), from Arpinum, the home-town of Marius, achieved the rare feat of rising from a non-senatorial family to win the consulship of 63 BC at the first attempt and at the minimum age [144–8]. Early in his year as consul, he demonstrated his credentials by leading successful campaigns against a series of popular tribunician bills, including a bill to deal with the chronic problem of debt and a bill for settling people on the land, which was one of the most enlightened pieces of legislation of the era. His campaigns centred largely around arousing fears of renewed disruption and ascribing personal motives to the bills' proposers. Nowhere does he acknowledge the existence of the social and economic problems which the bills were designed to settle. No surprise then to find a growing centre of open discontent in Etruria, the same region that had been the focus of the troubles led by Lepidus in 78 BC [61]. Men oppressed by 'the savagery of the money-lenders and of the Roman courts' (Sallust, *Catiline* 33) found a local leader in a certain C. Manlius and a vocal and forceful champion at Rome in the senator L. Sergius Catilina, who was making his second, and again unsuccessful, attempt to be elected consul. Frustration in Etruria threatened to, and eventually did, boil over into open revolt. The Senate responded with the usual declaration of the *senatus consultum ultimum*. In this atmosphere of heightened tension Cicero made an attack on Catiline in the Senate in a speech which was remarkable for its rhetoric as it was for Cicero's sparing

use of evidence. Catiline left Rome, pleading his innocence of any attempt to subvert the state, and eventually found his way to the camp of those whose cause he had sought to advocate. Towards the end of the year, with the defeat of the rebellion ever more likely, people began to doubt the seriousness of Cicero's claims. So it was with considerable glee that, following a tip-off, Cicero arrested a number of Roman aristocrats who were accused of conspiring in support of the rebels. They could have been prosecuted in the courts; but in an atmosphere of hysteria Cicero chose to bring the issue of their fate before the senate, thus turning it into a lynching court. When, after a see-saw debate, the Senate voted in favour of death, Cicero had the accused executed. Consuls had had men killed previously under the *senatus consultum ultimum*, but such men had been in some sense in arms and resisting. Cicero's victims were helpless in chains before the Senate [168]. Within a month Catiline was also dead, putting up a brave fight in battle. Cicero represented Catiline as an anarchist and portrayed himself as saving the state. More cynical observers, more aware of the social and economic issues which underlay the troubles, might point to his passing remark in a letter that in 63 BC 'he had rescued the money-lenders from a state of siege' (*Letters to Friends* 5.6.8).

Cicero's Rome

67. At the end of 63 BC Cicero dreamed of controlling the political scene in conjunction with Pompey, when he returned to Italy. It was not to be, partly because Pompey had little interest in such an idea and partly because Cicero, for all his rhetorical talent, did not command the following to claim a place among the leading figures. Cicero's later political career was one of disappointment. In 58 BC, the tribune, P. Clodius, a personal enemy, had him exiled for a time for his execution of the conspirators in 63 BC. Cicero had little to offer, except despair, in the run-up to the war between Caesar and Pompey. He never found life comfortable under the domination of Caesar. After Caesar's murder, his championing of the cause of the Republic, which led to his death, was both heroic and characteristically totally out of touch with what was really happening.

68. Yet in another way Cicero was the dominant figure of the age. It was his vision of Rome which was adopted by contemporaries and succeeding generations. He represents another stage in the process of adapting Greek ways and ideas for a Roman audience [435ff.]. His contemporaries, the poets Lucretius and Catullus, used Greek ideas and metres. Cicero's rhetoric reflected and rivalled the best Greek precedents. Disappointed in public life, he turned to writing philosophical works and developed Latin in a way that enabled the lan-

guage for the first time to cope adequately with the expression of the abstract ideas at the heart of philosophy [386ff.]. In these works (such as *On the Republic*, *On the Laws*, and *On Duties*) Cicero both presented the influential ideas of the Greek world to the Roman élite, and also employed Greek ideas to explain the Roman social and political system. He offered a vision of a Rome run by a senate with the willing support of good men and true of all classes (the *concordia ordinum*, 'concord of the orders'), where the senators recognised their obligations to serve the needs of others in society. But such a Rome had never existed and could never exist. At times Cicero was able to analyse contemporary ills clearly. For example, he provided devastating critiques of the appalling behaviour of Roman provincial government, which undermined Rome's case and right to rule. Yet, of the problems at home, the poverty, the indebtedness, the social distress in Italy, he showed no recognition, offered no solutions. In his work *On Duties* (2.84), he declares that debt is something which can endanger the state and 'it is something which can be averted in many ways'; but he cannot give any practical examples of what should be done.

Motum ex Metello . . . (Horace, *Odes* 2. 1.1: 'The civil conflict which originated in Metellus' consulship [60 BC.]')

69. Pompey returned from the East towards the end of 62 BC and, despite fears that he would attempt some sort of coup, went out of his way to be conciliatory by disbanding his army on landing in Italy. Pompey was never a revolutionary. He was happy to show nominal respect for a political system, provided it acknowledged his pre-eminence within it. In the next year came the celebration of his third triumph. Velleius Paterculus wrote (2.40) 'The three divisions of the world had become so many monuments to his greatness' (i.e. his triumphs over the anti-Sullans in Africa [62], over Sertorius in Europe [62], and Mithridates in Asia [65]). How was such a man to be dealt with? Despite Pompey's attempts to allay people's fears, he found himself the subject of sniping from a group of senators around the Younger Cato (M. Porcius Cato), great-grandson of the Elder Cato. They successfully thwarted attempts by Pompey to get his settlement of the East officially sanctioned by the Senate and to have a law passed to provide land for his veteran soldiers. Pompey was not the only target. Crassus was offended, when a bill he was sponsoring was held up by Cato, and Julius Caesar, then coming to prominence, was first deprived by Cato's manoeuvres of the triumph which he felt his campaign as praetor in Spain entitled him to and then of a major command to accompany his consulship of 59 BC. What Cato and his friends were doing can be interpreted as trying to assert control by the constitutional authorities over the arbitrary use of power by individuals. It provoked Caesar into bringing Pompey and Crassus together with himself to settle their differences and to use their combined influence to steamroller through a body of legislation in their own interests. This arrangement, secretly put together in late 60 BC, is often labelled by historians 'The First Triumvirate'. The title is misleading. The three did not gain any constitutional recognition. They would have seen their informal agreement to co-operate as an expression of friendship (*amicitia*). Opponents would have described it as a faction (*factio*), an unnatural compact designed to pervert the normal workings of politics. At any rate, in 59 BC, the three pushed through a body of legislation to meet their needs. All the bills which had been held up were now passed and Caesar was invested with command in Gaul. The opposition did what it could. Caesar's fellow consul, M. Bibulus, Cato's son-in-law, resorted to an unprecedented religious device to try to prevent the holding of public meetings [121]. Caesar simply ignored him. Pompey's veterans were used to threaten and, indeed, to use violence to intimidate attempts by tribunes to veto the proceedings.

70. The coalition of Caesar, Pompey and Crassus was formed for short-term objectives. Once these had been achieved, in 59 BC, it no longer needed to remain in existence. In no sense did it collectively dominate the politics of the 50s. However, when necessary, it could be reformed to counter any revived opposition. So, when Caesar was threatened with the possibility of recall and opponents seemed likely to win the consulships of 55 BC, the three came together again. They forced through the appointment of Pompey and Crassus as consuls for 55 BC. These two got an extension for five years to Caesar's command in Gaul, where Caesar was already planning his two expeditions into Britain. They in turn were granted major military commands. Crassus got Syria and its neighbouring regions and it was no secret that he intended to launch an attack on Parthia, which at that time was still technically a friend and ally of the Roman people. The opposition could only bluster and accompany Crassus' departure with abuse and reports of bad omens. The campaign ended in defeat and death for Crassus at Carrhae in 53 BC. Pompey, for his part, was given the two Spanish provinces. However, he chose to stay in the vicinity of Rome to look after his interests and sent his legates to manage affairs in Spain. Pompey's position of being in command of considerable military forces in the provinces and yet a dominant presence in Rome created another important precedent taken up later by the emperor Augustus. These events demonstrated clearly that control of foreign affairs had effectively passed from the hands of the constitutional powers in Rome into the grasp of a few powerful individuals.

71. At the same time constitutionalists could do little to prevent the slide of

Roman politics into anarchy and corruption. P. Clodius, as tribune in 58 BC, came closest of all popular tribunes to establishing a long-term power base among the urban population of Rome. Through the links which he fostered with the local leaders of the city's districts he was able to call into the streets large numbers of people to demonstrate on his behalf. His opponents countered by recruiting gangs of their own, frequently from the gladiatorial schools. This period of urban disorder culminated in 52 BC with the death of Clodius in an affray and the burning of his body in the forum [200]; the fire spread and destroyed the Senate-house. Bribery, corruption and factional rivalry also threatened the breakdown of the normal processes of government. The years 53 and 52 BC began without consuls through the failure to complete the elections without scandal or violence. As matters lurched from bad to worse, Cato and Bibulus proposed in 52 BC that Pompey should be appointed to the position of sole consul. At first sight it seems odd to see the arch constitutionalists giving Pompey an unprecedented position of power. But the alternative was likely to have been an offer of the dictatorship. At least the consulship lasted only a year and was within the nominal control of the constitutional powers of the Republic. Pompey rose to the challenge with some tough and sensible laws and restored normality by having a colleague appointed as fellow consul before the end of the year. He was rewarded with an extension of time for his command in Spain. With Pompey now drawn into the constitutionalists' fold, they could now turn to undermining Caesar's position. There was a determination that he would be brought back to Rome at the end of his time in Gaul and face prosecution. Caesar for his part sought the same treatment that had been given to Pompey: the right to remain in command of his province and also hold the consulship again. When matters came to a head in 50 BC, Caesar got a tribune to hold up public business to prevent his being superseded in his province. Pompey came increasingly to see Caesar's claims as a challenge to his own authority and sided with the constitutionalists, thus giving them what they needed, a charismatic leader able to summon up considerable resources. 'What we now see is a struggle for personal power at the state's peril', wrote Cicero (*Letters to Atticus* 7.3.4) in December 50 BC. Victory for either side would bring with it the certainty of tyranny. A terrified nobility, remembering Sulla, sought any compromise to avoid the war and then split down the middle in its support.

Crossing the Rubicon

72. 'The only thing that Caesar's cause lacks is a cause', noted Cicero in the same letter. Caesar was soon to find one, and in January 49 BC on the pretext

of defending the rights of tribunes he led his army across the stream Rubicon, which divided his province from Italy. Pompey hastily abandoned Rome and fled east to Greece, where he was close to his most powerful source of support in the eastern Mediterranean [65]. In 48 BC Caesar followed him there and defeated him decisively at the battle of Pharsalus. Pompey fled to Egypt, where he was murdered.

73. For much of the next three years Caesar was engaged in facing and defeating his opponents in many parts of the Roman world. During this time he had himself appointed to several consulships and also to the post of dictator, culminating in 44 BC with his appointment as perpetual dictator (*dictator perpetuus*). The period also saw an unprecedented legislative activity. Caesar sponsored nearly forty pieces of legislation which tackled all the problems which had bedevilled the previous era: debt, the corn supply, land settlements, government of the provinces, corruption at home, a revision of the calendar. There were grandiose building schemes, large-scale civil engineering projects, grants of citizenship to some provincials, and gifts to all sorts and conditions of men. In this way he 'bound himself to many men' (Cicero, *Letters to Friends* 9.17.2). In return he was himself piled high with honours, many of them unprecedented in Rome but familiar from the Hellenistic world, some befitting the gods. Julius Caesar should be counted the first Roman emperor. In practice the world treated him as a monarch, though he rejected in public the title of 'king'. He was well aware of the resentment such behaviour might arouse among the aristocracy. He deliberately sought to avoid the harshness which Sulla had shown to his defeated opponents. 'Let this be a new way of conquering, to make mildness (*misericordia*) and generosity (*liberalitas*) our shield' (Caesar in Cicero, *Letters to Atticus* 9.7C.1). This was the show of clemency (*clementia*) for which Caesar became famed. But this was a double-edged virtue. To forgive was the prerogative of the king or tyrant. Roman nobles resented the idea that their careers depended on any other person's whim. There were those who were not prepared to accept Caesar's gesture. The Younger Cato, hunted down in Africa in 46 BC, chose suicide rather than accept Caesar's forgiveness, and in so doing established a model of behaviour, empty gesture though it was, for some in future generations who could not bring themselves to live quietly under a monarchy. There was of course another way of opposing Caesar. On 15 March (the Ides in the Roman Calendar) 44 BC Caesar was assassinated at a meeting of the Senate by members of a large conspiracy, which included many who had benefited from his favour.

After the Ides

74. The personal motives of Caesar's assassins were mixed, but they were brought together by a desire to return to a Republican normality. But they were too late. Few shared their dream. The Republic of the past generations had done little to help the poor of the city, the landless, the indebted, or the oppressed provincials. Within days of the killing the assassins realised that they were extremely unpopular, that they commanded little support and had no real power base. There were those, like Cicero, who were to struggle for his Republican dream, but that was only a side-show. The real issue was who was going to succeed to the leadership of the huge group which Caesar had built up. Initially those who had benefited from Caesar were afraid that his killing might lead to the loss of what they had gained. To placate them the Senate quickly agreed that all that Caesar had decreed, and even things he had promised but had not had time to carry out, was to be confirmed. This was a curious position – as Cicero querulously noted, they had killed the man, but had retained what he had done – but it reflected the reality of the situation. There were three contenders to replace Caesar: Lepidus (M. Aemilius Lepidus, from a noble family, a loyal lieutenant of Caesar's, who happened to be in charge of the troops near Rome at the time of the murder), Mark Antony (M. Antonius, consul in 44 BC and one of Caesar's closest companions), and C. Octavius, the 18-year-old great-nephew of Caesar, who found himself adopted by Caesar as his son in Caesar's will and thus obtained the greatest asset for the contest to come – the name of Caesar (after the adoption his name became C. Julius Caesar Octavianus – Octavian: fig. 1.11). Mark Antony sought to exploit his position as consul to give himself an advantage in this race, while Octavius began to win over Caesar's veterans during a tour of their colonial settlements in Italy. During the year Cicero turned against Antony, whose actions he interpreted as a threat to the restoration of Republican normality, and by the end of 44 BC he was leading a hysterical crusade against the man whom he now identified with relish as the 'new Catiline'. Early in 43 BC, Cicero and the Senate turned for help to Octavian and the forces he had attracted to his cause. Ignoring the fact that Caesar's heir would hardly be likely to share the interests of those who had killed his father-by-adoption, they granted him a command to assist the consuls in fighting Antony. After two battles in northern Italy Antony was driven into Gaul. The Senate thanked Octavian for his assistance and effectively dismissed him. Octavian responded by marching on Rome and got himself elected consul. Then, even more ominously, he called Antony and Lepidus to a meeting at which they settled their differences and agreed to have themselves created

1.11 Coin (*denarius*) of Octavian (*c*. 36–29 BC): on the obverse a head of Octavian in his romantic early image, on the reverse a figure of Victory holding a wreath and palm-branch and standing on a globe. Cf. [477].

Triumuiri Rei Publicae Constituendae ('the three men in charge of establishing the *res publica*'), a position which was recognised by a law in November 43 BC. The three then turned to Sullan-style purges of their political enemies by proscription – at Antony's insistence Cicero's name headed the list of victims. The cause of the Republic was now dead in the West. Antony and Octavian moved east and in 42 BC at Philippi in Macedonia defeated the armies raised by the leading Republicans, Brutus (M. Brutus) and Cassius (C. Cassius), who both committed suicide.

75. The triumvirs ruled jointly, issuing edicts in all their names. But in practice they spread out across the Roman world to deal with its problems. Italy and the West faced a troubled period. Octavian had to deal with an uprising in Italy – the result of the confiscations of territory in Italy to provide settlements for the veterans from the triumvirs' armies. Sextus Pompeius, a son of Pompey, became a focus for the surviving opponents of the triumvirs and carried on an intermittent sea-based guerrilla campaign in the West until defeated in Sicily by concerted action between Octavian and Lepidus. In the East Mark Antony was faced in particular with problems with Parthia, whose advance for a time disrupted many of the eastern provinces. By 34 BC he had recovered the ground initially lost, and then made a new settlement of the East. It became notorious that among the main beneficiaries of the settlement were Cleopatra, the ruler of Egypt, who had become Antony's consort, and her children.

76. In this period the elements of the Republican system had to learn to deal with the fact that all power lay in the hands of the triumvirs. The record of a senatorial decree of this period vividly demonstrates the way in which the

constitutional authorities knuckled under: 'all those rewards, honours and privileges which the Triumvirs have given or shall give . . . all these should be accepted as having come about in due and regular manner' (J. Reynolds, *Aphrodisias and Rome*, Document 8). The Senate had become a rubber stamp. The way in which individuals too in the Roman world had to come to terms with arbitrary rule is illustrated in a most evocative inscription. In the so-called 'Eulogy of Turia', the author of this inscription recalls movingly the actions which his wife took on his behalf during this period. He had been pro-scribed, but his wife pleaded with Octavian to allow him to return. When this was granted, however, 'Marcus Lepidus, Octavian's colleague, intervened to prevent my recall. Then, when you, my wife, prostrated yourself at his feet, he not only did not raise you up, but dragged you along and abused you, as though a common slave. Your body was all covered with bruises, yet with unflinching steadfastness of purpose you reminded him of Octavian's edict and the letter of congratulations on my pardon. Braving Lepidus' taunts and suffering the most brutal insults and wounds, you denounced these cruelties publicly' (*ILS* 8393).

77. The incident recorded in the 'Eulogy of Turia' also reveals internal dis-agreements between the triumvirs. Within the triumvirate there was a con-stant jockeying for position and influence. Lepidus was always in the least secure position and in 36 BC, after helping in the defeat of Sextus Pompeius, he found his troops deserting to Octavian and was forced into retirement. On several occasions war threatened to break out between Octavian and Mark Antony, and it became almost inevitable in the late 30s. Eventually the clash came on 2 September 31 BC at Actium in north-west Greece, where Octavian faced the combined forces of Antony and Cleopatra. Octavian was victorious. Antony and Cleopatra fled to Egypt, where they committed suicide when Octavian followed them.

78. As the political order crumbled, those involved, especially Cicero, whose writings have shaped so much our perceptions of the period, naturally felt that they were at the end of things, the last stages of a dreadful decline. Consciousness of change and a sense of transition and danger were a funda-mental part of the Roman picture of themselves. The anxious mood of the last generation of the Republic interpreted each new record-breaking disaster, each innovation as the climax or turning-point, and began to seek for a saviour-hero. The military brilliance of Gaius Marius, the Good Fortune of Sulla, the Alexander-like achievements of Pompey were all bids for this role. Julius Caesar came nearest to success in 'refounding' Rome, the gesture that was required to reverse the decline. Murder ended his projects. After Actium the task fell to Octavian. Rome, at last, had found her new king.

FURTHER READING

M. Beard and M.H. Crawford, *Rome in the Late Republic* (London, 1984)
M.H. Crawford, *The Roman Republic* (Fontana paperback, 2nd edn, 1992)
W.V. Harris, *War and Imperialism in Republican Rome 327–70 BC* (London, 1980)
C. Nicolet, *The World of the Citizen in Republican Rome* (London, 1980)

Sourcebook:
N. Lewis and M. Reinhold, *Roman Civilization, Selected Readings*, vols. 1 and 2 (2nd edition, New York, 1990)

2
Rome's new kings (31 BC – AD 476)

The second Romulus

79. The historian Dio Cassius (51.1) carefully notes the date of the battle of Actium, 2 September 31 BC: 'At this point Octavian alone held all the power of the state for the first time, and accordingly the calculation of the years of his reign should, strictly speaking, be made from that day.' He was right. Long before any attempt at a constitutional settlement, people throughout the Roman world were acknowledging Octavian (fig. 1.11) as their ruler, the latest focus of their hopes for peace and renewed prosperity. Octavian gained power by force of arms, as some emperors were to do later, but he cannot, any more than any of the later emperors, be thought of as a military dictator. As he himself put it (*My Achievements* 34), at this time he was in control of everything 'by the consent of everybody'. Cynical historians would be foolish to dismiss this as pure propaganda. Those who gain power by military force usually want to find some other more stable and acceptable basis for their rule. So from 28 BC onwards Octavian began the search for a constitutional basis for his dominant position in the state. In doing so he wished to assert the legitimacy of his rule, so that his right to be in charge was widely and generally acknowledged. Secondly he wanted to emphasise that he was content with modest-seeming powers which he wielded in an untyrannical way (it is of the greatest significance that in his own account of his reign, his *My Achievements*, he lists not just the honours he received, but also the excessive ones he chose to refuse (*My Achievements* 5)). But perhaps most important of all, Octavian realised that he could not rule an empire on his own. He needed the senatorial élite to participate in the task of administration and they had to be persuaded that there was an established career pattern for them and that they still had the opportunity to express their views and use their influence. The satisfactory achievement of these aims came only after a period of experimentation. In January 27 BC Octavian handed over his powers and territory to the decision of the Senate, who duly confirmed his authority as a consul and granted him a huge *prouincia* in which to exercise his *imperium*. This consisted of most of the provinces which contained Roman military forces. He could not govern this far-flung *prouincia* in any conventional sense; so he adopted the technique which Pompey had used of sending out his legates to the individual regions to govern in his name. The rest of the provinces were distributed annually by lot to senior senators, as had been the normal practice in the late Republic. Along with this settlement came the restoration and regularisation of much of the traditional machinery of administration: annual elections of magistrates, meetings of the Senate and of the people in assembly. Octavian could now represent himself as an elected magistrate of the Roman people with a large *prouincia* granted in regular manner by the Senate. All this worked as long as Octavian continued to hold the consulship each year. But in 23 BC he became dissatisfied and resigned his consulship. The continuous holding of the post could come to look irregular and, most important, it meant that there was only one consulship each year for the senior aristocracy to aspire to. But without the consulship the question arose of what was to be the *imperium* he was to use to govern his huge *prouincia*. So he was invested with the *imperium* of a proconsul, but it was specifically stated to be greater (*maius*) than that of other proconsuls, thus clarifying his relationship with other magistrates of the Roman people. There remained some ambiguity in his relationship with the consuls and that was settled in 19 BC by giving him the power of a consul without his having to hold the consulship. In these years there was considerable tidying-up and sorting-out of his rights to enter the city without losing his *imperium*, of convening the Senate, of putting motions to the Senate and suchlike. But there was one other power granted in 23 BC which is particularly revealing of Octavian's aims. He was given the power of a tribune (*tribunicia potestas*). In itself this was hardly a major addition to his constitutional powers. Yet it was clearly important to him. He began the practice of dating the years of his reign from this grant. Only the emperor or someone designated as his successor ever held the power. Its significance lay in the way in which it associated the emperor with the tradition of the popular tribunes of the Republic and their role as protectors and promoters of the interests of the ordinary people. And with this came a veiled threat to the aristocracy that in the last analysis, whatever their attitude to the emperor, he ultimately was in power as the people's champion.

80. But no amount of study of the constitutional fine print can explain the realities of the emperor's power. Octavian recognised this himself in a famous remark at the end of his *My Achievements* (34) that after the constitutional

settlement of 27 BC: 'I excelled everyone in influence (*auctoritas*), but I had no more power (*potestas*) than the others who were my colleagues in the various magistracies.' He is not trying to hide the fact that his views were pre-eminent, but is emphasising that they were so not because people were forced to obey him as a result of any excessive powers he held, but because of his *auctoritas*, the acknowledged influence which senior senators wielded, the influence which came from being associated with success. Following the famous meeting of the Senate in January 27 BC, which granted him his large *prouincia*, another meeting three days later granted Octavian a series of unprecedented honours, the most notable of which was the name by which he was to be known thereafter, *Augustus*, a title which implied 'holy', 'associated with the gods'. As someone 'holy', Augustus could expect the same sort of reverence which people showed to the gods, as the Greek translation of Augustus, 'Sebastos', showed (it was derived from the Greek word for 'worship').

81. So Augustus technically had a grant of *imperium*, that personal power once held by the kings of Rome, and also granted to the consuls, judges and governors of the Republic. But Augustus' *imperium* outshone that of all these predecessors. The senate continued to appoint men every year to command those armies and run the provinces, which were not part of the *prouincia* granted to Augustus. But, although the formalities of their independence from the emperor were long respected, these officials came to be seen more and more as the emperor's deputies. The governor of Asia, chosen by the Senate, could be described in an honorific inscription, as 'sent to preserve this province by that god Augustus' right hand and purpose' (*OGIS* 458). Augustus never felt any restraints in intervening where he thought necessary in any area of the Roman world. In response to delegations from the North African province of Cyrene (not part of his *prouincia*), Augustus neatly summed up the realities of the situation by dictating a line of action which it would be 'right and proper' for the governor of the province to follow 'until the Senate makes a decision or I myself find some better solution' (*SEG* IX.8). This focusing of power in the hands of one single Roman authority made it possible for greater order and pattern to exist in the Roman world. In the cities of both East and West the local notables, councillors and magistrates of old families with regionally based power now had a uniform goal: petitioning the Roman emperor for privileges and favours for their communities. People with a sense of injustice or grievance now felt that 'somebody up there loves me'. If only they could bring their problems to the notice of the emperor, then their troubles would be over. But how could he be put under an obligation to help? Since in many ways the emperor was like a god, remote, all-powerful and capable of transforming your life, then treat him like a god: build temples in honour of

Rome and Augustus, include him and his family in elaborate prayers, initiate lavish annual festivals with parades and sacrifices for him. It was no accident that this cult of the emperor developed first in the Greek East [41, 65]. Here they had been used to making their rulers the object of worship since the time of Alexander. But much of the East had also supported Mark Antony in the civil war. They needed to find a way to express their new loyalty to the victor of Actium, if they were not to be left out of the rewards and honours which he would bestow on the communities which had supported him.

82. There was another way in which this concentration on one central power clarified the nature of the Roman empire. Although there were no longer any great kings left of the sort who succeeded to parts of Alexander's empire, kingship survived on a smaller scale. Herod in Judaea and Juba in a kingdom covering the coastlands of what is now Algeria and Morocco are examples, and technically they were free and independent 'friends and allies of the Roman people'. But now, by expressing loyalty to Augustus, they conceded unequivocally that they were part of the Roman empire, that they were among 'the dynasts, tribal chieftains and priestly rulers who are also subject to the Romans', as the Augustan geographer Strabo (17.3.24) put it. Towards the end of his *My Achievements* (26ff.), Augustus reviews the conquests under his auspices which extended the provinces of the empire and brought new peoples under the direct control of Rome. Without a break he goes on to list the embassies, from as far afield as India, who came to him. Although the delegations themselves would not have seen it in this way, there is no doubt that Augustus took their presence in Rome as an acknowledgement of his and Rome's *imperium* just as much as if they had been provinces. As his poet Horace put it, 'neither those who drink the deep waters of the Danube will break the Julian commands nor the Getae, neither the Chinese and the faithless Persians, nor those born near the river Don' (*Odes* 4.15). In this sense Augustus really did have an *imperium sine fine*, a rule that knew no bounds.

The new age of peace

83. In the Roman Forum Augustus set up a Golden Milestone. From it distances were measured along the roads which radiated from the city across Italy and into the provinces. This measuring of roads, and the laying-out of a web of routes across the world, tied the parts of the empire symbolically to the centre, where the supreme ruler lived. This was a change from the Republic, when, for all that the Senate had authority, Roman *imperium* had always lain primarily where its holders had been with their armies.

84. According to the biographer Suetonius (*Augustus* 28), Augustus could

'justly boast that he had found Rome a city of brick and left it a city of marble'. Over the long years of his reign Augustus transformed Rome into a city which was visibly worthy of being the capital of the whole Mediterranean world. He filled it with monuments which could rival the greatest cities of the Hellenistic East [475ff.]. To commemorate the capture of Egypt he dedicated a huge sundial set out in a large piazza (figs. 2.1 and 2.2; cf. [263]). It proclaimed Augustus' dominion over time and the motions of the heavenly bodies. It also commemorated the arrival of the Egyptian sun-god at Rome; the pointer of the dial was a great obelisk brought to Rome from Egypt as a trophy and the whole area was dedicated to the Sun. In this way Augustus proclaimed the conquest of the clever Alexandrian Greeks whose skill laid out the dial, and of Egypt, the last of the kingdoms of the successors to Alexander to fall to Rome. The monument stood where the main routes from the north by road and river entered Rome, in the shadow of the great dynastic mausoleum which Augustus had begun constructing as early as 28 BC, and beside the Altar of Peace, which proclaimed the beneficial outcome of Augustus' wars. This new Rome was constructed in Augustus' own image. It was *his* Rome. The new forum which he constructed was dominated by a huge statue of Augustus in a triumphal chariot in the centre. Here came the Senate to decide on matters of war and peace. In the temple Roman governors offered sacrifice before leaving for their provinces. Here victorious generals returned, to be rewarded with statues set up round the forum. At one end of the original Roman Forum Augustus set up a temple to Julius Caesar flanked by a triumphal arch, and within the arch on panels were listed all the triumphs celebrated by Romans from the time of Romulus onwards. Equally striking was the way in which the Roman aristocracy ceased financing great buildings and monuments in their own honour on the scale they had throughout the Republican period. Nothing could be seen to rival the emperor. They turned instead to beautifying their home-towns in Italy or building their great funerary monuments on their own country estates, as the Plautii did later on the road to Tibur (fig. 2.3).

85. Augustus transformed Roman history, by placing himself at its high point. Roman historical writing of the last two centuries of the Republic was shot through with a deep sense of pessimism and foreboding, a feeling that Rome was in an inescapable downward spiral of moral and political decline. With Augustus that process was reversed. Now the history of Rome could be presented as moving logically towards its high point in the Augustan age. One side of the Forum of Augustus (fig. 2.4, cf. [128, 475], and fig. 3.3) was lined with statues of Aeneas and his descendants, the family of the Julii [7]. On the opposite side were representations of Romulus, the kings of Rome, and a carefully selected number of great Romans with inscriptions which emphasised

2.1 Augustus' sun-dial in Rome: the obelisk whose shadow measured the passage of time now stands in front of the modern parliament building in Piazza Montecitorio. Cf. [263].

their contributions to Rome's success. In this way Augustus placed himself within this tradition. The same message came from putting the list of all Rome's triumphs within his own triumphal arch in the Roman Forum (cf. fig. 1.5). Each of the seven centuries of Rome's history were evoked in an elaborate ceremony in 17 BC, the *ludi saeculares,* 'the Century Games'; but the prayers composed for Augustus on this occasion looked not merely backwards but also towards the continuing prosperity of Rome in the new age inaugurated by Augustus. Augustus now controlled time itself. The calendar contained an ever-increasing number of days on which the auspicious moments of the lives of Augustus and his family were celebrated. One of the months was renamed August in his honour. The cities of Asia chose Augustus' birthday as their new year's day in their reformed calendar.

86. Augustus 'bewitched everybody with the sweet pleasures of peace' (Tacitus, *Annals* 1.2). Peace had played little or no part in the ideas of the aggressive militarism of the Republic. There were no shrines or temples dedicated to it. Significantly it was in the chaos of the last generation of the Republic that it made its first appearance in the propaganda of men like Sulla and Julius Caesar, whose programmes were designed to bring an end to the internal strife of the period. For Augustus it was a central idea. One of the most evocative monuments of this period is the Altar of Peace , vowed in 13 BC to mark the return of Augustus to Rome from a visit to Gaul and dedicated in 9 BC. It stood beside the Via Flaminia at just the point where a returning general would ceremonially take off his military dress and put on the civilian toga, the dress of the city. Running round the outer wall of the altar area was a repre-

2.2 Augustus' sun-dial: detail of pavement-markings excavated in the cellars of a modern building. A bronze line marks the meridian, along which the obelisk's shadow fell at noon, and the short cross-lines indicate the length of the shadow on different days of the year. The inscriptions refer to events of the calendar and signs of the zodiac. Cf. [263].

2.3 Mausoleum of the Plautii, near Tivoli.

sentation of the ceremonial procession in 13 BC with Augustus near its head, surrounded by the priests, but followed by the members of his family (fig. 2.5), for they too were an assurance that the peace and stability which Augustus had created would continue in their hands after him. For most ordinary people the creation of internal peace for the empire meant economic revival. Late in his life, Augustus was sailing by the port of Puteoli on the Bay of Naples; when the passengers and crew of a ship, which had just docked from Egypt, learned of the emperor's presence, they crowded on deck to cry out that 'it was thanks to him that they had lives to live, thanks to him that they sailed the seas, and thanks to him that they enjoyed their freedom and fortunes' (Suetonius, *Augustus* 98) [243].

87. The key to Augustus' creation of peace within the empire lay in his treatment of the military forces. In the last century of the Republic the legions were able to extort ever-increasing rewards as the price of their loyalty in times of civil war. This process accelerated in the period after Julius Caesar's murder, as Octavian and Mark Antony sought to outbid each other in their efforts to win the soldiers' support. The civil wars suggested that the legions had an interest in unrest. Augustus' great achievement was to give them a stake in stability. The huge forces which came under his control after Actium were reduced to a core army of, probably, 28 legions, based at the edges of the empire, and a powerful élite force, the Praetorian Guard, based in Rome. For some years retiring soldiers were to receive the traditional rewards of land and some money grants. But after 13 BC the system was gradually regularised. Eventually in return for 20 years' service (or 16 in the Praetorian Guard) the

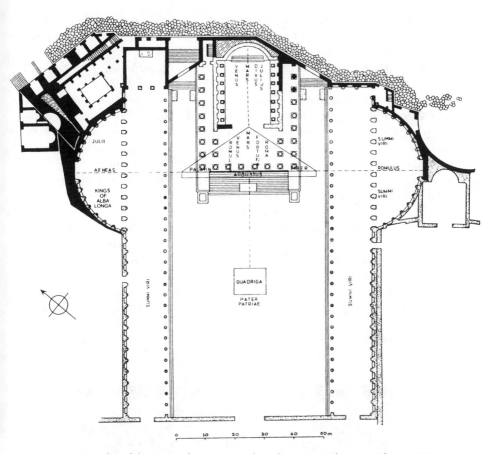

2.4 Plan of the Forum of Augustus marking the position of statues. Cf. [128, 475].

legionary received a lump sum on discharge which was the equivalent of some 13 years' pay. This was paid from a military treasury (*aerarium militare*) established by Augustus in AD 6 with a huge initial grant which was supplemented regularly by income from new taxes. Service in the legions now became a career, as it had never been before, with regular pay, significant privileges, the possibility of promotion, which could bring with it a rise up the social ladder, and the prospect of substantial rewards on retirement [238]. Of course, at moments of stress, for example at the moment of the succession of a new emperor, the armies were still capable of using threats to extort more, as happened in AD 14 on Augustus' death, when legions in Germany and Pannonia mutinied; but at most times the legionaries were not prepared to exchange the uncertainties of mutiny and revolt for the certain rewards which came with peace and loyalty to the emperor .

88. With these armies Rome's generals under Augustus' auspices added more territory to the provinces than anyone had ever done before. The whole of continental Europe from Portugal to the Rhine and north from the Mediterranean to the Danube was brought under Roman control and there were expeditions well beyond these rivers. In the East, Egypt was added to the empire and there were forays southwards into Ethiopia and east into Arabia. Displays of Roman force brought settlements with Armenia and Parthia (fig. 2.6). Yet at the end of his life one of the pieces of advice which Augustus left was that the empire should be kept within the bounds which it had reached under him. It is possible to see in this an uncharacteristic pessimism caused by a terrifying revolt in Pannonia in AD 6, which took three years to suppress and raised questions about whether Rome had overextended herself, given the available resources, and by the massacre of three legions in Germany beyond the Rhine in AD 9. But there may be more to it. Augustus may have realised early on that 28 legions were all he could afford and that this was scarcely sufficient to police the frontiers of the empire, let alone to engage in further expansion. Most campaigns can be seen as the securing of peace by keeping dangerous enemies far distant from the Mediterranean heart of the empire. Augustus revived an ancient tradition that the gates of the shrine of Janus

2.5 *Ara Pacis Augustae* (Altar of Augustan Peace), Rome (13–9 BC): representation of the imperial family in procession, featuring Agrippa with his head covered as a *pontifex* Cf. [476].

2.6 Settlement with Parthia. Relief on the breastplate of the statue of Augustus from Prima Porta, showing the handing back by the Parthians of the legionary standards which they had captured at the battle of Carrhae; all around are allegorical figures and deities relating to Augustan propaganda. Cf. frontispiece, [476].

were closed when the whole empire was at peace. Although this was supposed to have happened only twice in earlier history, the gates were closed on three occasions in Augustus' reign. One was after campaigns in Spain, and significantly Augustus himself describes what he did in Spain as 'pacification' (*My Achievements* 26). So his military campaigns tied in with the ultimate objective of his reign, peace. Even more notable were the opportunities for spectacular campaigns which Augustus did not take up. There were those who assumed that he was going to follow up Julius Caesar's campaigns in Britain; but he never showed any sign of doing so. Parthia could not be totally ignored; there were the defeats of Crassus and later of Mark Antony's generals to be avenged. However, in 19 BC a show of force was sufficient to obtain a diplomatic settlement with Parthia, which involved the return of the captured Roman standards. This was a great diplomatic achievement; but Augustus sought to present it to the Roman people as the equivalent of a military victory. This points to one of the most important consequences of an empire kept peaceful within defined frontiers. Although there were to be major campaigns to add territory – Claudius' invasion of Britain in AD 43 and Trajan's campaigns in Dacia in the early years of the second century – there were to be many fewer occasions for the use of military force. More and more what were

needed were not great generals but good administrators. Yet Roman aristocratic values, which set such great store on the winning of fame and glory, did
not adapt easily to acknowledging the quieter virtues of the bureaucrat. In his
biography of his father-in-law Agricola, the governor of Britain, which the
historian Tacitus wrote at the end of the first century, he praises those governors of Britain who pursued warfare with the tribes vigorously, but has nothing
but contempt for those 'idle' ones who sought simply to organise the territory
already won. What he could not come to terms with was the fact that men like
Agricola were increasingly an anachronism.

The inheritance of a single family

89. Augustus created a new era. The stability of the system owed much to the
fact that he lived so long. When he died in AD 14, most of those living at the
time had had no experience of any other way of running the empire. Yet
Augustus was frequently a sick man, and from time to time there had been
serious bouts of illness which he was not expected to survive, one as early as 23
BC. This raised the problem of what was to happen when he did die. There
were those who would wish to end the system Augustus had created and return
to the institutions of the Republic. As late as AD 41 the conspiracy against the
emperor Gaius and the revolt of Camillus Scribonianus in the following year
were determined attempts to put an end to the Principate. They achieved
nothing, and from then on 'Republicanism' became no more than an ineffective sentimental attachment to an imagined ideal past, which could be used to
criticise the tyrannical actions of emperors and to console those who failed to
make a success of their own careers under emperors. Republicanism had no
widespread support. Most people wanted an assured and undisputed transfer
of power, which would not disrupt the new stability. If Augustus had died
without taking any steps, then the likeliest outcome would be a renewed civil
war as contenders staked their claim for the empire – precisely what happened
on the death of Nero in AD 68. A successor needed to have what would be
widely acknowledged as a legitimate claim to the position. An important part
of such a claim was recognition by the Senate and People, whose task it was to
confer the various grants of *imperium* on each emperor. But in doing this, there
were good reasons why they could not ignore the emperor's family. First, the
heir to the emperor's vast personal wealth and patronage could not be set aside.
Secondly, the oath of loyalty, which everyone swore throughout the empire, was
to the emperor and his family ('I will be loyal to Caesar Augustus and to his
children and descendants all my life in word, in deed, and in thought'). So it
was easy for the people throughout the empire to transfer their loyalty to

another member of the family and see the legitimacy of his claim to rule over them. Augustus himself was determined to found a Julian family dynasty; cf. [419]. But he had no son, so attention turned to his daughter, Julia, who was married to Augustus' closest associate, Marcus Agrippa, and duly produced three sons, Gaius, Lucius and Agrippa Postumus. But Gaius and Lucius, in whom Augustus invested so much of his hopes, died young, and Agrippa Postumus, thought to be mentally unstable, never seems to have figured in Augustus' plans. After Marcus Agrippa died in 12 BC, Julia was married to Tiberius, Augustus' stepson, the son of his wife Livia. This loveless marriage produced a son who died in infancy. As he grew old and weak, Augustus turned to Tiberius and adopted him as his son and heir. There was another strand to Augustus' plans for a smooth succession. To prevent any power vacuum on his death, he had his potential successor invested with powers more or less the equivalent of his own. He had done this first with Agrippa, and by AD 13 Tiberius was virtually co-ruler with Augustus, invested by the Senate and People with an *imperium* the equal of Augustus'. This meant that on Augustus' death there was no doubt about his successor; Tiberius already had all the powers he needed to rule. The historian, Velleius Paterculus, a contemporary, testifies to the fears of people at the time and to the relief that the transition passed off peacefully: 'The world, whose ruin we had feared we saw, was not even disturbed, and such was the majesty of one man that there was no need to resort to arms either to defend the good or oppose the bad' (2.124).

90. Augustus had achieved much. The system which he developed formed the basis for the rule of emperors for centuries to come. But much still remained to be clarified and settled, in particular the role of the Senate in the administration of the empire. In the first weeks of Tiberius' reign there was a key meeting of the Senate. Seen from the distance of a century later, when the processes of the transfer of power were well established and conventional, the discussion could be branded as a 'shameless farce' by Suetonius. But at the time the issues were very real. Tiberius emphasised to the senate the scale of the task of running the empire, by producing documents prepared by Augustus, which outlined the state of the empire. Running it effectively was a job for more than one man, argued Tiberius. In this he was not seeking to lessen his power or to give up his supreme position; what he wanted was to be relieved of more of the day-to-day administration [188]. But he got nowhere with a Senate which was not prepared to co-operate. In the years that followed Tiberius tried to get his point over in another way. He referred every matter, whether important or insignificant, to the Senate for discussion and decision. Again the senators refused to play their part. Tiberius announced that he was going to be out of Rome; the Senate voted to suspend business until he

returned. Tiberius begged the Senate to appoint someone competent to command in Africa to deal with an uprising there; the Senate asked him who he thought should be sent. When at a meeting Tiberius lost his temper at the triviality of an issue and declared that he was ready to vote openly without further ado, a senator asked, 'Which position are you going to vote in, Caesar? If you vote first, then I will have your lead to follow. If you vote after everyone else, I am afraid that I might imprudently vote against you' (Tacitus, *Annals* 1.74). This went to the heart of the matter. By this date the emperor directly, or indirectly, controlled every aristocrat's career. His support could make or break a man's plans. So it was inevitable that ambitious men would avoid doing anything to offend the emperor; they would not want to take the initiative in controversial matters and would look to the emperor to provide a lead. What Tiberius was offering the Senate was responsibility without power, a gift the Senate was bound to reject. If decisions were to be made, they could be made only by the emperor or with a lead from him. If the work of the empire was to get done, the emperor could not avoid direct responsibility for it. In the second half of his reign Tiberius largely gave up his efforts to get the Senate to co-operate. His successors tried again from time to time. Claudius – or more probably the presiding consul – pleaded for real debate: 'It is altogether unsuited to the majesty of the Senate to have one man alone, the consul designate, state his view here, copying it word for word from the motion of the consuls; and the rest of you simply utter, "I agree", and leave saying, "Well, we had a debate"' (*Berlin Papyrus* 611). Nero made a real attempt in the early years of his reign to let the Senate get on with its duties. But nothing changed. Early in the second century, the senators, offered the opportunity for a secret ballot, treated the occasion as a joke, defacing their voting slips with obscene jokes. Not much later the formal speech, with which the emperor introduced matters in the Senate, itself came to be cited as a source of law; no one expected any debate to change the substance. If the Principate declined into autocracy, then the fault did not lie simply with the emperors, but also with the Senate.

91. There was another and more sinister constraint on the freedom of speech of senators. Under Tiberius there was a great increase in the number of cases of people being charged with 'diminishing the majesty of the Roman People', a vague accusation, first devised in the late second century BC [51]. But now the scope for employing the law was greatly increased: alleged criticism or abuse of Augustus, now a god, or Tiberius his successor could be construed as an attack on the majesty of the Roman People. Rome had no police force and no public prosecution service. So prosecution depended on private individuals who had to be rewarded for their efforts with a proportion of the

property of the accused person. This was a powerful incentive to bounty hunters. Even in the Republic one of the most effective ways of crippling the career of a political rival was to prosecute him successfully in the courts. Nothing changed under the Principate, and many of the cases may be seen as a continuation of this competitive rivalry among the upper class. Tiberius inevitably got the blame for the rise in the number of such cases. Yet he rarely initiated any himself and could only intervene to restrict the use of the law to serious cases, which he did for much of the first part of his reign. Nor could the Senate escape their share of the responsibility. As Tacitus admitted much later under Domitian, when there was another bout of treason trials before the Senate:

It was our hands, the hands of senators, which led Helvidius to prison. We were tortured by the looks which Mauricus and Rusticus gave us. It was us that Senecio drenched with his innocent blood. (*Agricola* 45)

It was a bold emperor who tried to do without some such law. There were sufficient real plots to make emperors keen to encourage people to expose them. Eventually, later in the century, most emperors were prepared to concede as part of the propaganda at the beginning of their reign that they would not allow any senator to be put to death, whatever the charge.

92. Tiberius was already 54 when he succeeded Augustus. He had seen and done most things, as a successful general and diplomat. One element in that early Senate debate on the task of running the empire may have been a world-weariness on Tiberius' part, a reluctance to involve himself in the burdens of office. At this time there was no great bureaucracy to help the emperor. Much depended on his own initiative and capacity for hard work. For a time, under Augustus, Tiberius had retired from public life to live on the island of Rhodes. In the first half of his reign he tried to escape from time to time, and then from AD 26 he retired to a spectacular palace on the tip of the island of Capri in the Bay of Naples. He was never to visit Rome again.

93. Every emperor had close advisers, to whom he turned for help and support. Marcus Agrippa had played that role for Augustus. Tiberius turned to his Prefect of the Praetorian Guard, L. Aelius Sejanus. The command of the Praetorian Guard [87] was the highest office a Roman *eques* ('knight') could reach; but because of the obvious favour in which Tiberius held him, Sejanus gained a power and influence which was deeply resented by the Roman aristocracy. That power grew in the years after Tiberius' retirement to Capri, because Sejanus could act as Tiberius' representative in Rome and the only means of communicating with the absent emperor. The aristocracy had to come to terms with fawning on Sejanus to get favours. As one of them was to

write later to Tiberius, 'I confess that I was Sejanus' friend; I sought his friendship and was happy when I obtained it . . . But we honoured not Sejanus of Volsinii, but your representative in state matters' (Tacitus, *Annals* 6.8). Sejanus became deeply involved in the struggles for power and influence within the imperial family. In AD 31 Tiberius was made to see that Sejanus was overreaching himself, and overthrew him in what was in effect an elaborate coup against his old friend. The years after AD 31 were a time of tension and uncertainty for the Roman aristocracy. Friendship with Sejanus could now lead to a prosecution. Tiberius became more and more ready to suspect disloyalty. In these years he increasingly lost interest in the affairs of empire and sank into despair. The empire was largely left to run itself. The *plebs* of Rome were deprived not just of the presence of the emperor, but of the games, shows and handouts associated with an emperor's appearances in public – not that Tiberius had ever been generous with these. When Tiberius died in AD 37, few mourned his passing.

The emperor Gaius

94. Tiberius was succeeded by Gaius Caligula (fig. 2.7), the 24-year-old grandson of Tiberius through Tiberius' adoption of Germanicus, Gaius' father, late in Augustus' reign. It may be that the seeds of Gaius' downfall lay in the enormous wave of support and enthusiasm which greeted his accession. Despite some pious remarks at the beginning of the reign about respect for the Senate, Gaius soon became suspicious of them and their role – with some justification, given their less than glorious record under Tiberius. Instead, Gaius sought to base his power directly on the support of the people, rather like many tyrants much earlier in Greece. But such a policy was extremely expensive and when, after two years, the money ran out, Gaius found himself increasingly isolated, unpopular, the object of suspicion and contempt from the Senate, and even the intended victim of plots formed within his own close family. The sources for Gaius' reign are full of lurid tales of sexual misdemeanours and irrational actions. This is the sort of material which was to grow up around every unpopular emperor. In all probability the truth cannot be recovered. Still less fruitful is speculation on whether Gaius was mentally deranged. The evidence needed is not available. However, it would be a mistake simply to dismiss or explain away all these stories and produce a 'whitewashed' version of Gaius' reign. The important fact in all this is that such stories were told about Gaius; people wanted to believe them. Gaius was doing something wrong. It is clear that his decisions were often arbitrary and lacked consistency. Lavish praise of the Senate at one meeting was to be fol-

2.7 Portrait of Caligula (AD 37–41).

lowed a year or two later by savage denunciation. People needed to know where they stood with an emperor; they needed a consistency on his part, so that they could calculate how he would react in any situation and what to do for the best to ensure his good will and support. A good example can be found in the record of Philo of an embassy of which he was a member, which came to Italy to attempt to get Gaius to secure the rights of the Jewish community in Alexandria. When eventually the envoys managed to get an audience with Gaius, it was while he was touring the building work being carried out on an extension to his palace. Gaius' only reaction to the Jewish embassy was to ask them about their attitude to eating pork and whether they worshipped him as a god. This was no way to carry out diplomacy.

95. In January AD 41 Gaius was assassinated in one of the passages which linked the various parts of the palace by a group of officers of the Praetorian Guard. But the plot may well have on a larger scale. Many senators may have been in the know. The brutal killing of Gaius' wife and baby daughter may be taken as an attempt to bring the dynasty to an end and restore the Republic. That attempt lasted overnight. Elements, particularly within the Praetorian Guard, who wanted to ensure the continuity of the Principate found a candidate in Claudius, Gaius' uncle, and proceeded to carry out a coup. If the normal laws of inheritance were applied to the imperial house, then there were others around who had a greater claim to inherit than Claudius. But Claudius had the support of the Praetorians. Much is made of the rewards which Claudius gave to them. But in reality these were no different, except in scale, from the grants regularly made at the beginning of reigns to ensure the loyalty of the troops to the new emperor.

2.8 Claudius' invasion of Britain. Coin (*aureus*) of Claudius with the emperor's head on the obverse and a representation of an arch built to celebrate the invasion on the reverse.

The reign of Claudius

96. The great project of the first years of Claudius' reign was the invasion of Britain (fig. 2.8). This did not in any way fit in with Augustus' advice to avoid major extensions to the empire. It is significant that the idea of an invasion of Britain was revived by Gaius, who got as far as the north coast of France before abandoning the expedition, and then carried out by Claudius in AD 43. Both these emperors lacked a military reputation, which was seen still as an essential part of an emperor's image. Claudius had suffered from crippling illnesses as a young man, which had prevented him gaining military experience. His desire also fitted the ambitions of the Roman aristocracy, who had been starved of opportunities to gain military glory under Tiberius. Anybody who was anybody was part of the invasion or served for part of their career in Britain. Yet there were no compelling strategic reasons to incorporate the island in the empire. A serious revolt by Boudicca under Nero led that emperor to contemplate withdrawing from the country, and later Domitian was to limit the ambitions of the general Agricola, who believed he was close to completing the conquest. These emperors recognised that Britain was an expensive luxury.

97. In some ways Claudius never managed to win general consent from the Senate for his reign. The first ten years of his rule were marked with a large number of executions of senators, often on extremely vague charges – indeed more aristocratic deaths are ascribed directly or indirectly to Claudius' reign than to any other first-century emperor. Yet it is clear from inscriptions that

the emperor was a highly effective administrator (cf. fig. 8.4), though the literary sources give him little credit for this. What the aristocracy found wrong with Claudius can be discovered from a speech which Nero made to the Senate, when he came to the throne. It often suited a new emperor to win favour by promising to put right bad features of his predecessor's rule (curiously, this led to the fact that many emperors' reputations suffered at the hands of their immediate successor). Nero promised that the affairs of the imperial household and the state would be kept separate and that there would be no place for bribery or corrupt favouritism in his palace, as there had been under Claudius (Tacitus, *Annals* 13.4). The origin of these charges lay in the contemporary perception of Claudius as a man dominated by his wives and freedmen. Once the emperor had become the sole source of influence and patronage, then those who surrounded him in his family gained reflected influence. If a subject, who sought help, could not get through to the emperor directly, then it might help to seek the aid of someone close to him, his wife or close relative for example. So the members of the emperor's family became power-brokers, acting as intermediaries between the emperor and his subjects. It is no surprise that the history of the Principate is full of powerful women, the mothers, wives, and daughters of the rulers. The same is true of the members of the emperor's household. Every great aristocrat had people to help his work; these were frequently slaves or freed slaves [243ff., 353]. Given the fact that more and more work was being piled on the emperor and that the Senate was reluctant and ineffective in taking on its share of the burdens, it was inevitable that emperors would turn to others to assist in the grind of day-to-day administration: letters to governors, replies to petitions, patronage of all sorts [193]. The freedmen who undertook this work are often described as part of an imperial bureaucracy; but in reality there was no great bureaucracy, only an element of administrative help [191]. Under Claudius a few of his freedmen became particularly prominent. What angered Roman aristocrats was the way in which such men, their social inferiors, intervened between themselves and the emperor, and played a considerable role in public affairs. One of them, Narcissus, was found helping with the organisation of the invasion of Britain, in charge of a major civil engineering project (from which inevitably he was alleged to have siphoned off massive illegal profits), speaking in the Senate, using patronage (the future emperor Vespasian is supposed to have had his early career boosted by him), and intervening in the jockeying for power within the imperial family. Worse still, the senators had to acknowledge and reward these men. Another freedman, Pallas, was offered an honorary praetorship and a small fortune by a obsequious Senate, 'because, despite his descent from the kings of Arcadia, he had put public service before his ancient lineage, and permitted himself to be regarded as one of the emperor's servants', as Tacitus (*Annals* 12.53), a bitter and resentful critic of freedmen, put it.

Whatever their true influence, Claudius could be seen as unlucky in his wives. One, Messalina, became the centre of a large conspiracy in AD 48, while her successor, Agrippina, worked assiduously behind the scenes to ensure that her own son, Nero, would succeed Claudius (she may also have been responsible for poisoning Claudius in AD 54).

Nero

98. Nero was still only 17 when he came to power. He was full of good intentions, which to an extent he carried into practice. The early years of his reign met with the approval of a wide range of people [398–9]. That was not to last. When Subrius Flavus, a tribune of the Praetorian Guard, was asked by Nero why he had broken his oath of loyalty by joining a great conspiracy in AD 65 to kill the emperor, Subrius replied, 'Because I hated you. No soldier was more loyal to you than I, while you deserved affection. I began to hate you when you murdered your mother and your wife and became a charioteer, actor, and arsonist!' (Tacitus, *Annals* 15.67). It is a startling list. In AD 59 Nero had ordered the killing of his mother, Agrippina, by a group of marines from the Roman naval base on the Bay of Naples. This event followed hard on what was seen as an earlier botched attempt to have her drowned in a collapsible boat. That may have been a genuine accident. Further, Nero claimed that his execution of Agrippina followed an attempt by her to have him killed. Again this may have been true, but it would never have been believed. Besides, ordering the killing of one's mother excited a horror among contemporaries. His divorce of his wife, Octavia, followed later by her execution brought people onto the streets of Rome to protest. These events demonstrated that Nero was above the law, answerable to no one; there was no way to restrain him and demand conformity to social norms. This also explains the other charges brought against Nero. After the murder of his mother, Nero, according to Tacitus (*Annals* 14.13), 'threw himself into all those lusts, which respect for his mother had held in check, even if they had been barely suppressed. He had a longstanding desire to drive in four-horse chariot races. Another no less disgusting passion was to sing to the accompaniment of the lyre in the manner of a professional artist.' To us these may hardly seem to be in the same class as family killings. But public performance was something the Roman upper class found demeaning. Yet there was another side to all this. Chariot races were the most popular

2.9 Chariot-race; the triple turning-posts and central obelisk of the Circus Maximus are visible in the background. Cf. [218].

spectator sport in Rome (fig. 2.9: cf. [218]) and Nero's involvement might be seen by the urban population as identification with their interests. As for the composition and singing of songs, here Nero was exhibiting a genuine interest in Greek culture, which was shown by the introduction of a five-yearly festival, the Neronia, based on Greek-style competitions in music and athletics. In AD 67 Nero was to visit Greece and take part in the specially arranged festivals. If this commitment to Greek culture seemed both eccentric and contemptible to a Roman aristocrat, the Greeks welcomed an emperor who shared their values and identified with them.

99. The devastating fire in the centre of Rome in July AD 64 was clearly an accident of a sort which happened all too often in Rome's largely unplanned environment. Yet even Tacitus, who describes the event in a way that shows he recognises its accidental nature, cannot resist also retelling the stories that Nero had deliberately started the fires. The cause of these stories was Nero's grandiose scheme to build an elaborate *domus aurea* ('Golden House': fig. 2.10) set in extensive grounds, complete with a large man-made lake, in one of the areas to the east of the Forum destroyed by the fire [483]. The exciting and novel architecture of the new palace was less likely to impress most people than Nero's exploitation of public distress for his own private benefit. It was easy then for gossip to suggest that the fire had been started deliberately to clear the area for this development. It is significant that the Flavian emperors

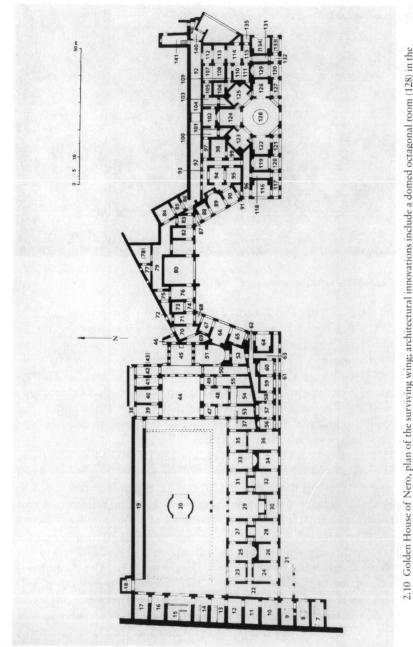

2.10 Golden House of Nero, plan of the surviving wing; architectural innovations include a domed octagonal room (128) in the eastern part. Cf. [483].

later ostentatiously returned much of the area to public use, draining the lake and using its excavated area for the foundations of the Colosseum, their new amphitheatre [484].

100. Here, then, was an emperor who did not obey the conventions and norms. But what could people do about him? He escaped a serious plot to assassinate him in AD 65 – the conspiracy of Piso. Other aristocrats ostentatiously chose to opt out of public life, so that they no longer had to associate with or show respect for the emperor. In the atmosphere of suspicion in the years after the Piso conspiracy it was easy for prosecutors to represent this sort of action as subversive. Nero had to do nothing other than stand by and watch their conviction. In a few notorious cases the victims chose to commit suicide and thus foster a myth about their brave opposition to tyranny, which their friends and family worked hard to keep alive through succeeding generations. In reality their deaths changed little. Nero remained popular in Rome. The armies remained loyal almost to the end. When in AD 68 there was a revolt in Gaul, which spread to the army in Spain, there can be little doubt that if Nero had acted promptly and resolutely, he could have recovered the situation. Instead he panicked, prepared to flee Rome, and committed suicide in a suburb of the capital.

Emperors made elsewhere than Rome

101. Nero left no heir or successor. This essentially left the empire up for grabs. In such a situation it was always the force of arms which would decide matters. The first claimant was the current governor of one of the Spanish provinces, Servius Sulpicius Galba. His distinguished Republican aristocratic ancestry was likely to win favour with his fellow senators, but he managed to squander his advantage by making every mistake it was possible to make. Where reconciliation was needed, he was fierce towards those who had not declared for his cause. Where senators and officials needed to be reassured that their future careers were secure, Galba surrounded himself with a narrow group of cronies. Where the army expected rewards for support, he took the line of high principle that he would not buy their support. Finally, a dramatic gesture on his arrival in Rome early in AD 69 of immediately announcing a young aristocrat as his successor led to a coup by one of his disappointed supporters, Marcus Salvius Otho. In any case, the army on the Rhine had already become suspicious of Galba and had sought its own candidate, Aulus Vitellius. He invaded Italy and defeated Otho, only to find that the armies of the East and a number of the forces in the Danube region had decided on their candidate, Titus Flavius Vespasianus, who at that time was engaged in

2.11 Portrait of Vespasian (AD 69–79) from Ostia. Cf. [484].

suppressing a major Jewish revolt. Vespasian was desperate to avoid being seen as bringing civil war back to Italy itself. But events had gained their own momentum. Forces invaded Italy in the name of Vespasian. The city of Cremona was sacked and in the last desperate days in Rome, fighting between supporters of Vitellius and of Vespasian led to the burning down of the temple of Jupiter on the Capitol. Vitellius was killed. The year AD 69 had seen four emperors, candidates of the armies rather than of the senate and people of Rome.

Pax Romana

102. With Vespasian (fig. 2.11) the Roman world drew back from an ever-continuing cycle of disorder. He was to establish a new dynasty [484]. Although they had had no say in the choice of Vespasian, the Senate and People of Rome eagerly accepted him in the hope of restoring stability. As Tacitus (*Histories* 4.3) put it, 'At Rome the Senate decreed to Vespasian all that was usually decreed to emperors.' One of the most remarkable inscriptions to survive from Roman antiquity is part of the law acknowledging Vespasian's powers. Among its clauses is one which startles at first glance: 'That he shall have the right and power . . . to transact and do whatever things divine, human,

public and private he deems to serve the advantage and the overriding interest of the state' (*Law on the Powers of Vespasian: ILS* 244). Does this represent the decline of the Principate into blatant autocracy? But, the clause adds, 'just as Augustus, Tiberius and Claudius had' (no one was likely to name Gaius or Nero as precedents). The ultimate power of the emperor to do whatever he wished had been there from the start, although some of the earlier emperors might have shied away from expressing it so blatantly. The price of peace and stability was, as it had been in 31 BC, that all power should reside in one man.

103. Many might have been apprehensive about the future in AD 70. No one could have anticipated that Vespasian had ushered in the remarkable period of peace and stability which lasted until AD 193, the period in which Rome became the Roman empire, an integrated whole. Not that there were no disruptions: a serious army revolt on the Rhine under Domitian and a revolt by the governor of Syria under Marcus Aurelius (both failures); many plots, including the successful assassinations of Domitian and Commodus; and constant scheming and jockeying for positions of influence within the emperors' families and advisors. Nevertheless, the empire gained a settled rhythm, which was hardly interrupted by such happenings.

104. The first part of the period was guided by the members of the Flavian family. In AD 79 Vespasian was succeeded by his son Titus, whose brief reign was chiefly remarkable for the devastating eruption of Vesuvius, which buried Pompeii and Herculaneum on the Bay of Naples. The representation of Titus' reign as brief but golden [485] was largely created as a stick with which to beat his brother Domitian, who succeeded him. Although an able administrator, Domitian earned an evil reputation in our sources. A solitary man by disposition, surrounded by a relatively narrow band of friends and advisors, he could appear remote. The vast new palace which was built in his reign to dominate the Palatine Hill (fig. 2.12) could been seen either as a fitting centre for the Roman world with its awe-inspiring audience chamber and hall or the lair of a wild beast, which roamed its dark corridors and feasted on the blood of its victims. The well-publicised trials and executions of a number of dissident senators towards the end of his reign had a disproportionate effect on Domitian's later reputation. It was under Domitian that men like Tacitus and Pliny the Younger, whose writings were to have so great a role in moulding later generations' view of the Principate, had their careers – successful careers at that, despite the fact that both would later distance themselves from the reign.

105. Domitian was murdered in a palace conspiracy in AD 96 and replaced by a senior but elderly senator, Nerva. There was a real threat that matters might disintegrate again as in AD 69, but Nerva moved quickly to adopt and

2.12 Palace of Domitian on the Palatine (Domus Augustana, completed AD 92): the so-called Stadium, a huge sunken garden. Cf. [483].

name as his successor, Trajan, an experienced senator, who at that time was in command of the armies of Upper Germany, and who duly took over on Nerva's death in AD 98. The emperors who reigned for much of the second century, Trajan, Hadrian, Antoninus Pius and Marcus Aurelius, were of very diverse character, but have uniformly been blessed with favourable assessments in our sources. There are two interlocked reasons for this. First, they were all 'one of us', as Pliny praised Trajan – that is they were members of the Senate. Secondly, although each was often kinsman of his predecessor, he was not in direct line of descent and was chosen by adoption by his predecessor as his son and heir. The importance of this process can be seen from a speech put in the mouth of Galba by Tacitus (*Histories* 1.16), when Galba adopted a certain Piso as his son in AD 69: 'Under Tiberius, Gaius and Claudius, we were the inherited property, so to speak, of a single family. The exercise of choice which begins with us will be our version of freedom. Now that the house of the Julians and the Claudians has come to an end, adoption will discover the worthiest successor in each case. To be begotten and born of emperors is a mere accident, and is reckoned as no more. In the process of adoption

2.13 Portrait of Hadrian (AD 117–38). Cf. [487].

there is free use of judgement, and if you wish to make a choice, a consensus points out the man.' It was not to be the accident of birth which decided who should be emperor. The choice was to be from the ranks of senators, and in theory many could aspire to the Principate. Further, an emperor's choice was expected to be informed by the views of the ruling class.

106. Trajan's distinctive achievements were his major military operations – two wars beyond the Danube in Dacia (celebrated on his column, set up in his forum in Rome [486]) and an invasion of Parthia. Hadrian (fig. 2.13) was a restless traveller around his empire and the sponsor of great building programmes in Rome and elsewhere [487]. Antoninus Pius' reign was marked by the effective administration of a largely peaceful empire. Marcus Aurelius was a sensitive and highly educated man, who affected the air of a Greek philosopher, even while conducting major wars on Rome's northern frontier. He was also the first emperor for a century to leave a son as heir. Commodus, 18 years old when he succeeded as sole ruler in AD 180, went a long way to prove to his contemporaries the inadvisability of natural, as opposed to adoptive, succession. His arbitrary decisions and exotic behaviour recalled the reigns of Gaius and Nero. He fell victim to a palace coup on the last day of AD 192, strangled in his bath by his masseur.

Efficient Rome

107. 'These will be your arts – to rule the peoples with your *imperium* and impose your custom on peace' is the way in which Virgil has Anchises prophesy a different future for the Romans from the attainments of the Greeks (*Aeneid* 6.851–2). It was in the period after AD 69 in particular that Romans sought to redefine themselves. The emphasis was away from the achievements of war to the arts of peace. It is to this period that we owe the picture of the Romans as practical geniuses. In a treatise on the aqueduct system of the city of Rome, a senator, Frontinus, wrote of his enthusiasm for the quantity and complexities of the water supply: 'compare this with the Pyramids or the useless, but celebrated, masterpieces of the Greeks' (*On the Water Supply of the City of Rome* 16). The great buildings of the age combined with texts such as Statius' poem on the building of a new road or the descriptions of architectural work in Pliny's letters to give a new sense of Roman skill in utilitarian matters. Pliny also wrote of his chores as Prefect of the Treasury in the same vein as our author on aqueducts, talking of the 'highly illiterate letters' that he must write as a dutiful public servant (*Letters* 1.10.9). This is the age that saw the first codification of Roman Law, under Hadrian, and the ever more numerous inscriptions from the cities of the empire seem to show the importance of the 'illiterate letters' of the Roman administration for the daily lives of hundreds of communities.

The Fortunes of Italy

108. The origins of the emperors in the century or so after AD 69 also reflected the transformations which were going on to the idea of Rome in this period of high empire. Vespasian, the son of an equestrian *publicanus* ('tax-collector'), came from Reate in Italy, north of Rome. Freed from direct taxation in 167 BC, given Roman citizenship in 89 BC, divided like the city of Rome into regions by Augustus, and increasingly regarded as the hinterland of the capital, Italy became more and more obviously the Roman homeland. Virgil celebrated its beauty, antiquity and fertility; like Horace, Ovid and Propertius he was one of the wave of well-to-do men from the towns of Italy who came to Rome to make their fortune. In the generations after the Social War, the families of the local gentry of the Italian towns flocked to stand for office in Rome, to fill its magistracies. Now, with Vespasian, the Italians had provided Rome with an emperor. Italians were at the very centre of Roman power. When the poet Statius at the end of the first century AD wrote in praise of one Septimius Severus, a Roman of Italian family from the city of Lepcis Magna in Libya, he

protested (perhaps too much), 'your heart is not that of an outsider, you are Italian through and through' (*externa non mens, Italus Italus*; *Siluae* 4.5.46). The credentials of men like Septimius needed to be established, and the crucial factor was membership of the ruling people defined in terms of the Italian peninsula. But Italianness never became the core of Roman imperialism like the nationalistic ideologies of the empires of the nineteenth and early twentieth centuries. It was more like a privileged inner circle, and as the centuries progressed the boundary between Italy and the provinces became blurred under the pressure of widening horizons.

The open élite

109. At the very end of the Republic men with Roman citizenship from the provinces were aspiring to great careers at Rome. Protégés of great politicians – Caesar's friend Balbus from Cadiz in Spain, or Pompey's adviser Theophanes, from Lesbos – could succeed even if they were from far-flung parts of the empire. This effect was greatly strengthened by the unifying of Rome's power under the authority of one man. All promotion at Rome and in the provinces and kingdoms was ultimately the emperor's decision. First Italians, whose families had moved to the provinces, then more and more provincials who had close ties with Rome and Italy, could expect successful senatorial careers if they had the favour of the emperor. The process is well illustrated by an inscription which records part of a speech which Claudius made in the Senate in AD 48 to justify the granting of permission to stand for senatorial office to the chieftains from the area of Gaul conquered a century earlier by Julius Caesar (*CIL* XIII.1668; cf. Tacitus, *Annals* 11.23). A rambling discussion on early Roman history – a favourite topic of Claudius – was designed to demonstrate that Rome had grown great from its willingness to absorb other peoples. By praising men from the parts of Gaul closest to Italy who had already entered the Senate, Claudius sought to show that the policy continued to pay off and that there was no longer any point in distinguishing between such men and those from the rest of Gaul: 'Not even provincials should be excluded provided they can add distinction to this Senate-house.'

110. The families of provincial élites, whether relatives of dependent kings or magistrates of free or provincial cities, now had other goals besides promoting the welfare of their home communities. During the years AD 70–117 many wealthy men from the eastern Mediterranean whose family connections covered both of these groups joined the inner circle of Roman power. Descendants of kings who had supported Augustus were consuls at Rome a hundred years later. With Trajan and Hadrian came the culmination of these sorts of process. Although both were brought up in Rome, their attachment was to the homeland of their families in a distant part of Spain. Provincials could now become emperors [367].

The Second Sophistic

111. What did it feel like to be born a wealthy potentate of Sardis in Asia and to be consul at Rome in AD 92? We can see how the consuls and the political life of Rome worked from the correspondence of Pliny the Younger. This life became the goal of many an Easterner, but in achieving it, they harnessed the power of that legacy of Greek philosophy, oratory, letters and art, which centuries before had given men like the historian Polybius and the philosopher Posidonius influence within the Roman élite. But instead of being hostages or dependants as they were, the new Hellenes used the same skills to enter the inner circles of Roman power. Once before in Antiquity philosophy and the pursuit of power had come together, the age of the philosophers and teachers, known as sophists, in fifth-century BC Athens (*WoA*, 4.44–8). Now again learning could be a passport to political power in the age which a third-century writer (Philostratus) called 'the Second Sophistic'. Greek culture could win power at Rome. In the second century AD, when this process was at its height, the cultural heartland of the Roman empire was the world of the cities which produced these scholar-statesmen. Success came through oratory, philosophy and patronage of the visual arts. Very wealthy men – such as Herodes Atticus at Athens – embellished their cities with buildings on a greater scale than ever before, and founded festival after festival in competition with each other. The mood was potent enough to affect emperors as well – Hadrian, who travelled like a wandering philosopher to every part of the empire, or Marcus Aurelius, who wrote philosophical reflections on the task of being emperor.

'Romanisation'

112. According to his son-in-law Tacitus, Agricola, the governor of Britain from AD 76 to 84, built public buildings, introduced the practice of bathing and taught the Britons to wear the toga and to speak Latin. This passage is often quoted as a key text for what is often described as 'Romanisation'. This is sometimes taken as the deliberate imposition of a coherent package of ideas that make up Roman civilisation. But as we have seen, the very concept of what was Roman changed over time and the interaction with the various peoples absorbed into the empire was a complex two-way process.

113. Local benefactors in the early second century AD built a grand new temple in the sanctuary of Asclepios, the god of healing, in the province of Asia, at Pergamum. They chose to imitate the great rotunda which Hadrian had dedicated in Rome, called the Pantheon, the shrine of all the gods. The way in which the vault was constructed came from the contemporary architecture of the capital. But the significance of the choice depended on the fact that so many people from Asia had been to Rome, including men who had reached the consulship. The particular impact of the shrine to Asclepios on the pilgrims to it must have been intended to owe something to the references to the great building in Rome.

114. She is seated in a high-backed wicker chair (fig. 2.14). Her dress is a simple, flowing robe with full sleeves and for ornament she wears an earring, a necklace and, on each arm, a patterned bracelet. In her left hand she holds a distaff and spindle, and by her side stands a basket full of balls of wool. Her right hand reaches down to open her sturdy jewellery casket. This scene is carved with loving care on one of the most evocative monuments from Roman Britain [306]. The tombstone comes from the northern frontier of the Roman empire, from the fort at South Shields, which overlooks the entrance to the River Tyne in the North of England. Under the scene her husband has had carved a dedication in imperfect Latin: 'To the spirits of the departed and to Regina, his freedwoman and wife, from the tribe of the

2.14 The tombstone of Regina, wife of Barates. See [114].

Catuvellauni, aged thirty, Barates of Palmyra set this up', and then in the Palmyrene script of his homeland: 'Regina, the freedwoman of Barates, alas'. So, at some point, perhaps late in the second century AD, Barates had travelled the length of the Roman world from his homeland, an important caravan city in the desert beyond Syria, to Britain, where he obtained a slave who came from Hertfordshire. He freed and then married her – a familiar story. They were both to end their days on the northern frontier of the empire, where Barates either served in the army or was a camp-follower. When Regina died, Barates ordered a monument which was reminiscent in style and content of the tombstones of his distant home at the other end of the empire. This extraordinary monument is demonstration that the complex interplay which made the distinctive culture of Roman society in this period was not confined simply to the élite, but could be found much further down in society [244].

Empire without end

115. There were more transformations to come, though they lie beyond the period which is central to this book. The assassination of Commodus led in early AD 193 to a situation similar to AD 68/69. Even more unedifying was the sight of the Praetorian Guard putting their loyalty up for auction to be won by the contender for the throne who paid the most. As before the matter was to be settled by force of arms, when Septimius Severus, a man of Italian descent from North Africa, emerged as victor.

116. The third century was seen by contemporaries and some modern scholars as a period of decline. Barbarian tribes broke through into the heart of the empire. In the East Rome failed in the face of resurgent Persian dynasty. But the reality was that Rome's forces were a thin line of defence round the empire. They had never been adequate to meet concerted large-scale pressure. The surprise was that they had been effective for so long. Parts of the empire, such as Gaul in the West and Palmyra in the East, for a time more or less seceded from the Roman empire and looked to their own defence. This should be taken as a sign of prosperity and growing local confidence. The crisis of the empire was gradually turned around by a new breed of Roman emperors. These were not from the senatorial class, but were tough professional soldiers; many of them had been born and had served in the lands along the Danube. At the end of the third century one of these, Diocletian, went a long way to restoring the empire and providing it with the administrative machinery and manpower which it needed to survive. He also

virtually acknowledged that the task had become too big for one man. He recruited three others and jointly all four divided up the job of administering the empire. That system did not really survive Diocletian. The civil wars which followed culminated in the success of Constantine at the battle of the Milvian Bridge in AD 312. This was truly one of the most important moments in the history of Europe, because Constantine chose to fight the battle under the banner of the Christian God. From that moment Christianity was transformed from an intermittently persecuted religion [383–4] into first the personal religion of the the Roman emperor, the recipient of imperial patronage and favour, and then by the end of the fourth century into the religion of the Roman state. When artists came to depict Christ in this period, more and more he appears as a Roman emperor, sitting in judgement on his people. So the emperor became Christ-like and Christ became a Roman emperor writ large.

117. With the death of Theodosius in AD 395, the empire virtually split in half: a western half, no longer really centred on Rome, but on the imperial residences in North Italy, Gaul and the Balkans, and an eastern half, centred on Constantinople, created by Constantine to meet the demands of the eastern élites for a Rome of their own. For much of the fourth century barbarians had been filtering into the Roman world; they had been settled in underpopulated areas and recruited into the army to defend the empire and to serve as military officers and administrators. It should not be thought that these barbarians came to destroy. For them the world of the Mediterranean was an El Dorado, a California. They wanted their slice of the good life. Since they could not keep them out, the Romans, particularly of the West, increasingly had to accommodate them. In AD 410 a band of these barbarian tribes quarrelled with the western court and sacked the city of Rome. Despite the fact that Rome had long sinced ceased to be at the heart of the empire, the event was seen as a shocking sign throughout the empire. What the barbarians did was to carve kingdoms out for themselves from parts of the western empire. Once again the idea of Rome was transformed. In many ways these German kings acted like Roman emperors. Roman orators, bishops, and poets could now find homes at their courts as they had previously done at the courts of the Roman emperors. When in AD 476 the German King Odoacer sent the latest holder of the title of emperor into retirement, and then saw no reason to replace him, the event seems to have caused but little stir. Did Odoacer have a sense of history, or indeed of humour? The name of that last western emperor was Romulus.

FURTHER READING

F. Millar, *The Emperor in the Roman World* (London, 1977)
Colin Wells, *The Roman Empire* (Fontana Paperback, 2nd edition, 1992)
P. Garnsey and R.P. Saller, *The Roman Empire, Economy, Society and Culture* (London, 1987)

Sourcebook:
N. Lewis and M. Reinhold, *Roman Civilization, Selected Readings*, vols. 1 and 2 (2nd edition, New York, 1990)

3
Princeps *and* imperator

The mixed constitution

118. The Romans not only secured a world empire but controlled it from the early second century BC to the fifth century AD, more than six hundred years. This achievement has been a source of admiration from the beginning of the process down to modern times. For example, when Benito Mussolini, the fascist leader of Italy, wanted to impress the world with the power of the new Italy that he claimed to be creating in the 1920s, it was to the symbols of the Roman empire that he turned to provide the images of Italian domination. The question how Rome rose to power fascinated ancient historians. The first person to tackle the problem, the Greek historian Polybius (*c*. 200 to after 118: see [43]), argued that the basis of Rome's rise to power lay in the peculiar constitutional arrangements that the Romans of his own period enjoyed: a mixture, as he put it, of monarchy, oligarchy and democracy (Polybius 6.11.11). Not surprisingly, these are Greek words expressing Greek concepts: rule by an individual (monarchy), by a small group (oligarchy) and by the mass of the people (democracy). The Romans of his own time probably would not have expressed the idea using these concepts. Nevertheless, it is certainly true that the relationship between the power exercised by great individuals, the power of the great families of the ruling classes and the power both of the people in general and of the city of Rome as a whole was essential to the working of the Roman state and to the Romans' own ideas about it.

119. We shall never know precisely how this 'mixed' constitution came about, but it is important to realise that, at least according to Roman tradition, the first move towards it was the expulsion of the kings in 510/509, and their replacement by two consuls who held the same power (*imperium*) which the kings had held [12–13]. By this means, so the Romans later believed, the power which the kings had exercised without any effective check (and which had been given to the first king, Romulus, by Jupiter, most powerful of the gods) was retained within the city of Rome. Moreover, abuse of that power was restricted by two means: first, it was divided equally between the two consuls, and second, the consuls (and all major office-holders) were 'magistrates', i.e. men who had been elected and who held office for only twelve months. None the less, when Polybius described the power of the consuls as almost royal, he was hardly exaggerating, and to that power, or *imperium*, we must now turn.

Imperium and *res publica*

120. Romans believed that *imperium* as exercised by their elected magistrates came originally from the kings. This gave this supreme power a surprisingly individual flavour. As we shall see, it was perceived as 'belonging' in a special sense to the particular person who exercised it and was, to a large extent, for him to use at his own discretion. There was, however, another heritage from the royal origin. The king, so it was believed, had been given his *imperium* as part of the establishment of the city of Rome, and often the word *imperium* is used by the Romans almost as if it could stand for Rome itself, or at least the power and influence of the Roman people. The *imperium* was seen as the power by which the *res publica* got things done; and *res publica* means not so much 'republic' (as we tend to translate it) as 'the activity of the Roman people'. Similarly the word *imperium* seems to originate not in an abstract notion of 'power' but in the ability to issue orders (from the Latin word *imperare*, 'to order'). It was this ability to issue orders which the kings had been given, according to the Romans' own myths, with the approval of the gods when the city itself was founded. Naturally, then, it was the holders of this power who formed the executive of the state, men who acted to get things done on behalf of the people. This too is why it was essential that the major magistrates who held this *imperium* should also be in a position to consult the gods (*auspicium*) about what should be done. Their power, after all, came from the gods [389]. Consequently, the two bases of the magistrates' powers were *imperium* and *auspicium*: the first was the ability to issue orders; the second the ability to ask questions of the gods. Indeed, properly speaking *auspicium* was more fundamental even than *imperium*; the first thing that a magistrate did on the day of his entry into office was to consult the gods, early in the morning at the break of day, as to whether he had divine approval for the exercise of his *imperium*. The answer was always in the affirmative; but it was only after that answer had been given that he could proceed to act as a magistrate.

3.1 The Roman triumph: Titus celebrating the defeat of the Jews in AD 70. Arch of Titus, Rome (soon after AD 81). Cf. [380, 485].

Imperium and the gods: *auspices* and triumphs

121. This combination of the activity of gods and men in the functioning of the state sounds curious to modern ears. We are often tempted to dismiss it as a superstitious remnant of early beliefs which cannot really have been held by the powerful race which created and maintained one of the greatest empires the world has ever seen. The temptation increases when we see how ruthlessly Romans actually tried to manipulate religion for political ends. For example, during the controversial consulship of Julius Caesar in 59, his fellow consul and political opponent Bibulus (M. Calpurnius Bibulus), unable to stop Caesar's legislation by other means, spent long hours observing the auspices, and declaring that the gods were opposed to any laws being passed. Despite the great political furore caused by Bibulus' attempts to block Caesar, he was completely unsuccessful, and his reporting of the unfavourable omens was effectively ignored (see also [69, 365]).

122. Roman ideas, then, of the relationship of the gods to politics were unlike ours; but that does not mean that they took religion lightly. To see more clearly how *imperium* and religion fit together, it is worth looking at the Roman triumph (fig. 3.1; cf. [380, 485]). This was a prize awarded to a successful Roman general and, by the second century BC, had become the highest he could be awarded. Since the main task of most holders of *imperium* was to command the armies of the Roman people, it is easy to see why it acquired such importance and prestige for the ruling class.

123. In the Republican period, when a holder of *imperium*, whether a magistrate or a pro-magistrate (that is someone acting as though a magistrate [150]) left the city to take up the command of an army, he had first to perform certain religious rites. These included (i) the confirmation (through *auspicia*) that he would be allowed to consult the gods while he was away from Rome, and (ii) the making of a solemn promise to Jupiter, who as the greatest of the gods protected the city of Rome, that if there was a successful outcome to the fighting in which he would be involved, he would return to the temple of Jupiter on the Capitol in Rome to give thanks. Only then could the commander, wearing the *paludamentum* (the cloak which was the official dress of a Roman commander in the field), cross the sacred boundary of the city, the *pomerium*, to join his army. The reason for this was that the carrying of arms and the presence of soldiers were not normally allowed within the *pomerium*, for fear of violating the sacred area of the city itself, which was protected by the gods, and which had originally been defined, so the story went, by Romulus at the foundation of Rome. The power that the general used to command troops outside the city was called *imperium militiae*, and was distinguished from that used by magistrates within the city, which was called *imperium domi*.

124. Once the commander had joined his army, he proceeded to his *prouincia*, the area in which he was to operate as a holder of *imperium* [171]. Once there, he would carry out such activities as were required, which nearly always involved some military action. At the end of his time in the *prouincia*, he would return home with his army, and encamp with it outside the city of Rome. Here he would consult with the Senate, which usually met for the purpose in the temple of the war-goddess Bellona, just outside the *pomerium*. By this means, he did not have to give up his *imperium militiae*, as he would have to do on entering the sacred boundary. If he had been victorious, or at least if he could claim that he had, he would ask the Senate to allow him a triumph. The Senate would normally do so if he could provide evidence that he had pacified his *prouincia* and killed a substantial number of the enemy. Once the Senate was satisfied, the commander was granted the right to hold his *imperium militiae* within the city for one day only, the day of his triumph, and was given money to pay for the expenses of the celebration. If not, a triumph could be refused, or, if the victory was not thought worthy of a triumph (if, for instance, the enemy involved had been slaves, not free men), a lesser triumph (*ouatio*) might be voted. But it is worth noticing at this point that there were two circumstances in which the will of the Senate could be ignored. First, a commander could celebrate at his own expense. Second, if he happened still to be in the year of his magistracy, for instance as consul, he held *imperium* as a magistrate. He could use this to celebrate a triumph within the *pomerium*. Thus in 143 BC the consul of the year, Appius Claudius Pulcher, who had been refused a triumph by the Senate over the north Italian tribe of the Salassi because of the disgraceful way he had treated them, still celebrated a triumph. But he took the precaution of entering Rome accompanied by his daughter, a Vestal virgin, in order to prevent one of the tribunes of the plebs from imposing a curse.

125. On the day of the triumph itself, a solemn procession, headed by the Senate and including prisoners of war, entered the city (cf. fig. 8.7). Behind this, leading his victorious army, came the commander himself, riding (as no one else in Rome was permitted to do) in a four-horse chariot. He was dressed in the *tunica palmata* and *toga picta*, garments of purple and gold normally worn by the statue of Jupiter in the temple on the Capitoline, and his face too, like Jupiter's, was reddened with dye. In his right hand he held a branch of laurel and in his left, an ivory sceptre, with an eagle, the bird most associated with Jupiter, on the top. On his head he wore a laurel wreath and over his head was held a crown made of gold and representing oak leaves, another symbol of Jupiter. Wearing this attire, he followed the *uia triumphalis* which ran alongside the Forum and up to the temple of Jupiter on the Capitol, where he made the necessary sacrifice and so fulfilled the promise made to the god before he left the city [123].

126. The precise significance of this ceremony has for long been a matter of dispute. Was the *triumphator* on the day of the triumph intended to be a personification of the god Jupiter himself? Or was he simply wearing the clothes of the ancient kings of Rome? For our purpose, however, the answer to this question is less important than the more obvious points (i) that the *imperium* which the commander held was seen to originate from the god, and (ii) that the recognition of success took the form of a powerful religious ceremony, which exalted both the god and the individual who had used the *imperium* on behalf of the Roman people.

127. The idea of *imperium* spans Roman history, and the first emperor of Rome, Augustus, was not slow to manipulate it for his own purposes [79]. From an early stage, Augustus used the theme of the continuity of *imperium* and its connection with the long history of the triumph as part of his presentation of his new regime. As early as 38, seven years before he became emperor, he used the title *imperator* as part of his name. Soldiers had acclaimed successful commanders in the field by this title since at least the late third century, and it became recognised as an informal preliminary stage to the claim by the commander to a triumph. The word is obviously connected with *imperium* and at an earlier stage may well have meant simply 'holder of

3.2 Arch of Augustus in the Roman Forum, erected in 19 BC after the recovery of the standards captured by the Parthians. Cf. [11] and 1.5.

imperium'. Augustus' use of it as part of his own name was clearly an attempt to harness the idea of military success to his own person.

128. The importance to Augustus of the tradition of *imperium* and the triumph can be seen at its clearest, however, in the way in which he used it in the great architectural remodelling of the centre of Rome. This led to his making the claim that he had found Rome built in brick and left it built in marble. For example, he had a triumphal arch built in the Forum (fig. 3.2), just beside the temple of the Deified Caesar (i.e. Julius Caesar, his adoptive father). This was inscribed not only with a list of all the consuls from the beginning of the Republic down to his own time, but also with a list of all those who had celebrated triumphs, beginning with Romulus (cf. [11] and fig. 1.5). Even more striking was the Forum of Augustus (cf. [85, 475] and fig. 2.4), which housed the temple of Mars the Avenger (fig. 3.3). Augustus had vowed to set up this temple during the campaign of Philippi, when he defeated Caesar's assassins Brutus and Cassius. When the temple was dedicated in 2 BC, it contained the statues of Mars and Venus, legendary ancestors of the Julian family, and of the deified Julius himself. But this was not simply a family shrine. The statues in front of the temple were of those who had served the city as military commanders and had been awarded triumphs. Further, it was here that, as Suetonius explains: 'Augustus decreed that the Senate should consider declarations of war or claims for triumphs; this should be both the starting-point for commanders holding *imperium*, when escorted to their provinces, and the repository of all triumphal tokens when they returned victorious' (Suetonius, *Augustus* 29.2). Thus Augustus appropriated to the Julian family the idea of the triumph and of the *imperium militiae* with which it was so closely connected. This is a typical example of the way in which Augustus presented his own new monarchy as the natural development of the entire history of Rome from its foundation.

Imperium and magistracy

129. From the time of the expulsion of the kings and the establishment of the republic, so the Romans themselves believed, the people who had held the *imperium* had been magistrates annually elected and holding office for that year only. The two consuls who were thought to have been instituted at the very beginning of the Republic shared between them the power that had previously belonged to the kings, and were at first drawn from the 'patricians', men who had been nobles during the regal period. But this tradition was soon challenged, and among the most fierce of the disputes of which we have reports from the early Republic was the question of who was to be allowed to become consul. This dispute was finally resolved in the early fourth century by a compromise which enacted that at least one consul each year should come from a plebeian (that is, non-patrician) family. Although this position had been reached by 367 BC, it is a sign of the political conservatism of the Romans that

3.3 Temple of Mars Ultor in the Forum of Augustus (dedicated in 2 BC).

it was not until 172 BC that two plebeian consuls held office together in a single year [16–19]. This conservatism was partly rooted in a conviction that the patricians had, through their links with the ancient cults, a closer connection with the gods. For example, in 215 BC, under the extreme conditions of the Hannibalic war, the plebeian M. Claudius Marcellus, already an experienced and successful general, was elected to fill a consulship left vacant by the death of a patrician consul designate. But he was not permitted to take up office, because thunder had been heard during his election and this was interpreted as a sign of the anger of the gods that two plebeian consuls were about to take office together (Livy 23.31.12–14). As often, we are probably right to suspect political dirty tricks, particularly when elections to office are concerned; but even so, the fact that this religious feeling about the necessity for patrician involvement in the running of the state could be used like this shows how important the hereditary element was in the mind of the Roman people.

Magistracies with *imperium* (see [15])

(1) Consuls

130. The first *imperium*-holders, both in point of time and of importance in the state, were the consuls. It was the consuls who gave their names to the year, and official dates in Rome always took the form 'when so-and-so and so-and-so were consuls'. They consulted and presided over the Senate [166], which was the main policy-making body in the state, and presented bills (*rogationes*) to the assemblies of the people to create legislation. In the earliest period of the Republic they were probably responsible for hearing legal cases between citizens, though this was delegated to the praetors at an relatively early stage [132]. In general, the consuls acted as the heads of state, wearing the purple-bordered *toga praetexta* and seated on a special seat, the *sella curialis* ('curule seat'). Both of these marks of distinction were shared with other magistrates, who held powers which seem to have been delegated to them from the consuls. Consuls were preceded by twelve attendants, called lictors, carrying the *fasces*, a bundle of rods tied together, to demonstrate their power to compel and punish.

131. The chief function of the consuls, however, even in the late Republic, was that of commanding the armies. 'In the elections for consuls,' Cicero said in a speech delivered in 63 BC, 'it is generals that are chosen, not legal experts' (*In Defence of Murena* 38). It was the consuls who recruited fresh troops for the army each year, and who went to the *prouinciae* assigned to them by the Senate in order to conduct the warfare which was the normal annual activity

of the Roman state. When they left the city, exercising the *imperium militiae*, their lictors carried *fasces* with axes in the middle of the bundle of rods. This emphasised that their *imperium* now allowed them to execute Roman citizens who disobeyed them [124, 173]. This military function of the consuls explains why, down to the end of the third century BC, the triumph was virtually the exclusive preserve of consuls or the dictators [134] who from time to time acted in their place.

(2) Praetors

132. In 366 BC, in the midst of the arguments about whether plebeians should be allowed to hold the consulship, a new magistracy was created. Its purpose was to relieve the consuls of the task of hearing legal cases. This was the praetorship, and its tenure was originally confined to patricians, no doubt in an attempt to keep this vital area of the consul's work out of the hands of the plebeians. In 242 BC, just before the end of the First Punic War, a second *praetor* was created, later called the *praetor peregrinus*, to look after cases involving foreigners (*peregrini*). From this time onwards the original *praetor* was known as the *praetor urbanus*, because he heard cases within the city of Rome. These men were responsible for what we would call private law cases, concerning the rights of persons and of property. Their exercise of their *imperium* in this legal context was to be of great historical significance: it was directly responsible for the development of Roman law through the late Republic and Empire. Praetors too held *imperium*, used the curule seat and were accompanied by six lictors, and also had the right to consult the gods through the *auspicia*. This makes them sound like a more restricted version of the consuls, and in many ways that is just what they were. The historian and antiquarian Messalla, writing in the late Republic, specifically describes them as 'colleagues of the consuls' (in Aulus Gellius, *Attic Nights* 13.15.4).

133. Probably because they could be seen as colleagues of the consuls, and thus essentially as holders of *imperium*, praetors developed two new functions – those of military commander and *prouincia* governor. During the first Punic war, praetors are found commanding armies, sometimes holding the praetorship at the end of their tenure of the consulship (for example, A. Atilius Caiatinus, consul in 258 and praetor in 257 BC). And in 227 BC, in the period between the two Punic wars, two additional praetorships were created, to provide commanders to go to the first two overseas *prouinciae* to be controlled by Roman officials on a regular basis, Sicily and Sardinia. In the aftermath of the war with Hannibal in 196 BC [31–3], two further praetors were created to take charge of the two Spanish provinces; and eventually Sulla made the total up to eight in his reforms of the whole magisterial system in 80 BC [59]. Of these eight men, two were still responsible for the law courts, as the first two praetors had been, but the remainder were sent out to command forces and govern provinces throughout the empire. In line with this shift to a more military role for the praetors, they too became eligible, from 200 BC, to celebrate a triumph.

(3) Dictators

134. Down to the time of the Second Punic War, there was also provision for an emergency situation in which it was considered necessary for a single magistrate to take control of affairs. This magistrate, the *dictator*, was usually nominated by one of the consuls, and his power was even greater [15]. This was indicated by the fact that twenty-four lictors preceded him, and that the *fasces* they carried always included the axe, even within the boundaries of the city. This shows that the period of a dictator's rule was in effect one of military law; and no doubt for the same reason, it was limited to six months only, rather than the twelve months of the other magistrates. During that period, the dictator was responsible for the running of the state; and indeed his full title appears to have been *dictator rei gerundae causa* ('dictator for the purpose of carrying on the business of the state'). The other magistrates acted as his subordinates. There could also be other forms of dictatorship, with more specific tasks. These were generally instituted when the two consuls were not available, and were given to the most senior magistrate available. Thus when both consuls were on campaign, a dictator was appointed to hold the elections; and once, after the slaughter of members of the Senate at the battle of Cannae in 216 BC [32], a dictator was appointed to make up the list of the Senate. In all cases except this last, dictators also had a junior colleague, the *magister equitum*, who had originally been (as his title suggests) a commander of cavalry, and who also held *imperium*.

135. After the end of the Second Punic War, for reasons which are not entirely clear, the *dictator* and *magister equitum* were effectively dropped. Only on two occasions after this was the title of dictator used again: once when Sulla was appointed dictator to revise the statutes governing the constitution; and again when Julius Caesar was appointed dictator on several occasions from 49 BC onwards, culminating in his appointment as perpetual dictator in February 44 BC, a month before his death [73]. In both these cases, although they were obviously not the same as the dictators of the earlier type, the title seems to have carried the implication of military law and of absolute control of the activity of the state. Just as in earlier times the establishment of a dictator had not meant the abolition of the *imperium* of the consuls and praetors, but its subjection to the greater *imperium* of the dictator, so too Sulla and Caesar used the title to show that they were supreme in the state.

Magistracies without *imperium*

(1) Quaestors

136. So far all the magistracies we have looked at have involved the holding of *imperium* and have been connected in some way or other with the consulship, either as a lesser colleague (*praetor*) or temporary superior (*dictator*). But there were other magistrates who did not hold *imperium*, even though they too seemed to owe the particular nature of their office to its relationship to the consulship. The oldest of these magistrates is the quaestorship, which, according to later authorities, was the earliest of all the magistracies, predating even the consulship in that it had been set up by the kings [15]. *Quaestor* means 'investigator' and this suggests that at some stage they acted in a legal capacity. Further, from the beginning they seem to have been assistants to the consuls. In the late Republic their duties were connected with the state treasury. This was not only a store for public money but also for copies of statutes and other state documents. It was called the *aerarium Saturni*, because it was in the basement of the temple of Saturn in the Forum. From the time of Sulla onwards there were twenty of these quaestors elected annually [59]. Two of them served in the city (*quaestores urbani*); one accompanied each holder of *imperium* to his overseas *prouincia* to act as financial officer; others performed administrative functions in Italy, one being in charge, for instance, of the corn supply coming to the city through the port of Ostia. This great variety of functions was probably the result of the fact that they were always in essence assistants to the holders of *imperium*, and consequently filled those roles which were necessary from time to time in different circumstances.

(2) Tribunes of the plebs

137. The magistracies which we have looked at so far were all held by men with *imperium*, or connected to the *imperium*-holding magistrates in some way. One other group of annual magistrates, however, were neither holders of *imperium* nor closely linked with *imperium*-holders, because they were not in origin officials of the Roman people (*populus Romanus*) at all. These were the officials of the *plebs*, of which the most important were the tribunes (*tribuni*

plebis). These had probably originated as magistrates of the plebeian 'state-within-a-state' during the so-called 'conflict of the orders' [21, 129], and by the time plebeians were admitted to the consulship in 366, there were ten of them. Although in many ways the tribunate became during the following centuries simply another magistracy, it retained many characteristics from its early connection with the plebs. For example, it could not be held by a patrician (in the late Republic Publius Clodius Pulcher, a member of the patrician family of the Claudii, had to have himself adopted into a plebeian famliy in order to be able to become tribune [71]); again, though tribunes were protected by a religious taboo against any attacks (*sacrosanctitas*), they were not accompanied (as e.g. consuls were) by attendants. The main function of the tribunate was to preside at the assembly of the plebs (*concilium plebis*); to present bills to it, in the same way consuls and praetors did to the other assemblies of the people (the *comitia centuriata* and *comitia tributa*, [130, 159–63]); to assist any plebeian who was seized by a magistrate; and to interpose a veto on any action of a magistrate or on any senatorial proposal put before the other two assemblies. From the time of the Hortensian law at the latest (287 BC), the decrees of the plebeian assembly, the *plebiscita*, had the force of a statute passed by the whole people. Consequently, the tribunes were influential as law-makers and so in a potentially powerful position. Further, they were able to bring a prosecution against an individual on a range of criminal charges. As such cases would be heard before an assembly of the people, tribunician prosecutions were often highly charged political events. For example, in 63 BC the consul Cicero threatened a tribune who had proposed a bill to distribute public land in Italy and other areas of the empire. Another tribune Titus Labienus reacted to this threat by bringing a prosecution against the elderly Gaius Rabirius. The charge was that, as consul thirty-seven years earlier, Rabirius had used military force to bring about the death of the tribune Saturninus (Lucius Appuleius Saturninus). The argument was: what powers did a consul have to use force in putting down a tribune of the people? The relevance of the case to Cicero was obvious, and it is no surprise that he defended Rabirius against the charge (though, in the event, the trial was abandoned). This illustrates one of the ways in which the powers of the tribune could be used to present a political stance in the popular tradition, which harked back to the days of the early Republic and the defence of the rights of the *plebs* against the patricians. Something of this tradition had probably always been present in the office of tribune, but it was undoubtedly reinforced by the activities of Tiberius and Gaius Gracchus in 133 and 123–2 [46–9] and was to play an important part in the problems that beset Rome for the next hundred years.

(3) Aediles

138. In addition to the tribunes, the plebeian assembly also elected two plebeian aediles each year. In origin these men seem to have been appointed to assist the tribunes, rather as the quaestors did the consuls [136]. Again, as with the quaestors, their title (probably something to do with the Latin *aed-* stem, which spans in meaning 'room', 'house' and 'temple') does not appear to relate to what they actually did. They were elected by the *concilium plebis* (like tribunes), wore no special clothes, and sat with the tribunes on the bench with other plebeian magistrates. But in time, the plebeian aediles became *de facto* largely divorced from their connection with the plebs, probably because they became closely associated with curule aediles. Curule aediles were established in 366 BC when the praetorship was set up and the consulship made accessible to plebeians as well as patricians. Curule aediles were originally patricians, no doubt to balance the plebeian officials of the same name, but by the last century of the republic the curule aediles were alternately patrician and plebeian on an annual basis. The curule aediles were elected by the *comitia tributa* as they were magistrates of the whole people; similarly they wore the distinctive dress of a Roman magistrate, the purple-edged *toga praetexta*, and sat on a curule seat (see [130], and compare their plebeian colleagues). But in function the two were identical: they had responsibility for the fabric of the city, the upkeep and cleaning of the roads and paths, the distribution of water from the public aqueducts and conduits and access to and behaviour in public places. They also had responsibility for control of prices, especially of corn. Rather surprisingly they also had certain judicial functions, some of which related to their other work, but some of which seems to have been ordinary criminal jurisdiction. They also had power to impose fines. They were responsible for putting on games, the *ludi plebei* being, as might be expected, the responsibility of the plebeian aediles, the *ludi Romani* of the curule aediles. In addition to these, which had been established at a early date, there were other games introduced from time to time, such as the *Megalesia*, set up in 204 in honour of the goddess called the 'Great Mother' (*Magna Mater*), the *Cerialia*, in honour of Ceres and the *Floralia*, for the goddess Flora. This gave the aediles the heavy financial responsibility of presenting large-scale public entertainment, mostly at their own expense; but this also provided an opportunity for lavish display, which might well help a political career. Suetonius comments on Julius Caesar's holding of the aedileship in 65 along with Marcus Bibulus in just such terms:

While he was aedile, he set up temporary porticoes in the *comitium*, the *forum* and its basilicas and even on the Capitol, in which he showed off, with a great profusion of objects, some of the splendid material prepared for the games. He put on wild-beast hunts and games, both with his colleague and independently of him, in such a way that he took all the credit even when the cost was shared. Bibulus admitted it, saying that he was treated just like Pollux; for just as the temple of the Twin Brothers [Castor and Pollux] in the *forum* was only called the temple of Castor, so the magnificent games put on by himself and Caesar were ascribed to Caesar only. (Suetonius, *Julius* 10)

(4) Censors

139. One further magistracy needs to be mentioned, though it is different from all those we have looked at so far in that it was not annual. The censors were normally appointed once every five years. Tradition had it that they were first appointed in 443 BC to relieve the consuls of one part of their work, i.e. counting the people. This count had both practical and religious significance, and explains why the censors' period of office was different, not only in the length of time allowed for it, but in the way that time was thought of. The censors finished their tenure of office when they had completed their work, which was called 'establishing the *lustrum*'. The *lustrum* was a sacrifice of a pig, a sheep and a bull (*suouetaurilia*) to ensure purification, and it is not certain why this was connected with the census (fig. 3.4). Perhaps, as in other religions, the actual process of numbering the people was considered sinful (as in the case of King David in counting the people of Israel and Judah (2 Samuel 24)); perhaps the censors were seen as in some sense refounding the city and wiping the slate clean for a new beginning. The process of completing the census was inevitably one which took a variable amount of time, and usually was done well within the five-year period. Indeed it was believed by the end of the first century BC that the period of tenure of office of the censors had been restricted by a statute, introduced almost as soon as the censorship itself, to eighteen months, in order to limit the length of time that they could exercise the power which they held. Whether or not this was true, it does seem to reflect the time actually taken. The censors belonged to the group of magistrates which was associated with the consuls, wearing the *toga praetexta* and sitting on curule chairs. They also held the *auspicia*, which allowed them to consult the gods [120].

140. The importance of the censors was much greater than might be expected from what has been said so far, and can be seen from the fact that the office was usually held by men who had already reached the consulship. The reason was that, in conducting the census, they also assigned individual members of the *populus Romanus* to different groups within the state. Thus down to the first century BC they were responsible for reviewing the membership of the Senate, and this meant both including new members (usually from

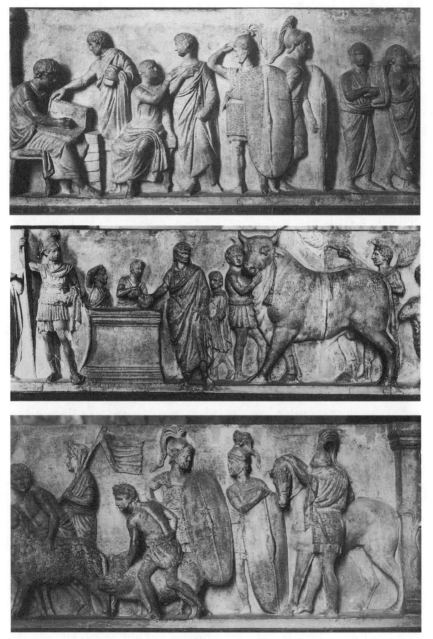

3.4 A census ceremony and *suouetaurilia*. Cf. [474].

among those who had held a magistracy) and excluding those who had offended against the moral standards of the state, as, for instance, by being convicted on a criminal charge. Once they had chosen the Senate, the censors turned to the people and summoned them to meet on the Campus Martius, where they and their property would be listed. The words of the summons are preserved by the first-century BC antiquarian writer Varro and suggest that these details may have been preserved in records held by officers of the thirty-five tribes to which all Roman citizens belonged. Even so, it does seem the censors scrutinised them carefully to check that those listed there actually were citizens (either because of Roman citizen parentage or by a grant of citizenship) and that their property was correctly registered. The census of property was vital for two reasons: first military, because service in the different sections of the army depended upon the amount of property owned [278], and second legislative, because one of the popular assemblies, the *comitia centuriata* [159ff.], was organised on the same basis. The census classified the citizens (i.e. those capable of serving in the army) into *centuriae*. These were originally military units but continued later to be used as voting units in the *comitia centuriata*. The censors also conducted a review of the *equites*, who had in the earliest period of the republic formed the cavalry. By the late republic the *equites* were required to hold a certain amount of property (400,000 sesterces) and to buy and maintain a horse with public money. There were eighteen *centuriae* of such *equites*, but by the second and first centuries BC, these *centuriae* were no longer of military significance, but they did have special voting privileges in the *comitia centuriata*. In this way the censors established the political basis of the state, not least because it was the *comitia centuriata* which elected the consuls and praetors. What is more, there was no check on what the censors did other than that there were two of them, and on occasion they could disagree violently about who should and who should not be included. The most notorious example happened in the censorship of Gaius Claudius Nero and Marcus Livius Salinator in 204 BC, when these two men, formerly enemies but allegedly reconciled with one another, proceeded to exclude each other from the list of *equites*; not satisfied with that, Nero excluded Salinator from the *centuriae* of the *comitia centuriata* altogether, and Salinator responded by excluding all but one of the thirty-five tribes, including Nero by name. This, as Livy remarks, was likely to damage the reputation of the censorship in the eyes of the people (Livy 29.37).

141. There were a number of other functions performed by the censors, of which the most important were the issuing of contracts for public works and the erection and repair of public buildings. The Roman state under the Republic had no directly employed work-force, with the exception of the

attendants and scribes of the magistrates and, of course, the army. Even the army was at first an unpaid militia and continued to be conscripted from the citizen body down to the end of the Republic [173]. The absence of such a work-force meant that all activities of the state which required organised labour were contracted to private individuals, who were allowed to form joint companies for the purpose, and, as a result of their involvement with the activities of the state, were called *publicani*. Their contracts, which covered such diverse matters as road-building, supplying the army and collecting certain provincial taxes, were allotted to the 'publican' companies every five years by the censors. Although senators could have no direct involvement with the publican companies, the sums of money involved were, at least by the second century BC, sufficiently large to be of considerable political importance. The censors also had a sum of money voted to them by the Senate and held by the quaestors which they could spend on the repair of public buildings, or the erection of new ones. This again was a matter of financial importance to the contractor, and an opportunity for the censors to gain prestige and popularity.

The ruling class: political careers and aristocratic ethos

142. Magistrates and *imperium* were of central importance to the Roman state and reflected the sort of society Rome was in the period of the Republic. In order to be a candidate for a magistracy, it was necessary to be a free Roman citizen (not, that is to say, a freed former slave); to have reached a specified age (in the late Republic, thirty was the minimum age for the quaestorship, forty for the praetorship and forty-three for the consulate); and (at least still in the second century) to have served ten campaigns in the army. More surprising to us, there was a rule excluding anyone who received regular payment for work done. These conditions would all have restricted candidature to the land-owning classes, especially since there was no payment for tenure of a magistracy. Not that even that made much difference. The way in which the elections took place anyway ensured that the chances of anyone without substantial wealth reaching the higher magistracies were very small indeed. Money and favours were, then as now, an essential part of the business of getting elected. The candidate had somehow to present himself to the attention of the voters who would gather in one of the popular assemblies for the purpose, and that would involve at the least the use of agents to spread information about the benefits that would result from voting for a particular individual. Sometimes candidates descended to outright bribery, using *sequestres* and *diuisores* to act as go-betweens, respectively collecting and distributing the bribes. Their activities were made illegal by a series of increasingly severe laws, which seem to have been universally ineffective.

143. Quintus Cicero, in a political pamphlet addressed to his famous brother Marcus Tullius Cicero as he mounted his election campaign for the consulship of 63 BC, provides considerable insight into the way in which an election campaign might be run:

A campaign for any of the magistracies is divided into attention paid to two separate considerations: the first is fostering the support of friends, the second the goodwill of the people. The support of friends ought to come from benefits given and duties done, from charm, ease of manner and a pleasant personality; but during a campaign the designation 'friend' has a wider application than in ordinary life. Anyone who might show you any goodwill, might show you any respect, might come to see you at home, is to be counted as a friend. On the other hand those who are more properly called friends, who are related to you by blood or marriage or connected with you by membership of the same group, to these people it is valuable to show as much affection as you can. Further, anyone who is close to you, and especially members of your own household, should be worked on to ensure that they are fond of you and want you to reach as high a position as you possibly can – this goes for your fellow tribesmen, your neighbours, your clients, even your freedmen, yes, and even your slaves. Virtually all conversation which spreads out from those close to you increases your reputation with the electorate. Then you ought to make sure that you have friends of various types: for appearance's sake, you need people famous for their achievements and reputation, who, even if they do not work practically at increasing the vote, none the less bring a candidate a certain esteem; to maintain your cause, you need magistrates, especially, and the tribunes of the plebs; to secure the votes of the *centuriae*, you need people of great influence. All those who have, or might hope to have, a tribe or a *centuria* or any other benefit at your hands, they especially are the ones that it is worth expending great labour on in order to establish yourself with them and make quite sure of your position. (Q. Cicero, *Pamphlet on Electioneering* 5.16–18)

144. As Quintus makes clear in this passage, to achieve the necessary influence over the voters, a candidate needed both direct contact with the voters and a reputation as an associate of those whom the voters thought highly of. This in turn meant reliance on the advice and help of friends (whether genuine or acquired for the purpose of the campaign), who were themselves members of the political élite. But that in itself would not be enough. It was the voters themselves, in the *centuriae* of the *comitia centuriata* and the tribes of the *comitia tributa* [159, 164] that counted in the last resort. For the members of the great families the matter was easier in that they had among the electorate numerous dependants (the clients referred to by Quintus), who owed them a duty of support, not least at election time, in return for favours shown them or expected by them. But not even a member of the greatest families could have

3.5 Statue of a Roman with busts of his ancestors; such busts came to replace the wax masks which *nobiles* kept in their atria and paraded in funeral processions. Cf. [304, 468].

relied entirely on these clients, since by the time of the late Republic the voters in the elections must have been numbered in tens of thousands [216]. There is no doubt, though, that the possession of great landed estates brought with it an immense advantage in the elections, and that, perhaps even more importantly, the Roman people had a pronounced tendency to vote for members of families which had provided magistrates in the past [10]. This was reflected among the aristocracy itself by the cult of the ancestors of the family. The title *nobilis* (that is, 'noble') was given only to members of a family which had an ancestor in the male line who had been consul; and in the hall of the house of such a *nobilis*, the wax masks of his ancestors, hung upon the walls, were a continual reminder of past glories and a claim to future recognition (fig. 3.5; cf. [304, 328, 468]). The term *nouus homo*, 'new man', was applied to the man who became consul from a completely non-consular background.

145. As the number of magistracies grew in the second and first centuries, an additional obstacle was placed before anyone aiming at the highest positions in Rome. After the number of praetors was increased to six in 197 BC, all those who intended to run for the consulship had to have held the praetorship

Table 1.

The Cornelii Scipiones, the Sempronii Gracchi and the Aemilii Paulli

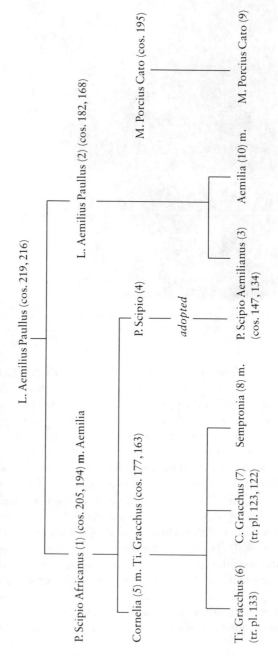

L. Aemilius Paullus (cos. 219, 216)

L. Aemilius Paullus (2) (cos. 182, 168)

M. Porcius Cato (cos. 195)

M. Porcius Cato (9)

P. Scipio Africanus (1) (cos. 205, 194) m. Aemilia

Cornelia (5) m. Ti. Gracchus (cos. 177, 163)

P. Scipio (4)

adopted

P. Scipio Aemilianus (3) (cos. 147, 134)

Aemilia (10) m.

Sempronia (8) m.

Ti. Gracchus (6) (tr. pl. 133)

C. Gracchus (7) (tr. pl. 123, 122)

beforehand; and, at least by the time of the *Lex Villia Annalis* (a statute introduced in 180 BC), a two-year gap was required between the two offices. After Sulla's legislation in 81–80 BC [59], it was also necessary to hold the quaestorship before the praetorship. No doubt this *cursus honorum* ('race for honours'), as it was called, was introduced partly to ensure that those holding the highest offices of state had had experience in the magistracies before they reached these top posts. But since would-be consuls needed to be elected several times over to a series of magistracies of which there were progressively fewer at each stage (twenty quaestors, eight praetors and two consuls by Sulla's time), those for whom election was comparatively easier had a great advantage. That increased the likelihood of the nobles holding the consulship, as opposed to those who had no consuls among their ancestors already. Further, magistrates were able not only to make financial gains (booty from military campaigns or money extracted legally or illegally from overseas *prouinciae*) but also to win more clients, in Rome or in Italy or among important people in foreign communities. The support of such people greatly enhanced the status and so the electability of the magistrate or pro-magistrate and his family. All this conspired to ensuring that, once you had held *imperium*, your descendants would be extremely likely to hold it as well.

146. After the reforms of 366 BC [19], at least one of the consuls each year was a plebeian, and therefore there was each year at least one opportunity for a plebeian to ennoble his family. As a result, by the middle and late Republic, there were great families of both patrician and plebeian origin. Further, since the circle of the governing classes of Rome was relatively restricted, it was inevitable that such families would intermarry, and it was by such marriages that political bonds were formed. Quintus Cicero indicated [143] how important those related by blood or marriage were when it came to looking for support at the elections. The network of one set of families can be seen in the table (Table 1), which shows the relationship in the third and second centuries between two of the very greatest patrician families, the Cornelii Scipiones and the Aemilii Paulli. Scipio Africanus (1 – this refers to numbers in the facing table), who defeated Hannibal at Zama in 202 BC [32] and Lucius Aemilius Paullus (2), whose victory at Pydna over Perseus of Macedon in 168 BC ended the Macedonian monarchy [38], were brothers-in-law, and one of Paullus' sons (3) was adopted by Africanus' son (4). Moreover (though this is not shown on the table) another of Paullus' sons was adopted into the family of the Fabii Maximi, thus providing a link with another great figure from the Hannibalic War [31–2], Quintus Fabius Maximus. The table also shows the close links that developed between the Scipiones and one of the great plebeian families, the Sempronii Gracchi, in the two generations after Scipio Africanus.

Cornelia, Africanus' daughter (5), married Tiberius Sempronius Gracchus, who was a major figure in the 170s and 160s, holding the consulship twice and also being censor in 167. She thus became the mother of the two famous tribunes, Tiberius (6)[46] and Gaius Gracchus (7) [48–9]; but also the mother-in-law of her own adoptive nephew, Scipio Aemilianus (3), by his marriage to her daughter, Sempronia (8). Close family connections of this sort were part of the background of political life in Rome.

147. Members of these great families were well aware of their own superiority. For example, in 62 BC, Cicero, who was not a member of a noble family but a *nouus homo* ('new man'), was faced with an attack on his consulship of 63 by the tribune, Quintus Metellus Nepos. Cicero attacked him in return, only to receive a blistering letter from Nepos' brother, Quintus Metellus Celer, serving as proconsular governor in Gaul, who had been praetor in 63:

If you are well, that is good. I would have expected, given our mutual interests and our restored good-will, that I would not be damaged with such derision, nor would my brother Metellus be threatened in his person and property by you because of what he said. Even if respect for him himself was not enough to restrain you, the dignity of our family and my services to you and to the state ought to have been enough to hold you back. Now I see that he is under attack, and that you have abandoned me: all this is most improper. So I, who am commanding an army and a province and am in the middle of a war, am in grief and distress. Since you have done all this quite unreasonably and without the benignity due to our ancestors, do not be surprised if you live to regret it. I had not expected such inconstancy in you towards me and the members of my family. As for me, however, neither grief for my family nor injuries done by any individual will distract me from serving the state. (Q. Metellus Celer, in Cicero, *Letters to his Friends* 5.1)

This hardly sounds like a letter from a more junior to a senior member of the Senate; but the difference between them, of course, was that Metellus' family could show consuls back to the time of the Hannibalic War, whereas Cicero was an upstart from a family from Arpinum. This meant that throughout the earlier part of his political career, Cicero as a *nouus homo* had, in electoral terms, to swim against the tide. True, it was possible to turn such *nouitas* to advantage. As Cicero's brother Quintus, in his advice on campaigning for the consulship, says, there are three things he must always keep in the forefront of his plans: 'I am a *nouus*; I am seeking the consulship; Rome is Rome' (Q. Cicero, *Pamphlet on Electioneering* 1.2). Quintus is hinting that an untarnished background could make up for noble pedigree. For a *nobilis* who disgraced the family name was in some ways in a worse position than a *nouus* who had no name to disgrace. For example, Scipio Aemilianus, when a young man, in a conversation with the historian Polybius, admitted that his family thought of him as not sufficiently engaged in the pursuits that would maintain the political supremacy of the Cornelii Scipiones: 'Everyone regards me as a quiet and lazy person, with no share in the energetic character of a Roman, because I do not choose to plead cases in court. They say that the family does not need the sort of representative that I am, but someone just the opposite. That is what hurts me most' (Polybius 31.23: [43]). Family pressure on a *nobilis* could be considerable.

148. For a *nouus homo*, energetic and successful public performance was even more necessary if he was to establish himself in political circles, and so gain the consulship which would bring nobility to his family. Cicero could not rely (as Aemilianus could) on connections that were ready-made for him by membership of a family, but had to establish them himself; and in Cicero's case this was done particularly by careful use of his gifts as an orator, in the political arena and in the law courts. These were precisely the activities which were also expected of Aemilianus. Other *noui homines* might make progress through outstanding military service, as did Gaius Marius in the last years of the second century BC [53]. Almost invariably, however, some connection with the established families of the nobility was necessary to launch a *nouus homo* on his political career. Marius, for instance, enjoyed the patronage of the Metelli, though he finally achieved the consulship in 107 BC through a campaign which involved an attack on one of his patrons, Quintus Metellus. Marius was serving under him in Numidia at the time, and his attack excited the anger and resentment of other *nobiles*. Again, the *nouus* the Elder Cato (Marcus Porcius Cato) first enjoyed the support of the family of the Valerii Flacci, and held both his consulship in 195 and his censorship in 184 with Lucius Valerius Flaccus as his colleague [43]. Then, after reaching the consulship, he married a member of the noble plebeian family, the Licinii. His son by this marriage (Table 1, (9)) subsequently married the daughter (10) of Lucius Aemilius Paullus and thus became a member of the important and influential group of noble families we have already examined [146]. This younger Marcus Porcius Cato died before entering office as praetor, but his eldest son held the consulship in 118 BC.

149. The basis of political life of the Republic was the magistracies of the Roman people, the *imperium* which they gave and the status, both political and social, which resulted for individual Romans and their families. The same Scipio Aemilianus who expressed such anxiety to Polybius about his unworthiness to represent his family [147] summarised the connection between these various elements in a speech given later in his career, of which a fragment has been preserved: 'The dignity of rank arises from integrity, the honour of a magistracy from dignity, *imperium* from a magistracy, and

freedom from *imperium*' (Scipio Aemilianus, from Isidore, *Etymologies* 2.21.4). The rank of the noble's family depends, in Aemilianus' formulation, on the propriety with which his ancestors have discharged the tasks given to them by the people, and this in turn gives access to the magistracies and *imperium*. From the holding of *imperium* comes not only the ability of the noble to do what he would wish but also the liberty which was the hallmark of the free republic, which the Romans, and especially the political classes, valued.

Imperium and magistracy: the developments of the third and second centuries

150. As we have seen [129–41], the magistracies and their relationship to the *imperium* that had come down from the kings changed through the period of the early Republic, as the city of Rome grew and the functions of the magistrates became more complex. In the third and second centuries, however, as Rome became not only an Italian but a Mediterranean power, the role of the magistrates grew immensely. On the military level, even during the period of Rome's expansion in Italy, it became clear that it was no longer enough to have Roman armies commanded only by the magistrates to whom the *imperium* was entrusted: for it was entrusted only annually. What if an important campaign (say) extended beyond the allotted year? Consequently, in 326 BC the consul of the previous year, Quintus Publilius Philo (see fig. 1.5), was appointed *pro consule* ('in place of the consul') by a vote of the people in order to allow him enough time to finish the siege of Naples, and during the war against the Samnites and the Etruscans early in the next century this extension of *imperium* beyond the allotted year was increasingly used. The giving of *imperium* in this way took two forms. First, if the commander was, as in the case of Publilius Philo, already holding a magistracy, his tenure of *imperium* was extended beyond the end of his tenure of the magistracy, in order not to disrupt a campaign by changing commander at a crucial stage. This was called 'prorogation' and became the normal method of creating pro-magistrates. It was the business of the Senate, who, when they were assigning commands to the holders of *imperium* at the beginning of the year, also decided whether to use this means to extend the *imperium* of those who had held it the previous year. Second, someone could be given *imperium* without currently holding a magistracy. This happened in the wars in the early third century, and again during the Hannibalic War, when this mechanism was used to provide commanders for Spain. But after the decision in 197 BC to create two new praetorships to provide commanders for the two Spanish *prouinciae* [133],

this was used only in exceptional circumstances, of which the most notable was the appointment of Pompey in 77 BC to fight against Sertorius in Spain [62]. From one important point of view, however, the two forms of pro-magistrate were the same. In both cases the men involved were holders of *imperium*, but were not magistrates of the Roman people.

151. These pro-magistrates were the men who, through the second and first centuries BC, extended the power and influence of the Roman state throughout the Mediterranean world and beyond. It was as pro-magistrates, even more than as magistrates, that the political élite commanded the armies which defeated the kings of Macedon and the tribes of Spain in the second century and controlled the *prouinciae* which were allotted to them for the exercise of their *imperium*. For the whole of the second century and for the first three decades of the first, this made little difference to the balance of power in the Republic, because they became pro-magistrates by the process of prorogation, and as such could think of their whole command as an extended form of magistracy. Prorogation therefore made the magistracies more important and more profitable than they would otherwise have been. In 53 BC, however, the Senate proposed a decree, ordering a five-year separation between the holding of a magistracy and the tenure of a *prouincia*. The purpose of this was to make it impossible for candidates for office to exploit their *prouinciae*, which they had done up till then by filling their pockets at provincial expense, or by pouring money into extravagant election campaigns knowing they would instantly recoup it (Dio Cassius 40.46.2). When in the following year Pompey passed a law on the holding of provinces, he incorporated this measure in his legislation.

152. By the time of Pompey's law, however, an important change had taken place in the relation between magistracy and pro-magistracy. When Marius was consul in 107 BC [52], he had used a law passed by a people's assembly to transfer to himself a *prouincia* which the Senate had already allotted to a different pro-magistrate. Ever since then, it had been clear that provincial commands could be assigned by other means than through the Senate. For example, in 67 BC Pompey (cf. fig. 1.10), who had held the consulship in 70 but had not gone to a *prouincia* after it, was appointed to a huge command against the pirates which extended throughout the Mediterranean and for fifty miles inland from the coast [64]. This appointment was made by a law proposed by a tribune of the plebs, Aulus Gabinius, and was in fact the appointment of a non-magistrate to a pro-magistracy, not unlike that which had sent Pompey to fight against Sertorius [150]. In 66 BC the same mechanism was used to send Pompey to complete the war against Mithridates, another extensive command, which ended in 62 BC with Pompey's reorganisation of the whole of Asia Minor, Syria and Palestine [65]. And the great commands of the 50s similarly depended on the assignment of provinces by laws passed in people's assemblies. For example, Caesar, when consul in 59, was given Cisalpine Gaul (i.e. northern Italy) and Illyricum for five years by a tribunician law, to which the Senate added Transalpine Gaul; and his command was renewed by a law proposed by Pompey and Marcus Licinius Crassus, in their consulship in 55 BC. In the same year, Pompey was given command in Spain and Crassus against the Parthians by a tribunician law [70]. The effect of this was twofold. First, it removed the control of the most important military commands from the Senate. Second, and more importantly, it separated the right to command from holding the magistracy. The changes were highly significant. In earlier years, the essential aim of any member of the political class was to reach the consulship, and to distinguish himself in the command that he would then receive. It was, of course, always the case that some consuls would get more important commands than others simply because they happened to reach the top at a more significant moment; but in principle all consuls were alike, and the *imperium* that they held was of equal value. In the time of Caesar and Pompey, this was self-evidently no longer the case. The great commands that they received by such unusual means in the 50s distinguished them clearly from the ordinary run of consuls. On top of this, the commands were so vast and complex (e.g. Pompey's over the pirates) that a large number of lower-level commanders had to be given *imperium* so that the job could be done at all. These were usually called *legati pro praetore* ('subordinate officers acting in place of praetors'). In essence, what was happening in the last decades of the Republic was the emergence of a small group of individuals at a superior level to that of the other members of the ruling class, whose position was reflected in the commands and the sort of *imperium* which they held [70–1]. These people (and in the 50s BC, they comprised the three members of the so-called 'First Triumvirate', Caesar, Pompey and Crassus) were called by Cicero *principes*, that is 'first citizens'. All of them were nobles, in that they came from 'consular' families [143]; but none (with the possible exception of Crassus) belonged to the small group of great families which had dominated the consulships over the past century and a half. Naturally their power depended on the control of armies, but those armies were not drawn from their own dependants: the armies and the *imperium* that went with them were voted to them by people's assemblies. Consequently the traditional pattern in which Scipio Aemilianus and others had placed their trust for the stability and freedom of the republic [149], was disrupted. In 56 BC Cicero complained that even men like Lucius Domitius Ahenobarbus, whom he describes as having been consul designate since his birth, could be excluded from the consulship, and that the three men who were in fact controlling the state had in their note-books lists of future consuls as long as those of consuls past. 'Whose situation could be more miserable than Domitius', except the republic's? There is no hope of any improvement for it' (Cicero, *Letters to Atticus*, 4.8a.2).

Augustus and *imperium*

153. The Roman historian Tacitus described Augustus' take-over of power, after his defeat of Mark Antony at Actium in 31 BC [77], in language which reflects the change in power which we have seen in the late Republic: 'Augustus, using the name *princeps*, took the whole state, worn out with the troubles of civil war, into his *imperium*' (Tacitus *Annals* 1.1). For obvious reasons, Augustus did not adopt the style of monarchical government which had led to the assassination of his adoptive father, Julius Caesar, but he was faced with a similar problem to Caesar's – how to find a way to hold and use *imperium*, the power to command essential to any Roman ruler. Caesar, logically enough, had chosen the one Republican magistracy which allowed for virtually monar-chic power, that of the dictatorship [134–5]. To that extent, Caesar was acting more within the tradition of the Republic than in the 50s, when, along with Crassus and Pompey, he controlled affairs from outside the structure of the magistracies, in the way which Cicero complained about [141]. But even so, he clearly caused great offence by declaring, the month before his death, that he intended to hold this office in perpetuity, because he thus effectively debarred the members of the old ruling class from their right (as they saw it) to control Rome through their tenure of the magistracies: he was depriving them of that freedom (*libertas*) which, in Scipio Aemilianus' words, depended on magis-tracy and *imperium* [150]. It is no accident that the assassins of Caesar took as their watchword on the day of the murder the word *libertas*.

154. Augustus was well advised, therefore, to avoid using the dictatorship. On at least one occasion during his reign, he actually refused it when in 22 BC the crowds in Rome clamoured for him to accept (Augustus, *My Achievements*, 5.1; Dio Cassius 54.1). Instead, when on 13 January 27 BC he laid down the unconstitutional powers which he had held during the war against Mark Antony, he initially functioned simply as consul, but with a huge area of the Roman world assigned to him by the Senate as his *prouincia*, and not for one but for ten years (Dio Cassius 53.4). In the longer term, however, this would not prove satisfactory. The simple reason was that the consulship had been designed specifically to limit the power of its holders, partly by being an annual magistracy, and partly by providing for two equal holders of the magistracy to be in power at any one time. The second limitation was fairly

easily circumvented by ensuring that Augustus' colleague was someone of his own choice; but the first was more difficult. After all, the emperor was not about to retire at the end of his year in office. So from 27 to 23 BC he was duly re-elected each year, but this must have begun to look like a perpetual consulship, which was hardly better than a perpetual dictatorship. Finally, in 23, Augustus, after a bout of illness, gave up the consulship. In place of it, he received *imperium pro consule*, since, like all others in that position before and after, he was 'in place of a consul', using the *imperium* of a consul without actually being one. In this way, he left the consulship open for competition among the members of the upper classes, and was able to suggest that he was doing no more than had been done before by his republican predecessors who had held *imperium pro consule* [79]. The suggestion was, of course, misleading. The forces he commanded through subordinates [188] and the areas they controlled were far greater than even the *principes* of the late Republic had had at their disposal; and more particularly he had a number of specific privileges granted to him which made his position far more like that of a consul than was true of any other proconsul [81]. Like a consul in the Republican period, he had the right to bring matters before the Senate, which no pro-magistrate had, since pro-magistrates were not magistrates; and like the consuls, but unlike pro-magistrates, he did not forfeit his *imperium* on crossing the sacred boundary of the city, the *pomerium* ([123–4]; Dio Cassius 53.32). All this meant that effectively he had all the power of a consul without actually holding the magistracy; and this was acknowledged when, in 19 BC, he was given the right to sit on a curule chair between the two consuls (Dio Cassius 54.10).

155. This pattern of separating power from office was the logical extension of the development we have already seen in the 50s BC (above 152); and Augustus used it in a variety of ways to fit his monarchical power into the structures of the republican magistracies. For example, on three occasions, as he himself says in *My Achievements*, he was asked to carry out the supervision of laws and morals. This was normally done by the censors, but Augustus did it without a colleague and without actually holding the censorship [139–41]. Still more remarkably, he held the power of a tribune (*tribunicia potestas*), even though, as a patrician (by adoption into the family of Julius Caesar), he was unable to hold the office itself [137]. Indeed the connections the tribunate had with the people of Rome made this 'pro-tribunate' (as we might call it, though the Romans never did) an especially valuable asset, and both Augustus and his successors used it to date the years of their reigns.

Imperium and empire

156. Augustus completely refashioned the power basis of Rome and in so doing laid the foundations for the constitutional position of the emperors who followed. As late as the fourth century AD, for example, the emperor Constantine [116] was still dating his reign by the number of years he had held the *tribunicia potestas*. The key lay in the care with which Augustus separated out the powers of the various magistracies, and in particular the *imperium* of the consuls, from the magistracies to which they were attached and concentrated them in his own hands. To us this may seem curiously legalistic and unnecessary. We are inclined to think that his control of the armies of the Roman state and of the vast quantities of wealth, both private and public, which he had seized, was more significant for his maintenance of his position as emperor than constitutional niceties. But it is worth remembering how central to the Roman understanding of state power these constitutional notions had been. Of course it was important for a ruler to keep a firm grip on the armed forces, but if he also wanted to be seen as a legitimate ruler and not just a military adventurer, he had to show that his hold over the Roman world was no different from that of traditional republican *imperium*-holders. But *imperium* was not only a link between the old Republic and the new Empire; it was also one of the basic notions behind the Romans' ideas of what an empire was. As a result of the concentration of so much *imperium* in the hands of one man, the emperor, it became natural to associate the empire of the Roman people with that *imperium*. This idea was, as we shall see in the next chapter, reflected in the way that empire was actually run; and it is interesting to note that it is only after Julius Caesar had shown how the *imperium* which had previously been divided up between a series of magistrates might be drawn together into the hands of one individual that the phrase *imperium Romanum* began to be used in the sense of 'Roman empire'. It was by adopting the methods of the late Republican *principes* that Augustus, the sole remaining *princeps*, was able to create for himself a wholly new position, that of monarchical emperor (or *princeps*, as Tacitus calls him) out of the constitutional material bequeathed to him by the determinedly non-monarchical magistrates of the Republic.

FURTHER READING

M. Gelzer, *The Roman Nobility*, tr. R. Seager (Oxford, Blackwell, 1969)
A.H.J. Greenidge, *Roman Public Life* (London, Macmillan, 1901)
T.P. Wiseman (ed.), *Roman Political Life 90 BC – AD 69* (Exeter Studies in History, no. 7, 1985)

4

Governing Rome

The development of the constitution

157. By the time of Augustus, the city of Rome alone contained about a million inhabitants, and the territory which Rome controlled stretched from the Atlantic to the Caspian and from the English Channel to the Sahara. However great the *imperium* which the emperor had gathered into his own hands, it simply was not possible for an individual to administer such a large and complex entity by himself. In any case, the tradition of the Republic which Augustus had inherited meant that the running of the state did not depend solely on holders of *imperium*. As Polybius saw in the second century BC, the Republic was a 'mixed' constitution, with a contribution from the 'oligarchic' Senate and the 'democratic' popular assemblies, as well as the almost 'monarchic' consulship and the other holders of *imperium* [118]. This analysis gives a clear picture of the 'constitution' of the Republic; but Greeks like Polybius tended to assume that, because they could give an explanation of the way in which things worked, they had been set up in the beginning in order to function in this way. The Romans, on the other hand, were well aware that their institutions emerged from a long history of continuous modification, and that they often showed signs of having originally been designed for purposes quite different from those for which they were finally used [23]. Cicero, for instance, quotes this remark of the Elder Cato, put into the mouth of Scipio Aemilianus in a dialogue about the Roman Republic: 'Cato used to say that the constitution of our city was better than those of others, because in the others the state was almost always founded by the laws and institutions of individual people ... whereas ours was not based on the ideas of one man but of many, and it was set up, not in the life-time of one man, but across many centuries and generations' (Cicero, *On the Republic* 2.1.3). Apart from anything else, this tradition of change and development made it possible for Augustus to reshape the

4.1 Casting of votes in the *Comitium*: the figure at the left receives a voting-tablet from an attendant, that at the right drops his tablet into the ballot-box.

'democratic' element of the people's assemblies and the 'oligarchic' element of the Senate so that the work they had done under the Republic continued in the new circumstances of the Principate.

The assemblies of the people

158. The long period of development of which Cato was so proud resulted in some curious oddities by the time in which Cicero was writing. One of the strangest was the way in which the people assembled and voted (fig. 4.1), both for elections and for passing laws. In theory the citizens, as listed every five years by the censors [140], formed the sovereign body, and it was they who chose the men who would hold the magistracies and exercise *imperium*; they too were the source of legislation, and though consuls, praetors and tribunes might propose measures, it was the people which, in one of the people's assemblies, had to pass the proposal for it to become law. And indeed, this sovereignty was acknowledged when Publius Valerius, one of the first consuls to hold office after the expulsion of the kings in 510/509 BC, ordered that the lictors who accompanied the consuls should lower the *fasces*, symbols of *imperium* [130], when the consul addressed the people (Cicero, *On the Republic* 2.31.54). So in practice [142ff.] the people's votes did count in the elections: they could not be ignored. The oddity of their position, however, becomes clear from the fact that by Cicero's time there was not one legislative and electoral assembly of the people, but three.

'*Comitia centuriata*'

159. The oldest of the three was the *comitia centuriata*, which had been set up, according to the story generally believed in the late Republic, by one of the kings, Servius Tullius, in the sixth century BC. This assembly originated in a meeting of the Roman army, and its organisation clearly reflects this. For example, in this *comitia* the people were divided into *centuriae* (whence the name), which were originally military units; the first eighteen *centuriae* consisted of cavalry, i.e. those who had been awarded a 'public horse' by the censors [140] and so had full entitlement to the rank of *equites*; there were *centuriae* of trumpet-players, flute-players, blacksmiths and attendants, each of whom had had a particular importance in the army of the kings; and so on (see [162] for more examples).

160. The *comitia centuriata* consisted of 193 *centuriae*, and the system was that of an electoral college, i.e. each *centuria* had one vote. The people were fitted into the *centuriae* in accordance with the amount of property they were registered by the census [140] as holding. Outside the eighteen *centuriae* of *equites*, which were the 'top' *centuriae* of the *comitia*, there were five property-groupings (or *classes*). The first *classis* had seventy *centuriae*, but we do not know how the *centuriae* were divided among *classes* 2–5. At the bottom there was one *centuria* not registered as a *classis* at all which was made up of all those who had no property registered in the census. These people were called the *proletarii*, because they could not produce agricultural goods but only children (*proles*). This group was probably far larger than those in any of the other census categories, even though efforts had been made through the third and second centuries to get more *proletarii* into the fifth *classis* by reducing the property qualifications yet further [173].

161. From this it is clear that the *centuriae* did not contain equal numbers of people; and it is even clearer that though the top, wealthy *centuriae* (the *equites* and the first *classis*) contained overall far fewer citizens than the lower, poorer ones, the 'one *centuria*, one vote' system meant that the votes of the wealthy counted for far more than those of the poor: the *equites* (18 *centuriae*) and first *classis* (70 *centuriae*) controlled 88 of the 193 votes. The system of voting further emphasised this, since voting began at the top of the hierarchy, each *centuria* declaring its decision in turn until a majority had been gained. Once that had happened, no others were asked. As the total number of votes/*centuriae* was 193, it would have been very rarely indeed that the last *centuria* of the *proletarii* was ever asked its opinion. Of course it did not make any difference to the result when any particular *centuria* was asked to give its vote, since it would not affect the size of the majority; but since their vote was almost never taken into account, the *proletarii* and members of the lower classes can hardly have felt intimately involved in the life of the state.

162. The *comitia centuriata* had as its main function the election of the consuls and praetors, and it could be summoned and presided over only by a magistrate holding *imperium*. It was also this assembly which was consulted before a full-scale war could be declared. This is another indication that the *comitia centuriata* was still regarded as being the army, meeting to be consulted on matters that concerned it. This is also the reason why it met outside the sacred boundary of the city, the *pomerium* [123–4]: no army was allowed to enter the city. Here is a good example of the way in which the Romans continued to use institutions whose original purpose had disappeared long before.

163. The advantage which the *comitia centuriata* gave to the richer citizens accurately reflected the way in which most of the members of the ruling class, which filled the magistracies and the Senate, thought the state should be run. Cicero puts this argument into Scipio Aemilianus' mouth in his discussion of the problems of democracy:

Equality of rights, which free peoples hold dear, cannot be maintained; for, although no check or restraint is placed on these peoples, they are particularly inclined to assign many functions to many people, and there is a great deal of choosing of men and offices among them; and this so-called equality is in fact most unequal. When both the best and the worst, who are bound to exist in every nation, are given equal honour, equality itself is most unequal; and this cannot happen in states which are governed by the best people in them. (Cicero, *On the Republic* 1.34.53)

For Scipio and for Cicero, one distinction between the 'good' and the 'bad', at least in political terms, was quantity of possessions, particularly land, which was what distinguished people from one another at the census [140]. Cicero had this distinction in mind when he called those politicians who generally supported the interests of the upper classes *optimates* and those who tried to mobilise the people as a political power-base *populares*.

'Comitia tributa' and 'concilium plebis'

164. There were however two other legislative and electoral assemblies in Rome, the *comitia tributa* and the *concilium plebis*. These two were similar in their internal organisation, and the voting unit in both cases was not the *centuria* but the tribe, of which there were thirty-five. Again, it was an electoral-college 'one tribe, one vote' system. In the beginning, these tribes were geographical divisions of the people. Originally there were four tribes, all in the city of Rome itself. But the tribes gradually grew in number in line with the

increasing numbers of Roman citizens outside the city, until the number was fixed at thirty-five in 241 BC. After that, even though many more Roman citizens were created in Italy (especially with the enfranchisement of the Italians after the Social War of 91–87 BC [54]) the number was kept constant. This meant that the wealthy did not have the same built-in advantage that they had in the *comitia centuriata*, though the richer members of the 31 rural tribes probably found it easier to get to Rome with their supporters than the poor [143]. The essential theoretical difference between the assemblies, however, was that the *comitia tributa* was an assembly of the whole people, while the *concilium plebis*, as its name implies, was an assembly of the *plebs* alone. The *comitia tributa* could be called by the curule magistrates (i.e. the consuls, praetors and aediles, though in practice, it was usually a consul or a praetor who did so); while the *concilium plebis* was convened and presided over by a plebeian magistrate, and normally by a tribune of the *plebs*. Similarly, the *comitia tributa* elected the curule aediles and quaestors, while the *concilium plebis* chose the plebeian magistrates, the tribunes and the plebeian aediles. In the earlier stages of the Republic, there had also been a distinction in the legislative activity of the two assemblies. The *comitia tributa* could approve laws of the Roman people, just as the *comitia centuriata* did, while the *concilium plebis* could only enact a decree binding on the *plebs* (*plebiscitum*, from which comes our word 'plebiscite'). But after the Hortensian law in 287 BC, which brought to an end the 'Conflict of the Orders', plebiscites were given the force of laws (*leges*) which bound the whole people, not just the *plebs* [23, 137].

165. The powers of the assemblies were great, but even so they depended both in theory and in practice on the magistrates. In elections, the presiding magistrate had a considerable amount of control over what went on, and that magistrate was a consul in the case of elections for the consuls, praetors, quaestors, censors and curule aediles; the tribunes presided over the elections by the *concilium plebis* of the plebeian magistrates, the plebeian aediles and the tribunes. During the Hannibalic War, for instance [31ff.], the redoubtable Quintus Fabius Maximus, then at the height of his power, while presiding at the consular elections in 215 BC, ordered the *centuria* which had cast the first votes to go back and reconsider because the candidates they favoured were unsuitable to lead the state against Hannibal. Perhaps not surprisingly, he himself was one of the consuls who were eventually elected (Livy 24.7.8–9.4; [129). This sort of direct intervention in the process of election was extremely rare, but it was in theory possible for a presiding magistrate either to refuse to accept the nomination of a candidate or even to declare a successful candidate not to have been elected. For example, in 67 BC the consul Gaius Calpurnius Piso was asked what he would do if the radical politician Marcus Lollius

Palicanus was elected by the people at the consular elections. 'I will not declare him', was the answer (Valerius Maximus 3.8.3). Perhaps fortunately, the question did not arise. When it came to legislation, however, the control exercised by the magistrates was more obvious. Only those magistrates who held *imperium* had the right to 'deal with the people' (that is to present measures to the *comitia centuriata* or the *comitia tributa*), and that meant normally the consul or praetor, or, when appointed, the dictator and his *magister equitum* [134]. So only these magistrates could ask the question of the people, 'Do you wish and order such and such to be a law?', which was the form in which a proposal (*rogatio*, literally an 'asking') was put to the assemblies of the whole people. The same was true of the relationship between the tribunes and the assembly of the *plebs*. There was no provision, as there was, for instance, in the Classical Athenian democracy, for a proposal from the floor of the assembly (*WoA*). The power of the people in republican Rome was limited to the decision on whether to approve or not approve what the presiding magistrates put to them.

The Senate

166. The other element in the threefold structure [118, 157] was the Senate. If the popular assemblies were less powerful in fact than might have been expected from their theoretical position, the reverse was true of the Senate. The story that was accepted in the late Republic was that Romulus had assembled the first Senate in order to have a body of advisers, drawn from the 'best' men in the state [162]. No doubt even the kings had a number of such advisers, perhaps drawns from the heads of the most important families. If this is true, it would explain why the name *patres* ('fathers') was often given to senators, though of course this may simply be a metaphorical use, the senators being regarded as 'City Fathers' of Rome [16]. What is surely the case is that they were thought to bring to their task the wisdom of age: this is clear from the very name of the body, since the word 'senate' comes from the Latin word *senex*, 'old man'. When the kings were expelled in 510/509 BC and replaced by consuls, the Senate remained part of the new order. The respect in which the Senate was held can be judged from the fact that in later times it was regarded as the state *consilium*. This word was regularly used to describe the body of friends and associates that any Roman in public life would gather round him for advice. In a similar way, the head of a family (the *paterfamilias*) had a *consilium* drawn from the family.

167. Until the censors took over the job, probably at some point in the late fourth century, it appears that the consuls chose a new Senate each year.

However, once the censors were given the responsiblity, the nature of the
Senate was bound to change, since senators were now appointed for life
(unless the censors subsequently removed them from the Senate for some mis-
demeanour). Further, it increasingly became a right of those who had been
elected to one of the curule magistracies to occupy a place in the Senate after
their tenure of office. Finally Sulla, in his reshaping of the constitution during
his dictatorship from 81 to 79 BC, took away the power of the censors to add
new senators by tying entry directly to election to the quaestorship, the lowest
of the offices on the *cursus honorum* [145].

168. The result of senators being appointed for life was to make the Senate
the most continuous element in the structure of the state, since the popular
assemblies tended, by their very nature, to be made up of different people on
different occasions, and the magistrates were only in office for a year. This,
combined with the fact that the members were all experienced ex-magistrates,
made it a repository of the collected wisdom of the Roman ruling class, and
thus gave it immense prestige [468]. In the late republic, Cicero could say: 'Our
ancestors made the Senate the guardian, the leader and the defender of the
state, and they wanted the magistrates to respect the authority of this order,
and to be, so to speak, the servants of this most weighty council' (Cicero, *In
Defence of Plancius* 65.137). Properly speaking, it remained what it had
always been, an advisory body for the chief magistrates, i.e. the consuls, the
praetors, and, by the late Republic, the tribunes (probably included because of
their role as proposers of measures to the *concilium plebis*). This is apparent
from the way in which Senate meetings were run. The Senate could only be
convened by the senior magistrate present in Rome, which usually meant one
of the consuls, or, in their absence, a praetor. In Cicero's time, the meeting
began, after the opening formalities, with the consul presenting to the Senate
the matter on which he required advice. He then proceeded to ask each senator
in turn to express his opinion. This was done according to rank, beginning
with the consuls designate for the following year, if the elections had already
taken place, and then those who had already held the consulship. The other
magistrates designate and ex-magistrates then followed in order, ending with
the former tribunes and quaestors. Within their group, the ex-consuls were
called in the same order throughout the year, according to a list published by
one of the consuls at the outset of the year. This was a matter of some importance. For example, in January 61 BC, Cicero wrote to his friend Atticus to say
that he had only been placed second on the list, and tries to make Atticus
believe that he is quite relieved: had he been placed first, he says, he would have
been under an obligation to the consul who had made up the order, Marcus
Pupius Piso, whom he describes as 'a perverse individual' (Cicero, *Letters to*

Atticus 1.12.2). This was not just a matter of personal pride, though no doubt that had a lot to do with Cicero's scarcely concealed irritation. Since the various ranks of magistrates were called in order of seniority, it is likely that the basic idea was that the more important people should be heard first; and indeed, as might be expected, they tended to set the tone of the debate for those who followed. Often, senators who were called later would simply respond to the consul's question by indicating agreement with an earlier speaker; and those who were at the very end of the list (and were often not called at all because the Senate could not continue its meeting after nightfall) expressed their opinion by walking across the floor of the Senate-house and sitting near the senator with whom they agreed. These were called *pediarii* or 'foot-soldiers', because they expressed themselves with their feet rather than their voices. At the end of the session, the consul took one of the opinions that had been given, and, if he had judged correctly that this was the view of the majority, the Senate would adopt this as its advice. It would then be issued as a *senatus consultum*, usually translated as 'decree of the Senate', but more properly 'the considered opinion of the Senate'. If there was doubt about the matter, the consul would direct the Senate to vote, either in favour of or against a particular proposal. More often than not, this second stage would not be necessary, but sometimes it could be crucial. For example, Cicero, at the end of the debate on the fate of those who had taken part in the Catilinarian conspiracy during his consulship in 63 BC, decided to take the opinion of Cato the Younger (Marcus Cato) as the basis of the resolution that the conspirators should be executed [66]. But since Cato was only tribune designate, he took the precaution of putting the matter to the vote (Sallust, *Catiline* 55.1).

169. It might be imagined that an advisory body of this sort, though very valuable for the magistrates who consulted it, would not have power of the sort that the assemblies of the people had: for the only way in which the Senate could exercise power was through the advice it gave to the magistrates. But their power was in practice substantial, simply because the magistrates virtually always took the 'advice' they were offered. In part this was no doubt because of the excellence of that advice; but it was also because of the relationship between the magistrates and the Senate within the world of Roman politics. As we have seen in the last chapter, the magistracy and the holding of *imperium* were the basis of the political life of a member of the Roman ruling classes during the Republic [120ff.]. However, though the holding of magistracies marked the high points of a political career, they lasted only one year each. Moreover, even if the praetorship and the consulship were extended by the use of pro-praetorian or pro-consular *imperium* [150], the total would still not

take up the whole of a politician's time, especially after he had reached the consulship. As a result, all the rest of his years as an active politician were spent in the Senate. This meant that the other people in the Senate had been or were likely before long to be in the same position that the current magistrates were in; and perhaps more importantly, that the body from which the magistrates were getting advice was one of which they had all been members before being elected magistrates, and which they would rejoin as soon as they laid down office. Consequently the magistrates and the Senate were very much part of the same grouping within the Roman political organisation. Not, of course, that they always agreed with one another, but at least they all worked within a single set of notions about how the state should function. This connection between the Senate and the magistrates is, incidentally, one reason why Polybius' neat analysis of the Roman constitution into three separate elements – consuls, senate and people – does not really fit the reality of political life at Rome [118, 157].

170. The 'power' of the Senate consisted therefore of the influence which it in turn exercised over the magistrates. As a result it could affect legislation: for by custom, though not by law, all legislation except that concerning the extension of citizenship, whether it came from a consul, a praetor or a tribune of the plebs, had to be brought to the Senate before being considered by the people's assemblies. For example, when Tiberius Gracchus took his agrarian bill to the *concilium plebis* in 133 BC without the approval of the Senate, he was acting in a way which, though not contrary to any law, was certainly out of step with the way the Senate and the people normally functioned [46–7]. Similarly, a consul who wished to celebrate a triumph asked permission from the Senate beforehand. Although it was possible for a consul who, for instance, was still in his year of office, to celebrate without such permission [124], generally speaking it was recognised that the triumph was a reward granted by the Senate.

171. The Senate's involvement with foreign policy was also based on its relationships with the magistracy. Although the Senate did not of course directly control the army – this was the task of those who held *imperium* [124–5] – it did decide both the *prouinciae* which were to be assigned to those holding *imperium* each year, and the size of the forces which each commander was allowed to levy. This gave the Senate considerable powers of patronage, since they could decide which commands the magistrates and pro-magistrates would hold. Indeed this power of patronage was sufficiently important for Gaius Gracchus to limit it [48–9]. As tribune in 123–122 BC, he passed a law that the consuls' *prouinciae* for the following year should be determined *before* the consuls were elected: when the consuls had been elected, they

decided who was to hold which *prouincia* by lot (the method always used to determine the holders of praetorian *prouinciae*) or by mutual agreement.

172. The result of all this was that the Senate had effective control over the foreign policy of the state: for in the last resort this policy depended on where Rome was prepared to send its armies to fight. It was therefore to the Senate that embassies from foreign states came to present their requests and complaints; and this is also the reason why the power of the magistracy and of the Senate was undermined in the last century of the Republic when people's assemblies began to appoint pro-magistrates to important commands [152]. It was of course open to the consul to ask the opinion of the Senate at any point on matters of foreign affairs, and provincial commanders would write to the Senate with reports of what they were doing in their *prouinciae* (two of Cicero's letters from his time in Cilicia are reports of this type [179]). But in the last analysis, it was the allocation of the *prouinciae* each year which gave the Senate the opportunity for a full-scale review of Rome's foreign policy commitments.

The commander and the army

173. It was through the command of the army (figs. 4.2 and 4.3) by the holders of *imperium* that the magistrates and pro-magistrates related to what was in theory the people as a whole. Just as the *comitia centuriata* was seen as the army assembled in a political capacity [159–63], so the army could also be regarded as equivalent to the people as a whole. Thus Polybius, in his account of the constitution, talks about the army as the Roman people, and says: 'when they [i.e. the Roman people] are on campaign, all of them, both as individuals and as whole, come under the power of the consuls' (Polybius 6.17). This illustrates that, again in theory, all the citizens of the Republic were liable for conscription into the army [57]. Cicero says that anyone who avoided conscription was liable to be sold as a slave, on the grounds that he was not facing up to danger as a free man should (Cicero, *In Defence of Caecina* 34.99) In practice though, through the early and middle Republic, the only people who were called up for army service were those who had a census qualification down to and including the fifth *classis* [160]. The reason for this was that during this period, soldiers had to provide their own equipment, which the *proletarii* (the group below the fifth *classis*) were reckoned incapable of. It is no doubt for this reason that the property-level that gave access to the fifth *classis* was progressively lowered, so that from 11,000 *asses* (a standard unit of coinage) before the Hannibalic War, it had fallen to 1,500 *asses* by the last quarter of the second century. This last represents a very small amount of

4.2 The Roman army in the field: at the bottom the shipping of supplies; above, the ritual sacrifice of a boar, ram and bull to purify the army before it set out on a campaign. Cf. [486].

property indeed, almost certainly insufficient to maintain an average-sized family. All the same, it was these property-owners, however small-scale their property may have been, who made up the citizen legions which fought and defeated Hannibal and the Hellenistic kings [33–4], and were engaged in almost continuous warfare in northern Italy down to the 170s and in Spain throughout the second century. But it must be emphasised that they did not make up the whole of the fighting force which Rome deployed through this period. The Latins and the other Italian allies provided soldiers who fought alongside the Romans, usually on the ratio of two allies to every Roman. It is difficult to calculate what proportion of the total available manpower this represents, but it is probable that more allies served in relation to their numbers than Romans.

174. The Roman army was, then, a citizen militia rather than a professional army, and in theory a new army was conscripted to serve with the new magistrates each year. For this reason, the *stipendium* that they were paid was not high, since it was intended only to be enough money to cover the expenses of citizens who were taken away from their normal livelihood. Indeed, it

remained low until Julius Caesar, as consul in 59 BC, doubled the amount they were paid (Suetonius, *Julius* 26.3). In practice, though, the long campaigns against Hannibal, followed by the no less demanding overseas wars of the second century, led to longer and longer periods of service becoming necessary. It was possible, if a man had a taste for the military life, to string together a series of campaigns, and even look forward to re-enlisting after he had returned home to his farmstead. Livy gives an account of such a man, admittedly in a context that makes it likely he was the exception, rather than the rule. In 171 BC, Rome was raising troops for the war against King Perseus of Macedon [38] and found itself short of experienced centurions. So a *senatus consultum* was passed, demanding service from all ex-centurions under fifty. Some ex-centurions objected to this compulsory inclusion; but at this point, according to Livy's story, one former centurion, called Spurius Ligustinus, who was well into his fifties, launched an equally fierce objection to his compulsory exclusion: he had fought for Rome in twenty-two annual campaigns, beginning in 200 BC, in Asia Minor, Macedonia, Italy and under three separate commanders in Spain, and wanted more (Livy 42.34). The existence of such people as Ligustinus makes it certain that others, perhaps not to the same

4.3 The emperor addresses his troops; building a fort. Cf. [486].

extent, were enthusiastic for the opportunity to get away from the life of a farmer to more exotic locations and kill people, enrich themselves on plunder and enjoy the excitement and the subsequent prestige of a successful campaign. It was only for campaigns in areas which promised little in the way of loot and where the enemy was known to be difficult to defeat that there was any problem in raising an army. One such case was the difficulty the consuls of 151 and 138 BC had in levying an army to fight in the central plateau of Spain against the Celtiberians of Numantia. In general, however, the people seem to have been eager to be enrolled.

175. The reduction in the qualification for the fifth *classis* [173] shows that, however keen the people may have been to serve, there were not enough of them to provide the forces needed to sustain Rome's military activity around the Mediterranean. Matters came to a head when in 107 BC Gaius Marius, who had been elected consul with much opposition from the established noble families in Rome, was allotted the *prouincia* of Numidia, where a war was being carried on against King Jugurtha [51]. The allotment was not done in the traditional way by the Senate, but by a tribune of the *plebs*, who had a plebiscite passed in the *concilium plebis*. This outraged the nobles still more, who saw that this weakened the position of the Senate. When Marius was elected, the campaign was proving a difficult one, and fighting in the uncongenial territory of north Africa with few cities to sack and only a remote chance of victory was not likely to prove popular. When therefore Marius announced his intention of recruiting additional forces, the Senate did not attempt to interfere. It was sure that in so doing he would put himself out of favour with the very people who had just voted him his command. Marius however circumvented the problem by the simple expedient of throwing the levy open to all, and taking volunteers from the very poorest members of the state, who had hitherto been excluded [52].

176. In some ways this was simply the logical extension of what had been happening over the previous hundred years, as the lower limit for membership of the fifth *classis* had been systematically reduced. It did, however, make quite clear what had apparently been concealed hitherto, that when the soldiers had completed their tour of duty and went home, they would need support from somewhere. This was more obviously true for Marius' volunteers than had been the case before, because Marius' men would not have a farm to go back to once they had been discharged. As a result, Marius tried to ensure that those soldiers who served with him in his three-year campaign in Numidia and subsequent campaigns were given land to go to when they returned. He persuaded the tribune Saturninus (Lucius Appuleius Saturninus) to have a land law to this effect passed through the *concilium*

4.4 The army gathers outside a fortified encampment in readiness for action. Cf. [486].

plebis in 100 BC [52]. But Saturninus was killed in riots and his whole legislative programme was annulled.

177. It does seem that Marius' opening of service in the army to volunteers from among the *proletarii* created a different relationship between a commander and his troops (fig. 4.4) from what had been the case before. When in 88 BC, Sulla marched against Rome to regain the command against Mithridates which Marius had taken from him [56], he apparently had little difficulty in persuading his newly recruited army to follow him; and through the period of the civil wars, down to the victory of Octavian over Mark Antony at Actium in 31 BC, a series of army commanders led troops which were prepared to follow their own general against the city itself. Sulla in 88 [56] and 82 BC [58], Marius in 87 [58], Caesar in 49 [72] and Octavian in 43 [74] all marched with Roman armies to seize the city which had not been taken since the Gallic sack of 390. It is, of course, too simplistic to put this down simply to Marius' change of recruitment policy in 107. The tradition of the independent power of a holder of *imperium* and the growth in the importance and extent (both in area and time) of the great commands also play a part. But there does also seem to be a change in the atmosphere, almost in the psychology of the armies of the last century of the Republic. It is as if the soldiers who had previously reckoned on getting land and booty for themselves by fighting the enemies of Rome on the instructions of the Senate had now decided that they were more likely to achieve this by backing one general against another. In some cases, this was no doubt the result of a long period of service under a commander that they had come to trust. For example, Caesar in 49 led an army that had served with him since he had begun the war against the Gauls ten years before. However, this was by no means always true. In particular, it was not true of Sulla. When he moved against Rome in 88, his army may have contained some soldiers who had fought with him during the war against the Italian allies from 91 onwards, when he served as a *legatus* [178]. But it was certainly not 'his' army in the way that it was to become by the time he marched back into Italy in 83 and 82, after five years of fighting against Mithridates [58].

There is one further change in the composition of the Roman legions which is worth noticing. After the granting, however reluctantly, of citizenship to the Italian allies after the war of 91 to 87 BC, there were no longer Latin and other allied contingents serving with the Roman forces, because all now held the citizenship [54–5]. This in turn meant that the legions contained those who had previously been Italians as well as those who had long held Roman citizenship. Although this change will not have affected the army that Sulla used against Rome in 88 and then took with him to fight againt Mithridates, it might explain why later Roman armies were less in awe of Rome than the earlier ones had been. Certainly whatever the reason or combination of reasons, the armies of the late Republic seem more 'professional', both in their technical expertise and in their attachment to their own leaders, than had been true in the second century.

Prouinciae and provinces

178. The allocation of *prouinciae* was one point at which the business of the Senate, the *imperium* of the magistrates and pro-magistrates, and the people as members of the army, all linked together [171–2]. This is of course because a *prouincia* was an area of responsibility for an *imperium*-holder, and one of the most frequent activities of *imperium*-holders was the fighting of wars. By the late Republic, however, fighting in the *prouinciae* was not the only activity, even for those whose *imperium* was to be held outside the city [123]. For many of the *prouinciae* which were allotted by the Senate in Cicero's time were what we would call 'provinces' in the sense of an area of overseas territory which was controlled and governed by the Romans, not fought for by them. It is easy to see how these two notions of *prouincia* came about. The earliest overseas provinces had all had their first contacts with the Romans as a result of Roman armies being sent there. Indeed, the first such three areas (Sicily, Sardinia and Spain) were all places to which they had gone to fight against the Carthaginians during the First and Second Punic wars. From the point of view of the allocations of *prouinciae* by the Senate, the only difference between a *prouincia* which was a military area in which a war was to be fought and one which was in our sense a 'province' was that the latter was allocated every year, while the former stopped being designated once the war was over. In other ways too the provincial governor and the army commander were dealt with in the same way. The staff that accompanied a governor was basically the same as that which served with an army commander. One of the quaestors elected each year looked after the governors' financial dealings, and one or more *legati*, assigned by the Senate on the recommendation of the *imperium*-holder, acted as his immediate subordinates. Again commander and governor both made use of groups of advisers which made up a *consilium* of the type normally consulted by any Roman who had important decisions to make [166]. There is a famous inscription recording the grant of citizenship to a group of Spanish cavalrymen by Pompey's father, Cnaeus Pompeius Strabo, during his campaign in the war against the Italian allies in 89 BC. This lists a *consilium* which includes, on the one hand, men who had already held the praetorship, and on the other, his own son, then only seventeen (*ILS* 8888).

The governor and the province

179. It was not only senatorial procedure that made the provincial governor (fig. 4.5) resemble the provincial commander in the republican period. When Cicero was governor of Cilicia in southern Asia Minor in 51 BC, his letters to the Senate, reporting what he had achieved (Cicero, *Letters to Friends* 15.2 and 15.14) are entirely taken up with military matters, even though most of his time was spent on administration and the law courts. In other words, the primary responsibility of the governor was still seen as ensuring the military security of the area to which he had been sent.

180. Although the origin of the provinces was military and the perception of them remained so to a considerable extent, the work done by a provincial governor had always included tasks which we would consider civilian. These became progressively more important as the empire expanded. One of the major functions of the governor in a province not under military threat was jurisdiction. As an *imperium*-holder, he was able to conduct cases between Roman citizens, but, simply because he was the representative of the power of

4.5 Portrait-statue of a general, perhaps a provincial commander or governor, from Tivoli.

Rome, he also dealt with those involving non-Romans. The extent of such jurisdiction varied from province to province, because it depended on the type and number of the provincial communities themselves. Rome had treaty relationships with some which explicitly excluded judicial interference; and in some provinces, a decree by a provincial governor, often rather misleadingly called a *lex prouinciae* ('law for the province') laid down the way in which cases between citizens of the various communities in the area were to be handled and the point at which the governor was expected to be involved. One example of this is Sicily, of which we know a certain amount, because of Cicero's speeches against Gaius Verres, the governor he prosecuted in 70 BC for extortion there. In Sicily, the *Lex Rupilia*, a measure laid down by Publius Rupilius when consul there in 132 BC, specified with some precision the governor's involvement with the local community, all of which, at least according to Cicero, was ignored by Verres. Certainly in the last century BC provincial governors posted edicts on their arrival in their province, stating the cases they would handle and the basis on which they would judge them, just as the *praetor urbanus* did in Rome [132]; and indeed Cicero in Cilicia based much of his edict on that of the urban praetor.

181. Another area of the governor's work that we would think of as civilian was the collection of taxes. In areas where the tax was a fixed amount (usually called *stipendium*), the governor's quaestor would collect the money directly from the local communities. But in other cases, where the return was variable (as for instance with customs dues at the ports, or tithes on grain), intermediaries were used to collect the taxes. Usually this was done by the *publicani*, who put in bids with the censors to collect taxes on a five-yearly basis [142]. The advantage for the Romans in this privatised tax-collection was that on winning the contract the tax-collector paid the tax due in advance of collecting it. The Romans had the money already. Consequently, even though the tax actually collected might go up or down depending on the level of trade or the quality of the harvest from year to year, the income of the state was assured. It also meant that the governor and his quaestor were relieved of the burden of having to make the arrangements for the actual collection. But as in all questions of administration, the Romans were not dogmatic about how things should be done, and often based their practice on what they found already in place. In Sicily, for instance, the corn tithe was collected not by Roman *publicani* but by local Sicilians. This was because the system on which the tax was levied, the *Lex Hieronica* dating back to the time when Hiero was king of Syracuse, was in place well before Sicily became a Roman province, and was perfectly efficient.

182. The variety of treatment that the provinces received, with different systems of taxation and different patterns of jurisdiction, came about because the Roman empire itself was not, at this stage, based on any imperial system. It was simply the aftermath of a series of military involvements, which had turned into longer-term commitments. The size of the governor's staff was really very small, if it is thought of as intended to administer a whole province. In addition to the staff mentioned above [178], the governor might appoint military commanders at a lower level than his *legati*, known as *praefecti*; and he was accompanied by a group of assistants (scribes, attendants and, of course, his lictors [130–1]). He also often took younger men, who might help with various tasks and at the same time gain some experience of Roman rule overseas, called *comites* ('companions'). All these people, however, seem very few compared with the task of governing large areas like Sicily, or half of Spain, or the province of Asia (the Aegean coast of modern Turkey), with its numerous and highly sophisticated Greek cities. The answer is that they did not 'govern' these areas in the modern sense. They took no interest in or responsibility for the day-to-day life of the people there. That was the task of the local provincial communities themselves, who looked after the upkeep of the cities, raised local taxes and provided the courts which judged the ordinary cases between their own citizens. To a large extent, the work of a governor was

still that of the commander of an occupying army, even if, as in the case of peaceful provinces like Sicily or Asia, the number of soldiers under his command was small.

183. The limited scope of the activity of the provincial governor did not mean, however, that he had little effect on the inhabitants of the province. The power that his *imperium* gave him was immense, and provided many opportunities for personal enrichment for the governor and his associates, and for the oppression of the provincial communities. Most of the direct evidence for such exploitation comes, it must be admitted, from Cicero's prosecution speeches against governors like Verres and so is hardly unbiased. None the less, the opportunities available for extraction of cash in return for favours given was enormous. Farmers, for instance, could be made to go to the expense and trouble of transporting across the province the grain that they owed for tax, if they did not bribe the governor; and, as the ultimate source of law, the governor could not only protect himself but also arrange matters to suit his friends. The likelihood of such powers undermining the resolve of even a well-disposed Roman governor was immense. Cicero wrote to his brother, Quintus, while the latter was proconsular governor of Asia from 61 to 59 BC: 'Actions which are honourable in the context of our ordinary daily life as private individuals must appear godlike when *imperium* is so great, moral standards so depraved and the *prouincia* such a temptation to corruption' (Cicero, *Letters to his Brother Quintus* 1.1.19). He goes on to observe that to show mildness when presiding over a court in Asia is far more admirable than it is in Rome: for in Rome, the magistrate is scrutinised by his colleagues, the Senate and people, while in Asia 'great numbers of citizens, allies, cities and states depend upon the nod of one man' (Cicero, *Letters to his Brother Quintus* 1.1.22).

184. The only check on provincial misgovernment during the Republic was the threat that, on his return to Rome, the governor would face trial on a charge of extortion, the *quaestio de repetundis* 'inquiry on the recovery of improper gains' [44]. Moreover, this was an important issue for the Senate, which in the last century and a half of the Republic seems genuinely to have desired that Rome's allies in the provinces should be treated fairly: after all, the Senate was well aware that governors came from among them and returned to them. This is the reason for the political struggles between the time of Gaius Gracchus and the consulship of Julius Caesar over who was to act on the jury of the *quaestio*, and in particular whether or not senators were to form all, part or none of its membership. It is notable, however, that this concern did not lead them to set up a means of controlling the governors while they were actually in their provinces, almost certainly because they were still regarded as

military commanders, with whom it would be quite improper to interfere during the tenure of their command. The notion of the supremacy of a holder of *imperium* was too important to allow anything else. In practice this meant that not only was it impossible to stop a governor while he was actually engaged in plundering the provincials, but it was also difficult for those provincials to get satisfactory redress afterwards. Although after Gaius Gracchus' law *de repetundis* in 123 BC [48] an accusation could be made by a provincial himself, he would have little or no chance of obtaining a conviction unless he had support from members of the Roman upper classes; and even then a former governor who was found guilty could simply go into exile outside Rome (or, in the late Republic, outside Italy). Verres himself took his profits with him into exile before the end of his trial, and survived to die in 43 BC, when Mark Antony, keen to get hold of his collection of Corinthian bronzes, had him proscribed.

Rome and its 'constitution'

185. The problem of controlling provincial governors was only one example of the difficulties that increasingly presented themselves during the late Republic. The means that the Roman state used to run its affairs throughout the Mediterranean had their origin in the structure of a city-state in central Italy in the sixth and fifth centuries BC In effect it had never had a constitution at all, in the sense of a coherent set of legal provisions by which to organise the state, and as Cicero's use of Cato's remark about the superiority of the Roman state shows, many Romans were not only aware of this but proud of it [157]. In some ways, not having a written constitution was a great advantage: it meant that Romans, especially those of the upper classes, could make substantial changes within the pattern of government so long as they stayed within the traditions which they claimed had been set by their forefathers, the famous *mos maiorum* ('the way the elders behaved'). The change in the functions of the various magistrates [130–41], the separation of *imperium* from the magistracies [150–2] and the way the Senate developed [168–9] are all examples of this. Two disadvantages, however, became increasingly apparent as the power of the Roman state grew in the last two centuries BC. The first was that Rome did not have a clear way of deciding on the overall policy of the state, in the way we expect a modern government to do. All they had was a clear-cut machinery, through the power of the holders of *imperium*, for getting things done and a way of determining who did them. In its heyday, it is true, policy was left to the Senate, but, as we have seen [166–8], the Senate was in theory only an advisory body. So both the

magistrates and pro-magistrates, in the executive decisions they took, and the people, when they were presented with laws to pass in their assemblies, could (within the rather vague limits of the *mos maiorum*) alter what the Senate had decided and make fresh policy decisions of their own. The second disadvantage of an unwritten constitution became obvious when the needs of the state for government outgrew what the 'traditions of the ancestors' could permit – or at least grew faster than the leaders of the Senate (who determined what counted as the 'tradition of the ancestors') were prepared for. When this happened in the last century of the Republic, some of the provisions of the *mos maiorum*, as it was interpreted at the time, were set down in the form of what might be called constitutional legislation. Sulla in particular produced a series of measures which put into written law what had earlier been assumed, and over the previous fifty years frequently challenged. This is what he was doing in the rules he enacted in 81–79 BC about what tribunes of the *plebs* could and could not do, and in his stricter definitions of the *cursus honorum* and the extent of the powers of magistrates and pro-magistrates. All this was designed to produce a strengthening of the control of policy by the Senate, which up till then had never been provided for in any written constitution [59–60]. As a result, when Augustus came to power and needed to find ways in which the position of the new monarchical Principate could be expressed in terms of the *mos maiorum*, he had a firmer basis from which to operate. As has been seen in the last chapter, he took as part of his pattern for his reformulated *res publica* an idea which had been developed under the old Republic, i.e. the separation of power from the offices to which it had traditionally been attached [153–4]. However, just as *imperium* by itself could not govern Rome and its empire, so Augustus needed to find new ways to shape the roles of Senate, people and the provinces, which had provided the policy-making and governmental structures of the Republic.

186. Augustus (fig. 4.6) solved the first problem of the unwritten constitution and the variety of methods of policy-making to which it gave rise by bringing all policy decisions into his own hands, just as he had done with the executive power [153–6]. The second problem, however, of the relationship between the *mos maiorum* and the powers of the various elements in the state (magistrates, Senate, people, provinces etc.) was genuinely problematic because it was a matter of the overall picture that the Romans had of their own government. Julius Caesar had been killed because he had created what looked like an overt autocracy from the material of the old Republic [74]. Further, the whole notion of one-man rule was clearly contrary to the traditions of the forefathers, who had begun the Republic in the aftermath of the overthrow of the autocratic kings. It was the way in which Augustus tackled

4.6 Augustus: portrait-statue from Via Labicana,
Rome. Cf. [79, 321, 477]

this side of the problem which more than anything gave the new Principate,
the reformulated Republic, its own particular shape.

Imperial senators and imperial Senate

187. The role of the Senate under Augustus was bound to be different from
what it had been in the days of the Republic, when it regarded itself as the
major policy-making body. It was, of course, still the advisory body for the
magistrates, especially the consuls and praetors, but as the real power now lay
not with the magistrates themselves but with the *princeps*, their own importance, which depended on their ability to instruct the magistrates, was severely
diminished. Moreover the continuity of the Senate, which had given it a particular significance when the executive power lay with annual magistrates, was
no longer an advantage in a state ruled by a monarch. Augustus did in fact pay
considerable respect to the Senate. No doubt the extension to his 'pro-
magisterial' position that he was given in 23 BC – the right to bring proposals
before the Senate – was intended to give the impression that in some sense the
relation between the Senate and the *princeps* would be similar to that with the
consuls [79, 153–4]. It became clear, however, by the end of his reign that the

reality was quite different. Although he did attend the Senate, he set up a separate advisory *consilium*, chosen by himself and including a number of senators, and also another group which acted as a steering committee for senatorial business [81].

188. The result of this was that the Senate became marginalised. For example, Augustus' successor, Tiberius, who seems to have been at the outset more inclined to follow the patterns of the old Republic, had considerable problems with the Senate early in his reign [90]. Tacitus describes how in AD 14, at the very beginning of his reign, Tiberius was thrown off balance by the Senate during the debate in which the powers to control the empire were formally voted to him:

> Amidst the most grovelling appeals from the Senate, Tiberius happened to say that, although he did not believe himself equal to the management of the whole state, he would undertake such of it as was entrusted to him. 'I ask you then, Caesar,' said Gaius Asinius Gallus, 'which part you want to have entrusted to you.' Put off his stride by this unexpected interruption, Tiberius was silent for a moment; then, recollecting himself, he answered that he felt it inappropriate to choose or reject anything in particular, since he would prefer to be excused from it altogether. (Tacitus, *Annals* 1.12.1–3)

Needless to say, Tiberius was rapidly persuaded to take on the whole burden of the state; but this uneasy relationship between *princeps* and Senate seems to have resulted in Tiberius' dislike of the Senate as a body, and a disinclination to use it, except for occasions such as the great show-trials for treason which marked the latter stages of his reign. The Senate clearly recognised (and this is implicit in Asinius Gallus' mischievous question in AD 14) that it had no effective control over the power which now ruled the empire; and this became obvious to all when, after the murder of the emperor Gaius Caligula in AD 41, the Senate spent forty-eight hours in debate as whether or not to restore the old Republic, while the Praetorian Guard was making Claudius the next emperor at its camp on the outskirts of the city ([95]; Suetonius, *Claudius* 10–11).

189. If there was little practical role for the Senate under the new regime, there was plenty for the senators in other parts of the administration of the empire. As with his rearrangement of constitutional matters, Augustus actually changed more than he appeared to do, though most of this change was to do with his control of the army. In 27 BC, he handed over to the Senate all the commands that he had held during the last stages of the civil war with Mark Antony, and received back from them a more limited command. That at least was the theory. In practice, the provinces which Augustus received were all those which contained substantial numbers of troops, and after some adjustment through his reign, consisted of: Spain (except for the relatively peaceful area of Baetica in the south); Gaul (except for the long-established southernmost area, modern Provence); the new *prouinciae* of the Rhine frontier; the eastern frontier provinces; and Egypt. In the remaining areas, which had only small-scale forces for internal 'police' duties, the pattern of sending out governors by the Senate remained as it had been: the provinces received an ex-magistrate with *imperium pro consule*, a quaestor and a minimal staff [179ff.]. There was some change in the methods of administration: the *publicani*, for instance, no longer had responsibilty for the large-scale taxes, whose collection was entrusted increasingly to the cities of the provinces themselves. On the whole, however, the pattern remained that of the Republican period. In the provinces allotted to Augustus, however, there was a change, in that the person who held the *imperium pro consule* was Augustus himself. Clearly it was not possible for Augustus to function as a governor in the sense that Cicero had done in Cilicia, and consequently he appointed *legati*, rather as had been done in the large-scale commands of the *principes* of the late Republic [152]. These *legati Augusti pro praetore*, 'pro-praetorian legates of Augustus', were, however, in other respects very like their predecessors, the provincial governors of the republican period. They were not only senators but ex-consuls, and in most respects at least as senior as the proconsuls in the senatorial provinces. They had the same administrative and juridical functions, and also the command of much larger military forces. In effect the only difference between the two was that Augustus chose his *legati* directly, while in theory the proconsular governors were appointed by the Senate. Even then, the emperor could influence the choice of such governors. One, known from an inscription, announced proudly that he had been sent as proconsul to Cyprus to organise the province, without use of the lot, on the authority of Augustus himself (E & J 197).

The emperor and the army

190. One change that did come about was in the conditions for the army. The gradual move towards a professional army which was taking place during the late Republic [174–5] was made the new policy by Augustus. By the end of his reign, he had laid down that the period of service for men entering the army (now composed of volunteers) would be sixteen years, with a further four years in a reserve to be drawn on in emergency; and that all soldiers, at the end of their service, would be given a fixed sum, in place of the land issued by some commanders after campaigns in the republican period. This cash payment was to come from a treasury set up for the purpose with money given

by Augustus, and was to be funded thereafter from taxes on inheritance and on auction sales. After the battle of Actium in 31 BC, Augustus retained twenty-eight out of his sixty legions to control and defend the empire. These were considerably more than the ten to fourteen that had been the norm during the late Republic. Of these twenty-eight, he lost three in the disaster in Germany in AD 9.

The new method of rewarding and controlling these legions was plainly intended to ensure that commanders would not be able, as Caesar, Pompey, Mark Antony and Augustus himself had done, to use the armies of the state for their own ends; and until the death of Nero in AD 68 this method was largely successful. Few army commanders rebelled against the emperor in this period, and those that did (as for example Lucius Arruntius Camillus Scribonianus, who attempted a *putsch* from Dalmatia in AD 42 against the newly installed emperor Claudius) were put down rapidly. Indeed it was only after the fall of emperors who had shown no interest in the army (Nero in AD 68 [100] and Commodus in 193 [115]) that army commanders posed a serious threat, and in each case the victorious commander (Vespasian in 70 [102] and Septimius Severus in 193) was able, after considerable bloodshed, to restore the Augustan position and regain the loyalty of the troops. Only in the third century did the mechanism which Augustus had set up really collapse, with a consequent period of half a century of military anarchy.

Imperial administrators: *equites* and freedmen

191. Because of their experience (and expectations) arising from their work in the Republican Senate, the senators clearly needed to be given a major public role under Augustus' new regime. But senators were not the only people whom the emperor used in the enormous task of running the empire. Augustus also used *equites* in a number of places, in ways which had no immediate precedent from the Republic. He appointed a number of men to posts which carried the title *praefectus*, which in the Republic had designated a minor military commander [182]. Some of these were very important jobs indeed, such as the *praefectus annonae* (in charge of the corn supply to Rome), the *praefectus uigilum* (who commanded the fire brigade and police force in Rome itself) and the *praefectus praetorio* (originally one but later two men, who commanded the Praetorian Guard, which protected the emperor himself). One of the greatest of these posts was that of *praefectus Aegypti*, an equestrian officer who acted as provincial governor of the very important province of Egypt, which it was forbidden for any senator to enter without explicit permission from the emperor. In some of the more difficult smaller

provinces, he also used *praefecti*. Pontius Pilatus, the Roman official in Judaea responsible for the crucifixion of Jesus of Nazareth under the reign of Tiberius, was one such.

192. The other officials of equestrian status whom Augustus used were called *procuratores*. The word basically meant an 'agent', who in private contexts could act on behalf of another person (the term was later applied to the provincial *praefecti* like Pilate, suggesting they were directly appointed agents of the emperor). As the emperor acquired properties throughout the empire by inheritance and confiscation, such procurators managed these properties, whether they were in senatorial provinces or the emperor's own. In the latter, *procuratores* also took care of the finances of the province, in the same way as the quaestor did in the senatorial provinces. The use of *procuratores* avoided the need to create a large number of extra magistrates, and also kept the finances of the imperial provinces firmly under the emperor's supervision. Not all these *procuratores* were *equites*. In some cases under Augustus, former slaves from the emperor's own household were appointed, though after his reign such appointments seem to have been restricted to running the imperial estates. The important point however is that the use of either *equites* or freedmen was the first case of people other than senators occupying official positions in the provinces.

193. It was not these men, however, who created the greatest stir among the senatorial classes in Rome. It was inevitable that, as more and more of the functions of the state were handled by the emperor or by his agents, the individuals who were part of the emperor's own household and so closest to him should come to play an increasingly significant part in the running of the empire. And it was natural too: in many wealthy families in Rome, slaves and freedmen were given responsiblity for the management of the family's affairs, particularly in the areas of accounts, correspondence and so on [97]. All Augustus was doing was enlarging their responsibility. Thus, Suetonius states that Augustus' own will was written partly in his own hand and partly in the hands of his freedmen, Polybius and Hilarion; and that he also left a short account of the military and financial state of the whole empire, to which he had appended the names of those slaves and freedmen who could give the details on which it was based (Suetonius, *Augustus* 101). It was the importance that these men gained through their closeness to the emperor which the senators found offensive, especially under the reign of Claudius, who was said to be completely under the thumb of his wives and his freedmen. None the less such men became so much a part of the imperial household that in AD 64 Nero compelled the suicide of a Roman noble who kept in his house freedmen with titles such as *ab epistulis* ('secretary in charge of correspondence'), *a*

libellis ('in charge of petitions') and *a rationibus* ('in charge of accounts'): the argument was that this alone showed he was intending to seize the throne. And Nero did the same to his nephew in the following year (Tacitus, *Annals* 15.35, 16.8).

The emperor and the Republic

194. However absurd Nero's actions appear to us to have been, they empha-sise one point that is undoubtedly true about the situation in Rome after Augustus had reshaped the Roman 'constitution'. Although much of the gov-erning of Rome and its empire was still undertaken after Augustus by the same sort of people as had been responsible for it under the old 'free' Republic, the decision-making role was now firmly in the hands of one individual, the emperor [80, 185–6]. It is true that Augustus took complex measures to confine as much as possible of his new-style government within the patterns of the old, and, as he did with his careful management of the magistracies, to organise the control of the armies and the provinces in such a way as to look as if nothing had changed. But the fact of the matter was that the Senate no longer controlled the world, even if it did have the privilege of voting to the man who did control it the power with which he did so. As the debate in the Senate at the beginning of Tiberius' reign showed, the senators had no real choice, and knew that they had not [188]. The question that this raises is – what did Augustus think he was doing? Did he really think that the Senate did not understand the realities of the new situation? Was he trying to fool the ruling class of Rome, and, if so, why were they apparently so prepared to be fooled?

195. These questions, though they seem real enough to us, were almost cer-tainly not the ones which concerned the contemporaries of Augustus. By the time Tacitus came to write his *Annals* in the early second century AD, the Principate was sufficiently clearly established for its origins to be discussed in the way in which he did in the opening sentences of his history [153]. For Tacitus, the emergence of the new monarchy under Augustus was something which could be noted and regretted. For the Romans of the 20s BC, living in the aftermath of two decades of civil war, Augustus' position was both inevitable and a relief from the mutual slaughter which had threatened to tear the empire apart. The Roman world needed some means to draw itself together again, and this could only be done through the agency of one man, and only then if that one man could show that he was the fulfilment of what had gone before, not its destruction. What Augustus suceeded in doing, by drawing both the power of the magistrates and the means of governing the empire into his hands, was to provide a focus for a state which was threatening to fragment. The fact that he was the commander of virtually all the armies and the source of massive patronage did of course mean that the liberty of the old ruling class was severely restricted; and the fact that to many in the provinces of the empire (especially in the Greek world) he was regarded as divine inevitably reduced the status of all other Romans. He had, however, given the old ruling class a role to play in the new scheme of things, so that, if they no longer ruled, at least they still governed, the world.

FURTHER READING

P. Garnsey and R. Saller, *The Roman Empire* (London, Duckworth, 1977)

A. Lintott, *Imperium Romanum; Politics and Administration* (London, Routledge, 1993)

J. Richardson, *Roman Provincial Administration* (London, Macmillan, 1976, repr. Bristol Classical Press, 1984)

Sourcebooks:

B. Campbell, *The Roman Army, 31 BC – AD 337* (London, Routledge, 1994)

B. Levick, *The Government of the Roman Empire* (London, Croom Helm, 1985)

5
The life of the city

The rhythms of the city

City without end

196. 'Rome wasn't built in a day.' 'All roads lead to Rome.' 'When in Rome
. . .' These proverbs about the Romans centre on a place: the city of Rome.
What was it like? The answers to that question will tell us much more than
what 'daily life' was like. As the proverbs imply, Rome had a very special position in the Roman world, through which we can understand important aspects
of how the whole culture worked. The Roman city is best approached through
two apparently contradictory statements:

(1) Roman society, culture and civilisation were urban.
(2) Rome cannot be understood without taking the country into full account
     [338].

The point is that the rich and powerful in Roman life, the pace-setters, were
active in both town and country at once. As a result, much of the country was
a kind of extension of the town, and, because of this, the affairs of the town
made their mark on the country more deeply than at any time in Europe before
the Industrial Revolution.

Country holidays

197.

In the consulship of Manius Acilius and Gaius Porcius [114 BC], Publius Helvius, a
Roman *eques*, was returning home to Apulia after the *ludi Romani* ['Roman Games', a
great Roman festival]. As they were passing through north Campania, on the Via

Appia, his maiden daughter, who was seated on a horse, was struck by lightning and killed. (Julius Obsequens, *On Prodigies*, 37)

Now here is our itinerary, so that you can make up your mind where to meet us. I want to go to Formiae for the *Parilia* [a festival of the goddess *Pales*, celebrated on 21 April]. Then, as you think I had better avoid that Bay of Luxury [i.e. the Bay of Naples] at the present time, we shall leave Formiae on 1 May [59 BC] so as to be at Antium on the 3rd. There are to be some games at Antium from the 4th to the 6th which Tullia wants to watch. From there I propose to go to Tusculum, then to Arpinum, returning to Rome by 1 June. (Cicero, *Letters to Atticus* 2.8, trans. Shackleton Bailey (adapted slightly), no. 29)

In these two passages we get tiny glimpses of people from the Roman upper classes engaged in and making decisions about their travel plans. We see how senators and *equites* (the second rank of the Roman élite, sometimes translated 'knights') would make quite long journeys with (and to some extent to suit) their families. We see how religious festivals dominated the year [363]. Helvius and his unfortunate daughter, for example, had been in Rome for the most splendid occasion of all, the Roman Games themselves, in honour of Rome's greatest God, *Jupiter Optimus Maximus Capitolinus* ('Jupiter the best and greatest, of the Capitoline Hill'). It is clear that there was a rush of people into the city for these celebrations, which lasted ten days in mid-September in Helvius' time. But the city was very hot at that time of year, and some went the opposite way precisely in order to *miss* the crowds. The end of summer, in other words, was a season in which you would expect to be on the move, and with all the families, friends and slaves of the rich moving too, it must have been fairly chaotic. To take the second passage, Cicero is one of those who would dodge the *ludi Romani*, but he and his daughter Tullia planned their movements in spring 59 around both the festival of the goddess of shepherds, *Pales* (which also commemorated the founding of Rome), and other entertainments in the towns of the countryside between Rome and the Bay of Naples, which was the favourite resort of the wealthy Roman, and equipped for luxurious living on the grandest scale. These places, though much more relaxed than Rome and a break from formal political life, were not remote hideaways. They would be transformed by the circulation of people like Cicero and Tullia – and their entourages.

198. The end of winter and the onset of pleasant spring weather, usually up to the end of April, formed another season for visiting your home-town – since most Romans, like Cicero, were not actually from Rome originally – or friends also staying away from the city, or attractive seaside-resort towns like Antium or Formiae, or – if you could afford it (as many could) – one of your own country-houses (*uillae*). Movements of this kind are one of the really impor-

tant facts of Roman life, and we can only begin to understand how Rome worked if we try to imagine the year divided into the two touring seasons (August–October, March–April) and the two working seasons (November–February, May–July) when most business was done. Such movements affected all those who were dependent on wealthy people like Cicero – their slaves, clients and the retailers who kept them all supplied.

199. But it was not only the rich who were on the move. The sailing season began in April and ended in September, and these months in particular attracted large amounts of skilled and casual labour into Rome to handle the cargoes of staple foods on which the city had come to depend by the late Republic [30, 220, 268–9]. Likewise, the harvest (principally in July) attracted workers to move out of Rome into the countryside (similar needs in the Middle Ages are the reason for University long vacations). While the élite enjoyed their breaks from business in the country, many other people were on the move, taking advantage of the seasonal labour shortages to win a bit of much-needed cash.

The suburb

200. But these are not the only patterns of movement that broke up the year. Many attractive places to visit – like Tusculum in the Alban Hills south of Rome, which Cicero mentioned in the letter quoted above [197], and where he had a favourite estate – were close enough to the city to be suburban and to encourage a sort of commuting. This comes over clearly in Cicero's colourful story of the murder of his enemy Clodius, also in the Alban Hills at Bovillae, about eleven miles out of the city. Cicero is defending his ally Milo on a charge of murdering Clodius [71]:

So when Clodius got to know of Milo's journey, he left Rome without delay himself to set up an ambush for Milo outside the Clodian estate. Clodius was in such a hurry that he walked out of a riotous public meeting – something which he could only have been induced to do by a pressing engagement of a criminal kind. I gather his frenzy was sorely missed. Milo spent the day in the senate. When the session ended he went home, changed his clothes and shoes, waited a while for his wife to get ready too, and finally set out. (*In Defence of Milo* 27–8)

Now Clodius could easily have been back in the city by now, if his excuse, which was a short trip out of Rome, had been genuine: but no, as things were, there he was, ready for anything, mounted, with no sign of a carriage or baggage, no Hellenic companions (unusual for Clodius) and no Mrs Clodius (which is unprecedented) – waiting for Milo. Along comes Milo – who, don't forget, please, is supposed to be on his way to an ambush of his own with murder in his mind – dressed for the country, wife in carriage, and with a long and uncontrollable retinue of giggling girls and boys.

Sunset still about an hour off. From his farm, out steps Clodius. Dozens of armed men spring down on Milo's carriage from above – they kill the driver – out jumps Milo, and flinging his cloak aside, gives quite a good account of himself, so that some of Clodius' pals think of going round the back of the carriage to stab him from behind. The rest meanwhile are finishing off a few slaves from the escort, on the assumption that the owner has already been killed. I am glad to say that some of Milo's slaves (though there were casualties) were alert and faithful. They saw the fight by the carriage but couldn't get to their master to help him. They heard Clodius shout 'Milo's had it.' Naturally enough they believed him. So, equally naturally, they did what it was their duty to do. Milo didn't know. He certainly didn't give any instructions. He could scarcely be said to have been there at all. But they did it. I'm not simply passing the buck; this is what happened. They did it: and what's more, there is not one of us who wouldn't want his own slaves to do just the same in the circumstances. (*In Defence of Milo* 29)

Vivid and – forensically speaking – implausible, this passage is full of insights into late Republican life. The readiness with which the wealthy moved between Rome and country is striking, even after a working day and even though it clearly involved moving the whole household. Equally remarkable is the distinction between city and country life-styles, even down to the different clothes. Life in the country, in other words, became a carefully cultivated alternative to life in the town, and this is what gives rise to much of the imagery of rustic bliss in Latin literature [372–3].

201. That said, this 'countryside' of the area round Rome itself is not physically far removed from the city, and the cultural leisure-activities of people like Clodius and Milo in their villas, as we see from Cicero's allusion to the string of Hellenic companions, are just like those of the city, but on a more expansive scale. In both town and country, then, the rich called the tune and shaped much of what went on: by their movements, and, still more, by their tastes. Even rural violence had its source in the greed of the landowners [47], breaking out like the political hatred that brought Clodius to his end on the Via Appia.

202. Like so much of our evidence, these stories which show Romans on the move are mainly about the upper classes, and we see their inferiors only as supporting cast. To conclude this section with a slight corrective, we can look at the tomb inscription of a man of a different position in society, but which reflects the same bustling and restless suburban life. A retailer who had probably once been a slave, he was buried in a community in the Tiber valley about 45 miles north of Rome. With the easy connections offered by the river, this was still a place very closely in contact with the city, as the text shows.

I am now free from care, who once was well known in the Holy City [Rome] for selling leather goods. I displayed wares suited to popular use. My exceptional good faith was always praised everywhere. When doing work on contract, I always kept my accounts straight, and was on the level in all my dealings, as fair to all as I could be, and sometimes a help to a persistently needy person – always generous, and always going shares with my friends. (*ILS* 7542)

Such is the atmosphere of the life and business practices of the small retailer in the big city, on view miles away in the not-so-remote 'suburbia'.

A year of festivals

203. Romans did not have weeks or weekends, but the Roman year was divided into smaller sections by sequences of 'special days'. Some, like the three named month-days, the Kalends (1st), Nones (5th/7th) and Ides (13th/15th), came round twelve times a year. Others, notably the *nundinae* ('ninth-day') when markets were held, came round at more frequent intervals [282]. Such days were related to the life of the countryside. During the *nundinae*, for example, all kinds of agricultural produce were bought and sold, the sort of occasion when the leather merchant [202] will have found much business. Again, in a treatise on the running of a rural estate (*c*. 160 BC), the elder Cato recommends Rome among other cities as a good place for buying the sort of equipment that could not easily be made on every estate: the *nundinae* would be the time to do this. The *Parilia* and even the *ludi Romani* [197] were also related to the country life: in origin at least, they reflected the cycle of tasks in the year of the agriculturalist. As in all pre-industrial societies, the seasons of the year were closely tied in with agricultural production. In the Mediterranean, the only really idle season is the summer drought, and even then, some landscapes will still receive attention – where irrigation is possible, or where there are high pastures where summer grass is available for animals. Otherwise, there is a constant round of sowing and harvest, the time for each depending on the choices of crop made by the farmer – whether to plant legumes or other vegetables, which kind of grain, whether to go for dense planting or to grow for high quality and low bulk. One of the reasons why the festival year is so complex is that the season's weather is unpredictable. So the wise farmer diversifies his crops as much as possible to spread his risks.

204. One important set of festivals was tied to the beginning and end of the summer, when the agricultural labour-force could be available for other things, in particular military expeditions against neighbours. Raids and effective self-defence are another way of keeping the larder well stocked in an unpredictable world, and the Romans, as we saw at [6], believed that their first

forefathers had been particularly good at that sort of thing. The *feriae Latinae*, usually held during April (the date was determined from year to year), marked the beginning of the fighting season; the *ludi Romani* at the end of the summer were the celebration of its successful close. By the late Republic both had become major excuses for the display of power and wealth, the occasion when military success across the whole Mediterranean world, and the pretensions of the political leaders of a world-empire, were on show.

205. From an early age Rome had forged complex political bonds with neighbouring communities like the Latins and these links too were commemorated in festivals [24]. That was why the *feriae Latinae*, as their name ('Latin holidays') implies, took place on the highest summit of the Alban Hills, 13 miles from Rome. That in turn was why people from the towns that had originally joined in the festival mixed so easily with the Romans, and why these parts could so easily become welded to the city in the kind of suburban matrix that we have described. Festivals of this sort drew city-dwellers out into the countryside and helped to give the whole area of west central Italy a feeling of unity. In this a sense of history had a part to play too; commemoration is an important feature of many festivals, one of the ways in which the important events and developments of the past could be brought to the attention of subsequent generations.

206. So the calendar was very complicated, reflecting a bewildering variety of activities, events and localities in a single system; there were never long gaps without some significant day. Indeed, by the second century AD there were so many 'special days' that the emperor Marcus Aurelius passed a decree to limit them to 135 a year! When we come to think about the working and relaxation of the city in its imperial heyday [217, 225–7, 244], we must bear in mind the effect and meaning of these significant days.

Privilege and dependence

Belonging

207. One of the things that is hardest to work out about a world as distant as that of the Romans is how much independence people enjoyed. Almost certainly, self-determination for most people was severely limited in comparison with that of Western societies today. Shortage and hardship were the most obvious signs of this. They were normal occurrences in a society in which very many people were dependent on others, and this dependence is one of the central aspects of Roman life that need to be understood. This is why the movements and choices of the rich were so important. If it had been normal to be poor but independent, if most Romans had been citizen householders keen not to play at being politicians and aristocrats, but preferring to maintain a popular culture of their own, we would be wrong to focus so much on the determining choices of the powerful. But although the Romans believed, rightly or wrongly, that that is how the city had worked in its early days, by the second century BC it was no longer true. Even when writers of later years talked about the 'good old days' when Romans were all small farmers and stalwart soldiers, they could not resist imagining in those earlier years the pride and privilege of the well-born and some of the forms of dependence that were important in their own day, when they read of the arrogance of the last kings and their families, or the disdainful pride of some of the first members of the aristocratic lineages (like the Claudii), that still had great power at Rome in the late Republic. Of these forms of dependence, the most important was being a client, *cliens* [10, 213ff.].

The retainer

208. We have already seen how rough life could be in the countryside near the city in the troubled last years of the Republic [200]. In the following passage, Cicero shows what could happen in the remoter parts of Italy. He is defending a man called Tullius (no relation) who has been engaged in a land dispute with his neighbour Fabius, who

brought down to the ranchland some youths chosen for their spirit and their muscle, and equipped them with whatever form of weapon was best suited to each. No one could have had the slightest doubt that they were being procured for fighting and killing rather than for agriculture ... Armed to the teeth and without bothering to hide what they were up to, they were wandering about the place. The land and the roads themselves were not safe. Meanwhile Tullius takes up residence on his farm, and one day Fabius, our convert to arable farming and cattle-rearing, takes a stroll around on the property. There he notices a not particularly large building on the disputed land, and a slave of Tullius' called Philinus. 'What business have you lot got on my property?' he says. The slave replies politely – not being stupid – that his master was at the villa, and if there was anything that he could do for him, that was the place to discuss it. (Cicero, *In Defence of Tullius* 8.18–20)

Although the meeting goes fairly smoothly, the next night, just before dawn, Fabius' mob breaks into the building on the disputed land, pulls it down and cuts the throats of a group of Tullius' valuable slaves. Philinus escapes, badly hurt. The uncomfortable position of the owned workforce comes across vividly. Valued in proportion to their price, they are caught between the need to defend their master's interests and their own skins. Slave-owning bosses, however fair-minded, are well used to ensuring that their own interests are maintained in a place far from law and order, at whatever cost to others. Even in less troubled times than the late Republic, the countryside was a place of violence. Friends of the younger Pliny – one an *eques*, and one a centurion – had disappeared without trace when making a journey on major Roman highways.

209. Here too town and country have very similar experiences. The jury listening to Cicero knew many of the people involved in this dispute, since they moved households regularly from one domain to another. The violence in the country may have been particularly blatant, but it is all of a piece with the equally dangerous state of affairs in the streets of Rome [489].

210. Quite apart from everyday violence, the actual crowds in the city could cause problems even for the powerful. For example, just before his downfall, the emperor Tiberius' minister Sejanus was descending from sacrificing on the Capitol and ran into such a crowd that his bodyguards had to take a detour. Hurrying to catch him up on the other side of the crowded sector, they fell down the steep steps that led to the prison – the steps on which the bodies of executed criminals were exposed, as Sejanus' was to be in a few weeks' time ([93]; Dio Cassius 58.5.6).

211. The already hectic and anxious atmosphere in the centre of the city cannot have been improved by the presence there of such ugly reminders of the precariousness of life and death as these stairs, and the prison where malefactors were strangled, and the Tarpeian rock off which criminals were pushed, to end up on the paving stones right beside the Senate-house and the Speakers' Platform of the Forum. Certainly small-scale private violence happened all the time. Night-time was especially dangerous. Many instances could be given of victims of casual attacks. Here is a particularly sad one from Salonae, a great port city on the coast of what is now Croatia.

> To the spirit of Julia Restituta, unluckiest of people: in her 10th year she was killed for the sake of her jewellery. Julius Restitutus and Statia Pudentilla, her parents [set this up]. (*CIL*.III 2399)

The client and the slave

212. In a treatise aimed at a reform of agricultural methods, the mid-first-century writer Columella outlines the problem:

> If a rich man buys a farm, out of his footmen and litter-carriers he chooses the man most decrepit in years and strength and packs him off to the countryside. (*On Agriculture* 1, *Preface* 12)

So when a slave was worn out at a physically demanding job like carrying his owner around in a litter (a preferred form of transportation for the rich), he might end up as a slave farm-hand, doing back-breaking work on the soil until a premature death. Life expectancy among slaves was not high. There is no reason to suppose that the sort of exhaustion that Columella is describing was the result of what we would call old age. The close tie between the rural estate and the owner's town interests is again apparent [272]. Slaves are the most obvious sort of dependant, and there were very many of them. A city which had a reasonable number of wealthy families could almost be called a city of slaves.

213. Columella continues:

or else a proprietor of moderate means chooses one of his dependants who is no longer willing to make his daily financial contribution, and since he is no longer a source of revenue, puts him in charge of a farm even though he knows nothing about the business that he is to run.

This is more surprising. It shows us the client whose daily financial contribution to a patron of middling means really matters. Rather than lose out altogether when the client is too hard up to pay his daily stint, the patron employs him and takes his labour instead of his cash. True, such a dependant is not demeaned or worn out like the slave; but he still cannot escape. He knows that he needs his patron, whether he has to buy his patron with his money or his work, and he no doubt thanks his stars that his patron is sufficiently needy not to be able to afford the luxury – as the rich man would – of abandoning him to look after himself without any of the security that the patron–client relation might give.

214. An ironic grave-inscription, popular enough for us to know it in two versions, says of the tomb:

All a person needs. Bones reposing sweetly, I am not anxious about suddenly being short of food. I do not suffer from arthritis, and I am not indebted because of being behind in my rent. In fact my lodgings are permanent – and free! (*CIL* VI.7193a, cf. 33241)

This text summarises well the plight of thousands in the city. People there were dependent because the necessities of life could not be guaranteed. What is particularly revealing here is that the hand-to-mouth existence was not just a matter of finding food; accommodation was precarious too, since all the property available to the poor was rented, and rents were exacted mercilessly. Contracts, moreover, covered very short periods, and some premises were let even by the day. Winter in Rome is harsh, and not knowing where the next month's rent was coming from must have been a familiar anxiety. This unpredictability added to the confusion and instability of life at Rome. The result was a paradox. The city of all those festivals, famous for being a place of stylish leisure, Rome was a place where it was hard to survive without work.

215. Even when work was obtainable, it was organised with very short-term contracts (compare the parable of the labourers in the vineyard, Matthew 20.1–7). A horrifying story has reached us from a philosopher with social interests who wrote in the early first century BC (Posidonius, quoted by Strabo 3.4.17, cf. Diodorus 4.70). It tells of a woman who gave birth while working on a day-contract in a gang doing heavy agricultural digging, probably to tend high-quality vines. She wrapped her baby in leaves, hid it and went straight on with her work, scared of losing the day's wages. A humane overseer ordered that she should be paid in full and sent home; but this was clearly not considered normal.

216. The appeal of the city was that the free handouts available there could serve as your wages for being seen to be dependent. At that price it was worth paying court with a mob of others to a great man and making yourself a visible sign of what an extraordinary place Rome was, and how grand its great men [144, 329–30]. Hence the daily attendance at the greeting of the patron in the morning, the 'greeting' (*salutatio*); hence the *sportula*, a small sum of money handed out to deserving clients in the afternoon. Another consequence was that a considerable portion of each day was devoted to these civilities rather than to business:

> The first and second hour [just after dawn: the Romans divided the daylight hours into twelve segments that varied in length with the season] wear down the men making the *salutatio*, and the third is business time for the rasping lawyers. Rome prolongs its different employments to the fifth hour. The sixth offers rest for the exhausted and the seventh is the end of the working day. The eighth and some of the ninth are bath-time, and the rest of the ninth sees the couches filled with the reclining dinner-guest. (Martial 4.8.1–6, going on to say that after dinner is the time to bother the emperor with the gift of his volume of slight poetry)

217. For those who were not lucky enough to enjoy the security of clientage, the burden of work was more like that of the labourers in the vineyard. Most of Rome's great buildings were constructed not by slave-labour but by the daily contracted labour of the free dependent population. But there were other buffers against need. One was to co-operate with others in the same position. An inscription (*CIL* VI. 30983) gives us the names and status of 49 men and 4 women involved in the running of the grain warehouses of Galba. They got together to form an association dedicated, appropriately enough in the dirty, overcrowded city, to the Divinity of the Emperor and the Gods of

Good Health. Four were officers, three were honorary members who paid no dues; there were six slaves, six slaves born in the emperor's ownership, one other imperial slave, and the rest were ex-slaves. Most of the slaves were the property of other members of the society. This sort of arrangement reproduced the advantages of being in the entourage of a great senator, and was probably more typical of the normal person's everyday life than clientage was. In 'friendly societies' of this kind we can see glimpses of a theory of the need for solidarity and mutual help among the lowly, reminiscent also of the virtues of honesty and generosity proclaimed on the epitaph of the leather-dealer that we met before [202]. Most of the dependent at Rome, slave or free, were dependent not just on the great but on each other.

Privilege

218. Undoubtedly the best-known feature of Roman 'daily life' is the games, *ludi*. These took place on those special occasions, in a complicated calendar, when holidays occurred [203]. The *ludi*, like the 'circuses' in the satirist Juvenal's famous phrase *panem et circenses* ('bread and chariot-races'; cf. [98] and fig. 2.9), were part of the 'pay-off' for dependence. We shall come to 'bread' in section [220]. What the élite offered the masses in *ludi* was rather different, and neither was it simply 'entertainment' in a modern sense, or even distraction from the awfulness of precarious city life: rather it was a small and momentary taste of the world that the rich permanently enjoyed. There was a repertoire of these 'perks' (the Latin term was *commoda*). All of them were timeless ingredients of their own aristocratic lifestyle watered down for mass consumption. Take literary, musical, cultural entertainments. Their main purpose was the amusement of the rich, as we have already seen in Cicero's sneers at Clodius. Take the competitive games. The masses could share in the exciting activities of aristocrats as they fought and hunted (figs. 5.1, 5.2). Take the baths. Hot water and fine oil had been the reward of a hero as far back as Homer's *Odyssey*, and the minstrels and the competitions at games belonged in a Homeric setting too (*Odyssey* 4.39–51, 8.62–130). Dependency made these features of aristocratic life briefly available to the whole Roman people. But the reason was not altruism. It was a truly remarkable city in which the poor were able to share in some of the goodies of the rulers, and the culture of the *commoda*, through promoting dependence and advertising the wealth and felicity of the state, helped the wealthy to go on living in a self-congratulatory cocoon.

5.1 The *ludi*: a gladiatorial combat.

5.2 The *ludi*: scene from a wild-beast hunt.

Survival and luxury.

To those who have shall be given . . .

219. The normal inhabitant of Rome spent an anxious day hoping that his expressions of dependence would be rewarded by immunity from the worst dangers and anxieties of the urban condition [334]. At one extreme there was the possibility of starvation, at the other consumption of the most spectacular and luxurious food. In particular, one of the most common signs of people's dependence on those who ran Rome was the right to enjoy free handouts of grain. But there was more to this than welfare. The handout did not aim at providing basic minima, which it often surpassed in both quantity and quality; it was not means-tested. As well as simply keeping starvation at bay, it also helped to confirm the position of the Roman citizen at the top of the great hierarchical structures that kept the Roman world together. Eating good bread-wheat from Africa or Egypt, rather than cheap and nasty locally-grown cereals, gave the thousands of people in the city of Rome who were entitled to receive it the (justifiable) feeling that they were better off than those who had toiled to produce it in its place of origin [252–3].

Daily bread

220. One of the seasonal events that we have already alluded to [199] was the arrival of the fleet that brought the wheat of Egypt to Rome. It was eagerly awaited in the Bay of Naples at the port of Puteoli. Here is a set-piece description of the scene by Seneca the Younger:

Today, without warning, the Alexandrian *tabellariae* came into view. These are the ships which they always send on ahead to give the news that the fleet is on its way. This is a very welcome sight for the Campanians; the whole population of Puteoli settles down on the quayside and tries to spot the Alexandrian ships by the type of rigging. They can do it too, even though the whole bay is full of ships, because only the corn-fleet is allowed to use the sail called *siparum*, and all the ships hoist it high on their masts . . . Within the strait between Capri and the headland which is 'the high and stormy watchtower of Pallas' other ships are instructed to use only an ordinary sail, with the result that the *siparum* is a sure sign of an Alexandrian. Everyone was in such a rush to get down to the sea, and it was a great satisfaction to me to control myself and not to be in a hurry to get the business letters that I was expecting with the fleet. (Seneca, *Letters to Lucilius on Moral Topics* 77. 1 – about AD 64)

221. The event was spectacular: where else could you see such great ships? The geographer Strabo, in the Augustan period, judged the prosperity of the

chief city of Egypt, Alexandria, by the same spectacular shipping: either at Puteoli or at Alexandria you could easily see the eloquent difference between the heavily laden cargo-ships sailing Romewards, low in the water, and the lightness of the vessels riding high on their return journey (Strabo 17.1.17). The thought that the better-quality wheat grown so far away was brought across the dangerous sea for the benefit of Rome was amazing. But the show also demonstrated how the day-to-day existence of the population was dependent on the whim of the rulers of the world. The stuff of life was available, and that was wonderful, but getting it still depended on others. As the empire lasted, the ostentatious distributions escalated. More and more foodstuffs – wine, oil, meat – were added to the routine of the distributions, and the wheat came to be made available in the form of bread: further savings for the city population, further indications of how great Roman power must be to make such complex and lavish distributions mere day-to-day routine. It always remains essential to see these distributions to the poor in the same light as the other ways in which food was used as a lure and a reward by those seeking to assert their status in the city [269].

Problems with breakfast

222. 'Have you had breakfast yet?' So the short-reigning emperor Vitellius [101] on his way to the Rhine army to bid to become emperor, buttering up the servants of the public post, embracing the soldiers and muleteers and messengers at the posting-stations, and belching to show that *he* had started the day with some food (Suetonius, *Vitellius* 7.3). Gossip about this most hedonistic of emperors can help us to understand the precarious balance between riches and poverty so typical of life in Rome.

So short of money was his household that it is generally agreed that he had no money at all for the journey to Germany, and had to rent a garret for his wife and children whom he was leaving behind in Rome, and let out his own house for the remaining part of the year. He also took the pearl ear-ring from his mother's very ear to pawn it for the expenses of the journey. Nor could he get away from the crowd of creditors who waylaid him (and who included the people of Sinuessa and Formiae, whose public revenues he had embezzled), until he threatened them with prosecution for personal insult on the grounds that an ex-slave who was claiming a particularly large sum had kicked him . . .

So the future emperor leaves the capital, in telling contrast with the usual lavish scenes of farewell or welcome at the gates which the great men usually received. But the money raised on the pledge of the ear-ring left plenty over for breakfasts.

223. The anecdotes reveal another vital point about Roman life. Cash was in short supply (cf. [238]). As Columella and Martial indicate [213, 216] the daily existence of the dependent revolved around a few coins to pay for the baths or the tavern or the rent. This story, however, shows us the other side of the picture. The life of the wealthy too depended on supplies of ready currency of which even the wealthiest – even an emperor – might run short. In the case of Vitellius, he had been plundering the revenues of the resort-towns of the Roman countryside like Formiae (where Cicero and Tullia had been heading for the *Parilia*, [197]); he raised money through the rental market; and he pledged *objets d'art* for further cash, while his family lived in – relative – squalor. The cash thus raised he used for displays of conspicuous consumption inseparable from the life of privilege, and Vitellius put himself on show on his journey by his over-familiarity with the inferior functionaries whom he was trying to impress. For them breakfast is a *commodum*, a 'perk', a 'handout'. Meals shaped the Roman day as they do ours. But breakfast could never be guaranteed.

224. Here the satirist Martial mocks Caecilianus, who always comes to lunch far too early:

The slaveboy has still to announce the fifth hour to you, and out you come to lunch (*prandium*), Caecilianus. The courts are still in session, the morning-games of Flora are still going on. 'Callistus! Quick! In with the slaves, never mind their bath! Spread the couches! Ah, Caecilianus, *do* come in and sit down!' You ask for hot water, but they haven't yet brought in any cold; the kitchen is closed and chilly, the hearth bare. Next time why not come really early, Caecilianus? No need to wait for the fifth hour – what you are after is clearly a late breakfast. (Martial 8.67)

Amid the usual banter about the discourteously early guest of moneyed society, the beginnings of the Roman day emerge. Once again breakfast appears an indulgence, an extra meal for the privileged. Then there are the ablutions of the household, the need to fetch any water consumed from outside the house, the kitchen unused at the start of the day, and the public life of the city – including religious rites – going on well before the first planned meal, the *prandium*, at which wine might be served and guests invited. For most people the day began not with breakfast – the baker's *adipata*, pies or pastries cooked overnight and eaten by boys at daybreak (Martial 14.223) – but with the duties of the *salutatio* that we have already met [216].

Banquets for all

225. In many cultures one of the ways in which people express their sense of community is to eat food together. Ancient Greece and Rome were no exception. The people of a Greek city felt at one when they shared in the sacrificial meal, and the public festivals of the Romans continued that tradition. Because of the vast number of Roman citizens (5,000,000 by the death of Augustus in AD 14), however, it was small sub-groups of the citizen body that shared a meal or a commemoration. Here too the dependence of lower-status groups on the generosity of the rich could be seen on every occasion. From the emperor giving a feast to the Senate, or his wife hosting the *matronae* (respectable married women) in the same way, down to a group of slaves meeting to honour the birthday of their owner, these occasions expressed the same order that we have seen in other contexts. When the imperial system started, loyalty to the emperor and to his family was regularly built into commemorations of such events, when inscriptions were set up to record the generosity of the donor of the banquet (we have already seen the staff of the Granaries of Galba making a dedication to the imperial cult as part of their activities as a social club [217]). Here is a typical example of AD 18:

... and further that on the birthday of the emperor Tiberius for ever the town-councillors and the people should have a dinner – an expense which Quintus Cascellius Labeo promised to meet in perpetuity, thanks being also voted for his generosity – and that on that birthday each year a calf should be sacrificed. Further, that on the birthdays of Augustus and Tiberius, before the town-councillors go for their dinner, the spirits of those emperors should be invited to the dinner with incense and wine at the Altar of the Godhead of Augustus. We have set up that altar with our own funds; we have set up games for six days following 13 August out of our own funds. On the birthday of Livia we gave sweet wine and cakes to the women of the villages at the Temple of the Good Goddess out of our own funds ... (*ILS* 154, from Forum Clodii, about twenty miles north-west of Rome).

226. Not many years afterwards an inscription records the much more lavish benefaction given in Roman style at a small Greek country town, Acraephia in Boeotia. The benefactor here gives grain and wine to the country people and the landed proprietors, and distributes meat and sweetmeats with sweet wine, at breakfast (significantly) as well as dinner, while his wife gives a special breakfast to the children, the slaves, the wives, the female slaves and the maidens – an interesting pecking-order – and to the performers who had been hired for the part of the entertainments that the Romans would have called *ludi*: the inscription specifies that that had never been done before. It is easy to see how such activity maintained people's dependence and interdependence while reinforcing everyone's position within the community. Despite their numbers, the whole population could on occasion be treated to celebrate something as important as an imperial triumph. The huge colonnades and precincts that were laid out in public spaces in Roman

5.3 Hadrian's Villa at Tivoli (between AD 124 and 133): the so-called Canopus and Serapeum, an artificial lake and semi-domed grotto named after monuments in Alexandria. Cf. [487].

cities and, on a (usually) lesser scale, in imperial and senatorial villas were used for these occasions, and at the focal point of the whole design the patron could be dimly seen in a safe place participating – but not at too close quarters. In the emperor Hadrian's villa at Tivoli (fig. 5.3; [487]) the colonnades which housed the guests run the whole length of an artificial lake decorated in Egyptian taste: there is a place for guests of honour in a great artificial cave at the end, below the place where a stream of water runs out of the shadows to cascade down into the lake. A little way up this it is bridged by the imperial dais, on full view to the assembled diners but only accessible by a route through a door in the wall of the cave!

227. The public banquets are very impressive, and quite unfamiliar to us. We take for granted, on the other hand, the tavern, a common feature (as we think) of the medieval and early modern city. But that is wrong. A semi-public place where poorer inhabitants of the city can go to eat and drink, mix socially and enjoy other pleasures such as gambling (fig. 5.4) or bought sex is not something that the economic and social circumstances of every urbanised civilisation produce. And though, at first sight, they may not look like another favour from the rich, that is in fact what the taverns of a Roman city amounted

to. The property market which made the necessary building available, the customers' cash which paid for the services, the sources of production and supply which made food and drink (especially wine) available at affordable prices – all these were spin-offs from the working of the system of keeping the urban élite in the style to which they were accustomed. In the turmoil and movement of population that was normal in Rome, such outlets, the sort of place where the society of employees of the Galban warehouses [217] met, generating a sense of belonging and community, fufilled an important social need. In a city on the move, any stability was very valuable. And to the causes and nature of that fluidity of the city population we must now turn.

The cosmopolis

A mobile world

228. Frequent coming and going have been part of the picture of life in a Roman town that we have been putting together in the earlier parts of this chapter [269]. It was, above all, part of the feel of Rome itself. The rhythms that we discussed [197–202] obviously involved thousands of people in jour-

5.4 Dice-players in a tavern.

neys of considerable length. Even when the city was at its most crowded, it depended for survival on people on the move to bring in the staples for the food of the masses, and the luxuries of life for the wealthy – a good deal of which filtered out in the different ways, direct and indirect, that we have examined, into the life of the community as a whole. The materials for all this came from all over the Roman world. Praising the city in the second century AD, the Greek orator Aelius Aristides called it 'the common workshop of the world'. He did not mean that Rome was experiencing an early Industrial Revolution, but that it was the place where raw produce from all over the world was transformed into the stuff of civilisation. One might even say that supplying Rome, like paying tribute to imperial Persia or to the Athenian empire of the fifth century BC, was one of the things that defined the empire.

229. Likewise, the movements of people that went with this great accumulation of every kind of goods were not just an accidental part of the experience of living in the city that ruled the empire. What went on at Rome was very markedly shaped and influenced by the fact that it was at the centre of the world. Inhabitants of Rome behaved as they did because their city was one in which horizons were really wide and travel a constant feature. When the Pope to this day issues a communication *urbi et orbi* 'to the city [of Rome] and the [rest of the] world' the point about Rome's centrality is eloquently made. But it was not true only of Rome. Cities in the Roman empire were foci in a world of movement, and without that movement they would have lost their purpose, function and character.

230. There was a very high degree of interdependence in the Roman world. Place intermeshed with place, mobility was the order of the day, and the atmosphere that resulted was cosmopolitan. Yet danger and insecurity were as common as the anecdotes in the earlier parts of this chapter have already shown. This makes Rome a fascinating study for us, who live in a world where for all the speed and relative safety of communication we still feel parochial and divided. Rome's is a history with particularly singular characteristics in comparison with other human experiences. There are two general points that may help us to understand this phenomenon.

231. There is a familiar commonplace in ancient poetry: that the golden age at the beginning of time was ended when the first ship-timber was felled and the ship *Argo* constructed. The journey of Jason was used as a type of all the later communications which brought war and corruption and greed to a world that had previously been happily parochial. There is an equally well-known theme in Roman history, that the Romans were landlubbers who wanted nothing at all to do with the sea and had no experience of it until they were forced to fight the Carthaginians [29ff.]. At that point they demonstrated a

versatility as laudable as their previous hostility to the sea had been relentless, and through a do-it-yourself approach to naval warfare succeeded in somehow beating even the greatest maritime power of the Mediterranean. These two ideas are clearly connected: the Romans wanted to be thought to have shunned the sea because their early history was full of sturdy agricultural virtue, which was incompatible with the trouble that seafaring brought to those communities that were involved with it. But both ideas are actually reflections of the fact that in the real world the sea was absolutely central to economy and politics, and its importance had grown steadily from the period that we usually think of as 'Greek colonisation' (eighth/seventh century BC) onwards: the sea was at the heart of everything that we know as classical civilisation.

232. Not surprisingly, Rome had been deeply involved with the sea from the earliest period, and there were many signs of that in the city [4–5]. The cult of Hercules at the Greatest Altar in the river-harbour area of Rome had close affinities with that of Melqart, god of that great trading people the Phoenicians (whose origins lay in the area of modern Lebanon); not far away was a pair of temples whose cults, since their foundation in the sixth century BC, had had close ties with divinities who supported the maritime power of the Greek city of Corinth. Pottery from the excavations here shows how close Rome's contacts with the eastern Mediterranean were from the very earliest period of the city's existence.

233. Cicero would have been shocked. In a famous set-piece in his *On the Republic* (2.3.5–10), he praised Romulus for his judgement in avoiding the coastal sites that almost all Greek cities had, and so keeping it clear of all the corruption and danger that the sea stands for. Even he wants to have his cake and eat it, though, since he cannot resist adding praise for the site on the Tiber. As the pots from the river harbour (fig. 5.5 and 5.6; cf. [294]) show, it was indeed the Tiber that made Rome important from the beginning, and we may identify the river as the most distinctive and important feature of the site of the city, central to many of the aspects of its society and economy. Not all Roman writers were coy about its importance: the elder Pliny called it the 'most placid of traders in all the goods of the world' (*Natural History* 3.54), linking it to the tradition of praising Rome through its focal role in the trade of the Mediterranean. That role was naturally most developed when Rome was at its most powerful, but Rome had been involved in long-distance trade well before the challenge of Carthage.

234. As a result of meeting the Carthaginian challenge and that of the fleets of the kingdoms of the eastern Mediterranean, Rome's power extended over both land and sea [34ff.]. The supposedly landlocked Romans based their

5.5 The river-harbour in Rome. Excavation of the quayside below the Aventine, showing mooring holes for boats. Cf. [294].

5.6 Model of the harbour area in Rome, with the Porticus Aemilia at the lower right. Cf. [42, 294, 465].

5.7 Mausoleum of Hadrian, built AD 135–9 (now Castel Sant'Angelo).

power in the Mediterranean, as much as the Carthaginians had done, on harbours, shipyards and sailors. If the empire and the place of Rome in it are often symbolised for us in terms of roads, milestones and bridges, it would have seemed to its subjects to be summed up just as well in docks, jetties, granaries and lighthouses. We can still sense something of this dimension of Rome's life by looking at the two surviving craggy fragments of the vast early second century BC warehouse complex at the Porticus Aemilia in Rome, or reflecting that the enormous imperial mausolea of Augustus and Hadrian are sited so as to impress passers-by on the river (fig. 5.7). But the Tiber itself has severely damaged the remains of the important monuments of the city on its banks and helped to obscure the vital fact that despite Cicero, Rome was a great port, and a great maritime power. Take one instance of what has been lost – the main shipyard, the Navalia. This was clearly a major monument to Rome's control of the seaways, a kind of exhibition place for the exotic. It was here (Pliny, *Natural History* 36.40) that the artist Pasiteles narrowly escaped being eaten by an African panther while he was drawing a lion from life; and it was here that you would go if you wanted to see the ship that had brought Aeneas from Troy to the shores of Latium. But we can't even tell with precision where this significant and impressive complex stood.

235. So the river and its activities were central to the activities of the city populace. For both skilled and unskilled work, very many people depended on the Tiber, just as they depended on it to import their food, or to provide them with a place for the disposal of their refuse. And in the wider sense, Rome depended for its power on its place in a web of seaborne communications, and its inhabitants well understood the control that Rome exerted over it. Being a Cosmopolis had a deep effect on who the inhabitants thought they were.

236. One of the aspects of the cultures of the ancient Mediterranean that is most different from ours is that of ethnic identity – your sense of what kind of person you are in what kind of community (cf. chapter 8). First, there was nothing like nations in the sense that we are used to – states whose character is shaped by a belief in a rough racial kinship reflected in language, culture and institutions and their evolution together alongside other similar entities. Second, because of the wide, all-inclusive horizons of the Mediterranean world, descriptive terms for social groups tended to be looser and less exclusive than we might expect. For example, Greeks and Jews lived all round the Mediterranean, not just in Greece and Judaea. So being 'Greek' or 'Jewish' could not be easily defined either in terms of geography or kinship, but rather in terms of cultural attitude – Greeks contrasted themselves with 'barbarians', Jews with 'gentiles' – and their relationship to political power, since they were subject to dozens of different state-authorities, large and small, was far from straightforward. *Romanitas* too, the idea of being Roman, was equally broad, open as it was to (the more fortunate) former slaves from all over the world and, increasingly under the Empire, to other categories of former aliens to whom the citizenship was made available, usually in return for military assistance. Romans contrasted themselves with those who did not possess Roman citizenship, *peregrini* ('foreigners'), people living in a fragmented ethnic world outside the group. But apart from shared loyalty to Rome there was very little that all Romans had in common, and the label 'Roman' was more like the somewhat self-satisfied terms 'Western' or 'First World' in modern parlance than it was like 'Iraqi' or 'German'. Here is a testimony from Rome:

To Mercury, the eternal god Jupiter, Queen Juno, Minerva, Sun, Moon, Apollo, Diana, Fortune . . . , Wealth, Isis, Piety . . . Divine Fates: that it may be good, auspicious and happy for Imperator Caesar Augustus and his family . . . and for the Senate and People of Rome, and for the Peoples [i.e. non-Roman citizens]! In the year [AD 1], Lucius Lucretius Zethus, ex-slave of Lucretius, set up this Augustan Altar at the bidding of Jupiter (*ILS* 3090).

237. The attitude was not necessarily benevolent, and certainly not egalitarian; Rome had, after all, conquered 'the peoples' of this summary of the world. But they had their place in the structure of the system that resulted, and there was no reason to think that if they survived long enough they or their children might not be as Roman as the next person. The resulting tendency to inclusiveness is a key to understanding the ancient city. Romans did not think of foreigners in Rome in quite the way that the French today, for example, might think of foreigners – whether tourists, business people or immigrants – in Paris.

Moving for opportunity

238.

The young adults, moreover, who had been prepared to put up with poverty doing manual labour for a wage in the countryside, were attracted to the city by handouts from the state and from private individuals, and had opted for the life of leisure there in preference to their thankless toil. (Sallust, *Catiline* 37.7)

On the shore at Baiae with a lucky reed, catching fishes. (Marble gaming-board, from Rome)

Bathe here like you do in the big city! (Bath-house advert, in a village north of Rome)

In the city there was much more money – literally, more *coins* – than in the country [271]. That means not just that the city was where the rich lived for much of the time and where they did their spending, but that cash as a medium of exchange was something that you would be more likely to find in the city. More people would actually depend on coin in the city, rather than on exchange of goods through barter and the return of favours [283–4]. As a result of this [223] the city was a place where dependence was much more obvious, since that dependence was most efficiently expressed in terms of money, and the ways in which you could get money were relatively limited. The dependence was all the worse because the prospect of freedom, of self-determination, was always so tantalisingly close if only you could somehow amass enough of the precious currency to be your own boss. Self-improvement required cash. Whether you were a slave accumulating the *peculium* (a personal hoard of savings) to buy your freedom one day, or a free person calculating the constant demands for money for rent, clothing, food, the games, the baths and the tavern, it was coin, *nummi*, that you needed.

To qualify as a senator or as an equestrian required huge sums – 1,000,000 sesterces for one, 400,000 for the other. That can disguise how much difference even a small accumulation of coin could make to your life. A litre measure of wheat at Rome cost between one and two sesterces during the Empire. Those who received salaries in coin, like soldiers, for instance, were fairly comfortably off by comparison with wage-labourers, like the young men fleeing the countryside in the passage of Sallust just quoted. The soldiers who served in Rome in the Praetorian Guard or the other cohorts whose duties included maintaining order in the capital received higher rates than those who served in the legions in the provinces ([87, 174]). As far as we can tell from the inscriptions, these soldiers do not come from the poorest backgrounds. This sort of recruitment seems to have become a kind of privilege for the middling citizens of towns in Italy. Serving in Rome was an honour in its own right.

239. For even more lowly people there were less predictable ways of collecting cash. If you became a dependent, the handouts could be in cash; the emperor gave out a dole in coin from time to time too, and it was sometimes substantial. Alongside your wages for fetching and carrying or for other transient unskilled labour, often in what we would call 'service industries', there were further possibilities for accumulating cash through bribes, windfalls, theft, and that major feature of pre-industrial money societies, private gambling. This other aspect of the life of the city that the élite affected to despise and to condemn – while enjoying it themselves – was regarded by outsiders as a real characteristic of the way Rome worked. Its centre, as we have already said, was the tavern. The second text quoted at [238] is a typical slogan from a gaming-board from a tavern in the city of Rome, and it refers to the excitement of the play as if it were a predatory sport like hunting or fishing, set in that most famous centre of luxurious living, the resort of Baiae on the Bay of Naples. In holiday resorts of our own time, too, the wealthy like to flaunt their riches in conspicuous display, and one way of doing this is to gamble with it, in the hope of getting even more, without effort, to show off. The tavern, as we saw above, represents the other pleasures of the privileged city, and these were a major attraction alongside the possibilities of raising cash. The third text at [238] shows how others might aspire to the imitation of the attractions for which Rome was famous, the attractions which led people to journey to the capital, and in pursuit of which they turned to gambling when they were there.

240. The problem of the poor flooding into the city that Sallust outlined was handled by the Roman authorities so as to limit eligibility to the free handouts: only those whose address was in a formal sense the city of Rome could qualify. But the stability inherent in a 'fixed address' was hard to come by in the world of coming and going that has been described. Cicero complains in a letter that some of the builders at work on his villa twelve miles from the city are knocking off to go down to Rome for their handout of grain, and no doubt the eligible actually spread out in the countryside and small towns around Rome for miles in every direction, coming into the city when they knew that there was something to be gained: a process further complicating the rhythms of movement in the neighbourhood of Rome [197ff.]. Identifying the eligible, always difficult in a mass society, must have been extremely difficult in Rome, especially since the state was not too bothered about which particular economic group received the grain anyway. So the benefits of the city were probably in practice much more widely shared than they should have been in law, and that helps to account for the pull that the city exerted. Another solution was to resettle parts of the population of the city by force in settings where they might have more to do with good honest agricultural production, like depopulated bits of Italian countryside. On one occasion, interestingly, Julius Caesar tried a more intelligent plan: since most of the populace was heavily implicated in sordid economic activity, why not settle a great number of them at the great seaport of Corinth, where they would have more opportunity to make money, well away from Rome? But such attempts were infrequent and affected only relatively small numbers. Like the occasional recruitment to the army that still went on from the city of Rome even under the Empire, it was the more respectable members of the community who would be eligible for such initiatives. But much of the poverty and the violence that went with it came from those who were dependent and struggling precariously to become self-determining. For our purposes, Rome must be recognised as Caesar saw it, as a place of turbulent ambition, of an aggressive population constantly 'on the make'. Perhaps the distaste of the rich for marketing and the world of the *taberna* (the units in which the economic life of the urban populace went on, including the taverns which have inherited its name), like their affected distaste for gambling, derived from the inevitable contrast between their own privileged lives and this hectic world: a world whose atmosphere is most simply summed up in the floor mosaic in a Pompeian house which attracts good omen through its words *salue lucru[m]*, 'Welcome, Profit!' (fig. 5.8; cf. [300]).

Moving for business

241. Just as the rich men of the city moved in and out, to and from their estates, so the dependants who ran their affairs in the wider world came and went from the city. The dependants of the emperor in particular must have made up an extremely mobile part of the population. Even if they were slaves themselves, they could have their own dependants:

To Musicus Scurranus, slave of the emperor Tiberius Caesar Augustus, chief cashier to the Gallic revenue department (imperial) with responsibility for the province of Lugdunensis: some of his team who were with him in Rome when he died set this up to a man who deserved well of them. Venustus, business rep.; Agathopus, physician; Facilis, footman; Decimianus, special expenses; Epaphra, cashier; Anthus, cashier;

5.8 Remains of the mosaic inscription SALVE LVCRV ('Welcome, Profit!') in the doorway of the House of Syricus at Pompeii. Cf. [240].

Dicaeus, attendant; Primio, valet; Hedylus, chamberlain; Mutatus, attendant; Communis, chamberlain; Firmus, cook; Creticus, attendant; Pothus, footman; Tiasus, cook; Secunda. (*ILS* 1514)

Here is a slave of the kind that we mentioned before, one whose master's status gives him a position enviable by most of the free. His visit to Rome swelled the population by at least 14, and their spending-power was clearly not trivial (we should consider the possibility that they are arranged in this list in some order of seniority). Only one was a woman: was this imbalance a general feature of life in the city? Nine of them had Greek names, and it is worth asking in passing in what, if any, sense were they 'Romans'?

242. Others on the move for business were the entrepreneur, shipowner or merchant who intended to sell to the Roman market. He was a very significant visitor. His interests were looked after partly through his membership of the city community in his home-port – we have an inscription from Puteoli describing the headquarters and clubhouse there of the traders from Tyre on the coast of Phoenicia – and partly in Italy. At Ostia, for example, there was a whole portico – probably a private rather than a public foundation – devoted to premises for the representatives of the business communities of towns across the Mediterranean, with their insignia picked out in black and white mosaic on the floor (fig. 5.9; cf. [269]).

243. Shipping took place on many different scales, but it is worth noting that many of those involved in commerce were just as likely to travel in groups as an imperial slave like Musicus. There was obviously the crew of the ship; but the business of trade involved the same sort of personal assistants and staff. Each ship that put in at Rome or its ports represented a temporary change in the population. Here – from Puteoli once again – is a vivid scene by way of illustration:

When Augustus was sailing across the bay he happened upon an Alexandrian ship. Just as he put in beside it the sailors and crew in white clothes and with garlands on, burning incense, heaped on him auspicious greetings and the greatest of praise, saying that it was through him that they lived, through him that they sailed, through him that they had benefit of freedom and financial success. This cheered him up so much that he gave his companions 40 gold pieces each to spend specifically on Alexandrian goods (they had to swear individually not to spend it on anything else). (Suetonius, *Augustus* 98.2)

The glimpse is revealing – not least of the rather special role played by cash [238]. The Alexandrians had an opportunity to express directly the role of the order maintained through the rule of the great men of the state in their own ambitions; but they were combining in their personal greeting respect for the emperor and their own prayers for themselves in exactly the way that we have met before in the inscriptions [236]. The romance of the exotic trade with the East is something that we have also come across more than once, a testimonial to the power of Rome and the success of Augustus [220–1, 228].

244. The trader was one type of professional. Rome also attracted many other kinds of expert – literary figures, religious sages, doctors, philosophers, orators, entertainers – who no doubt enjoyed varying fortunes from their stay in Rome. One of the most successful was Claudius Galen, the famous Greek

5.9 Insignia of the Carthaginian shipmasters. Cf. [242, 269]

doctor from Pergamum in western Turkey, who lived in great style with a house in Rome and one in the suburbs, and mixed in high society in the second century AD. His fame and success were due to his celebrated diagnoses which he took care to publicise himself, like the occasion when he proved that the ailment of a senator's wife was a case of love-sickness for a dancer at the theatre! Entertainers on the professional circuit naturally came to Rome for the many festivals, and the movements recorded in some of their commemorative epitaphs are amazing, often involving long stays in distant parts of the empire. Here a musician of some kind of the third century AD is being celebrated:

> He won at the Sebasmia at Damascus three times, at the Actia at Bostra twice, at the Pythia and Asclepia at Carthage, at the Severia and Commodia at Caesarea in Mauretania. In his honour – as never before – the most excellent city council of Ostia, at popular demand, and because of his extraordinary skill and very great loyalty to his home-town, decreed that a statue should be set up at public expense. (*ILS* 5233)

Local boy makes good: here was a man from Ostia (cf. fig. 6.1) whose ability had taken him all round the Mediterranean, from what is now Algeria to Syria [114]. Once again, as those prizes came rolling in, we can assume that the retinue of this hero of Rome's port-town continued to expand. In fact, the style in which these new grandees of the performing world were honoured as they travelled recalls the honours paid to ambassadors and visiting potentates in earlier times, before the empire developed into the single cultural continuum that it became by the second century AD. They too had brought retinues with them who became part of the transient population. Some, like the hostages of eastern kings, stayed more or less permanently; others made brief but spectacular visits, like that of King Tiridates of Armenia to Nero. Embassy and artistic performance here come together, since the state visit of a prince like Tiridates was the occasion for great artistic displays involving people like our Ostian artiste, festivals like the ones at Acraephia or Forum Clodii [225–6], but on the most enormous scale. But it was not only the performers who were on show, and not only the actors who performed. The people applauded both the artists and those who had paid for them and made their presence possible; and the visitors witnessed not just the show on stage but also the show consisting of the vast and pampered population of the Italian cities – all made possible by conquest, wealth and the benevolence of great Romans. A powerful visitor owned wealth to compare with any senator, and could see good pantomimes at home. But nowhere else could he see a display like the massed Roman populace in its spectacular setting.

Moving involuntarily: the life of the slave

245. 'If Italy is only your stepmother, keep your opinions to yourself.' The famous words of Scipio Aemilianus to a turbulent Roman crowd in the second century BC are telling. Already at that date the crowd was to an important extent composed of people who had come to Rome as slaves and could not claim Italy as their real 'mother'. But in this anecdote, they were clearly taking on themselves a more active role since they actually needed the great man's reproof.

246. One of the principal causes of the mobility of populations in the Roman world was undoubtedly slavery [334, 350]. The slave-trade brought a substantial proportion of its human cargo to Italy through slave-markets like the Greek island of Delos or Side in southern Turkey, and it was this that perhaps did most to maintain the cosmopolitan atmosphere of the city of Rome. Since in the imperial period most slaves came from trade rather than war, and since the sources of supply were mainly in parts of the Mediterranean where the *lingua franca* was Greek, this had the important and perhaps surprising result that the main language of the common people in imperial Rome was not Latin but Greek. That was why, for instance, the liturgy of the early Christian church in Rome was in Greek (Latin was adopted as a liturgical language only in the fourth century: hence the retention to this day of the prayer *Kyrie eleison,* 'Lord, have mercy . . . ').

247. Naturally, the life-histories of the slaves of Rome are almost wholly unknowable now. But one we do know is a man, from Phrygia in what is now Turkey, who was brought to Rome as a slave to one of Nero's former slaves, the powerful and infamous freedman Epaphroditus. His name was Epictetus (the name means 'extra acquisition': it was contemptuous and patronising, like so many slave-names – try translating some of the other slave-names mentioned in the inscriptions quoted in this chapter). Though a place at the imperial court was in theory a highly desirable position for a slave, we know something of the difficulties and humiliations he experienced, because Epictetus was freed himself and became a famous moral philosopher. He used some of his experiences to illustrate his lectures, which were avidly written down by his élite audience and eventually published. By that time Epictetus had moved – in what was probably a fairly typical way, since mobility took the survivors out of Rome as well as bringing the hopeful in – out of the capital once more, to settle in Nicopolis ('Victory City'), which Augustus had built in north-west Greece to commemorate the battle of Actium. Slaves with this sort of position who lived beyond the age of 30 might have a reasonable chance of being freed and ultimately winning their independence, though clearly some aspects of Epictetus' experience were very exceptional.

248. Being a slave of an ex-slave of the emperor (cf. Musicus the financier [241]) meant that you were in a strange position. You had access every day to the pinnacles of wealth, power, status, information; you naturally moved to some extent in the same surroundings as your owner [97]. But you were still subject to the terrifying dangers of slavery. The doctor Galen tells a story which illustrates this in the context – yet again – of travelling with a retinue. He had a friend who was normally a gentle and reasonable soul, but prone to rages. One day, they were travelling from Corinth to Athens when it turned out that a case containing something that this man particularly wanted had been left behind. In fury, he took a sword in its scabbard and struck the two slave-boys who were responsible on the head, so hard that the blade split the sheath and horribly injured them. Horrified at what he had done, he galloped away, leaving Galen to bring the party safely to Athens. It is fair to record that, according to Galen, he was later filled with remorse. It is also noteworthy that he panicked partly because if the slaves had died it would have caused serious trouble for him with the authorities. But the story does demonstrate the vulnerability of the slave to abuse of every kind.

249. It is a sombre thought that, despite this, many people actually opted for slavery to better their circumstances and create new opportunities for them-selves (cf. [412ff.]). Epictetus and Musicus may be examples of this: the liter-ate and the intelligent had some chance of avoiding the worst sorts of slave-employments, like service in the quarries or mines. Voluntary slavery is a reality in the imperial period: to be born free was not necessarily an advantage. In the countryside, in particular, education and voluntary enslavement might be the only escape route from oppression and grinding poverty. The city of opportunity could be much further away for some than it was for the young men of Sallust's analysis [238].

250. This route into the city introduces yet another important characteristic of Roman city life. Rome was a place where writing was abundant: some 50,000 inscriptions have survived, particularly on tombstones; cf. [415]. This too was an important sign, impressive even to the illiterate, of how different the city and its inhabitants were. There is a relation between this fact and the fact the Rome was a place where most of the population was composed of slaves and ex-slaves. People like Musicus and his slaves [242], literate outsiders doing for their owner a job which clearly involved writing, and probably not without some financial resources, were, we may guess, more likely than the free poor to choose to set up a long written record in memory of the dead. Musicus' inscription was a list, with full details recorded of the dedicators and their occupations. The inscription of those running Galba's grain warehouses likewise [217] was a display of order and organisation. Rome was a city of lists and rosters (which have greatly increased our evidence for its society). We should not, however, take the literacy implied by the inscriptions or the order-liness of the records as evidence for too high a level of efficiency in Roman public life. There were no administrative examinations, and the level of book-keeping required did not necessarily require the intellect of an Epictetus. That lists were kept is no guarantee that they were kept well or that they were of much practical use.

251. The inscriptions and the freedman-world that they show us are mis-leading in another way too. They tend to omit not only the free poor, but also the less well-off slaves. A slave who wanted his freedom helped his cause if he could save up enough (the *peculium*) to give his master to buy a younger replacement, and to do that it helped if he had been involved in his master's business affairs. The relatively able and literate were therefore at some advan-tage, and many of them probably had fairly realistic hopes of manumission. There were many times that number of less skilled slaves, people whose crush-ing physical loads saw to it that they did not reach the age when they might have been freed [212]. Skeletons of a couple of hundred of victims of the erup-tion of Vesuvius caught at the harbour at Herculaneum as they were trying to escape by sea show a marked variation in physical health. Many of the young adults (aged about 25) are in a fine state, fit and healthy; others show an unexpectedly early onset of bone degeneration and arthritis – which must have been caused by exceptional and continuous manual labour. Even without the arbitrary violence of Galen's friend [248], the outlook for a general-purpose slave was not good.

252. The city depended on people like this, however. In the ancient world the main source of energy was human. Animals, it is true, carried loads and turned mills, but they never threatened to replace slave labour (they also took up a great deal more space in an already very crowded urban environment). This human energy-source was provided by the slave-trade, which worked across imperial frontiers and was also fed by the illegal involuntary enslave-ment of children and the victims of robbers and pirates – like the unfortunate acquaintances of Pliny, perhaps, who disappeared without trace while travel-ling [208]. More or less voluntary slavery no doubt could sometimes be hard to distinguish from this.

253. The central point is that compared with the large numbers of free, dependent people needed to provide the services which would maintain classi-cal civilisation and the comfort of those who ran it, the slave-population was relatively small. Only a few dozen million people in all rattled around in the whole of Europe and the Mediterranean. Slaves were a very precious commod-ity: in bulk, they were a very lucrative resource to those who traded in them.

This trade was centred on the ancient city, which is why there were so many slaves in Rome. Rome was where the people-brokers lived.

City of the Gods

Mobile deities

254. Rome collected cults as it collected people, but only in part *because* it collected people. First, Romans of the Republic had thought of themselves as especially loved by the Gods, and their success as a clear sign of divine favour [360ff.]. Second, they systematically invited the Gods of their enemies to join them and give up protecting their former clients. Third, they cemented the relationship between themselves and their subjects by encouraging them to worship the gods of Rome with equal loyalty and reverence. Fourth, since so many thousands of foreigners came to Rome anyway, it was inevitable that Rome would become a centre of many different cults. But immigrant communities did not bring their gods merely as an accompaniment. Rome was the sacred capital of the world. Immigrants who practised their religion there could argue that this gave their cult precedence over that of others. This is certainly what happened with Christianity.

255. These foreign cults were important in the life of the city. Particularly numerous in the more important centres, they were in Rome itself another visible sign of the cosmopolitanism that went with power. Even if they were very exotic, some were officially recognised by the state. The classic case is Cybele, *Magna Mater* ('the Great Mother'), who had been invited to come from Asia Minor to Rome to help in the war against Hannibal. Her cult centred on a sacred monolith and was attended by self-castrated priests, and we may guess that it was attractive partly because it was so very different from other Roman religious experiences. In this case, the introduction of the cult was done at the highest level. But there were other rites that, though equally alien, were actually practised by foreigners living in Rome but were not officially welcomed; again Christianity is an obvious example, but the religion of the god Mithras (fig. 5.10) fits into this category too. Sometimes the reception of a cult was ambiguous. Deities like Isis (fig. 5.11) and Serapis from Egypt, for example, did receive very widespread cult from individuals (we saw Isis on the dedication of Lucius Lucretius Zethus [236]), and having been associated with the great Hellenistic kingdom of Egypt [84] were of some interest to the Roman emperors and to the upper classes: but they could also be regarded with very great suspicion.

256. This happened even to the Great Mother who, for all her official

5.10 Mithraeum: the cave-like form with benches at the sides and cult-reliefs at the end is standard.

5.11 Rites of Isis.

welcome, sometimes had her rites regulated, while adherents of other cults found themselves periodically the victims of repression and expulsions. One particularly well-known occasion was the suppression of what the Romans believed to be a sinister network of cults of the Greek god Dionysus in Rome and South Italy in 186 BC. The Roman state liked to be in charge of religion, and a variety of small cults did not pose a threat; when the cults co-operated and seemed to offer an alternative community to the ordered one run by Rome, it was a different matter, as the Christians were to find [383ff.].

257. It is easy to see how confusing loyalties might be. The followers of Dionysus were persecuted, but under the name Liber, he had a perfectly acceptable cult near the river-harbour and Circus Maximus at Rome; he shared a temple with Ceres, the goddess who provided cereals, which was not surprisingly a sanctuary with strong associations with the urban populace. Or take Juno, for example, wife of Jupiter, who had various ancient cults in Rome but was also patroness of Rome's neighbour and enemy Veii, in Etruria. When the Romans defeated Veii at the beginning of the fourth century BC, they asked her statue if she wanted to come back to Rome with them: the statue nodded in agreement. Then again, it was typical of ancient cultures to assimilate their own gods to those of foreign enemies. Thus, for example, Juno was associated with the Carthaginian Heavenly Queen Tanit, and as such was worshipped at Carthage and in Africa even when both were thoroughly Roman: and her cult came to the capital too, perhaps already after the Romans destroyed her city in 146 BC. This identification is part of the background to Juno's role in Virgil's *Aeneid*. To take another example: Egyptian Isis protected seafarers and therefore traders (the slave-dealers of Republican Rome seem to have been prominent among her adherents, setting up a sanctuary to her on the Capitoline Hill itself). If you dealt with Alexandria, like the grain shippers that we have encountered, a little Isis-worship was obviously in your interests. On the other hand she was a representative of an alien land of animal-headed gods whose proud and frightening queen (Cleopatra) had corrupted a great Roman (Mark Antony) and nearly prevented Augustan Rome from coming about. Should you worship her or not?

258. As a result, the religious life of the city was as complex as its society, and fluid and shifting in very much the same way. The evidence suggests that cult-practices even influenced each other, and that there was a good deal of borrowing of elements from other traditions. Under the church of San Stefano Rotondo in Rome a sanctuary of Mithras has been found, and in it a dedication of the third century AD in very unliterary Latin:

Eternal Lord! Cascelia Elegans asks thee, by thy mercy, on her own behalf and that of all those who are hers, since thou hast had pity on all these creatures. She asks thee, Eternal One, by the land and the divine sea, by all that thou hast created of good, by salt and the sacred seeds – for me and mine, I ask, have mercy on them, by thy dutifulness, by the living law, by thy creatures, Eternal One, be kind to my fellow slave, and my daughter, and to my master Primus and Celia my patrons, my Lord. (*La soteriologia dei culti orientali nell' impero romano*, edd. U. Bianchi and M. Vermaseren, 1984, pp. 156–7)

The language sounds a bit like the first Latin Christian liturgy; the 'living law' sounds like Judaism; salt is a familiar ritual substance in Greek and Roman religion; 'sacred seeds' sound like the religion of the Great Mother – and so on. Most puzzlingly, this touching glimpse of a Roman household where two slaves (who could not marry under Roman law) have a marital partnership and a daughter, and where Cascelia can pray so feelingly about her owners as well as her relatives, is dedicated by a woman in a Mithraeum attached to a cavalry barracks, and one rule that we thought we knew was fundamental to the worship of Mithras was that it rigorously excluded women! So despite the famous conservatism of Romans in religious matters, seen primarily in the nit-picking attention to the detail of correct performance in even the most obscure ritual, there was a considerable place for innovation and creativity. The variety of religious experience available in Rome was all of a piece with the kaleidoscopic life of the city and that variety is probably one of the dimensions of the life of a city like Rome that an outsider would find most striking.

259. The spontaneity of city religion reflected the complexity and mobility of Roman life. It also, not surprisingly, mirrored the other preoccupations of the inhabitants of the city. At street-corners each neighbourhood had its own shrine with its own particular deities, which helped one feel more secure and that one belonged. You might find among the statuettes of the deities a statue of the *Stata Mater*, the 'Mother Set Firm'. A lexicographer and some of the dedicatory inscriptions explain:

The statue of *Stata Mater* was worshipped in the Forum, but after Cotta paved it, a very considerable part of the populace transferred the cult of this goddess to their own districts, so that the new paving would not be damaged by the fires that used very often to be lit there at night. (Festus 416L)

Sacred to quiescent and imperial Fire and to the imperial Mother Set Firm: Publius Pinarius Thiasus and Marcus Rabutius Berullus, district magistrates of the Street of the Purification-place of Weapons, year 5. (*ILS* 3306)

The material is familiar by now. In the inscription, two ex-slaves (slave-names 'Band of religious devotees' and 'Beryl'), who lived in a district of Rome named from the place where the festival of the purifying and putting away of the blood-polluted weapons of the previous year's campaigns took place every year on 19 October [204], are making a dedication to protect their neighbourhood from fire. It is five years after Augustus reorganised the districts of the city, so about 2 BC, and they blend their loyalty to the emperor with their religious hopes that fire will be kept under control. The explanatory passage shows us an earlier stage, when the people used to come out into the Forum in the dangerous night-time and light propitiatory bonfires with the same end in mind. Religious behaviour here goes hand-in-hand with the preoccupations and anxieties of life in the perilous environment of a Roman city. We have already seen another example of that in the association for honouring the deities of good health [217]. This sort of spontaneous cult is easy to parallel in Islamic or Indian cities today. In ancient Rome it extended to living individuals; it is a testimony to the real vitality of popular politics that the leaders of causes dear to the urban masses, like the Gracchi [46ff.], received very attentive worship with incense and candles at their statues when they had met violent ends in the general interest. Something similar can be seen in the rich diversity of the urban cults which multiplied around Augustus and his family and their successors, and of which we have now met several examples.

The religion of daily life

260. Religion, therefore, reflects the composition and movement of the city population, and the difficulties of managing the urban environment. It is also closely linked with all the other facets of 'daily life' that we have studied – with corn-supply, games, baths, houses, crossroads, ships, and so on. One of the commonest forms of religious veneration was what we might call 'blank cheque' cults where a highly adaptable deity with a relatively settled ritual could be moulded to fit any needs. Take, for example, 'The Good Goddess', *Bona Dea* (whom we met in the record of the festivals at Forum Clodii [225]), a deity whose cult was primarily practised by women, and which had a particular part to play in ensuring their place in the social system). One inscription shows us an official called Zmaragdus ('Emerald'), in charge of the three detachments of workers in the grain warehouses of Galba [217], and his wife Fenia Onesime (her slave-name means 'purchased') dedicating to 'the little *Bona Dea* of Galba's warehouses' – *Bona Dea Galbilla* (*CIL* VI.30855). Elsewhere, however, *Bona Dea* is linked with Aphrodite. Rome was full of real or copied works of art (another ingredient of its special atmosphere, another sign of its ability to ransack all that was best from everywhere else) and one particular favourite was the famous statue of Aphrodite from Cnidus in Asia

Minor by the great Greek sculptor Praxiteles. At some stage, there grew up alongside one of the copies of this statue a cult to *Bona Dea Veneris Cnidiae*, 'Bona Dea of the Venus (i.e. Aphrodite) of Cnidus'. This is a good example of how extreme the adaptation of monuments could become: *Bona Dea* and Venus/Aphrodite existed in completely different religious frameworks – the spontaneous worship of the back streets, with its crossroads shrines, and the grand literary religion of the élite and their temples – but were here joined. The process is quite like the way that the cult of the emperor and his family intruded, as we keep seeing, into cult centring on places and buildings, dwellings, workplaces or public monuments.

261. While we shall probably never get very far in understanding much of the feeling that went with this sort of religion, we can get further than simply saying that colourful religion was an accidental accompaniment of Roman daily life. We should note that the places and activities to which ritual was attached were exactly those where uncertainty, constant change, danger and a high degree of dependence – the main themes of this chapter – were prevalent. By including the place where they worked or lived in the relationship between themselves and the gods, Romans tried to confirm and maintain some stability and predictability in their lives from one day to the next. By worshipping the domestic deities of a household, the *Lares*, in which slaves and freedmen joined with the free family (fig. 7.6; cf. [328]), or by joining in the communal observances at the crossroads (the focus of any densely built-up neighbour-hood) Romans helped define where they belonged in a perilous world. Further, the power of the patron, and behind that the power of the state, most easily recognised as the emperor himself, held the whole thing together. So it was perfectly natural to weave these too into the pattern of one's worship. Thus the slave honoured the personal 'genius' of his master, the client that of his patron, and everyone that of their ultimate ruler, the emperor.

262. At this point it is important to stress that many, maybe most, religious acts were performed by, in, or on behalf of, some sort of group. Group worship, of course, strengthened the sense of 'belonging' in the city. The cult places of the city, like the shrines at the heart of each city-district, were usually the preserve of an association of worshippers, and worship there expressed the inclusiveness and solidarity of the membership of the association. Through such bodies, as we saw [217], the favour and patronage of the better-off could be gained and the dependent could try to improve their position. Many of the units which made up the city – associations of foreigners like the Tyrians at Puteoli [242], groups of worshippers of *Bona Dea* or *Stata Mater* or of the Genius of the Emperor – were established within a religious setting. In such groups, people who lacked important patrons or a secure place in the life of the city could find some sort of stability and sense of identity. As members of groups they had a place, however humble, in relation to the powerful, and could echo the Alexandrian sailors hailing the emperor [243]: 'through you we live . . . , through you we enjoy liberty and our fortunes'.

Religion of time and space

263. In the Roman city even the more abstract aspects of life – the counting of years, the naming of months, the passing of the festivals – all revolved, in a way quite unfamiliar to us, around the political structure of the state. Those who travelled to Rome for the *ludi Romani* [204], for example, were living proof of the world's allegiance to the capital. Again, when the imperial system was in place, the power of Augustus was enshrined not just in the great sundial (cf. [84] and figs. 2.1 and 2.2) which showed his conquest of Egyptian learning, or in the month of August (named after him), or in the way of counting years from the battle of Actium (31 BC: see [77, 79]) but in the movements of the stars themselves. Augustus was born at the highly auspicious moment of the autumnal equinox, and Capricorn became an imperial symbol. In other words, neither history nor the experience of passing time could ever be wholly free of the evocation of the imperial system.

264. A *monumentum* is a reminder, and Rome was a place where the practice of reminding the people of the past was very highly developed: in this sense, 'history' is far from being a literary pursuit confined to an educated élite in which the rest of the city-population did not participate. For example, in Interamna (Terni), a small town north of Rome, there is a dedication to the 'Foresight of Tiberius in crushing Sejanus' [93]. This is dated with reference to the year 851 'after the foundation of Interamna', and the loyal dedicator is a former slave. A gaming-board from the city of Rome from the third century AD has the inscription 'The Parthians are dead, the Briton conquered; Romans, play on!' In other words, it was impossible to enjoy the privileges and run the risks of the city without being constantly reminded of how it had been set up and how it was maintained. When the poet Gallus looked forward to the day when 'Caesar' (either Julius or Augustus) would 'become a great part of Roman history' (fig. 9.6) he was describing a process that did actually occur and was clearly understood by his all contemporaries, not just the narrow literary élite.

265. For residents and visitors alike, Rome was a city that expected the question 'why?' It was a place of wonders, waiting for explanation. The games, the great monuments usually set up through the generosity of the powerful, like Augustus' Mausoleum, or the Navalia, or the Temple of

Bona Dea ('The Good Goddess'), or the warehouses of Galba, the teeming population, the huge quantities of free food, the inscriptions to be seen everywhere – all invited admiration, comment, and explanation of what they meant. Further, every part of the world had some interest in Rome: there was certain to be some commemoration of its subjection and incorporation there, whether it was herbs for the remedies of doctors like Galen, a looted work of art, a fierce exotic animal on its way to the arena, a cult that had once been foreign, or simply sacks of grain waiting for distribution to lucky Romans. Those who wanted to answer the question of how so much magnificence had come about had only to look to the temples: it was the Romans' skill at eliciting the good will of the gods over vast passages of time that was most responsible for the *status quo*. It is typical that the first emperor to proclaim himself a Christian, Constantine [116], at once began to enrich the city with great churches, beginning with Old St Peter's. These are the Christian monuments, helping to square the Christian sense of the meaning of history with the record of the Roman tradition (see [502–3] and fig. Ep.1).

266. The study of 'Daily Life in Ancient Rome' is not just a kind of entertaining exercise to get under the skin of and try to come to terms with a vanished and utterly different world. The way in which most people live or lived, all the accidental and trivial-seeming aspects of what goes on in most places most of the time, are not a sort of background noise. In fact they reveal in their patterns and currents the real outlines, the actual substance of the same history that we learn more conventionally through consuls and emperors, dates, battles and decrees.

267. Rome is especially important in another sense too. The ordinary people of the city are not simply passive, a clean sheet being written on by the rich and powerful. In being actively involved, individuals like Cascelia Elegans [258] or Zmaragdus from the warehouses of Galba [260] brought about change that was not determined by their masters. Each contribution may have been tiny – but for every one Cicero, there were tens of thousands of ordinary people like these, whose participation shaped the Romanness of the Roman world. In the end even the rich and powerful individuals were all part of the process of Roman history in which the 'greatest part' was always played by the *populus Romanus*.

FURTHER READING

M. Beard and M.H. Crawford, *Rome in the Late Republic* (London, 1985)
K. Bradley, *Slavery and Society at Rome* (Cambridge, 1994)

F. Dupont, *Daily Life in Ancient Rome* (Oxford: Blackwell, 1992)

N. Purcell, 'The city of Rome and the *plebs urbana* in the late Republic', *Cambridge Ancient History* IX^2 (1994), pp. 644–88

Sourcebook:

B.M. Levick, *The Government of the Roman Empire, a Sourcebook* (London, 1985)

6
Production and consumption

Introduction

268. About the end of the first century AD a loyal adopted son recorded in a fine inscription the achievements of his father in the community of Ostia, the port at the mouth of the Tiber, which served Rome (fig. 6.1; cf. [244]):

> In honour of Gnaeus Sentius Felix, son of Gnaeus, grandson of Gnaeus, of the Terentina tribe, co-opted with the status of an aedile by decree of the decurions [the town councillors], co-opted as a decurion by decree of the decurions, quaestor of the treasury of the community of Ostia, *duouir* [senior magistrate], quaestor of the company of young men. He was the first man ever who in the year in which he was co-opted to the decurions and was appointed quaestor of the treasury, was also designated as *duouir* for the following year. He was a *quinquennalis* [senior official] of the guild of superintendents of sea-going ships. He was co-opted without payment into the guild of the Adriatic sea shippers and of the guild which meets at the statue of the chariot in the wine forum. He was patron of the companies of principal secretaries of the public records, and of the junior clerks, of the attendants, of the official messengers, of the town criers, of the bankers, of the wine-dealers from the city of Rome, of the corn-measurers (fig. 6.2) of Augustan Ceres, and of the corporation of the rowers, and of the ferryboat-men of the Lucullus Crossing, of the *dendrophori* [officials of the cult of Cybele], and of the citizens from the forum and the public weigh-house, and of the freedmen, of the public slaves, and of the oil-dealers, and of the young cabmen, of the Augustan veterans, and of the staff of the procurator of Augustus, and of the guild of the catchers and sellers of fish. He was in charge of the official parade of the young men. Gnaeus Sentius Lucilius Gamala Clodianus his son dedicates this to his most indulgent father. (*CIL* XIV 409)

269. You can hear the hum and sense the bustle of life in an important port (cf. [219, 234–5, 242] and fig. 5.9). The inscription illustrates the complex network of people required at just one link, albeit an important one, in the chain of trade in the Roman empire. In the city of Rome itself there is a start-

6.1 The port of Ostia: aerial view, showing the hexagonal harbour of Trajan. Claudius' harbour lay immediately to the north (top), the city of Ostia off the photograph at the bottom. Cf. [244].

ling monument to the scale of the trade that passed through Ostia and up the Tiber. It is Monte Testaccio ('the Hill of Pots'), a huge mound consisting of the fragments of the *amphorae*, the large pottery jars, used to transport olive oil in bulk from the valley of the Baetis (Guadalquivir) in southern Spain. Once the oil had been unloaded and transferred, the empty amphorae, which could not be reused, were dumped behind the docks. It has been estimated that at least 53 million such amphorae, each carrying 73 kilograms of oil, must have been imported to Rome in the first two centuries AD. The huge scale of this operation was matched by the trade in wine, also carried in amphorae, to meet the city's demand for up to 1.8 million hectolitres of wine per year. All this had to be supplied by the free market. Grain was such an important part of the ancient diet that the Roman authorities intervened from the late second century BC onwards to ensure a steady supply to the city. The city would require something like 200,000 tonnes of grain to be imported annually to feed its population [221]. It was transported by huge ships originally to Puteoli on the Bay of Naples, because it was not until the time of the emperor Claudius that a relatively safe harbour was created at Ostia, and not until improvements made by Trajan at the beginning of the second century AD that the major grain fleets regularly docked at the mouth of the Tiber. There the grain had to be transhipped into a kind of barge (*nauis codicaria*) to be carried up the river to Rome. It could take three days to cover the 22 miles and it would have taken up to 4,000 barge-loads to move the annual requirement. The Tiber must frequently have been packed with boats and in the area south-west of the Aventine on the right bank of the Tiber there grew up from the second century BC a port area with vast warehouses (*horrea*), parts of which survive or are illustrated on the Marble Plan of Rome (fig. 6.3).

270. All this suggests that Roman trade must have been on a scale which was unprecedented. This is confirmed by the fact that the number of recorded shipwrecks round the Mediterranean is far higher for the late Republic and early Empire than for either earlier or later periods. This is an indication that the overall volume of trade was of a size which was not to be seen again until at least the Renaissance.

But Rome was a freakish exception. No other city in antiquity was larger

6.2 A corn-measurer (*mensor*) checking the contents of a corn-measure (*modius*).

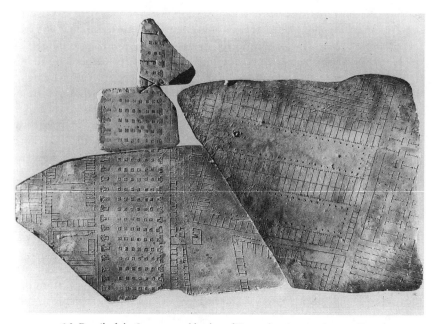

6.3 Detail of the Severan marble plan of Rome showing warehouses (*Porticus Aemilia* at the left and *Horrea* of Galba at the right).

and only a very few even approached being in the same league. So it could be argued that all this evidence of a high level of commerce is misleading, that it hardly touched the lives of the families of the peasants who made up the vast majority of the population of the Roman empire. They, struggling to make ends meet, sought self-sufficiency and had little use for markets or exotic imports [214, 260].

271. These two snapshots (Rome with its bustling wharves, piled high with cargo from distant parts, even from beyond the frontiers of the empire, and on the other hand the limited horizons of the peasant, who matched needs to what could be produced from the locality) are at the heart of a long-standing debate among historians about the nature of the Roman economy. There are those who emphasise the simple or 'primitive' nature of economic activity. They point to the central importance of peasant agriculture, seeking to play down the scale and significance of markets, to a lack of concern with markets in ancient writers on agriculture, and to the upper-class snobbishness about trade, which pervades the literary evidence. On the other hand, there are those historians who are impressed by the evidence for trade on a large scale and, in

particular, by the widespread use of money as the normal means of carrying out transactions [237]. For them the Roman empire created a unique 'world economy', unparalleled until the modern era. The reason why this is likely to continue to be a hotly disputed subject is that, although people in the Roman world engaged every day in economic activity, they never sought to describe what we would call 'the economy'. What the ancient economy lacked was economists, so that we are forced to construct a model of it for ourselves.

The land

272. There can be no dispute that land was the key to most people's lives [212ff.], whether they were the family of peasant farmers, the aristocratic owners of grand estates (fig. 6.4), or the speculators and investors in large-scale trade, who, as Cicero (*On Duties* 2.88) put it, 'make their way from the port to land and country estates' (i.e. invested the profits of trade in land). Yet the historian is faced with a problem. For the countryside hardly exists in Roman literature as a closely observed phenomenon. Descriptions are mediated by the conventions of rhetoric and a sentimental idealisation of the coun-

6.4 A country estate: the villa is at the centre, amid scenes of estate activities and peasants bringing seasonal offerings to the lord and lady.

tryside. People saw what they wanted to see. Pliny's description of his estate at Tifernum Tiberinum (*Letters* 5.6) conforms all too closely and suspiciously to the ideal estate set out by the Roman writer on agriculture, Columella. So, too, the lives of those engaged in agriculture can take on an almost romantic picturesqueness, as in Virgil's *Georgics*. Peasants at work added to the pleasures of the scenery (*pulchre laborantes* ('labouring prettily') in the telling phrase of a late Roman author, Cassiodorus, *Variae* ('Miscellany') 12.15).

273. A profound sentimentality could suffuse descriptions of the ideal life of the small peasant – perhaps most beautifully in Virgil's account (*Georgics* 4.127ff.) of the life of the old Cilician pirate, resettled on land in southern Italy:

> who had a few acres of left-over land, and this a soil not fertile enough for bullocks to plough, nor right for sheep, nor suitable for vines. Yet he planted herbs here and there amid the thickets, with white lilies for a border, and vervain, and the slender poppy, and matched in contentment the wealth of kings. Returning home late at night, he would pile his table with a feast for which he had paid nothing.

Modern historians, too, frequently have their own sentimental view of the peasant farmer, leading a self-sufficient life on a small farm, until either driven off by grasping, wealthy landowners or reduced progressively to a state of near serfdom. The truth is far more complex. The large estate, so far from being a threat to the survival of its peasant neighbours, may frequently have been a lifeline. In turn, the success of the big estate may often have been dependent upon a ready supply of labour. Varro, the writer on agriculture in the second half of the first century BC, neatly sets out the choices:

> All agriculture is carried out by human beings, either by slaves, or by free persons, or a mixture of both. (Varro, *On Agriculture*, 1.17)

He points out that there were the many poor free farmers who worked their farms with their families. Then there were the free men who hired themselves out (*mercennarii*) for farm operations. In many provinces of the empire (although not in Italy, where it was banned) there were men in a state of debt-bondage, working off their debts on their creditors' estates. Finally, there were slaves. Varro shows that the choice of manpower was not a simple one. He particularly advocates the use of hired hands for the intensive annual labour of the harvest and the vintage (fig. 6.5). It would be wholly uneconomic for a landowner to keep sufficient slaves to meet the considerable demands of these short, but vital, periods of the year. So too, the earlier writer on agriculture, Cato, has contracts with individuals who worked parts of an estate in return for a share of the produce, which could have been an important supplement to their income (*On Agriculture*, 136 and 137).

6.5 Agricultural labours (at the top ploughing and sowing, at the bottom tending the vines in winter).

274. It is interesting that in the first century AD Columella, when he reaches the same point as Varro, and outlines the manpower issue, stresses the importance of tenants. It is sometimes claimed that tenancy only became popular when the supply of slaves began to dry up after the period of great conquests. However, it is clear that it was always an option and, indeed, a very advantageous one. It provided the landowner with some assurance that the land was being worked effectively, because it was in the interest of the tenant to do so. So, it was a good way to exploit distant properties, which the owner only visited infrequently. It provided some return, although tenants could not always have been counted on to pay up promptly. The tenant gained access to housing and equipment, which might not otherwise be available. There was a distribution of the risks between the landlord and tenant.

275. So the stability of the rural economy was dependent upon a complex network of economic and personal relations. The peasants were involved in a subsistence economy. What is meant by this term is not that the peasants necessarily lived on the margin of subsistence, rather their economic aim was subsistence. The peasant household produced much of what it consumed, and also produced for the market, primarily to buy the goods and services needed to subsist. When setting goals for themselves, peasant families kept in mind their average productivity in bad years. So if demand for the crops which they produced for the market went down, the peasant resorted to strategies to increase output and so ensure a basic target income. Of course, the range of manoeuvre for many was very limited. On the other hand, in years when the demand for the peasant's crops increased and the price went up, the typical peasant responded by decreasing his output, since he could more easily and with less effort meet the target he had set himself for the cash or goods he required to subsist. It is this form of behaviour which over the centuries has baffled attempts of economists to get agrarian economies to 'take off' and turn themselves into mature market economies.

276. In many ways this peasant economy was very stable and long-lasting. Individual peasant families could, of course, fail. Bad weather, a bad harvest could force them to borrow. Rural debt was to be an important problem throughout the Roman period. A greater, perennial problem was that a farm which was adequate for a small family would come under stress, once the sons had married and had families of their own. The laws of inheritance would tend to bring about the fragmentation of the property, which would solve nothing. The alternative was for some of the children to find new land of their own. Such a model predicts that, given an expanding population, every two generations or so there will be a demand for new land. This is exactly what the evidence suggests throughout Roman history. Furthermore for much of the Republic the state recognised the need to respond to this demand for land. As a result, Rome annexed the territory of defeated neighbours as *ager publicus*, 'state-owned land', which was sometimes used to settle colonies of Roman citizens on, and sometimes simply distributed as individual plots to those who applied. In the late Republic and the Empire a land grant was an important part of the rewards for military service. When it became difficult to find land in Italy, then settlements were made on land throughout the empire [46].

277. At the other end of the scale were the great landowners, among whom could be counted all the senatorial aristocracy. For them land was the most respectable and the most secure investment (cf. [203]); *sum quidem prope totus in praediis* ('I am almost completely bound up in estates'), said Pliny the Younger (*Letters* 3.19). He was to help friends, like Suetonius the biographer, buy modest estates to meet their needs (*Letters* 1.24). Men like Cicero or Pliny did not usually own just one single large estate; rather they accumulated a number of farms, sometimes in the same general locality, but more usually

scattered over Italy. These estates were sometimes acquired by purchase, but frequently were the result of gifts or inherited under the wills of friends or grateful clients. For these landowners were written the handbooks on agriculture, which form one of the largest bodies of technical literature to survive from antiquity (the works of Cato the Elder from the mid second century BC, Varro (M. Terentius Varro), the great scholar who was a contemporary of Cicero, Columella of the first century AD, and Palladius in the late Empire). These were the most notable examples of a vast literary output on agriculture from the Hellenistic period onwards, of which we know little in detail except the names of the authors. They tended to contain a mixture of received wisdom, derived from other books, and personal observation; but above all else they reveal the complexity of the Roman élite's attitudes to their estates. The emperor Marcus Aurelius in a letter to Fronto (*Letters to Marcus Caesar* 2.5) likened the noted orator, M. Antonius Palaemon, to the kind of hardworking, shrewd farmer who with remarkable singleness of purpose devotes the whole of his estate to corn and vines in order to get the greatest return. Not for such a man are the frivolities and novelties of the Pompeian fig, of the Arician cabbage, or of the Tarentine rose; nor is there room on his estate for pleasurable retreats and groves. In short, 'everything was planned for utility rather than pleasure – the sort of thing which ought to excite praise, but may not inspire affection'. *Utilitas* ('profitability') and *uoluptas* ('pleasure') are constant themes in the Roman agricultural writers [431]. Indeed, Varro's work (*On Agriculture* 1.2.12) begins with the question: 'What is the goal of agriculture: profit, pleasure, or both?' It is clear from all the agricultural writers that for the élite the answer was both and that, although, of course, they required a return from their estates, profitability was rarely the sole objective and in some cases not even the primary one. An example of such patterns of thought can be found in a letter of Pliny the Younger (*Letters* 3.19). In it Pliny asks the advice of his friend, Calvisius Rufus, about the desirability of Pliny's purchasing the next-door estate which adjoined his large property at Tifernum on the Tiber. Pliny was primarily inspired by the *pulchritudo iungendi* ('the pretty effect of joining the properties together'); but he was also aware of the issue of profitability. The estate contained good agricultural land and woods which provided a moderate income; but it was also run down and was worked by an indebted tenantry. This was the nub of Pliny's problem: was it going to be worth the considerable extra expenditure which would be needed to set these tenants on their feet again? It is worth noting in passing that if Pliny's scheme had worked then the lot of the peasant tenants would have improved and that the joining together of the two estates would not necessarily have disrupted the local pattern of agriculture. Pliny wanted to buy the property because the addition to his own would have created a new, attractive and pleasurable whole. What he sought advice on was whether, in view of the need for extra investment to solve the estate's problems, he was justified in indulging his whim.

278. A passing remark of Cato illustrates another aspect of aristocratic attitudes towards the land. In his work on agriculture (3.2), he states that the wise owner will ensure that his farmstead has ample storage for his crops, because that will be 'to the benefit of his wealth, his *uirtus* (virtue) and his *gloria* (fame)'. The desire to get the best price for one's crops by storing them for a time of higher prices is a strategy common to all farmers in all ages. It is the last clause which startles: success contributes to the landowner's *uirtus* and *gloria*, social values which were central to the thinking of the Roman élite, but which were normally displayed in politics and on the battlefield. The statement becomes less surprising when it is recognised that the ownership and exploitation of land was an important facet of what it was to be a respectable Roman gentleman. After all, land was essential to one's classification in the census [140] and failure to look after one's estates had been punished in the past by the censors (Aulus Gellius, *Attic Nights* 4.12.1). Just as the search for glory in public life stimulated fierce competition among aristocrats, the same was true on their estates. Pliny (*Natural History* 15.49) commented on the practice of designating new strains of fruit by the family name, thus establishing an 'everlasting memorial' to their discoverers 'as though they had achieved something distinguished in life'. Indeed, returning generals were often responsible for the introduction of new plants collected on their campaigns, such as the cherry, the pistachio and the jujube, and cartloads of exotic plants regularly formed important parts of triumphal processions, following the example of Pompey on his return from the East in 61 BC.

279. Nevertheless, the estate owner expected his property to provide him with income. So it seems odd to find Pliny (*Natural History* 18.37–8) quoting with approval the traditional dictum 'Nothing is less profitable than farming in the best possible way.' The reason for this advice becomes clearer when we understand the estate owner's view of his role in Roman society. The task of a *paterfamilias* ('head of a household') was to manage his *patrimonium* ('the family property') in such a way that it did not decline and affect the social standing and *fides* ('credit' in a broad sense, but including what we would call 'credit-worthiness') of his family. He would hope to hand his property on to his heirs enlarged, but certainly not significantly diminished. The squandering of one's patrimony was a charge by Roman prosecutors (as frequently in Cicero, e.g. *In Defence of Flaccus* 90, *Against Catiline* 2.10, *Philippics* 2.67). Once an estate had been bought, or received as a gift or inheritance, the essential requirement was to ensure that it paid its way, so that it would not become a continuing drain of the owner's limited cash resources. That cash was needed far more to enable people of substance to live successful lives in Rome, where conspicuous consumption and displays of *liberalitas* ('liberality') were an essential part of public life, the *dignitas sumptuosa* ('costly status') of Pliny (*Letters* 2.4; [216]). The surplus produced on estates was a necessary and welcome addition to the owner's income, but few were willing to tie up their precious cash in projects which in the long term might increase significantly the level of return from their estates. There were those who were more adventurous than others. Occasionally such people were successful (see Cicero, *In Defence of Roscius the Comic Actor* 33: 'Roscius obtained a farm at a time when prices of properties were low. It contained no villa and was entirely uncultivated; today it is worth far more than it was then'). Sometimes they met with honourable failure (see Cicero, *In Defence of Rabirius Postumus* 43: Rabirius helped a friend who 'was slipping down not through disgraceful expenditure and waste to satisfy his lusts, but through endeavour to increase his patrimony (*experientia patrimonii amplificandi*)'. Sometimes, again, there were serious consequences (L. Tarius Rufus, Augustus' admiral, spent a huge sum which he had received from Augustus on buying and bringing to a high state of cultivation land in Picenum. His wealth became so bound up in the enterprise that his heir refused to take up the inheritance (Pliny, *Natural History* 18.37)). The avoidance of costs and additional expenditure was a constant theme in all the agricultural writers, much more so than the search for extra profit. In the middle of the first century AD, at a time when Italian wines were facing increasing competition from those produced in Spain and southern Gaul, Columella had to argue elaborately that viticulture, despite its initial and continuing costs, could still provide in the medium term a good return on the investment (the passage, *On Agriculture* 3.3, is probably the nearest anyone came in antiquity to providing what we would recognise as an economic argument). It was not only that he had to argue against those who abandoned existing vineyards, 'because they sought to avoid the annual expenditure and thought that the foremost and most assured income was to outlay nothing' (Columella, *On Agriculture* 4.3). But Columella recognises that in all these cases he was arguing against current opinion, and elsewhere in his work he is a cautious as anyone else. There were at times very considerable profits to be made in wine and oil-production particularly, but the initial expenditure in establishing a vineyard or olive-grove was considerable and there were no immediate returns. A vineyard might take five years to come to maturity, olives three times that period.

280. The attitude of the great landowners towards their estates was a complex one. It was not purely economic. Land gave prestige and social status; no wonder then that the language used to describe their attitudes is social and moral rather than economic. Secondly, although the income from their estates was vital, simple maximisation of that income was not the primary aim. It is sometimes said that this outlook cannot be described in modern economic terms. This is not so. The behaviour of the great landowners was perfectly rational, given their goals. In the language of the economist they were 'profit-satisficing' and 'risk-averse'. The landowner set a level of return with which he would be satisfied; provided he achieved that, he was not interested in additional effort or expenditure to increase the returns further. The establishment of what would constitute a satisfactory return was not necessarily a complex calculation. Often farmers looked to how their neighbours were doing and judged their own success or failure by comparison with them. On visiting a new estate, the first thing to do, according to Cato (*On Agriculture* 1) was to observe how the neighbouring properties were faring. There was little inclination to buy run-down property and improve it. When this approach is combined with the reluctance to take risks and to invest in a change of land-use which might in the long term bring in larger profits, then the owners of large estates were unlikely to inspire a significant revolution in the methods of farming or in the pattern of land-use. Men with money were more likely to buy more land rather than radically improve their existing properties.

Markets

281. All landowners needed access to markets (fig. 6.6) both for their own products and to provide their estates with what they could not produce for themselves. This applied as much to the peasant farmer as to anyone else. Markets gave them some of the necessities of life, which they could not obtain in other ways, such as salt, a vital ingredient of the ancient diet. Further the presence of markets tempted even small-scale farmers to devote part of their land, which might otherwise have been used for subsistence crops, to production for that market. In the poem, the *Moretum* ('a dish of herbs and cheese'), ascribed to Virgil, the peasant Simylus, 'the rustic tiller of a meagre farm', gives over part of his farm to garden produce. But the cabbages, beets, sorrel, mallow and radishes were not for his own use: 'every market day he carried on his shoulder bundles of produce for sale to the city; and returned home from there, his neck relieved of its burden, but his pocket heavy with money' (*Moretum* 78–80).

282. Most towns of any size would hold regular markets (*nundinae*) and in some cases had a permanent market hall (*macellum*) built [203]. But markets

6.6 Market-scene (shoe-seller at the right, seller of pots and pans at the left).

could also be held at smaller, conveniently sited communities, or on large estates, and there were less regular fairs, often associated with religious sites. In the town centres there was likely to be an inscription set up with a list of places for markets in sequence with holes next to them into which a peg could be put to indicate the day of each market (fig. 6.7). Several such inscriptions have survived from central Italy. Such lists were important to farmers and also to the many tradesmen who probably moved regularly from market to market. The inscriptions also show that local markets were held in a traditional sequence, which avoided clashes of dates. This may help to explain why permission to hold a market had to be secured from the Senate and was strictly controlled. The emperor Claudius, a stickler for legal niceties, actually sought permission to hold markets on his estates (Suetonius, *Claudius* 12). One of the main reasons for this central control was to protect existing markets from undue competition. So, for example, when a senator petitioned to hold a market on his estate in northern Italy, the local town filed an objection with the Senate (Pliny, *Letters* 5.4); and in some cases known from inscriptions elsewhere in the empire the petitioner is careful to emphasise that the date for his market will not clash with already existing markets and will not result in a loss of trade to the local city. The increasing number of requests to hold *nundinae* meant there was an increase in trade; but its scale should not be exaggerated. The fear of the effects on already existing markets suggests that the overall level of demand at the regional level remained somewhat limited.

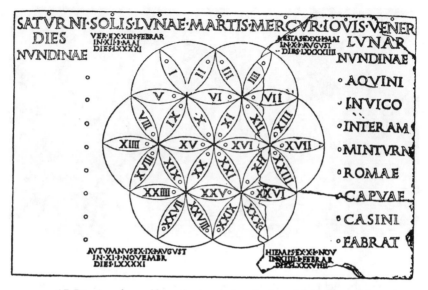

SATVRNI·SOLIS·LVNAE·MARTIS·MERCVR·IOVIS·VENER

DIES

NVNDINAE

VER·E·X·XIII·FEBRAR

IN·XII··MAI

DIES·LXXXXI

ASTAS·DEX·HMAI

IN·XI··AVGVST

DIES·DOOOIIII

LVNAR

NVNDINAE

° AQVINI

· INVICO

° INTERAM

° MINTVRN

° ROMAE

°CAPVAE

° CASINI

° FABRAT

AVTVMNVS·EX·IX·AVGVST

IN·XI··NOVEMBR

DIES·LXXXXI

HIEMAIS·EX·XI·NOV

IN·IIII·FEBRAR

DIES·LXXXVIII

6.7 Drawing of a marble market inscription: the days of the week are written along the top, the days of the month in the circles and eight towns of central Italy are named at the right. The board has holes for bronze pegs to be inserted to mark dates and places of the next market.

Money

283. There can be no doubt that trade at all levels was aided by the fact that the Roman world, at least by the early Imperial period, had a monetarised economy. This is sometimes contested (cf. [222–3, 237]); but the comment by the geographer Strabo (7.5.5) on the Dalmatians and other barbarians not using coinage suggests that by the time of Augustus coinage was the normal means of exchange within the empire – and not just within the cities. Papyri from Egypt show that even small transactions in villages normally used money. Confirmation from the other end of the empire comes from a letter (*Tab. Vindol.* II.343) recently discovered at the Roman fort of Vindolanda, near Hadrian's Wall in northern England, in which an Octavius begs his correspondent to 'send me some *denarii* as soon as possible' to finance a sizeable grain deal he has set up (fig. 6.8; cf. [415]). Of course, barter and payment in kind could, and did, continue where appropriate. Further, the availability of suitable coin could vary greatly over time and from place to place, as the jurist Gaius (*Digest* 13.4.3) noted: 'we know how the prices, particularly of wine, oil and grain, vary from community to community and region to region. It may

6.8 Letter from Octavius to Candidus, found at Vindolanda (Chesterholm) on Hadrian's Wall. Written in ink on wooden tablets, this refers to a number of commercial transactions, including purchases of corn and hides, and demonstrates that a full market economy was in operation on Britain's northern frontier. Cf. [415].

seem that money has one and the same value everywhere; but in some places it can be found more easily and at a low level of interest, while in others it is more difficult to come by and at a substantial rate of interest.' The reason for this is that the Roman authorities did not have what we would recognise as economic policies. Coins were struck and put into circulation primarily to pay for the state's needs, above all else Rome's armies. There was little or no appreciation of the overall effects of the money supply, and no real understanding of price inflation, which was frequently put down to the greed of the traders.

284. However, the passage of Gaius also points to a vital way in which temporary shortages of coin could be overcome by the presence of a system of credit, money-lending and banking. This can be shown to be an important part of the economy by the fact that debt seems to have been a prevalent problem at all levels of society, so much so that at times, particularly in the

Republican period, it could inspire violent political action. At the everyday level the circulation of money could be aided by *nummularii*, 'money-changers' (fig. 6.9), and more particularly by *argentarii* and *coactores argentarii*, 'money-lenders', who provided banking services, such as deposits and loans. We can see an *argentarius* at work in Pompeii, where part of the records of L. Caecilius Jucundus survive, written on wooden tablets. Many of these deal with a particular sort of transaction. Jucundus facilitated trading deals by acting as an intermediary between sellers and buyers. He organised auctions. Following a sale he would make over the total of the sale price to the seller, for which action he received a commission. He also acted as a banker by offering credit. The deals were often comparatively modest, the sale of a mule or a slave for instance. Jucundus seems to have been been ready to arrange deals in anything. On the other hand there were those *argentarii* who assisted the trade in the markets for specific goods. The funeral monument set up to L. Calpurnius Daphnus (fig. 6.10) described him as an *argentarius* in the *Macellum Magnum* ('the Big Market') on the Caelian Hill in Rome and showed him at work in a scene carved on the monument. On either side of Calpurnius were two porters carrying large baskets of fish; Calpurnius himself stands in the middle, holding a fish in his right hand, and in his left what is unmistakably the sort of jointed wooden tablet on which Jucundus kept his records. Calpurnius held auctions of fish in one of Rome's main markets.

Negotiatores

285. Men like Calpurnius and Jucundus operated at the comparatively modest, everyday level of trade. When we turn to larger-scale deals and international trade, then the key figures are those who *negotia gerunt* or *negotiantur* ('carry out business deals'), the *negotiatores* ([242–4]). It is clear from the evidence of Cicero that some, though not necessarily all, such businessmen were of high status – demonstrably *equites* in some cases – and possessed considerable wealth. It is significant that many of them were based in the Roman provinces, where they clearly played an important role. Cicero includes them among the key groups with which his brother Quintus had to deal in Asia, when he was out there as propraetor (Cicero, *Letters to his Brother Quintus* 1.1.6):

Your province includes that type of citizen who, either because they are *publicani* ('tax farmers') attached to us by the closest ties, or because they are so involved in *negotia* ('business deals') that they have become rich, consider that the security of the fortunes they enjoy is due to the blessing of my consulship.

6.9 Money-changing (or rent-collection?).

6.10 Funerary monument of L. Calpurnius Daphnus.

286. The *negotia* ('business deals') in which these men were involved are rarely defined in Cicero. It is clear that they could cover a whole range of transactions, including land, agricultural goods, shipping and the collection of taxes. It was often to them that the élite turned for loans of cash. What links all these activities is money. They are also closely involved in trade on a large scale. Concentrations of *negotiatores* are found in all the major ports. What they did was to set up the deals and finance them. These were the people who had the connections in overseas markets. This close involvement in trade may also explain why in the first century AD we find men for the first time defining their specialities: *negotiator olearius* ('dealer in oil'), *negotiator uinarius* ('dealer in wine'), and suchlike. It is much less easy to be sure of the social status of such people. There are signs that the term *negotiator* had gradually moved down-market and been appropriated by traders of all sorts. The expansion of trade throughout the empire is testimony primarily to the enterprise of men like A. Herennuleius Cestus (*CIL* IX.4680), who, though he died at Reate, was during his life a *negotiator* at the important wine depot at the place on the outskirts of Rome known as 'The Seven Caesars' and also *mercator omnis generis mercium transmarinarum* ('merchant who dealt in every kind of overseas product').

'Trade on a grand and abundant scale' (*mercatura magna et copiosa*) (Cicero, On Duties 1.151)

287. The existence of *negotiatores* also helps to explain another curious feature of the agricultural handbooks written for the rich landowners. Despite the fact that the landowners clearly expected to sell at a profit the majority of their cash crops, there is little or no interest in the trade and marketing of those products. It is true that they stress the advantages of the estate being near good communications by road or by water; but Varro (*On Agriculture* 1.16) shows that he is more concerned with the problem of supplying the estate with what it lacked and had to import than he was with the transport of his crops. Senators were not usually directly involved in trade. There was a curious law of 218 BC which actually forbade their ownership of large ships, although it is unclear how long it remained in effect. It is frequently argued that élite landowners had an aristocratic contempt for trade. Yet this is less than clear. Cato in the preface to his book on agriculture praises the trader as 'energetic' and 'committed to the acquisition of wealth'; his objection to involvement in trade is not moral or snobbish, but the practical one that such investments were *periculosum et calamitosum* ('risky and at the mercy of the winds'). No aristocrat, whose status depended on his wealth, could afford to have much of that wealth tied up in a form of investment which could easily go wrong. In the same way Cicero in a famous passage (*On Duties* 1. 151) goes out of his way to state that trade on a grand scale is praiseworthy. No, the reason for the apparent lack of interest in the markets for the estate's produce is that the *negotiator* frequently intervened at a very early stage. Consider the important trade in wine. Cato [147] includes a contract for the sale of grapes on the vine. It was a contract of this type which much later Pliny used with some *negotiatores* (*Letters* 8.2). It had many potential advantages for the estate-owner. The grape harvest required considerable manpower, which the estate was unlikely to have available. Under the contract it was the *negotiator* who had to provide the men to do the picking and pressing. The estate's presses would be used and the contract would allow the wine to be stored for up to a year in the storage jars on the estate. It was the *negotiator*'s job to bring in the amphorae, which would be used to transport the wine, to organise the transport, the shipping, and the marketing of the wine. We know a great deal about this because all the stages of this complex process involved serious legal problems, which were discussed in minute detail by the Roman jurists (the *negotiator* stores the wine in your jars: whose wine is it, who is responsible for its quality, what happens if the wine is not removed in time for the next vintage, when the jars are needed again?). Such deals sometimes went wrong. In the case of Pliny's *negotiatores*, they gave him a good price for his vintage in anticipation of a profitable market, which did not materialise. The businessmen came back to Pliny and asked for a rebate, which, surprising as it may seem, he gave them. Perhaps Pliny knew that he had to keep them happy and willing to take his vintages in future years. This illustrates the power of such *negotiatores*, which is also reflected in Roman law, where gradually there was a shift away from protecting the interests of the estate-owner towards minimising the risks for the large-scale buyer. Nevertheless the activities of the *negotiatores* insulated, as it were, the aristocratic owner from direct involvement in the world of trade. In many cases it was the *negotiator* who dealt with *nauicularii* ('the shippers') or the *mercatores* ('merchants'), who hired space on ships for their cargoes.

288. We can now trace the patterns of some of this trade in ever greater detail. Goods like wine, oil, and *garum* ('fish sauce') were transported in bulky amphorae. In many places the kilns which produced those amphorae have been discovered. Cargoes of the amphorae have been recovered from the wrecks which litter the coastal regions of the Mediterranean (fig. 6.11). Fragments of the amphorae, or more informatively the name stamps which the potters put on the jars before they were fired, have been catalogued by archaeologists from sites throughout the Roman world. It is impossible to judge exactly the scale of such trade. After all, we have no ideas what percentage of

the whole trade is represented by the surviving amphorae. But we are left with an impression of trade on a large scale.

289. From the second century BC to the first century AD large markets for wine opened up. First, there was the growing city of Rome itself. Then there was the notorious love of wine among the Celtic tribes of Europe, even before regions such as Gaul had been absorbed into the Roman empire. Some areas of Italy, particularly in coastal regions, close to convenient ports, responded by expanding viticulture in a way which undoubtedly affected the local economy and the pattern of land-use. In northern Campania the slopes of Mons Massicus (Monte Massico) produced Massic and Falernian wine of considerable distinction. Much of it was produced for export in the late Republic. At the height of the trade, close to the local ports of Minturnae, Sinuessa and Volturnum, there was a vast array of potteries, which produced the amphorae which the *negotiatores* needed to carry the wine. Such was the scale of production that in Sinuessa they even developed a style of building which made use of the rejected pottery from the kilns. Massic and Falernian travelled in these amphorae to markets throughout the western Mediterranean. But by the first century AD there were signs of change. The potteries are now found on a more modest scale inland on individual estates. The scale of production seems more modest. By this date the wines of Italy were having to compete with those from the vineyards of southern Spain and Gaul.

6.11 Amphorae in a shipwreck at La Madrague de Giens, near Toulon.

290. Similar accounts could be given for other areas of coastal Italy. Elsewhere, the production and trade in olive oil had even more profound and long-lasting effects on the economy of the valley of the River Baetis (the Guadalquivir) in southern Spain in the first three centuries AD. But once again historians need to be careful not to exaggerate the economic processes involved. They are limited in area. Much of inland Italy was untouched by the opening-up of new international markets. Secondly, the length of time during which a regional economy, such as that around Monte Massico, took advantage of the wider international economy was often quite short. There are even just enough archaeological clues to suggest that the estate owners and *negotiatores,* responsible for the success of the export of wine from the Monte Massico region, moved on to develop the viticulture of Spain and Gaul; that is to say that what they exported was not just wine, but a whole system of production.

291. Trade was not limited by the frontiers of the Roman empire. The most dramatic example was the trade in valuable exotic spices of the East, frankincense, myrrh, ivory, pearls, gemstones, and silk from as far afield as China, a trade which Pliny (*Natural History* 6.101) tells us drained coin on a huge scale from within the empire. Every year, about July, large ships would leave ports on the Red Sea bound either for the east coast of Africa or to catch the Southwest monsoon off the coast of the Yemen to be blown across to near the mouth of the Ganges or to the Malabar coast of southern India. Having loaded up with their valuable cargoes, the ships caught the north-east monsoon in November to cross back to the Red Sea, up which they battled to return to port. Their cargoes were transferred to caravans of camels which carried them to Coptos on the Nile and then up to Alexandria and beyond. All this is documented in a handbook for traders, written in the mid first century AD, the *Periplus Maris Erythraei* ('Voyage round the Erythraean Sea'). The value of this trade is shown by a papyrus which documents a shipment of 4,700 pounds of ivory, nearly 790 of textiles, and a large quantity of nard, an aromatic resin; this cargo was worth some 131 talents, a considerable fortune. The figure is even more startling, when it is realised that just one of the large ships on the Red Sea run might carry over 100 such cargoes on its annual voyage.

292. The picture presented here is of trade on a large scale, vigorous and profitable. The regional economies of the empire found from time to time that they could produce goods for which there were valuable markets overseas. The scale and nature of their involvement varied over time. Yet, it has been argued that even this is too positive and modern assessment of the scale of trade in the empire. There were other ways in which goods circulated, which might explain the pattern in the archaeological record. The great

aristocratic landowners frequently moved produce from property to property, to supply their town houses, their families, retainers and friends. No
doubt this happened, but hardly on a scale to explain all the evidence. More
significant is the argument that large-scale trade was predominantly state-
sponsored redistribution. The Roman state had to supply its armies, and
from the late second century BC took on the task of providing corn for the
huge population of Rome. This, it is claimed, was the cause of most movements of goods, not private trading; indeed, state intervention was necessary
precisely because there was no large-scale trade to meet these needs. The
argument is misguided. The only way in which the Roman state could supply
its needs was to attract private traders to become involved in the supply
chain. From the Second Punic War onwards, it was *negotiatores* and *mercatores* who controlled the supply of arms, food, and equipment to the armies.
As for corn, only something like half the needs of the population of Rome
were met by the state dole [219–20]; the rest had to come from the normal
workings of the market. The only way the Roman authorities could provide
their part of the supply was by involving private traders. The emperor
Claudius offered inducements to traders to provide ships for the transport of
the state corn. State redistribution would have been impossible without
already flourishing large-scale private trading.

293. Confirmation of the importance of the trade which Rome inspired
throughout the empire comes from a startling source, the mystical vision of
the Revelation of John, composed in Asia Minor towards the end of the first
century AD. The author contemplates the end of earthly power and the
destruction of the great city (Revelation 18.11):

The merchants of the earth also will weep and mourn for her, because no one any
longer buys their cargoes, cargoes of gold and silver, jewels and pearls, cloths of purple
and scarlet, silks and fine linens; all kinds of scented woods, ivories, and every sort of
thing made of costly woods, bronze, iron, or marble; cinnamon and spice, incense, per-
fumes and frankincense; wine, oil, flour, and wheat, sheep and cattle, horses, chariots,
slaves, and the lives of men.

Cities, consumers and craftsmen

294. So the ships and barges docked at the port of Rome on the Tiber (cf.
figs. 5.5, 5.6; [233]). They tied up to the pairs of mooring rings, which can still
be seen in the retaining walls of the Tiber. The goods were run up concrete
ramps onto the wharves and then into the huge warehouses which dominated
the area around the Aventine. There were numerous wholesale markets (*forum
uinarium*, 'the wine-merchants' market', *forum piscatorium*, 'the fish market'

etc.). The retail of goods took place in the market halls (*macella*), such as the *Macellum* near the Roman Forum, or later under the Empire the *Macellum Magnum* on the Caelian Hill), or there were the smaller local bazaars, groups of shops clustered round a courtyard. On market days open spaces were crowded with temporary stalls. Above all, there were the *tabernae* (fig. 6.12), the single rooms on the ground floor, which, to judge from the fragments of the Marble Plan of Rome, lined many of the streets. These shops often had a balcony at the back which served as living quarters, along with space for a workshop. The displays of goods frequently cluttered the pavements outside until imperial legislation banned this nuisance. 'The barber, innkeeper, cook, and butcher keep within their own doors. What was recently one great shop (*taberna*), is now the city of Rome again', wrote Martial (7.61) in praise of the law.

295. The cities and towns of Italy and the empire mirrored all this, though on a smaller scale. For all this activity, the cities of the ancient world have been seen as essentially places of consumption rather than production. They lived off the agricultural production of their surrounding territory or, in the case of Rome especially, were parasitic on the whole empire. The contrast is

6.12 A shopping-complex in Rome (Trajan's 'markets'); the shops and offices were terraced into the hillside behind Trajan's Forum (in the foreground). Cf. [489].

6.13 Tomb of M. Virgilius Eurysaces, Rome.

always made with the great cities of the Industrial Revolution. Yet, Rome and other cities were communities of productive craftsmen. They appear all too infrequently in the literary record, but they proudly proclaim their skills on their tombstones. Over 150 different trades appear in the inscriptions of Rome, some highly specialised. Nor did they always try to hide their involvement, when their skills brought them wealth. Marcus Vergilius Eurysaces, *pistor et redemptor* ('baker and public contractor'), had his large tomb constructed like a bread store (a *panarium*), with a frieze which illustrated the work in his bakeries (fig. 6.13). Many of the craftsmen and women were in origin freed slaves, set up in business by their ex-masters. Frequently they would be managers of the businesses, while their patrons retained an interest.

296. Estate owners would have shopping lists like the one recommended by Cato (*On Agriculture* 135):

Tunics, togas, blankets, patchwork, and shoes should be bought at Rome; caps, iron tools, scythes, spades, mattocks, axes, harness, ornaments, and small chains at Cales and Minturnae; spades at Venafrum; carts and sledges at Suessa and in Lucania; storage jars and pots at Alba and Rome; tiles at Venafrum . . . oil mills at Pompeii, and at Rufrius' yard at Nola, nails and bars at Rome, buckets, oil-vessels, water carriers, wine urns, other bronze vessels at Capua and Nola . . .

All this suggests a lively regional market for the craftsmen of the communities of central Italy. Some of what they produced might go further afield.

297. One of the most travelled products and one which was at times produced on something approaching an industrial scale was pottery. One of the most interesting results of Augustus' settlement of the empire and making the sea-ways safe was the sudden dominance throughout the empire and beyond of the red gloss pottery (known as Arretine or *terra sigillata*) produced at Arretium (Arezzo) in Umbria (fig. 9.7). For a short period in the reigns of Augustus and Tiberius there was an extraordinary fashion for this pottery and it was transported in large quantities over great distances. At first sight this is surprising. Pottery is not a product of such value that it could easily carry the costs of long-distance transport. Although wrecks have been discovered with whole cargoes of pottery, more normally pottery formed part-loads along with primary products. It should also be remembered that ships bringing wine, oil or corn needed to find cargoes for the return voyage. However, it also needs to be noted that by the middle of the first century, the pottery produced at Arretium had just as quickly lost its widespread market. The technology of producing red gloss pottery moved to southern and central Gaul, and later to eastern Gaul, and North Africa. It can be demonstrated that workshop owners from Arretium were responsible for bringing their skills to the new regions. Cn. Ateius, who had a workshop in Arretium, seems to have opened branches in Lyon and southern Gaul. Further the potters of southern Gaul occasionally stamped their pottery 'Arretine', thus acknowledging the origins of the style. The quantities of pottery produced at these centres were on an industrial scale; but this does not presuppose organisation as a modern industry. Study of the stamps of workshop owners and craftsmen suggest the pottery was produced by large numbers of independent potteries which rarely employed more than about 20 slave craftsmen.

Dynamic growth or stagnation?

298. Some, perhaps most, readers will by this stage be puzzled or infuriated. Where in all this were the slaves? For some historians, slavery was the defining characteristic of the Roman economy [245ff., 350ff.]. The neglect of the topic up to now is deliberate. The numbers of slaves were vast, but they were not to be found in equal numbers across the whole empire, nor at all periods. Further, a very high percentage of the total number of slaves were not employed directly in economic production, but in service in the houses of the great or as part of what passed for a civil service for government at local and imperial level. But those who participated in the chain of economic production are to be found everywhere, and their presence is taken for granted by our sources as the account above has also done. They are there on the estates, whether as chained workers or supervisors. They are there in the hills, herding great flocks. They staff the offices of merchants. They provide the skilled craftsmanship of the potteries. Finally, as freedmen and women, they dominate the urban economy of Rome. But it needs to be remembered that slavery is only one of a number of ways of exploiting the labour-power of individuals and that it has costs which need to be taken into account. The slave, particularly a skilled one, was expensive. He or she had to be fed, clothed and housed. At the end of their productive life they had to be replaced. This did not make the employment of slaves automatic. It was an economic choice and in many circumstances was not seen as the inevitable one. This may in part explain why there is hardly any evidence of the free population protesting that work was being taken from them by the use of slaves.

299. We have tried to reconstruct the elaborate networks of people involved in the processes of production and consumption, the links in the chains which led from the wine-growing estates of central Italy to the feasts of the Celtic aristocracy of Gaul, or from the shores of southern India to the emperor's table in Rome. These networks also linked the social classes. While the élite might hold aloof from direct involvement, they never missed a chance of a profit, through indirect investment and setting up their freedmen in business, as the Elder Cato did (Plutarch, *Cato* 21):

He used to loan money in the most criticised of ways, that is in shipping, in the following way. He required his many borrowers to form an association, and when there were fifty partners and as many ships, he took one share in the company through the intermediary of Quintio, his freedman, who dealt with the business and accompanied the ships on their voyages. In this way the risk did not fall on Cato entirely, but only a small part of it, and the profits were large.

300. The picture presented is a relatively dynamic one. At all stages in production and trade men were making rational economic decisions to better themselves, from the aristocrat who 'sought to acquire great wealth by honourable means' (Pliny, *Natural History* 7.140) to the greeting written in the entrance to a Pompeian house: *salue lucru* ('Welcome, Profit!': fig. 5.8; cf. [239]). The opportunities were there. Indeed, the scale and complexity of the economy of the Roman empire was not going to be equalled until Italy in the High Renaissance. But there were limits, which explain why the economy never 'took off'. The main limitation was the market itself. Vast wealth was concentrated in the hands of a tiny minority. Their desires and needs undoubtedly stimulated sectors of the economy. But elsewhere the resources of the majority were so limited and their immediate needs so simply met, that there was no base for consistent growth over time.

FURTHER READING

K. Greene, *The Archaeology of the Roman Economy* (London, 1986)
M.I. Finley, *The Ancient Economy* (London, 1973)

7

The Roman family

Introduction

301. Aeneas, the founding figure of the Roman people, was the mythological embodiment of Roman family values [7]. The standard image of Aeneas escaping from Troy is of a man with his old father on his shoulders and his young son in his hand (fig. 7.1). As developed by Virgil, this becomes the icon of Roman *pietas* ('respect'): the family man who looks back respectfully to the past generation and fights to secure the hope of the next. With his family, he carries the sacred symbols of its continuity, the Penates. Even if we find *pius Aeneas* ('pious Aeneas') a dull hero, his message comes through clearly enough: for the Roman, family values lay at the heart of respect for the gods and for the Roman community that was itself a family, the *patria* ('fatherland').

302. But what does it mean to talk about the 'Roman family'? Our word 'family' derives from the Latin *familia*, and that may lull us into thinking the two ideas are much the same. In fact *familia* has some significant differences. Strictly, it is a legal term, referring to those under the legal control of the head of household, the *paterfamilias*. As we will see, the *familia* covered the slaves of a household, but frequently did not include the wife; so that even if many Romans lived in groupings resembling the modern 'nuclear family', that was not what they referred to in talking about the *familia*.

303. Yet it is difficult to offer generalisations that cater for the vast cultural diversity of a Mediterranean empire that thought of itself as 'Roman'. Even within Italy itself at the height of the empire, we might expect substantial contrasts, between the metropolis and small provincial towns, between town and country (see chapter 5), between the aristocracy and the slave-born, between rich and poor. Again, if generalisations were possible, it is not clear we could ever find the sort of documentary evidence on which family historians of the

7.1 Coin (*denarius*) of Julius Caesar showing Aeneas fleeing from Troy with Anchises on his shoulder and the sacred image of Athena (Palladium) in his right hand. 47–46 BC Cf. [7, 475].

modern world depend. Surveys and statistics that allow one to generalise about birth rates, average life expectations, divorce rates and the like are the product of modern statistical mentalities and practices quite foreign to the Roman.

304. One answer is to look not at the bewildering diversity of actual practice, but at the ideals and norms which created the framework for actual practice. From this viewpoint, what makes the *Roman* family (as opposed to the family in the Roman world) is its success in passing itself off as complying with patterns of behaviour that were thought of as typically 'Roman'. A vivid example of such an ideal transformed by practice is in the use of family portraits. A well-known tradition among the Republican aristocracy of Rome was the preservation of portraits of their ancestors (sometimes derived from death masks: cf. [144, 468]). Displayed in the *atrium* ('hall') with lists of their achievements and linked by red threads to mark their relationship within the family tree, and paraded in the forum in a masquerade procession at the funeral of a family member, these *imagines* ('portraits') were the ultimate symbol of Roman family pride [328, 468–9]. The figure of the Barberini *togatus*, a toga-clad Roman holding in each hand the portrait of an ancestor [3.5], embodies this tradition. But though this figure is often taken for the typical Roman noble, he might equally be a freedman holding the portraits of his patrons, keen to *look* like a traditional Roman [97].

305. Thousands of funerary portraits survive, mostly of humble or otherwise unheard-of people, which echo, at a remove, the aristocratic tradition of *imagines*; however obscure they may be, we can tell at a glance that these people are Roman. A beautifully carved pair from the Capitoline museum in Rome (fig. 7.2) seem so typically aristocratic that they are traditionally known as Cato and Porcia; their inscription reveals them as two ex-slaves, Gratidius Libanus and Gratidia Carite. Such family groups are extraordinarily effective as testimony to the 'Roman family'. Another husband–wife couple identify themselves by a touching verse inscription: he, L. Aurelius Hermia, is a butcher from the Viminal hill in Rome; she, Philematium, his wife, 'chaste in body, who loved me and possessed my loving heart', had been the faithful companion of her fellow freedman since the age of seven, to die at forty. Larger family groups are also found, like the head of the young son between his craggy-faced parents or the long line-up of the Furii. Even the humblest might have their substitute portraits, like the group of slaves from Pompeii whose graves are marked by rudimentary gravestones with the outline of a portrait head (fig. 7.3).

306. All these images reflect the anxiety of the Roman family to project itself as a family in public, in death as in life. Just as an aristocratic funeral made visible and advertised the descent-group of a family, and its claims to continuing fame and respect, so the tombs with their portraits that lined the approach roads to a Roman city advertised the families within, and proclaimed their adherence to good Roman tradition. Even those who had no portraits, but were identified in death by inscribed words alone, achieved this effect. Gravestones, in a variety of shapes and sizes, are some of the most telling signs of the spread of Roman culture across the empire. It has been calculated that of some quarter of a million inscriptions in Latin recorded from across the empire, three-quarters are funerary commemorations. They are the best source of information about family life across the empire that we have. They give clues to demographic questions like life expectancy. Some carry words of affection, however conventional, that hint at the expected sentimental life of the family. Together they are testimony of the way the 'Roman' family made itself so, by reference to shared and understood norms of Roman behaviour [114].

307. For this reason it makes sense to put together a variety of sources of information to gain a picture of the Roman family. The portraits and tombstones can be related to the world of the Roman aristocracy known from historical accounts, biographies, and private letters; to the imaginary world of Roman literature that so often seems to offer an image of 'real life'; to the legal sources that define the framework of behaviour open to a Roman citizen operating under Roman law; and to the archaeological remains of the domestic settings within which the family operated. Rather than attempt to construct a

7.2 Funerary busts popularly called Cato and Porcia, actually M. Gratidius and his wife.

7.3 Pompeii, gravestone of N. Istacidius Helenus, one of a series carved to suggest the outline of a rudimentary portrait bust.

delusory picture of how the Roman family really was, it is better to look at the common frameworks within which, in an infinite variety of ways, different family groups constructed their own experience of being Roman. The three frameworks we shall look at are the legal (what were the rules?), the architectural (what were their houses like?), and the sentimental (what sort of emotional relationships were expected?).

The legal framework

308. The most persistent, and in the eyes of the Romans the most quintessentially Roman, feature of the family was the power of the father, *patria potestas*. Not only were they aware that the Roman father had powers over his family, and especially his adult children, that were exceptional, but it was a proud tradition to which they clung tenaciously. The second-century AD lawyer Gaius commented that 'this right is peculiar to Roman citizens, for there are virtually no other men who have such power over their sons as we have', and cited the views of the emperor Hadrian in support [410].

309. Stated at its most dramatic, the power of the *paterfamilias* was absolute: the power of life and death over his *familia*, that is his legitimate children, his slaves, and his wife if married in a form that transferred paternal control (*manus*, lit. 'hand') to the husband [314]. The *familia* could be seen as a state within a state: its members were subject to the judgement and absolute authority of the *pater* ('father') just as citizens were subject to the judgement and absolute authority of the citizen body. In exceptional circumstances sons or wives might be handed over by the state to paternal authority, as happened on the occasion of the scandal of the cult of Bacchus in 186 BC, or again under Augustus. But even if this awesome power was occasionally invoked, and its memory was kept alive, in practical terms it was not the most significant aspect of *potestas* ('power').

310. Much more immediate was the incapacity of anyone under paternal power to act as a fully independent agent under Roman law, above all in financial matters and the making of contracts. In theory the *filiusfamilias*, the son under paternal power, had little more independence than a slave. Exactly like a slave, the only way he could own property was as *peculium* – a private fund conceded to his use by his father, but revocable at any point, and automatically reverting to the father in the case of death. He could not make a will, nor inherit property in his own right. In practice, a father might allow his son (or his slave) considerable freedom, the establishment of a separate household, the running of agricultural estates, or the running of a business. And lawyers found a variety of devices to enable sons-in-power to do business and pursue legal contracts without having the requisite independence. But in the end, everything depended on the father's good will, and all could be clawed back.

311. This legally-enshrined custom led to situations the oddity of which the Romans relished. Most dramatically, it might be the case that a son-in-power might hold the highest public office while still under his father's control: as consul he held supreme *potestas* ('power') in the state, yet at home he remained like a slave under his father's *potestas*. The situation attracted anecdotes, like that of Fabius Maximus, father and son, who held the consulship in two successive years. The father approached his son on horseback: he demanded (as a father) that his son (as consul) use his powers to order him (the father) to dismount. It was, of course, as a talking-point, a neat way of drawing attention to the family's success.

312. How this affected people psychologically will be discussed below. But we should not overdramatise the incidence of *patria potestas*. It has been calculated on the basis of comparative figures that by the age of 10, nearly one-third of children will have lost their fathers; by the age of 25 (a standard age of marriage) over two-thirds will have gained their independence; and by the age of 41, the legal minimum for holding the consulship, as few as 6 per cent would have still-surviving fathers. The small minority who had to endure paternal control into their maturity had even so an escape route. The father could 'emancipate' his son, releasing him from his *familia* and his control (*manus*). Whether Romans flocked to take this option we do not know; but the fact that it is so little discussed outside the legal sources suggests that it was not generally seen as a big issue. The reasons for taking this option are likely to have been specifically legal. The Younger Pliny's rival at the bar, Regulus, emancipated his son in order to enable him to inherit property from his mother. That sort of legal technicality may have weighed more heavily than any frustration at heavy-handed paternal control (a circumstance under which in any case the father was less likely to release his son).

313. The legal relationship of husband and wife was more complicated. Roman myth heroised the husband who kept his wife under strictest control. One Egnatius Metennius is supposed to have cudgelled his wife to death for drinking wine, and thereby earned the praise of Romulus. But though the Romans took a perverse pleasure in such tales of brutal authority (just as mythically Manlius Torquatus Imperiosus was heroised for executing his son for stepping out of line in battle), it is historically more remarkable how far Roman law allowed wives to escape from the husband's authority.

314. Again, the crucial legal framework was *patria potestas*. Whether a wife was subject to this depended on the form under which she was married. Two ancient ceremonials, the offering of an emmer-wheat cake in joint sacrifice before ten witnesses (*confarreatio*), and the fictitious sale of a daughter with scales and balance before five witnesses to the husband (*coemptio*) had the effect of transferring a woman from the control (*manus*) of her father to her husband. In this case she became as a daughter-in-power to her husband: all her property and acquisitions were automatically his, and he had the theoretical right of life-and-death over her.

315. Dramatic though this sounds, what is much more remarkable (given the historical tendency in many societies to subject a wife to the husband's control) is that it was purely optional, and by the late Republic apparently not even normal. The lawyers explain that there had always been a third way by which a wife could come under her husband's control, by 'usage' (*usus*). To live together as man and wife for a year was already enough, and the wife automatically passed into the husband's control. In theory, this should have resulted in all Roman wives passing into their husband's legal control. But a legal loophole was found. If husband and wife spent three nights of the year apart it broke *usus*, 'usage', and the requirement to pass into control was waived. It is an extraordinary example of the capacity of the Romans for radical transformation of their laws and traditions without ever in appearance abandoning the previous practice. By a legal fiction, the majority of wives were freed from their husbands' legal powers.

316. One feature of Roman marriage that seems most surprising to us was the informality with which it could be both made and unmade. A legal marriage (*iustum matrimonium*) was a union between two Roman citizens not otherwise legally disqualified from marriage. Simply to live together by consent as man and wife made a marriage, without any formalities, ceremonials before witnesses or signing of registers; and simply to separate constituted legal divorce. Either partner could leave the other, without discussion or consent; and though it was conventional to offer reasons for doing so (which ranged from failure to produce offspring to finding the partner's behaviour irritating), and it might be prudent to satisfy public opinion or the censor that you had not behaved irresponsibly, there were no legal formalities involved, nor courts to be satisfied.

317. Along with this remarkable freedom of consent went an equally remarkable arrangement about the problem of joint marital property. It simply did not exist. Either the wife was under the *manus* of her husband, in which case everything she had or acquired was his; or she was not, in which case there was a total separation of ownership. It was specifically disallowed for husband and wife to make donations to one another ('lest by mutual affection they despoil themselves'). The husband might provide his wife with a maintenance allowance, and certain expenses, but even these were reclaimable

if beyond certain levels. If the wife's father was alive, she was in his power; but for the vast majority of wives of mature years whose fathers had died and who had become independent (*sui iuris*), their property was their own, with the proviso that they normally must have a male *tutor* ('guardian') with whose backing any legal contract would be made. By custom the wife brought with her to the marriage a dowry which passed to her husband's control; but it was not fully his since it was (with certain provisos) returnable in the case of divorce.

318. The point of this is not that women enjoyed the sort of freedoms available in modern society. They did not, and social convention ensured that on the whole women remained at least notionally subject to male authority, of the father, husband or *tutor* (the justification offered for tutorship was the 'feebleness of the female sex'). But it does mean that the Roman family was virtually free of some of the typical traumas of modern Western marriages. No man or wife found themselves under a legal or religious compulsion to remain together. There was no need for painful and expensive divorce cases in the courts; there could be no arguments over the financial settlements of a divorce (except over the return of the dowry); there could not even be agonising suits for custody of the children, who were automatically in the *potestas* of the father, unless he had emancipated them, giving them total independence. One might say that it gave the wife far greater freedom; she could walk out of a disagreeable marriage at will. But it also left her more exposed: her husband could tell her at will to leave her home and her children. *Uxor, uade foras*, 'Wife, get out of the house', was enough to terminate her marriage.

319. One consequence was that divorce and remarriage seem to have been very frequent, at least among the upper classes for whom we have biographical details. Although myth held (incredibly) that no Roman before a certain Carvilius Ruga in 230 BC divorced his wife, by Cicero's lifetime it is normal to hear of senators that they married three or four times. Equally, women bore children by a succession of husbands: one Vistilia broke records under the early Empire by having six different sons and one daughter by six different fathers (four of the sons became consuls, and the daughter married an emperor). 'Serial marriage' on this scale must have produced relationships of half-brothers and sisters of extraordinary complexity. Yet it is no contradiction to state that ideals of fidelity and lifelong commitment survived alongside legal ease and frequency of divorce and remarriage; the ideal wife was *uniuira*, possessed by only one man.

320. By our standards, Roman law was not much concerned with regulating the personal relations of individuals, and more concerned with control and transmission of property. Lawyers were not much concerned to discuss how

and why the alarming paternal 'right of life and death' could be used; but they do discuss inheritance at great length. Here too we may be struck by the great flexibility of Roman law in comparison with that of many other societies. Ancient tradition laid down a strict line of succession: on the death of the *paterfamilias* (the only member of the family with property), sons, daughters (if not emancipated) and the wife (if under *manus*), inherited in equal portions. In the absence of such heirs (called *sui heredes*), the property passed to the nearest relative in the male line ('agnate'). But these rules only applied when there was no will; and it became standard to leave a will. And although there was a strong expectation that sons and daughters would be remembered (more or less equally), and a will could be overthrown in court if they were passed over without good cause, the only strict requirement (this from 40 BC) was that the heir should receive at least a quarter of the estate. Women were in theory banned by the *Lex Voconia* of 169 BC from inheriting as heirs; this soon came to be seen as unjust, and was evaded by leaving them property as a legacy or a trust (*fideicommissum*). In general, the Roman writing a will had an astonishing freedom to leave property outside the family as well as within, to females as well as males, provided of course that the beneficiaries were Roman citizens.

321. Another striking freedom was over adoption. European aristocracies operating under feudal rules have been much encumbered by primogeniture (the automatic privileging of the elder son), absence of female succession, and impossibility of adoption. Roman rules not only treated all children more equally, but made it easy to produce substitute sons and heirs by adoption. By given rituals, a son passed from one *familia* to another (interestingly, the rituals might involve the same use of weights and scales as for the acquisition of a wife under *coemptio*, or a slave). But even if the formalities had not been completed, it was possible to use your will to nominate someone as heir to your property and name. Though this was not technically an adoption, the ease with which Caesar's testamentary heir (Octavian: fig. 1.11) passed himself off as his son shows that custom accepted the situation.

322. One point that must be clear about Roman family law is its capacity for progressive modification over time. If there was once a time when the father of the family held awesome sway over wife and children, with no escape except his death, a series of modifications, while preserving the ideal of *patria potestas,* had produced a much more flexible situation by the late Republic. A further major change came with the reign of Augustus. Legislating, on the face of it, to preserve and restore the traditional Roman family, he generated a set of new rules that played a central role for the next three centuries. The legislation was double-pronged. One prong imposed public control on family moral-

ity by making adultery and extra-marital sex a public offence. The other made marriage and the production of children a duty of the citizen to the state, by offering incentives to those who complied, and imposing disabilities, especially in the area of inheritance or property, on those who did not.

323. There has been endless debate about what Augustus was trying to achieve by this package of laws, and many different viewpoints are possible. It may be seen as a response to a perceived 'breakdown of marriage' and growth of 'immorality'. It may have been an attempt to reverse a perceived decline in the freeborn population. It may be seen as a cynical attempt by the state to raise revenue, by usurping the inheritances of the unmarried and childless. The intentions of the legislator are only partially recoverable; and whatever they were, it is characteristic of legislation to have unanticipated effects not intended by the legislator.

324. The question here is how it changed the legal framework within which 'the Roman family' was constructed. One vital point to make is that it shifted the relationship between state and individual family. The Republic may be seen as a collective of autonomous households, each under its sovereign *paterfamilias*. Though the community imposed plenty of expectations – about how sons or wives should be treated, about who ought to inherit, about the desirability of producing children and the anti-social effects of adultery – the law of the community provided few instruments by which to enforce its expectations on the head of the house. Imperial rule brought a new ethos. The welfare of the state took priority over the independence of the family. It limited the power of the *paterfamilias* to kill a daughter taken in adultery. It enforced public prosecution of the adulteress on the husband, and required divorce before witnesses. It gave public privileges to those who complied with the duty of producing children (for freeborn men advantages in seeking office, for freedmen release of their property from reversion to the patron, for women release from the control of the *tutor*); and it intervened in the private rights of inheritance of the childless. Moreover, the emperor gave himself the right to intervene, as ultimate legal arbiter, in family lawsuits, in order to enforce what he saw as morality. The net effect was not quite a transformation of the Republican family and its independence, but a very significant qualification.

Domestic settings

325. Houses and households varied enormously through time and across the empire. Even if we restrict our focus, as is convenient, to the highly visible remains of Pompeii and Herculaneum, reflecting conditions close to Rome in the late Republic and early Empire, habitations come in all shapes and sizes,

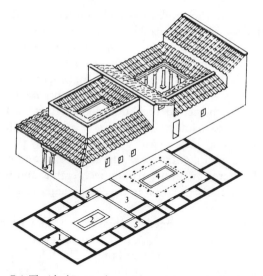

7.4 The ideal Roman house (*domus*): isometric drawing.

from the spreading mansions of the rich [471ff.], through apartments in brick-and-concrete blocks, to single-room garrets above shops. Nevertheless, we rapidly become aware as we visit these sites that there is some sort of ideal of the 'proper' Roman house (fig. 7.4); that the richest and finest houses offer the most explicit realisations of the ideal, and that the little garrets fall away from it most dramatically.

326. The central feature of this 'Roman house' is the generous central circulation space of the *atrium*. Roman discussions of the house underline the importance of this feature in setting their houses apart: the architect Vitruvius not only gives great attention to the rules and proportions of construction of the *atrium*, but when he turns to contrast the Greek with the Italian house, the first point he has to make is that Greek houses do not have the *atrium*. The evidence now suggests that the type goes back to the Rome of the Tarquins; certainly it had the status of a revered Roman tradition. Its importance was not so much practical as ideological: it stood for so much of what the Roman family was meant to be about.

327. The typical *atrium* is entered directly from the street, separated only by the long, narrow 'throat' of the *fauces* (fig. 7.5). That transition marked an important boundary between two worlds: *domi* and *foris*, 'inside the home' and 'outside the doors' (*fores*). The separation of the domestic and the public spheres was a separation of spheres of authority. Inside the house the

7.5 View from the street, through the *fauces*, into an *atrium* with its central roof-opening (*compluuium*).

paterfamilias held sway: beyond his doors, he was a citizen doing business with his fellow-citizens in the common outside space, notably the *forum*, or perhaps meeting in the Senate with other *patres* (so senators were addressed) to take counsel for the common good, the *res publica*.

328. But the division of private and public was reproduced within the house. As the *forum* was the common meeting-space of the city, so the *atrium* was the common space of the house, by contrast with the private spaces of individual rooms. It was the point at which all the users of the house converged: the family, its visitors, the remembered presence of its ancestors, and its gods. Literary sources describe as a feature of the *atrium* area the *lectus genialis*, the symbolic marriage-bed on which was consummated the union of man and wife through which the *familia* was reproduced (in practice, archaeology has yet to discover such a bed). It is here in the *atrium* that the images of the ancestors, linked by their red threads (*stemmata*), were supposed to be displayed [144]; here too the household gods might be worshipped, including the *genius*, the birth-spirit of the master to which the slaves made offerings (again, archaeological evidence only partly bears out these ideals – fig. 7.6; cf. [261]).

329. Even without marriage-bed, ancestors and *genius*, the *atrium* was the ideal space in which the *paterfamilias* might hold court, stationed presumably in the *tablinum*, so carefully framed by the traditional layout of the vista,

7.6 Shrine of the household gods. Cf. [261].

perhaps traditionally enthroned on his chair of state, the *solium*. This was the location for the much-satirised morning ritual of reception of callers, the *salutatio* [216, 428]. Here outsiders came inside, and met the *paterfamilias* on his own ground, on his own terms. They might be relatively social equals, friends (*amici*), even intimate friends (*familiares*); they might be clear social inferiors, and be prepared to acknowledge formal dependency, as *clientes*, though few except freed slaves, foreign dependants or legal clients normally used this label. Whatever their status, the act of salutation in itself was an acknowledgement of some sort of superiority (a social superior came calling only under special circumstances, for a betrothal or an illness, not in the morning salutation). The *paterfamilias* in his home thus became a quasi-father even to outsiders: a *patronus*. Under the Empire, social convention might require you to address him as 'Master', *domine*, even if by rising from his chair and greeting you with a kiss he marked you as an equal, not a dependant.

330. All this is best seen idealistically, not legalistically. Patronage used to bulk large in discussions of Roman politics, and the noble patron was sometimes presented as wielding a sort of block-vote from a faithful army of *clientes* [10]. More recently, historians have come to see that, at least by the late Republic, the votes of humble clients can have had only a trivial political impact. Few of the social exchanges that took place in the real-life *atrium* can have been strictly speaking between patron and client. But that would not

7.7 Statue of a Roman matron; the pose and dress conform to a standard type signifying modesty (*Pudicitia*).

affect the potency of the image. The *atrium* created the setting for the paternalistic head of house to receive the homage of the outside world. It was a stage on to which the freedman too, lording it in his new house, might step, whatever the limitations of his clout in the world outside. Patronage was more an image of how good Romans behaved than a precisely defined set of practices. Placing behaviour in this framework helped the participants to feel like true 'Romans'.

331. The *atrium* was not exclusively a man's world. The wife, *materfamilias* to her family, and *matrona*, respected married woman in her long skirts (*instita*), to the outside world, was also a figure who carried authority and respect (fig. 7.7). Indeed, she was normally independent of the authority of her husband, not even technically part of his *familia*, enjoying financial and legal independence from his affairs. The matron too held court in the *atrium*. Cornelius Nepos, writing biographies of famous Greeks and Romans in the 40s BC, explains that one of the major contrasts between the two cultures lies in their treatment of women: whereas the Greek household segregates women in the *gynaeconitis*, 'the women's quarters', the Roman matron is found at the heart of the house, and shares her husband's social life. This contrast of Greek and Roman ways is borne out in detail by Vitruvius' prescriptions for the

7.8 Pompeian peristyle garden.

Greek and Italian house. Indeed, he comments that the Greek idea of the separate men's area, *andron*, is so strange to the Romans that they apply the word to a corridor. Far too little is known of how in practice the males and females of the Roman household organised their use of space: they may for instance have used the same spaces, but at different times, the *matrona* receiving her visitors or attending to the practicalities of household management after the man had departed for the *forum*. But the important point is that Roman family ideology did not distinguish the *atrium* as a male area. It was the hub of the activity of the whole house.

332. The *atrium* was not the only 'public' space of the house. From the second century BC onwards it became normal for the house to offer a second open space beyond the *atrium*. It formed a conscious contrast. If the *atrium* was like a *forum*, the heart of the business of the family as mini-city, the second space was like the country. This space should carry the characteristics of a garden – as can be seen even in the smallest houses which have room for no more than a plant tub and a painting of a garden on the walls. Ideally it would be surrounded by a colonnade, whence its label of 'peristyle'(fig. 7.8); houses with too little space for columned porticoes on all four sides might make do with at least a couple of brick pillars. Planted out with a rich variety of

flowers, shrubs and trees – roses, lilies, viburnum, daphne, strawberry-trees, oleanders, and in larger gardens fruit-trees and planes – the garden could be kitted out with 'luxury' accoutrements, particularly fountains and marble statuary of animals and rural gods.

333. This artificially constructed world of 'nature' provided a suitable context for a given range of activities. Roman life was divided between *negotium* and *otium*, 'business' and 'leisure' [429]. *Negotium* belongs to the sphere of public life, *otium* to private life; and within the house if the *atrium* is the place of business, the peristyle garden is the place of leisure, of pleasure and luxury rather than work and profit. Typically, the finest reception rooms of the house open on this area. They might have a variety of shapes and names, *triclinia*, *oeci*, *cenationes*, but all fulfilled the same function as places of entertainment, of communal eating and drinking in the afternoon and evening. The richer the household, the more such entertainment areas could be multiplied (a choice of *triclinia* is common) and extended, with private bath suites, libraries and other facilities.

334. Reception and entertainment were only one function of the house. It was also a place of work, in many senses. In a world without offices and factories, the house was where much manufacture and commerce took place [219]. There is no division of residential from commercial and industrial quarters of the city. Shops and workshops are found in the frontages of private residences. Where more space-consuming processes are needed, as in bakeries (fig. 7.9) and fulleries, they are incorporated into the house. Equally in the countryside, wine-presses (fig. 7.10) and reception rooms are found under the same roof even in luxurious villas. And pervasively the world of work was present in the persons of slaves [246]: supplying domestic services from portering to food preparation and from service at table to personal attendance, but also providing the workforce for commerce, manufacture and agriculture. Just as slaves were legally incorporated within the *familia*, they were physically part of the household. In larger houses we may guess at separable slave quarters, but even in those they will have been omnipresent. They were crucial too, as we shall see, to its sentimental structure.

335. The traditional Roman house with its double focus of *atrium* and peristyle is built around some of the primary oppositions of Roman social life: of public and private, town and country, business and leisure, industry and luxury, and temporally of morning and afternoon. It is less revealing than we might hope about the activities of the 'family' as we think of it, the nuclear unit of husband, wife and children. Thus the standard *triclinium* layout of three couches at right angles, each with room for three, reflects its conception not as a *family* eating-space for parents and children, but as the area where the family received its visitors at leisure. Children were supposed, if present, to

7.9 Bakery with mills for grinding flour in the background and a sales counter at the front.

7.10 Reconstructed wine-press. The horizontal beam carved with a ram's head was forced down by winding the rope at the front end and inserting wedges at the back, so as to put pressure on the box containing the grapes (at the middle).

remain at the foot of the couch, not recumbent like the adults. Even the Greek house, with its division in principle of women's quarters (i.e. private family area) from men's (i.e. entertainment area for outsiders) seems more focused on domesticity than the Roman.

336. This means that the architecture of the house casts little light on other questions one might like to put about family structure. Could, for instance, the house accommodate an extended family in which sons or daughters remained resident in the parental house after marriage, and married brothers and sisters continued to cohabit after the death of the parents? Doubtless some of the larger houses with several suites of rooms *could* have done so, but it is impossible to say of the large Roman house, with its scatter of bedrooms round both *atrium* and peristyle, and in upper rooms front and back, whether the extra bodies would have been extended family, guests, slaves, freedmen and other dependants, lodgers or what. Perhaps the most important asset of these larger houses, which in Pompeii at least seem to have been common, was the flexibility that allowed them to accommodate any of these possible categories.

337. The discussion has focused on the *atrium* house not because all or even most Romans lived in houses of this type, but because the Romans themselves thought of this house-type as representing Roman ideals. In a city like Pompeii, we find a wide range of other types. There are the one- or two-room shops incorporated in the façades of larger houses, often including a stairway to an upper apartment, which will have been not just the place of work but home to the shopkeeper and family. There are narrow, terraced houses with a front room, a covered central circulation space corresponding to the *atrium*, a back room, a kitchen and a small garden plot. But all of these live cheek by jowl with the *atrium* houses of which they are fragments or down-market versions.

338. Turn to the metropolis of Rome, and the situation is rather different. The port site of Ostia preserves the best examples of metropolitan housing types, and what makes the impression there are the imposing brick and concrete high-rise blocks, of as many as five or six storeys, which are subdivided by several doors and stairways, often leading straight upstairs from the street, to separate apartments which could be sublet to tenants (fig. 7.11). In Ostia we find a majority of such *insulae*, and a minority of *atrium* houses. Correspondingly, we learn from a register of the City of Rome in late antiquity that the *insulae* numbered around 44,000 against only about 1,700 *domus*, presumably houses of the *atrium* type. It is therefore common to suggest that it was only the well-off Romans who inhabited *atrium* houses, whereas the majority of ordinary and poor people lived as tenants packed into squalid high-rise blocks. But the metropolis was special, notorious for its exorbitant house prices and rents: we should not expect similar blocks in the majority of

7.11 Ostian high-rise architecture, with shops on the ground floor and apartments above: reconstruction drawing. Cf. [489].

Italian towns (there are none in Pompeii). And it is clear that at Rome it was not only the poor who lived in high-rise blocks: the bourgeoisie too lived like this, and even equestrians and senators are attested as renting *cenacula*, 'apartments'. As in many European cities today, rich and poor could live in the same apartment block, the poor in the smaller, darker, less desirable parts, the rich on the *piano nobile* (the grand first floor) or in penthouse suites. In Rome itself, then, the *atrium* house gradually became restricted to the super-rich, while in country towns it probably remained the norm. That helped the Roman conviction that Rome was degenerate and unnatural: *real* Romans lived in the country. And indeed, countryside rather than town was where the majority of the population must have lived. The *atrium* house, then, should be thought of as an ideal, not a norm.

The sentimental framework

Introduction

339. Law and domestic architecture played a clear part in dictating the context in which the family operated. What is much harder to define is the

series of ideals and expectations against which its emotional life was shaped. Because many of the laws and norms of the Roman family are so different from our own, it is easy to leap to the conclusion that the Roman family was a cold and heartless institution. It is harder to grasp that morality, sentiment and affection played a vital part in the Roman family too, but in different ways and distributed in different patterns from those familiar to ourselves.

340. One suggestion has been that there was a major shift in pattern between Republic and Empire; that the Republican family was essentially patriarchal and authoritarian, without much room for affection, and that under the Empire there was a shift to a 'companionate' marriage held together by a sense of moral obligation and affection. Although there may indeed have been some shift in expectations, this suggestion oversimplifies the relationship between the framework of sentimental ideals and expectations on the one hand, and practice on the other. Sentimental ideals and harsh legal powers may sit alongside each other, in potential conflict. They act as reference points by which the family may define itself and its own success and happiness. In the vast variety of individual experience, what the 'norm' was, as judged against these standards, was neither known to them, nor knowable to us. Bearing in mind this caution, we may look at the three dominant relationships of the family, of husband and wife, parent and child, and master and slave.

Husband and wife

341. Some of the arrangements of the Roman marriage appear to us heartless and unfeeling. In particular many now find marriage arrangements for political and financial ends alien and shocking. In theory, *patria potestas* meant that a father could hand over his daughter in marriage to anyone he liked to construct an alliance. The young Pompey's first marriage was to the daughter of his trial judge; the bystanders are supposed to have sung the wedding hymn when he was acquitted. Several marriages later, his union with Caesar's daughter sealed their alliance in the triumvirate. In law, a girl could be married at the onset of puberty, or even before, and there are numerous cases of girls married as young as 12. Cicero betrothed his daughter Tullia at 9; when she died aged 30, she had been married three times. No less cynical seems the casual way in which happy unions might be dissolved for political purposes. A notable victim of this was the future emperor Tiberius: when his son-in-law Agrippa died, Augustus made his stepson Tiberius divorce Agrippa's daughter Vipsania, to marry his widow Julia. The story goes that Tiberius was particularly fond of Vipsania (and suspicious of Julia), and missed her so badly that Augustus took steps to prevent them meeting again.

342. It is not difficult, therefore, to build up a picture of the Roman marriage as an emotional wilderness in which romance and affection had no place. Augustus, in urging his marriage laws, read out an old speech by a censor: the message was that though marriage was a disagreeable burden, it was nevertheless what the citizen owed to his country. One may point, for instance, to the plot of Virgil's *Aeneid*, which assumes that romance and duty pull in different directions; if Aeneas' heart draws him to Dido, his duty drags him off to Latium and a political match made (to the fury of an old suitor) with Lavinia. No less, the rich tradition of Roman love poetry from Catullus to Ovid turns on the assumption that the poet-lover's mistress is not, and could not be, his wife (whether because married to someone else, or of too low status). Ovid, indeed, put it bluntly: frustration and singing at closed doors is what keeps love going; wives can't be loved, because their husbands can have them when they want (*The Technique of Love* 3.585–6).

343. But these assumptions are contradicted by abundant evidence that strong marital affection both existed in reality, and was an ideal. If Tiberius' forced union to Julia shows political convenience overriding human feelings, his attitude towards Vipsania, no less the result of political matchmaking, shows that affection could grow even in such stony ground. At the least, marital harmony, *concordia*, was a standard expectation; and though matchmaking doubtless reduced the chances of *prior* affection, separation was an easier remedy to discord. But the ideal of a happy marriage was actual affection. Catullus' wedding hymn for two members of ancient noble families, Torquatus and Junia (poem 61), not only prays for the growth of love, *amor*, to entangle her mind like ivy in a tree, but explicitly urges sexual fidelity on the husband, to avoid adultery, abandon male favourites, and sleep close to the tender breasts of his wife. And it is hard to imagine a better image of the companionate marriage than the scenario which Lucretius imagines men fear to lose on their death:

No more will your happy home welcome you, nor your excellent wife and sweet children rush up to snatch your kisses and touch your heart with secret sweetness. (3.894–5)

Nor could we ask for a more tender picture of lifetime affection than Ovid's telling of the story of Baucis and Philemon, rewarded by the gods for their piety and mutual affection by transformation into intertwined trees (*Metamorphoses* 8.704ff.).

344. A good range of sources attest marital affection in action. When Cicero writes to his wife Terentia as 'light of my life' or 'most faithful and best of wives' and expresses his longing to see her (*Letters to Friends* 14.4) or when

Pliny writes to his Calpurnia in even more gushing terms ('I am seized by
unbelievable longing for you . . . I spend the greater part of the night haunted
by your image . . .', *Letters* 7.5), it makes little difference whether they really
meant it, or were just putting it on. This was an appropriate way of addressing
a Roman wife. Similarly the hundreds of gravestones that celebrate a wife's
long fidelity, and address her as *carissima*, 'dearest', *dulcissima*, 'sweetest',
rarissima, 'rarest', and the like, however conventional and stilted the sentiments expressed, demonstrate at least the envisaged possibility of strong
affection in marriage.

To Urbana, the sweetest, chastest and rarest of wives, who certainly has never been surpassed, and deserves to be honoured for living with me to her last day in the greatest
pleasantness and simplicity, with equal conjugal affection and hard work. I added these
words so that readers should understand how much we loved each other. (*CIL*
VI.29580, Rome)

345. There would be no point in attempting to weigh such passages against
others that indicate the opposite, such as Cicero's sad account to his friend
Atticus of the quarrelsome and unpleasant behaviour of Atticus' sister
Pomponia to Cicero's brother Quintus (*Letters to Atticus* 5.1), or Juvenal's
sixth satire, an extended diatribe against marriage, in which the conjugal bed
is depicted as a tigress' lair where the wife lies in wait to savage her spouse for
imagined infidelities, covering up her own affairs with her lovers (6.268ff.).
The question of whether more Romans were happy or sad in marriage would
be wholly unanswerable. The point is that the Roman marriage was a human
relationship susceptible to strong emotion, for good or bad. It was not normally contracted *because of* emotion, nor *for the purpose of* satisfying it (yet
Augustus is said to have been led to his marriage to the already married and
pregnant Livia by passion). But it was a circumstance in which man and
woman lived closely enough together to develop strong sentiment; and for
them as for us that sentiment could make or break a relationship.

Parent and child

346. We are equally liable to be misled about the parent–child bond. *Patria
potestas* sounds so oppressive as to give any child good ground for hating the
father, and it has been suggested that a deep resentment against paternal
authority was normal, and that parricide was a frequent result. That is pure
speculation: reports of sons actually murdering fathers are scarce, and little
evidence suggests widespread resentment. Again, horror stories can be bal-
anced against examples of strong affection, such as the extremely close

relationship between Cicero and Tullia, or the doting of the orator Regulus on his son which Pliny thought so overdone.

347. Certainly, there were several factors which might tend to make the parent–child bond more distant than in modern circumstances. A high rate of infant mortality may have led to parents hardening their hearts against loss. More important, child-care was extensively delegated to slaves: from the wet-nurse who suckled, to the nurses and minders who cared for the infant, to the pedagogues who superintended the growing child and its education. Gravestones of such *mammae* and *tatae* show that they certainly could be the focus of strong affection for the child. Moreover, at social levels where 'serial marriage' was common, children may have found themselves frequently separated from their mothers – though not necessarily so, for Augustus' daughter Julia remained close to her mother Scribonia despite the parental divorce within a year of her birth.

348. The Romans evidently had a highly authoritarian image of how a father should behave. Perhaps we should not take it too seriously when a father-figure like Seneca the Elder expostulates about the misbehaviour of the young: 'Our young men are lazy, their intellects asleep: no one can stay awake to take pains over a single honest pursuit. Libidinous delight in song and dance transfixes these effeminates. Braiding the hair, refining the voice till it caresses like a woman's, competing in bodily softness with a woman, beautifying themselves with disgusting fineries – this is the pattern our young men have set themselves' (*Controversies*, preface). Seneca is harping simultaneously on the theme of the moral decline of education in Imperial Rome, and on the perennial parental theme of children not being like what they were in *his* day. But his own sons seem to have learnt their lesson, and we find his most famous son, Seneca the Younger (tutor to the young Nero) expressing appreciation of such parental discipline:

When at last we have acquired some wisdom, and it becomes evident that we ought to love our parents for the very things that kept us from loving them – their admonitions, strictness and careful watch over our heedless youth – they are snatched away from us. Few parents reach the age when they can reap some reward from their children: the rest are aware of their sons only as burdens. (*On Benefits* 5.5.2)

349. Some have seen a particularly close bond in the father–daughter relationship (the fact that Cicero reveals so much of his feelings tips the scales here); others have laid emphasis on the Roman mother. Study of gravestones points to the particular poignancy felt by parents bereaved of teenage children. But even were we able to conduct a survey of such sentiment, it could scarcely reveal more than the deep diversity also experienced in the modern family. One can only say that strong affection, in spite of what seem to us unfavourable circumstances, was perfectly possible. What Roman morality demanded of the child was *pietas*, respectful obedience of the type also demanded by fatherland and gods. Affection was neither an alternative to respect for authority, nor incompatible with it. The resolution of the issue of how a father should best treat his sons offered by Terence's comedy *Adelphi* 'Brothers', allows affection to sit alongside authoritarianism. The strict brother Demea has proved no better than the indulgent brother Micio in producing a responsibly behaved son. At the end Demea pretends to see the light, and to abandon his pose of heavy father, and to win back everyone's affection by indulgence. But he is only parodying the slack Micio; and the children end up by agreeing that they would rather he corrected their adolescent excesses, and disciplined them, since he knows better.

Master and slave

350. To grasp the emotional alienness of the Roman family, we do best to focus on the slave [258, 245ff.]. Here if anywhere is the breeding-ground of hatred, and *patria potestas* in its least palatable form. It is fascinating that wives and children could in some limited ways be legally assimilated to slaves, for instance in marriage or adoption by sale, or in the shared institution of *peculium*. But the very similarities merely underlined the differences: no father was going to treat a son or a wife like a slave, for that would be a humiliation to the whole family. The status divide between slave and free was one of the fundamentals around which they organised their lives [411]. For a slave, the paternal power of life and death was not a legal fiction, but a daily reality. If we were in danger of forgetting that Roman slavery depended on the rule of fear, we need only recall that the penalty for a slave killing a master was the execution of the *whole* slave household. It is unnecessary to dramatise the regimen of beatings and torture, or to insist on the massive evidence for resistance, not just in the dramatic but rare form of armed insurrection on the Spartacus model, but also in the persistent and ubiquitous form of sullen non-cooperation, decried by frustrated owners as typical servile laziness and stupidity [298].

351. But given all this, it is much more remarkable to discover the extent of the evidence for affection between slave and owner, and far more of a challenge to our powers of interpretation. When confronted with the real friendship between Cicero and Tiro, the unfeigned grief of a Pliny or a Martial at the death of a young favourite, or the widespread signs of affection on tombstones, for nannies and nurses, for young favourites (*deliciae*) and concubines

or trusted old retainers, for slave foster-children (*alumni*), or on the part of slaves for beloved patrons, the temptation is to say that perhaps slavery cannot have been that bad after all. But to use the happiness of some to offset the misery of others (surely the majority) is pointless. What is illuminating is to see the place occupied by the slave in the Roman family structure and the light that casts on the family itself.

352. Legally, as we have seen, the concept of *familia* embraced the slave as much as the child. The family was defined by the control of the *paterfamilias*; those outside his *potestas*, the wife not under *manus*, the emancipated child, or the emancipated slave, were not part of the *familia*, though they might remain part of the household, the *domus* [412]. The emancipated slave (provided the act of giving freedom followed legal form) acquired the family name of the ex-owner and their civil status (i.e. Roman citizenship), and continued under limited obligation, but to a *patronus* not a *dominus*. On the other hand, a slave could not marry and form a family of his/her own while in slavery. In practice, masters allowed slaves to form unions; but the offspring of any slave-woman was automatically the slave of the *paterfamilias*, even if he subsequently gave freedom to the mother. Homebred slaves (*uernae*) were a vital way of keeping the household staffed, and could be treated as objects of special affection – they might indeed be fathered by the master himself, or might be brought up with his own children.

353. Slavery was embedded into family structure. Slaves could fulfil parallel functions to children and wives. If most Roman business was 'family business', the workforce and partners were supplied by slaves and freedmen [191]. An archive of business records like the dossier of the Sulpicii from Murecine near Pompeii shows not only how slaves acted for their masters in important financial transactions, but also how difficult it is to distinguish freedmen from freeborn among the principal actors. A freedman, like a son, might inherit the family business; even a slave could be left his freedom together with an inheritance in a will, though this might be as a dirty trick to saddle him with a bankrupt estate. Equally, slave-women acted as concubines to the master, and might on acquiring freedom become their wives: that was a specific circumstance under which freedom could be granted below the legal age of 30, and gravestones suggest it was common.

354. Slaves, that is to say, belonged to the sentimental as well as the legal structure of the family. The universal bond that held the family together was power and authority, the ability to reward and punish. Within that was the potential for every type of emotional relationship: hatred and resentment, love and devotion. Slaves willingly died for their owners, as the Romans were anxious to advertise (there are no cases of masters dying for slaves). Slaves

suckled, nursed, and brought up their future masters; attended and made love to them; assisted in their business ventures and catered for their pleasures. That close bonding took place in some cases was a welcome bonus, just as it was between husband and wife, or between parent and child. That does not mean that it was a normal or necessary condition of family life.

355. Slavery played a crucial role in the reproduction of the Roman family, as well as in its structure. We noted at the beginning of the chapter that an extraordinary proportion of the funerary commemorations of Roman Italy under the Empire seem to be of freedmen, and that they create our image of the Roman family as much as the freeborn or the nobility. The successful slave was the one who made him or herself thoroughly part of the owner's family: learning to speak Latin like a native, and to internalise Roman standards and values. This is where the legal equivalence of the father's power over children and slaves is important: though there was a world of difference between a freeborn child and a slave, the family was a structure which treated a slave *like* a child, and could consequently give membership of society. Though the stigma of slavery lasted, there was nobody so anxious to be a good Roman as a freedman. In this way, slavery and birth acted as alternative structures for reproducing the family: a freedman's freedman's freedman was as much of a Roman as a son's son's son, and a proud freeborn child (*ingenuus*) might himself be an ex-slave's child.

356. One final case-study may illustrate the strangeness of these legal and emotional relationships. In an upper apartment in the House of the Bicentenary at Herculaneum was found a basketful of documents recording a legal case held at Rome only a few years before the eruption of AD 79. The case was about the civil status of a girl calling herself Petronia Justa: was she freeborn or slaveborn? Her mother, Petronia Vitalis, had been slave to a couple, Petronius Stephanus and Calatoria Themis, who to judge from their names could have been ex-slaves themselves. Vitalis had been given her freedom many years before; but her daughter had been brought up in the household of Stephanus and Themis. Technically, the case turned on whether Justa was born before her mother was freed (in which case she remained a slave) or after (in which case she was free).

357. There were no documents to prove matters either way, and testimonies conflicted. One Petronius Telesphorus declares that he is a fellow-freedman of Vitalis, and knows that the daughter was born free, and recalls the negotiations with Stephanus and Themis to the effect that as they had brought up the girl, Vitalis should compensate them for the expenses of upbringing and take her back. Two other witnesses swear they were present at a discussion between Vitalis and Themis, and had heard Stephanus declare, 'Why do you begrudge

your daughter, since we treat her like a daughter?', which they think proves the girl was born free. But another witness, Calatorius Marullus, swears he was given his freedom by Themis at the same time as the girl, and so knows she is Themis' freedwoman.

358. Behind the legal case we can see a longer-standing battle between two women, the natural mother, Vitalis, and the foster-mother, Themis. It is not that the affection is all on the side of the natural mother, and that her former owner and his wife wish to brutalise the daughter. On the contrary, Vitalis has abandoned her child to their care (on her account willingly), and Stephanus and Themis openly declare that they regard her as their daughter, and indeed have eventually given her freedom. It is late in the day that Vitalis tries to take her child back, and finds that Themis doesn't want to let go. The battle for emotional possession between natural mother and foster-parent is familiar enough to us; what transforms the situation and makes it so alien is the legal and social background of slavery and manumission against which it takes place.

FURTHER READING

Keith R. Bradley, *Discovering the Roman Family* (New York, 1991)
Suzanne Dixon, *The Roman Family* (Baltimore, Md, 1992)
Jane F. Gardner and Thomas Wiedemann, *The Roman Household: A Sourcebook* (London, 1991)
Richard Saller, *Patriarchy, Property and Death in the Roman Family* (Cambridge, 1994)
Susan Treggiari, *Roman Marriage* (Oxford, 1991)

8
The Roman mind

Introduction

359. This chapter explores the way Romans defined themselves in a changing and expanding world, by means of religion, education and 'civilisation', attitudes to Western 'barbarians', to Greeks, Jews and Christians, philosophy and law [236–7]. The Romans are often seen as admirable, because they are the source of our own civilisation. But were the Romans really so decent as we imagine, and how like us were they? The study will draw mainly on the work of two educated, upper-class males, Cicero and the Younger Pliny. It is not necessarily valid for the whole of Roman society.

Gods and mortals

360. In the late 50s, at the height of the turmoil of the Republic [68], Cicero wrote *On the Laws*, a blueprint for an ideal, yet practical society. His model was a Greek one, *The Laws* of the philosopher Plato (fourth century BC), and Cicero's work combined Greek theory with Roman practice. The first laws with which Cicero deals are those governing the relations between gods and mortals (2.19–22). Cicero stresses the need for pious behaviour, but insists there is to be no private worship of unofficial deities. Festivals are to be duly performed and the Vestal Virgins are to guard the eternal flame. And to make all this possible, priests are to be appointed, some in charge of rites, others in charge of interpreting the signs sent from the gods. Cicero thus restates the principle that an ideal Roman society would give a prominent place to religion [254–5].

361. The religious system of Rome was indeed seen in the mid-second century BC by an informed outsider, the Greek historian Polybius, as a distinctive and admirable aspect of the state (6.56.6–15). The elaboration of the

235

rituals and the integration of religion into public and private life was far more extensive than in the Greek states familiar to Polybius. Though he puts his own gloss on all this, by saying that religion was an opiate for the Roman masses, he also argues that it helped to maintain the probity of the upper-class magistrates, who, unlike their Greek counterparts, were constrained by respect for the gods from stealing public money.

362. Roman self-consciousness about their religion was enhanced by the extraordinary growth of Roman power (the phenomenon that Polybius had set out to explain in his *History* [118]). By the early second century BC the Romans could say to a Greek city: 'that we are people who set quite the highest store on reverence towards the gods, one might surmise especially from the favour vouchsafed to us by the divine power on that account; indeed, we are persuaded also by many other considerations that our high regard for the divine power has been manifest'. The Romans might, not unreasonably, believe that their stupendous success was due to their peculiar piety towards the gods (see e.g. [125]).

363. Religious festivals helped to define the identity of Rome and her citizens [197–8]. The *Parilia*, for example, celebrated on 21 April, was a festival which was associated with Romulus and the founding of the city. And these associations were very much alive in the changed political circumstances of the first century BC. When news of a decisive victory by Caesar reached Rome while the Parilia was being celebrated, the coincidence (if that is what it was) was exploited in favour of Caesar, the new Romulus: an extra day of games was added to the Parilia at which crowns were worn in Caesar's honour. Cults also related to gender roles. The official cults of Rome were run principally by men, but some cults demanded the participation of women. For example, the flame of Vesta had to be tended by the six Vestal Virgins; the cult of the *Bona Dea* was in the hands of the wives of senators; and 110 matrons took part in the ceremonies of the Secular Games, one for each year of the *saeculum*. The system drew on women so far as was necessary for cults and rites of a peculiarly 'female' nature, and were one way of defining what women, and men, were.

364. The official cults of Rome were intimately bound up with the political life of the city. There was no distinction between Church and State. Indeed the major priests of Rome were senators, and were answerable ultimately to the Senate. The Senate itself held debates on major religious issues, and if a portent, such as the birth of a two-headed cow, occurred, it was the Senate that had to decide whether to refer it to one of the priestly college for their advice. In other words, the political hierarchy of the Roman republic [121ff.] was the *religious* hierarchy too.

365. An example of the link between religion and politics in the Republic is the rules for meetings of the Senate and people. The Senate had to meet in a specially defined ritual space, a *templum*, whether that was the ordinary Senate-house in the Forum or an actual temple of a god. This was designed to ensure that discussions of the Senate met with divine favour. Meetings of the people also needed divine favour. The consuls had to watch the skies at the meeting in case there was an unfavourable divine portent, such as a flash of lightning; if they saw one, they had immediately to dissolve the meeting. This procedure came under severe pressure in the late Republic. In 59 BC, when Caesar was pushing through some controversial land legislation, his fellow consul, who opposed it, fearing for his life, stayed at home to watch the skies, and declared that he had indeed seen an unfavourable portent, which invalidated the legislation. (see also [69, 121]). Scholars used to see this as blatant manipulation of religion for political ends. In fact it shows the intimate connection between the two: when political life was in turmoil, religious rules inevitably came under strain.

366. With the ending of the Republic the role of the Senate changed [187ff.]. It of course retained much prestige, and the Younger Pliny was very proud to have been appointed to one of the priesthoods, even younger than Cicero (*Letters* 4.8), but the emperor, as *pontifex maximus*, was believed to control all sacred and religious matters. Appropriately enough, the portents of the two-headed-cow type, which signified general disruption of the religious system, were largely replaced by the reporting of portents at the birth or death of emperors. The emperor was now seen as the central figure of the religious, as of the political, system.

Civilisation and barbarism

Introduction

367. One way in which the Roman élite sought to define themselves in a changing world around them was by their education and culture [421–2]. Since the earliest times non-Romans had acquired Roman citizenship and political rights at Rome [27]. Though most never achieved any prominence in Rome, some of those from well-established families from other towns did: Cicero from Arpinum in Umbria (consul 63 BC [67]); the Younger Pliny from Comum in northern Italy (consul AD 100); the historian Dio Cassius from Prusa in Bithynia (consul *c.* AD 205 and 229). This remarkable absorption of local élites into the Roman élite, so unlike either the Athenian or the British empires, rested on cultural foundations [109–10].

8.1 Mosaic showing the rape of Europa, accompanied by an elegiac couplet referring to Virgil's *Aeneid*: 'If jealous Juno had seen the swimming of the bull, more justly would she have gone to the house of Aeolus.'

Roman education

368. The spread of Roman culture in the West was made possible by the teaching of a fairly standard curriculum to sons of the local élites. The first step was the learning of Latin. In most of Italy by the time of Augustus this was learned at home as the first and only language, but in recently conquered lands it was a language to be laboriously acquired by anyone who desired advancement. And pronunciation had to be watched. The future emperor Hadrian, who came from an Italian family settled in Spain, was laughed at in the Senate for his reading of a speech in an uncultured manner, and promptly applied himself to improving his Latin (Writers of Imperial History, *Hadrian* 3.1).

369. Between roughly the ages of 7 and 11 children learned to read and write Latin: some also began to learn Greek. The backbone of the next stage, from age 12 to 15, was the study of language and literature either at home with a personal tutor or (for boys only) in public with a *grammaticus*. Under the Empire a primary position was given to Virgil's *Aeneid*. Knowledge of this can be seen in mosaics from Britain (fig. 8.1) and in graffiti from Pompeii quoting

8.2 A school-scene. Cf. [421].

the opening lines of the first two books [415]. The *Aeneid* and other works were used by students both to practise their reading aloud, and to develop their ability to comment on grammar, figures of speech, and the writer's use of mythology. The value ascribed to such minute examination, a world apart from our contemporary emphasis on 'empathy', was itself reflected in the way that new works of literature were composed; cf. [448].

370. From literature boys moved on at 16 or so to rhetoric, which they studied in public lectures. Pliny himself attended lectures at Rome in Latin rhetoric from Quintilian and in Greek from one Nicetes (*Letters* 2.14, 6.6). The spread of such schools (fig. 8.2; cf. [370]) is illustrated by Pliny's concern to establish one in his native Comum, so that boys could be educated there rather than in Milan, some 25 miles away; he asked his friend Tacitus to find a suitable teacher of Latin from among his current pupils (4.13). Similar schools are found in central Gaul in the early first century AD, and in Britain in the generation after the Roman conquest.

371. Rhetoric generally has a bad name today. We value 'sincerity' over 'artifice', and our modern preference poses real problems for our appreciation both of Latin and of Renaissance English literature (see [445]). As C.S. Lewis once said, 'Rhetoric is the greatest barrier between us and our ancestors . . . Nearly all our older poetry was written and read by men to whom the distinction between poetry and rhetoric, in its modern form, would have been meaningless.' Some Romans too questioned the details of rhetorical education and considered whether with the death of political freedom under the Empire, rhetoric still had an important role. And yet a good case can be made in favour of rhetoric. There were two main types of rhetorical exercise: *suasoriae* and *controuersiae*. In *suasoriae* pupils took incidents from myth or history and argued over them: should Scipio cross to Africa [32]? Should Caesar accept the kingship [73]? These exercises obviously helped to develop boys' skills in con-

structing arguments. In *controuersiae*, pupils argued difficult cases in law, many of which were clearly fictitious. Pliny's teacher Quintilian gave an example familiar in his day (*An Orator's Education* 7.2.17): a son banished from home studies medicine. When his father falls ill, and all the other doctors despair of saving him, the son is summoned and says that he can cure him, if the father drinks the medicine he gives him. The father, having drunk part of the medicine, says that he has been poisoned. The son drinks the rest, but the father dies, and the son is accused of parricide. The pupil had to devise arguments for and against the accused. Pliny himself in middle age attended lectures by a visiting Greek rhetorician and noted the relative unreality of the cases, but he still defended the practice. 'The imaginary cases in the schools and lecture-halls do no harm with their blunted foils and are none the less enjoyable, especially to the old, who like nothing so much as to witness the joys of their youth' (*Letters* 2.3). And some could be less irrelevant than they seemed at first sight. Rome saw many cases of alleged poisoning, and Cicero, facing the rise to power of Caesar, took his mind off the current crisis by composing arguments, in Greek and Latin, about whether a man should remain in his country under a tyranny (*Letters to Atticus* 9.4). The apparently artificial world of the rhetorical school did positively prepare its pupils for both the law courts and political life. The value of this educational system gradually received official recognition. At Rome from the time of Julius Caesar onwards, there were privileges for teachers who were also Roman citizens, and the emperor Vespasian founded two chairs for the teaching of Greek and Latin rhetoric (Quintilian was the first holder of the Latin chair). Outside Rome, teachers of grammar and rhetoric were granted exemption from civic obligation, again by Vespasian. The point is that the emperors wanted to provide access to education, which they hoped would help to integrate local élites into the Roman élite. They also hoped that their patronage of rhetoric, a fundamental characteristic of Roman civilisation, would help to legitimate their rule.

Town and country

372. Another way in which the Roman élite reinforced its identity was by self-consciously adopting 'urbane' values. In the late Republic there was a strong sense of the merits of the city as against the countryside [200–1]. Catullus' poems are full of the terms 'urbane', 'witty', and 'charming'; Suffenus unfortunately lost the right to these qualities by writing too many verses (poem 22), while Asinius Marrucinus was told firmly that it was not amusing to steal napkins at dinner parties (poem 12). But the counterpart to

this positive evaluation of the city and denigration of rustic boors was a sense that the city was over-refined, and even depraved, while the countryside was the repository of real virtue. So Cicero once defended one Roscius from Ameria on a charge of murdering his father. He argued that Roscius, a mere country bumpkin, who had allegedly been banished by his father to the countryside, was in fact framed by the Roman city-dwellers who had actually committed the murder, and he went on to allude to the idea that the luxury of the city bred such crimes (*In Defence of Roscius of Ameria* 20.44.74–5). Virgil's *Georgics*, written after the civil wars that ended the Republic, contains an idealisation of the Italian countryside.

373. Pliny had genuine difficulty in reconciling these values. On the one hand, he is conscious that Rome is the real focus for living. He once castigated an acquaintance who had withdrawn from Rome to a distant part of Italy: 'When are you ever returning to the city, back to our duties and honours, your friendships with superiors and inferiors? How much longer will you be your own master, stay up when you feel inclined, and sleep as long as you like?' (*Letters* 7.3). And he was amazed to find that another acquaintance who had retired to the countryside turned out to be not just a fine father and farmer, but also a formidable scholar in both Latin and Greek (*Letters* 7.25). On the other hand, Pliny himself values his two country retreats, one near Rome, the other at Tifernum Tiberinum; two long letters are devoted to showing how they were the setting for an appropriate form of relaxation (*Letters* 2.17, 5.6; fig. 8.3). *Otium* ('leisure'), for Pliny, made sense only as a temporary escape from *negotium* ('non-leisure'), the daily round in Rome [428].

Rome and the Western provinces

374. The position of the Roman élite had also to be defined and defended in relation to other groups in the Roman empire. In general there was a sense of self-righteousness. Roman civilisation justified the empire, and hence the Roman élite. Pliny's uncle, the Elder Pliny, wrote that Italy was

a land which is the nurseling and mother of all other lands, chosen by the divine might of the gods, to make heaven itself more glorious, to unite dispersed empires, to temper manners, to draw together in mutual comprehension by community of language the warring and uncouth tongues of so many nations, to give mankind *humanitas* and in a word to become throughout the world the single fatherland of all peoples. (*Natural History* 3.5.39)

375. The sense of Italy as the conveyer of humane values is summed up in Tacitus' description of an incident in the conquest of Britain. When the

Romans engaged with British forces on the island of Anglesey, off the north coast of Wales, they found themselves facing women brandishing torches like Furies, and Druids calling down dreadful curses. Having conquered the island, the Romans at once suppressed the Druids and destroyed the groves which had been dedicated to the gruesome practice of human sacrifice (Tacitus, *Annals* 14.30). For the Elder Pliny, the suppression of such 'superstition' was a key example of Roman *humanitas*. 'One cannot calculate how great a debt is owed to the Romans for having swept away these monstrosities in which to kill a person was an extremely religious act, and to eat him guaranteed one's well-being' (*Natural History* 30.4.13). The Roman empire had a civilising purpose and hence rationale.

376. It was, then, easy to define the Roman élite in relation to the population of recently conquered Western provinces: they were uncivilised and barbarous, hardly deserving a relationship with mighty Rome. The year after Cicero had prosecuted Verres for extortion in Sicily [180], he undertook the defence of another provincial governor on the same charge. Fonteius, a governor of Gallia Transalpina (southern France), had allegedly plundered the local population but (unlike Verres) he had been careful to collaborate with the

8.3 Model of Pliny's Laurentine villa, based on the description in one of his letters.

8.4 Claudius' speech on the admission of Gauls to the Roman Senate. Cf. [97].

Roman businessmen in the province. Cicero dismissed the accusers as mere barbarian natives:

If we just look at the individuals concerned – and that surely ought to count most in weighing up a witness – can any Gaul however respectable be compared, I will not say with the leading men of our own country, but even with the humblest citizen of Rome? Does Indutiomarus really *know* what it is to give evidence? When he comes before this court, does that same awe which strikes each one of us strike him? (*In Defence of Fonteius* 12.27)

Of course this is the line that Cicero had to adopt in defence of his client, but its success illustrates the fatal flaw in the legal procedure designed to prevent extortion by Roman officials [44, 184]. And this attitude to provincials persisted to some extent under the empire. When in AD 48 leading men from Gallia Comata ('Long-haired Gaul', i.e. the part of France conquered by Caesar) sought the right to stand for senatorial office in Rome, some senators felt that such men, whose ancestors resisted Caesar, should not usurp the position of senators from Rome and the neighbouring parts of Italy. The emperor Claudius spoke in favour of the Gauls' application, and some did win the *right* to hold senatorial office (Tacitus, *Annals* 11.23–5: fig. 8.4, cf. [97]). But it is perhaps telling that we do not hear of any who actually did. Few senators would vote for a Gaul over one of their own kind.

377. As with the opposition between urban and rural values, the usual evaluation of Rome and Western barbarians could be inverted. Some Romans used barbarian values to highlight deficiencies in Roman ones. Tacitus, for example, composed an ethnographic treatise on the Germans, who were never part of the Roman empire, and described them as quite different from Romans, but also as in some ways superior: they were the repositories of a simpler and superior set of moral values that had been lost at Rome. And in his biography of his father-in-law Agricola (governor of Britain AD 78–85), Tacitus puts into the mouth of the British leader Calgacus a brilliant denunciation of Roman imperialism which includes the famous saying 'To robbery, murder and pillage they give the false name of Empire, and when they make a wilderness they call it Peace' (*Agricola* 30–2). But Calgacus' speech does not represent Tacitus' final judgement on Roman imperialism. Tacitus was giving Calgacus a speech appropriate to the occasion; and he gave Agricola an answering speech too. Calgacus lost the following battle.

Romans and Greeks

378. Relations between Romans and Greeks were a much more complex matter. On the one hand the Greeks were a conquered people, suspected of effeteness, and indeed effeminacy. Pliny as governor of Pontus–Bithynia can talk condescendingly about how Greeklings go in for gymnastics (*Letters* 10.40), and (somewhat like Cicero before him) denigrated the Greek witness accusing a senator of provincial extortion (*Letters* 4.9). But on the other hand Romans had an immense respect for Greek culture [40–3, 436, 439]. Cicero, defending the Greek poet Archias on a charge of illegally claiming Roman citizenship, makes great play of the greater glory gained by writing Greek rather than Latin poetry:

For Greek literature is read in nearly every nation under heaven, while Latin is confined to its own boundaries, and they are, we must grant, narrow. (*In Defence of Archias* 10.23)

Indeed, Archias had started on a Greek poem in celebration of Cicero's own consulship. Not only might contemporary Greek poets be prized, but, as we have seen, Romans themselves, who boasted of their proficiency in both languages, might compose in Greek. Pliny reports his precocious writing at the age of 14 of a Greek tragedy (*Letters* 7.4). As for art, copies of Greek sculpture were to be found in upper-class Roman homes from the first century BC onwards (fig. 8.5), and sculptors who created work for the Romans, whether

8.5 Artemis: Roman copy of a Greek statue, perhaps by the great
Athenian artist Praxiteles (fourth century BC). Cf. [470].

portable or monumental relief sculptures, were themselves all Greek. Further,
intellectual life in Rome was marked by borrowings from Greek predecessors
and a sense of the merits of Roman ways (we shall return shortly to the question of philosophy).

379. These fluctuating feelings about Greeks are most evident in the sphere
of Roman government. Pliny, writing to a friend going out to govern the affairs
of mainland Greece, advised him to remember that he was to be dealing with
the place where *humanitas*, writing and even agriculture itself were believed to
have been discovered (*Letters* 8.24). But the respect that Pliny thought he was
showing this ancient 'theme park' is deeply condescending; there was no
doubt where power and ultimate superiority lay. Only gradually did Greeks
come to hold office in Rome (a good example is Dio Cassius [367]). It was
unthinkable in Cicero's day, and still a rarity in the time of Pliny. For example,
apart from the descendants of Italian families settled in the Greek world (like
Pliny's friend and coeval Cornutus Tertullus), the only Greeks to achieve the
consulate in the early second century came either from one or two extraordinarily wealthy families (e.g. Gaius Antius Aulus Julius Quadratus, consul AD
94 and 105) or were descendants of former client kings loyal to Rome
(e.g. Gaius Julius Antiochus Philopappus, consul AD 109) (fig. 8.6). Greeks
generally were kept in their proper place.

8.6 Funerary monument of Philopappus on the Hill of the Muses,
Athens (AD 114–16).

Romans and Jews

380. Romans were even more ambivalent about Jews. Defending Lucius
Flaccus, governor of the Greek-speaking province of Asia, on a charge of
extortion, Cicero first denigrates the Greeks of Asia as unreliable, unstable
and greedy. He then tackles the hatred Flaccus had incurred when he confiscated and gave to the treasury gold which the Jews (as was traditional) were
sending from Asia to Jerusalem. Cicero falls into a mock whisper, so as not to
incite the Jewish bystanders who were allegedly capable of inciting public
meetings, and then argues that Jewish ways were a barbarian *superstitio*,
incompatible with the majesty of the Roman empire, which Flaccus was perfectly entitled to overrule (*In Defence of Flaccus* 27.64–28.69). The subsequent troubles Rome had with its province of Judaea only hardened the
attitudes of some Romans. Tacitus prefaced his account of Rome's suppression of the Jewish revolt (AD 66–70) (fig. 8.7; cf. fig. 3.1 and [122, 485]) with an
ethnography of the Jews, which is an extraordinary mixture of good information and garbled assertions. Some 'bizarre' Jewish practices, such as abstain-
ing from pork or resting on the seventh day, are sanctioned by their antiquity,
'but other practices, such as misanthropy or circumcision, are completely
without justification' (Tacitus, *Histories* 5.4–5).

381. But such hostility was not the whole story. Only a decade after Cicero

8.7 The spoils from the defeat of the Jews in AD 70. Cf. [125, 485].

was defending Flaccus, the learned antiquarian writer Varro identified the god of the Jews with Jupiter, seemingly on the grounds that, like Jupiter, Jahweh was their supreme god. He also quoted Jewish condemnation of religious images in support of his view that in the good old days the Romans had worshipped the gods without any images. This sympathetic understanding of Jewish religion was taken further by other Romans in the early Empire. Some began to observe aspects of the Jewish law, such as abstinence from pork and resting on the sabbath, while others actually became full proselytes, underwent circumcision and considered themselves as bound by the whole Jewish code. But in the eyes of people like Tacitus and Pliny either position was an unacceptable abandonment of traditional Roman ways.

Romans and Christians

382. Roman reactions to the Christians have always been a problem for apologists of the Roman empire. If the Romans were in general tolerant imperialists, not aiming to impose Roman ways on their subjects, why did they execute people for being Christians? But in fact Romans often *did* seek to regulate religious practices. Their repugnance toward Druidic human sacrifice led to its prohibition in Gaul and Britain. Jewish practices, bizarre though some were felt to be, were defensible by their antiquity, but a Roman who adopted

them was seen as a threat, and pressure to conform to Roman ways sometimes took legal form. For example, Tacitus records the trial of Pomponia Graecina, wife of Claudius' general Aulus Plautius, on a charge of foreign *superstitio*. She underwent a preliminary hearing before the Senate, and was then tried by her husband (*Annals* 13.32). A good guess is that she was suspected (wrongly as it turned out) of having converted to Judaism.

383. This background helps to explain the way Pliny treated the Christians. When as governor he was doing the legal circuit of Pontus–Bithynia, some locals denounced before him a group of (alleged) Christians (*Letters* 10.96–7). Pliny, who elsewhere seems so decent and even kind, had in general no doubts as to what he should do. He executed non-Roman citizens who admitted that they were Christians, and sent Roman citizens to Rome for trial. He was uncertain on only two points: first, what constituted guilt? (Was it enough merely to profess Christianity? Or was evidence of other criminal actions necessary? He decided on the former.) And, what should be done with those who had once been Christians, but were no longer? (The emperor Trajan agreed that they should be pardoned.)

384. The evidence of Pliny shows that by the early second century AD the execution of confessed Christians was a normal (if not necessarily common) practice. Both Roman citizens and non-Roman citizens were perceived to have transgressed some boundary. The test which Pliny imposed on those before him helps to show what the problems were for the Romans. He demanded that alleged Christians invoke the gods and perform a sacrifice of incense and wine to the image of the emperor. Praying to 'our gods', as Trajan calls them, and making an offering for the emperor were made the criteria for both political and religious propriety. Those who refused to conform must hate the Roman race, surely indulged in monstrous practices, and were generally hostile to the accepted (i.e. Roman) order of things. The execution of Christians thus has a frightening logic [256–7].

Philosophy and society

385. The tension between Roman and Greek noted above [378–9] is particularly striking in the context of philosophical thought. Here Romans of the late Republic and early Empire were faced with well-established and extremely articulate systems of Greek thought. How could Romans make this thought their own, and reshape Greek philosophy to serve Roman ends?

386. Cicero is the key figure in the story, the first person to write philosophy in Latin prose [67–8]. He was faced with three major Greek philosophical schools. The Epicureans, named after their founder Epicurus (341–274 BC:

fig. 8.8, App. 2 (Epicurus)), argued that pleasure was the goal of life, and that the virtues were important only if they resulted in pleasure. They also claimed that the gods had no involvement in human affairs. Though the Roman poet Lucretius had made a passionate defence of Epicurean doctrines about the gods (see App. 2), Cicero firmly rejected both Epicurean positions. First, Epicurean official doctrines conflicted with his sense that pleasure was contrary to decency; second, their view of the gods was tantamount to atheism. Despite Lucretius' work, Epicureans never became popular at Rome.

387. The second major school was that of the Stoics, founded by Zeno of Citium (335–263 BC: App. 2 (Zeno)). Under the influence of Panaetius (*c.* 185–109 BC: App. 2 (Panaetius)), Stoicism had a major influence on upper-class Romans. Panaetius held that the philosopher should help those who aimed to progress in virtue and wisdom, rather than just the wise man, and he made Stoic ethics relevant to the demands of public life. In the first century AD some Roman senators who felt that their personal position had been made intolerable by the almost tyrannical power of the emperor justified their opposition to particular emperors in terms of Stoic philosophy. Under Nero, for example, Thrasea Paetus was notorious for his adherence to Stoicism, and was finally forced by the emperor to commit suicide. Not that Stoicism was necessarily a subversive philosophy. It was perfectly compatible with the

8.8 Bust of Epicurus.

'proper' exercise of imperial power, and offered many reflections on matters of practical ethics. Seneca, for example, also under Nero, wrote treatises on such matters as the control of anger and the performance of good deeds (cf. [398] on his *On Clemency*).

388. Cicero was at times greatly impressed by Stoic writings, but his own position was that of the Academy, the third major school in his day. For the Peripatetic School, which took its lead from Aristotle (384–322 BC), was unimportant in the late Republic, though it was to revive under the Empire. The traditions of the Academy went back to Plato (*c.* 429–347 BC), but by Cicero's day, Plato's works were seen as posing questions rather than imposing answers, and Academicians themselves came to be sceptical about the possibility of attaining the truth. They were thus hostile to the certainties claimed by other schools, especially the Stoics. Their followers, however, did not merely sit on the fence. In the late Republic one of their most illustrious pupils was Brutus, who led the conspiracy against Caesar [73–4]. Brutus' family traditions and familiarity with the Greek philosophical arguments against tyranny combined to force him into action against the 'tyrant' Caesar, and for 'freedom'. Cicero adopted the position of his own teachers that though certainty was impossible, one should carefully consider the arguments of others and provisionally accept the position that seemed the best.

389. Two topics will illustrate the use of philosophy by Cicero and by later Roman writers: religion and politics. Cicero's work *On Divination* is particularly interesting. The work is in two books. The first argues in favour of divination. It takes many of its arguments from Stoicism, which saw divination as an aspect of divine providence, but roots them firmly in Roman practice. For example, just before Caesar's assassination [73], at sacrifices on consecutive days the sacrificial animal was found to lack a heart and a crucial part of the liver. 'These portents were sent by the immortal gods to Caesar that he might foresee his death, not that he might prevent it' (1.52.119). Though Caesar ignored the warning, this and numerous other examples of portents were, at least in retrospect, accurate warnings of the future. Divination did actually work. Indeed, Cicero was himself an *augur*, responsible for the interpretation of some signs from the gods, and many thought the prosperity of the Roman State depended on the maintenance of its system of divination [120].

390. The second book, bewilderingly, seems to take the opposite view and argue that, though divination may *seem* to work, it is theoretically indefensible. The heart could not have been missing from Caesar's first sacrificial animal. The living animal of course needed one, and it could hardly have disappeared into the air at the moment of sacrifice. No scientist could accept that there are some things that just suddenly become nothing (2.16.36–7). Thus

book 2 takes up most of the positive Stoic arguments advanced in book 1 and asserts they are wrong.

391. There is clearly a problem in understanding the relations between books 1 and 2 of *On Divination*. Scholars used to assume that it was evidence for a general decline in belief in traditional Roman religion, but that is too simple an answer: the theoretical arguments of book 2 would not worry any Roman who was sure that divination did in practice work. The point surely is that book 2 is in part the product of Cicero's Academic position:

It is the character of the Academy to put forward no conclusion of its own, but to approve that which seems to approach nearest the truth; to compare arguments; to draw forth all that may be said on behalf of any opinion; and, without asserting any authority of its own, to leave the judgement of the enquirer wholly free. (2.72.150)

But that position, which results in Cicero's failure to produce positive arguments of his own, is itself symptomatic of the difficulty of reconciling Roman practice with Greek theories.

392. That difficulty was, however, much reduced by subsequent Roman authors who developed the Stoic position so that it became generally compatible with traditional Roman practices. The basic doctrine was that a benevolent providence governed the world, and was compatible with the gods, with the fates and with nature. Consequently there was no clash between traditional beliefs about the gods and theoretical arguments against them, and it was possible for a Roman emperor, Marcus Aurelius (AD 121–80), to be a convinced Stoic, and indeed to write the *Communings with Himself*. Rather as Dag Hammarskjöld wrote his *Markings* when he was Secretary General of the United Nations, Marcus composed a series of philosophical reflections which abstracted the general from the particular and were designed to relate Stoic philosophy to his actual life. He was convinced that the gods, with providence, fortune and nature, were jointly responsible for the well-being of the world, and that it was his duty to display piety to the gods:

To those who ask the question, 'Where have you seen the gods, or from where have you learned that they exist, that you worship them in this manner?' I answer: First, they are visible even to the eyes; secondly, I have not seen my own soul and yet I honour it; and so, too, with the gods, from my own experiences every instant of their power I apprehend that they exist and I do them reverence. (12.28)

Marcus' work, which has inspired subsequent generations, epitomises the differences between the religious impasse reached by Cicero's philosophy and the justification of religious practices provided by subsequent Roman Stoicism.

393. Roman philosophical writing on politics is also very instructive. Here there was no theoretical difficulty of the sort faced by Cicero on divination: instead there were various more or less theoretical arguments addressed to the contemporary political system. Philosophy helped to define a position from which the present could be criticised.

394. Cicero's treatise *On Duties* is a general formulation of Roman political and ethical values, and very influential on subsequent Western political thought. This last philosophical work by Cicero was written during the crisis that followed the assassination of Caesar.

> I only wish that the Republic had remained in its original condition, rather than fall into the hands of men greedy not merely for change, but for revolution. For first I would be devoting my energies to action rather than writing, as I used to while the Republic was still standing. Secondly, it would be my own speeches rather than my present subject matter that I would be putting on paper, as I have often done before. (2.1.3)

Against this background Cicero set out his views of how society ought to work. However, this is no lament by a failed politician, but a rigorous philosophic tract. Though book 2 of *On Divination* had attacked Stoic views, in accordance with his general Academic position, Cicero here presents Stoic arguments (first advanced a century before by Panaetius) as those which are the most convincing.

395. According to Cicero, there are four principal virtues: wisdom, or the search for truth; social virtue, concerned with fellowship between individuals; the greatness and strength of a lofty and unconquered spirit; and seemliness, or an order and limit in everything that is said and done. Book 1 shows how duties are based on the four virtues; book 2 investigates the class of duties that relates to civilised living and to the availability of the influence and wealth that people find beneficial; and book 3 handles the apparent conflicts between what is good and what is advantageous.

396. Cicero is clear about the duty to participate as fully as possible in public life (1.20.69–26.91). One should not snootily despise holding office and civic magistracies and simply devote oneself to a life of philosophic learning. (This sentiment chimes in with other statements of the proper place for *otium* [373].) Nor should one rate military higher than civic affairs in a deluded pursuit of glory. (This view ran counter to the whole recent history of Rome in which pursuit of military glory had been paramount [61–6].) And those who do engage in politics should act for the benefit not of themselves, but of the citizens, and should care for the whole body of the republic rather than promote one factional interest. Here too Cicero stands against the naked ambition of contemporary dynasts who incited the people against the senatorial class for their own personal gain [45, 63–70]. So, for example, when Cicero argues that

liberality to the community is a proper means of gaining support only if it is
properly directed (2.21.72–24.85), he is able to quote many examples of mis-
directed liberality from the recent history of Rome: 'those who wish to present
themselves as *populares*, and for that reason attempt agrarian legislation so
that landholders are driven from their dwellings [46–7], or propose that
debtors ought to be excused from the money they owe, are undermining the
very foundations of the political community' (2.22.78).

397. As for the conflict between apparent advantage and goodness, Cicero
comes down firmly on the side of the virtues. 'Is there any matter so valuable
or any advantage so desirable that you would abandon the name and splen-
dour of a good name for it? . . . Why do we collect petty examples – fraudulent
inheritances, trading and sales? Here you have a man [Caesar] who longed to
be king of the Roman people and master of every nation; and he achieved it! If
anyone says that such greed is honourable, he is out of his mind; for he is
approving the death of laws and liberty and counting their oppression – a foul
and hateful thing – as something glorious' (3.20.82–21.83). It is thus hardly
surprising that Cicero held that it was honourable to kill such tyrants (3.4.19,
3.6.32). Cicero the Academic thus propounds the view of his friend Brutus,
and it was understandable (if inexcusable) that Mark Antony should have
Cicero executed the year after *On Duties* was written.

398. A century later the Stoic philosopher Seneca addressed a treatise *On
Clemency* to the young emperor Nero [98–100]. This, the first extant piece of
Roman political philosophy since Cicero, also brings Greek philosophic arguments to bear on contemporary politics. The premise from which Seneca
begins is that Nero has absolute power. He suggests that if Nero considers his
position he will say: 'I am the arbiter of life and death for the nations; it rests in
my power what each person's lot and state shall be; by my lips Fortune pro-
claims what gifts she would bestow on each human being . . .' (1.1.2). This bold
statement, which runs counter to many of our expectations about the low
profile of good emperors [78–118], expresses Seneca's view of the realities of
power. The issue for him was how this power was to be exercised. He hoped
that Nero would say to himself: 'With all things thus at my disposal, I have been
moved neither by anger nor by youthful impulse to unjust punishment, nor by
others' rashness and obstinacy, which have often broken the patience of even
the most easy-going people, nor yet by that self-display which employs terror
for the display of might, a fearsome practice, common among mighty powers'
(1.1.3). Clemency, for Seneca, consisted in restraint in the exercise of absolute
power. If Nero possessed that virtue, he would be a king; if not, a tyrant. This
contrast made perfect sense at Rome. Caesar, as we have seen, could be condemned and even killed as a tyrant, while 'king' could be seen as an honourable

title. (The tradition about the original kings of Rome was not unanimous, but at least some of them such as Numa and Servius Tullius were unambiguously admirable figures [8–9].) Seneca thus locates Nero's options both in a Greek philosophical tradition and in the memories of the Roman past.

399. The hope that Nero would abstain from abuse of his power was sadly not realised, and Seneca himself was later forced to commit suicide because of his implication in a failed plot against Nero. The principles underlying his treatise had always been very risky; too much hung on the moral character of the individual emperor. But they were all too appropriate for the Julio-Claudian period, which was characterised by the actions of extremely colour-ful emperors [89–100]; Tacitus was quite right in his *Annals*, written two generations later, to focus on the characters of Tiberius, Claudius and Nero.

400. By the time Tacitus was writing, emperors had realised their absolute power could make them unpopular and they reverted to an Augustan empha-sis on the subordination of the emperor to the institutions of the state. This new ideology is expressed for us most clearly in Pliny's *Panegyric*, whose origi-nal version was delivered in AD 100 in the Senate before the emperor Trajan (*Letters* 3.18). This speech is not a philosophical statement, but it is a good example of Roman political thought. Apparently complacent, the speech in fact offers up a political ideal to which Pliny hopes Trajan will conform (105–6).

401. The leading idea of the speech is that of *ciuilitas*, that the emperor behaves, or should behave, like an ordinary citizen or at least like an ordinary senator. At his first entry to Rome as emperor in the previous year, Trajan entered on foot (not in a grand triumphal carriage), mingled fully with the crowd (without an entourage of toadies), and embraced members of the Senate, members of the equestrian order and his own private *clientes* as when he had been a private citizen (*Panegyric* 22–4). Throughout the speech Pliny stresses the role of Trajan not as emperor but as consul, which he was in AD 99. For example, during the three-day trial for extortion (described by Pliny in *Letters* 2.11), Pliny emphasises that Trajan presided over the Senate solely in his capacity as consul, and that each senator called on to speak was free to speak his mind, without anxiety about Trajan's own views (*Panegyric* 76). In this world of low-key emperors, though senators knew that nothing had changed institutionally, they could still hope that their own freedom of speech or action could co-exist with that of the emperor. Pliny knew the tyrannical age of the Julio-Claudians could return; meanwhile the best he could do was to attempt to mould Trajan in the likeness of his political ideal.

Law and society

402. Roman Law is one of the most important products of Roman thought [308–9]. The reason is that, while the Greeks exerted some influence over styles of argument, they had no written body of law or theory of jurisprudence for Romans to draw on. Roman Law, therefore, is to be seen as a largely Roman achievement, which developed over our period as society grew more complex and the empire expanded. It has formed the basis for the laws of subsequent societies for a millennium and more, and is still a part of some university law courses [499].

403. Roman Law was codified for the first time in the Twelve Tables of 451/450 BC. Somewhat like the Ten Commandments, the Twelve Tables presented the basic legal procedures and punishments, and though much was later improved, they were not formally abolished until the sixth century AD, and in Cicero's youth schoolboys still learnt them by heart. But by the late Republic procedures had changed. In the criminal law new courts were created in addition to the original people's courts. In the civil law new institutions were not required, but a new procedure was developed, in the hands of the presiding magistrate, normally a praetor; cf. [132]. In place of the ancient procedure which was tied to the wording of the Twelve Tables, the magistrate was empowered to define the legal issue in terms appropriate to the case in hand. That is, he issued a *formula* (hence the name for this procedure 'the formulary system'). He then appointed a person or persons (*iudices*) to hear the case in accordance with his *formula*. The new system was very flexible and adaptable to new circumstances.

404. There was also new personnel, of two types. First, those who had made their name by speaking on behalf of clients in the courts. Advocacy was supposed to be an activity any gentleman might undertake, for which his rhetorical education would have trained him, and no doubt many 'gentlemen' did plead occasionally in the courts. Advocates were also supposed to receive little in the way of remuneration from their clients (on Jersey, today, advocates who undertake legal aid work receive no pay at all). But clearly some made legal work their speciality, and did in various ways profit greatly thereby. Cicero made his political name by his successful prosecution of Verres for extortion, and about half of his speeches (whether published or not) were originally delivered in the courts, and half had a political setting. He seems, however, to have ceased to speak for private clients in 69 BC. In *On Duties* he commended the proper exercise of eloquence, as follows:

Our ancestors gave to eloquence the foremost standing among civil professions. If a man is both a skilful speaker, and takes hard work lightly, and if he undertakes without reluctance or remuneration to defend a large number of clients (as was the habit of our forefathers), the opportunity for kind services and for patronage at law will be wide open for him. (2.19.66)

This was, for Cicero, compatible with his own claim that he had received the vast sum of 20 million sesterces by bequests from former clients (*Philippics* 2.16.40). Bequests as a form of indirect and deferred 'payment' for services rendered were perfectly acceptable to the ethos of the 'gentleman' advocate.

405. Pliny too was a very successful advocate, though in his day it was rarely possible to make political capital out of the courts. Some people still tried to restrict payment of advocates, but they seem to have been largely ineffective (*Letters* 5.9). Whereas Cicero had moved from private cases to ones involving criminal charges with political overtones (bribery, extortion, murder: fig. 8.9), Pliny's expertise was the complex area of inheritance law, and his favourite stamping-ground was the Centumviral Court, the scene of some of his greatest orations (*Letters* 2.14, 6.12, 9.23). He was thus able to win general acclaim and to establish his position within the patronage system [212ff.].

406. Secondly, whereas legal thinking had once been the preserve of a college of priests, the *pontifices*, by the first century BC there had emerged

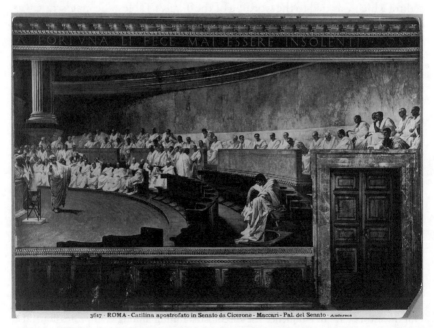

3617 · ROMA - Catilina apostrofato in Senato da Cicerone - Maccari - Pal. del Senato · Anderson

8.9 Painting by Cesare Maccari: *Catiline denounced by Cicero.*

specialist legal consultants, most of whom, in this period, were not even senators, a development that Cicero himself deplored (*On Duties* 2.19.65). He gave a vivid picture of the work of one such consultant, who did (exceptionally) manage to make his way to a consulship in 51 BC:

> Servius [Sulpicius Rufus] did his service in the city here with me, giving legal opinions, preparing documents, and giving advice, a life full of worry and anxiety. He learned the civil law, worked long hours, helped many people, put up with their stupidity, suffered their arrogance, swallowed their cantankerousness. He was at the beck and call of others, not his own master. A person wins widespread praise and credit with others when he works hard at a discipline which will benefit so many. (*In Defence of Murena* 9.19)

This type of independent legal figure still remained important in Pliny's day. One of his letters excuses Javolenus Priscus for a comic intervention at a poet's recitation as follows: 'he does however take part in public functions, acts as an assessor, and is one of the official experts on civil law' (*Letters* 6.15). But the trend was towards jurists holding imperial office. The great lawyer Ulpian, for example, was secretary to the emperor Caracalla (AD 212–17). Though Servius is represented by Cicero as merely assisting clients through the thickets of the civil law, jurists both in his day and later also published books on aspects of law. Javolenus wrote both summaries of earlier jurists and also lengthy *Epistulae* ('Letters') on aspects of property and inheritance; Ulpian wrote massively, almost 280 books, summing up many aspects of Roman Law.

407. The only work of these jurists to survive largely complete is the *Institutes* of the jurist Gaius. Written in the mid-second century AD, it long served as a textbook of Roman Law (a function it sometimes still serves). Much of the substance of the *Institutes* would also have been familiar a generation earlier to Pliny. The remaining works of the classical Roman jurists are known to us, if at all, through the final codification of Roman Law ordered by the emperor Justinian in AD 530, his *Digest*. This huge work, covering everything from legal procedure to divorce and inheritance, to murder and the regulation of provincial communities, was excerpted from 2,000 books, mainly of the period AD 100–250. Nearly a third of the *Digest* was taken from the works of Ulpian, but it also draws on Javolenus' *Epistulae* ('Letters') and on Gaius' *Institutes*.

408. The sources of Roman Law are clearly stated at the beginning of the *Institutes* (1.1–7): specific *leges*, popular enactments, senatorial decrees, magistrates' edicts, decisions of emperors, and the answers of jurists. Gaius cites all these sources in the course of the *Institutes*. For example, he cites an opinion of Javolenus Priscus on a disputed point of inheritance law (3.70).

The authority of the decisions of the people, Senate, magistrates and emperor was clear, but Gaius notes that the answers of jurists have the force of law only if they agree; if they disagree, the judge may decide which to follow. He also gave a full account of legal procedures (book 4), which shows a strong sense of the changing nature of Roman Law. For example, he describes the development of the 'formulary' procedure ([403]; *Institutes* 4.11.30–1).

409. He is also alert to the workings of Roman Law in the empire (he himself may have come from one of the Eastern provinces). Roman civil law was primarily for Roman citizens, but by the mid-second century AD they were perhaps as numerous in the provinces as in Rome and Italy. Provincial governors are noted among the magistrates whose edicts have the force of law (1.6), and are also mentioned as officials who consulted the emperor on points of law (1.53), as Pliny did when governor of Pontus–Bithynia. Some procedures differed in the provinces. Gaius explains that the composition of the council needed by a master to manumit a slave differed in Rome and in the provinces, as did the dates on which it sat (1.20). Some aspects of Roman law applied both to Roman citizens and to 'those subject to the rule of the Roman people', i.e. provincials: neither category are 'allowed to treat their slaves with excessive and causeless harshness' (1.53; cf. 3.128–43 for problems arising out of relations between Romans and non-Romans).

410. Gaius also brings out some of the peculiarities of Roman Law in comparison with other legal codes: the strong legal right of fathers over their children (*patria potestas*) 'is peculiar to Roman citizens . . . I am not forgetting that the Galatians regard children as being in the *potestas* of their parents' (1.55; see [308]). Similarly 'among non-Romans women are not in *tutela* ('wardship') in the same way as with us; still, in general, they are in a sort of *tutela*: a law of the Bithynians, for example, ordains that if a woman enter into any transaction, it must be authorised by her husband or full-grown son' (1.193).

411. The fundamental principle of Roman Law is the distinction between different statuses. Modern laws operate on the assumption that it does not matter if the parties to a case are rich or poor, male or female, citizen or noncitizen. Roman Law was entirely different. It held that the status of the individual was basic, and affected most of that person's rights and duties; cf. [350]. So book 1 of the *Institutes* is devoted to the law of persons, and distinguishes slave from free (both ex-slave and freeborn), and different categories of free: those subject to another (master, father or husband) and those legally independent but still subject to wardship (children and women). So an outrage (*iniuria*) may be committed not only against a man, but also against his children in *potestas* (lit. 'power': see [308ff.]) and his wife. 'Accordingly, if

you commit an outrage on my daughter (in *potestas*) who is married to Titius, an *actio iniuriae* ('charge of outrage') lies against you not only in her name, but also in mine and Titius" (3.221). And outrage was regarded as aggravated by the person affected: if, for example, an outrage is inflicted on a magistrate, or on a senator, by a person of low status (3.225). So, according to Pliny, a good governor administering justice in his province will pay especial care to ensure that the distinctions of status and dignity are preserved (*Letters* 9.5). *Dignitas* (lit. 'dignity') was not simple snobbery, but the principle of appropriate respect for people of different statuses.

412. Changing status was therefore very significant, and considerable pains were taken over the proper legal forms [245–6]. Under the empire there were two types of ex-slaves: Junian Latins and those with full Roman citizenship [352]. If a master wanted to free a slave in his lifetime as a full citizen he had in effect to do so before a magistrate with *imperium* (and meet other conditions as well, *Institutes* 1.17). Gaining access was obviously not easy, especially outside Rome, as Pliny illustrates (*Letters* 7.16). His wife's grandfather in Ticinum in northern Italy had earlier manumitted some slaves informally, so that they were just Junian Latins, but Pliny asked a friend, who was on his way to Spain as governor, to make a detour, and carry out the full procedure. Such repetition was sufficiently common to be discussed in the *Institutes* (1.35). Another way a master could upgrade ex-slaves was for him, or someone else, to petition the emperor for a special grant of citizenship, as Pliny does on behalf of others (*Letters* 10.5, 104). And again the *Institutes* notes the practice (3.72). In addition, Junian Latins could obtain Roman citizenship themselves by various forms of service to the Roman state (1.32–4).

413. An important consequence of differences of status was the effect on one's ability to make a will or to receive property as an heir or as a legatee. Inheritances and legacies were very important. About half of Gaius' account of the law of things is devoted to the acquisition of property upon the death of the owner (2.97–3.87), and it seems that 60–70% of Roman civil litigation arose from problems connected with the acquisition of property on death. Inheritances went naturally within the family in the first instance, and normally both to sons and daughters, followed by the wife; legacies went to ex-slaves and to one's friends. Wills thus also have a symbolic importance, as maps of the relationships of the testator to family and friends. But from a legal point of view status is again important. In general, non-citizens could receive neither inheritances nor legacies from Roman citizens. Under Augustan rules, Junian Latins [412] were similarly restricted; the unmarried could again receive neither, while the childless could receive only half of each (*Institutes*

2.110–11). None the less, within this basic framework, there was enough leeway for the practice of 'legacy-hunting' to emerge, even if it was often condemned (see e.g. Horace, *Satires* 2.5). In order to make a will, one had to be legally independent, which meant that Junian Latins could not (when they died, their property reverted to their master), but that women could, as Pliny illustrates (*Letters* 2.20, 7.24).

Conclusions

414. Roman Law has been one of the themes running through this chapter. Boys were trained at school in part on fictitious legal cases (*controuersiae*); every gentleman was expected to be able to argue logically. Following the proper procedures was crucially important. Failure to do so invalidated a will. It might also invalidate decisions of the people or the Senate. Law was fundamental to the well-being of the Roman state; Cicero argued this in *On the Laws*; Pliny's *Panegyric* expressed the hope that the laws were now superior to the emperor rather than the other way round. Roman Law was known to have features peculiar to the Romans, and not shared by the laws of those subject to Rome, and in the first instance it applied to Roman citizens and Roman land. So, all Roman citizens anywhere in the empire, from the emperor downwards, could make wills in exactly the same format, but as Trajan tells Pliny in Pontus–Bithynia, Roman Law on the dedication of temples did not apply to foreign soil (*Letters* 10.49–50; cf. *Letters* 10.68–9). But Roman governors could apply Roman rules to all those in their province, while respecting the statuses of those before them. Pliny sent Roman citizens who admitted that they were Christians to Rome for trial, but simply executed the equivalent non-Roman citizens. One can hardly ask for a more vivid illustration of the importance of law and status in Rome's 'civilising mission'.

FURTHER READING

Law:
J.A. Crook, *Law and Life of Rome* (London, 1967)

Education:
S.F. Bonner, *Education in Ancient Rome* (London, 1977)
H.I. Marrou, *A History of Education in Antiquity* (New York, 1956).

Religion:
M. Beard, J. North and S. Price, *Religions of Rome* (2 vols., Cambridge, 1997 – vol. 2 is a sourcebook)

Philosophy:
M.L. Clarke, *The Roman Mind: Studies in the History of Thought from Cicero to Marcus Aurelius* (London, 1956 and Cambridge, Mass., 1960)
A.A. Long, *Hellenistic Philosophy* (London and New York, 1974)
A.A. Long and D.N. Sedley, *The Hellenistic Philosophers*, 2 vols. (Cambridge, 1987) (a sourcebook).

Foreigners:
J.P.V.D. Balsdon, *Romans and Aliens* (London and Chapel Hill, 1979)

9
Roman literature

Literacy, literature and power

415.

> ADMIROR, O PARIES, TE NON CECIDISSE [RVINIS],
> QVI TOT SCRIPTORVM TAEDIA SVSTINEAS.

I wonder, O wall, that you have not yet collapsed [in a heap], so many writers' cliches do you bear. (Pompeian graffito, before AD 79, CIL IV.1904: cf. IV.2461, IV.2487)

This elegiac verse inscription occurs crudely scratched on walls at Pompeii in a number of different versions – some incomplete, some with mistakes in metre (as this one: *admiror* is scanned with a short 'i', when it is normally long), some illiterate. It argues that some (but it is impossible to judge how many) of the inhabitants of a small Italian provincial town in the second half of the first century AD, could read and write (fig. 9.1: see [250–1]). Other evidence for general literacy emerges from, for example, the soldiers' letters unearthed at Vindolanda (fig. 6.8 and [283]) in the far north of the province of Britain and from the inscriptions which occur on curse-tablets (*defixiones*) such as those discovered in the sacred spring at *Aquae Sulis* (Bath) (fig. 9.2).

There were public libraries (fig. 9.3). The first was set up by Asinius Pollio in 39 BC. By the end of the Empire there were 29 in Rome alone. Since Rome was the pattern for other urban centres, we can assume they were available elsewhere. One example is the public library donated by Pliny the Younger to Comum (Como in Northern Italy: *Letters* 1.8). The rich, of course, had private book collections. Cicero's correspondence is full of references to them, and of requests for books. The ruins of Herculaneum brought to light in 1752 a private library of 1,800 book rolls. Finally, if this is evidence of literacy, knowledge of stories from literary texts was certainly common, as we can tell from the way graffiti-writers and mosaic-makers (presumably at the command of their masters) used Virgil's *Aeneid* (fig. 8.1 and [369]).

416. In the absence of anything but anecdote (e.g. the poet Propertius' comment that his first book of poetry 'is read all over the Forum': Propertius 2.24a.1–3), we cannot conduct a survey into readership. But we can try to understand what reading meant to Romans. We must begin by attempting to answer three important questions about the place of literature in Roman society.

(1) Who wrote 'literature' and at what periods?

417. The answer to this is 'more or less any male who was educated in Latin, from any social background, from anywhere Latin was known, and in any political climate'. For example, an ex-slave from Africa wrote comedies for the Roman stage in the second century BC. In the same period, a member of the ruling aristocracy wrote a seminal work of Roman history. A trilingual Calabrian from a non-aristocratic background produced the first hexameter epic poem in Latin to deal with the Roman myth. A Mantuan, originally well-off, but dispossessed of his family estates after Philippi (42 BC[74]), wrote the quintessential Roman epic. A freedman's son from Venusia in south-east Italy became the foremost lyric poet of Augustan Rome [79ff.]. The son of a school-master of Greek ancestry from Naples had a successful poetic career, writing epic and occasional poetry in the darkest days of Domitian's tyranny [104].

In order of appearance, these writers are: Terence (P. Terentius Afer, 184–159); Cato (M. Porcius Cato, 234–149 BC; consul 195, censor 184: the work was called *Origines*, 'Roots'); Ennius (Q. Ennius, *c.* 239–169 BC; the *Annales*, 'Annals'); Virgil (P. Vergilius Maro, 70–19 BC; the 'Aeneid'); Horace (Q. Horatius Flaccus, 65–8 BC; *Carmina*, 'The Odes'); Statius (P. Papinius Statius, *c.* AD 45–96; the 'Thebaid', the *Siluae*).

(2) How were these works disseminated?

418. There were two major modes of dissemination – the author could speak direct to a listening audience, or he could circulate a written text.

Speaking to an audience

Audiences listened to stage plays at the *ludi* ('games'), eleven days' worth *c.* 200 BC, to 43 in Augustus' time. The size of the surviving theatres, none built earlier than the first century BC, seems to suggest large audiences (fig. 9.4) (the

9.1 Literacy among the ordinary people. Portraits from Pompeii of a man with a scroll and a woman with a pen and tablets ('Baker and his wife').

first permanent theatre built at Rome was Pompey's, in 55 BC). Likewise people could hear oratory in the *curia* ('Senate-house': fig. 9.5), law courts and popular political assemblies [158–65].

419. Most poetry and other literature too (e.g. history), even though designed eventually for readers, was also presented to a listening audience first. There were two ways this was done. One was the *recitatio*, a sort of 'book launch'. The satirist Juvenal speaks with horror of such an occasion (*Satires* 1.1–2): 'Will I always be a listener? Am I never to get my own back, bothered so often by the "Theseis" of Cordus with the frog in his throat?' The other was the 'literary dinner'. The epigrammatist Martial mocks such occasions (3.50): 'There's only one reason you invite people to dinner, Ligurinus. You want the opportunity to recite your awful poems.' But the ancient commentator Servius reports a moving example. Virgil used to give readings of 'work in progress' from the *Aeneid* to the emperor Augustus. On one occasion he read the funeral of Marcellus from *Aeneid* 6 (lines 860–86). Augustus had placed great hope for the future on this nephew (son of his sister Octavia), but he had died in 23 BC aged only 20. Augustus' wife was reduced to tears and fainted as she heard Virgil's portrayal of Anchises predicting the burial ceremony her husband had but recently performed (cf. [89]).

9.2 Lead curse-tablet from Bath.

9.3 Roman library, with recesses for cupboards to contain book-rolls. Apse in the Baths of Trajan, Rome (inaugurated in AD 109).

9.4 Roman theatre: model of the theatre of Marcellus, Rome (dedicated in 11 BC).

Circulating a text

420. In Classical Rome, the book was a roll made out of sheets of papyrus, glued together. It was awkward to handle; and writing, with quill and ink, was not easy either (fig. 9.6). Multiple copies, however, could be produced. Cicero, for example, sent volumes of his work to his friend Atticus, who had a troop of slaves working for him (the first person we know to go into the publishing business). Horace tells us of another bookseller/publisher, the brothers Sosii, and implies that they made money out of the books they produced (*Epistle to the Pisos* 345). But we cannot assume that they indulged in the same type of commissioning procedures as modern publishers do to find best-sellers, since we have no idea how many copies of a work might be produced, and we can only guess at the true price. Martial, for example, tells us that his first book of epigrams, about 700 lines, sold for 20 *sestertii* (=5 *denarii*), and his thirteenth (276 lines) for 4 (=1 *denarius*). It is impossible to say what these figures really mean. But one notes that elsewhere (1.103.10) Martial tells us that you could get a chick-pea dinner *and* a woman for an *as* each. Since an *as* was worth 1/18 of a *denarius*, you could have had 45 chick-pea dinners plus 45 nights of love for the price of a copy of Martial's first book of epigrams! Books might well have been beyond the pocket of most ordinary Roman citizens.

9.5 The *curia* (Senate-house) in Rome, originally built by Julius Caesar, restored by Diocletian after a fire in AD 283.

(3) What underlying forces controlled the production and dissemination of literature?

421. Publishing a book bestowed status. Consequently, authorship was not quite as open to all as (1) above may have suggested. There were unspoken 'rules' to the game, designed to ensure that entry to the 'club' was restricted and controlled. First of all, education was required and this had to be paid for (fig. 8.2; [367ff.). So Horace praised his father's foresight in using his hard-earned cash (he was an auctioneer) to give him the very best:

> He was a poor man with a few scrappy acres, yet he wouldn't send me to Flavius' school, where the important boys, the sons of important centurions, used to go, with satchel and slate swinging from their left arm, carrying their eight asses fee on the Ides of every month, but sent me to Rome. (*Satires* 1.6.71ff., tr. Niall Rudd)

In the passage of Horace just cited, the picture of the centurions' sons off to school with their satchels and writing-tablet, clutching their lesson-money, is important evidence for the level of wealth a family needed to educate its children. Centurions – a cross between tenured civil servants and members of the communist party in the former USSR – were always Roman citizens, and the backbone of the army which kept the grip of Roman power on the empire.

9.6 Fragment of a book-roll: papyrus from Qasr Ibrim (Egypt) carrying part of a poem by the Augustan love-poet Gallus.

Moreover, they earned between five and ten times what lower ranks did. In other words, they were the class which had that scarce commodity, hard cash, available to it [238]. Since education came at a price, there was a natural barrier to the aspirations of others in, for example, subsistence farming, who would rarely, if ever, have the spare cash to buy education for their children.

422. Secondly, both writing and reading required time. That is, time free (*otium*) from the irksome and intrusive business of life (*negotium*). The only people who had this of right (and considered it the *norm*) were the aristocratic landowning élite. It is no coincidence that these were among the most prolific producers of literature (for example Cato, Cicero, Pliny the Younger and Seneca). Further, they were not in it for the money. Horace remarks on one occasion that a book will make money for the (publishers) Sosii (*Epistle to the Pisos* 345). But the passage rules out the notion that cash was the *writer's* motive. What follows shows that what the writers were after was *fame*. Hence,

a writer who did not have independent means had to find ways of being supported.

423. The standard way was to find a patron or patrons who would repay your literary efforts with financial support. A writer might even be made secure and financially independent by his patron, as Horace was by Maecenas (*Satires* 2.6). It is difficult to determine how, for example, dramatists like Plautus (third century BC) supported themselves. They may have made money by selling plays on the open market to the agents of the curule aediles [138] who put on the *ludi* at which they were performed, but we do not know.

424. It is worth commenting that no really active measures were taken by the state to control what was written and disseminated. The legal code known as the Twelve Tables prohibited defamatory verses (cf. Horace, *Satires* 2.1.82) and it is reported that Augustus, though he took no notice of lampoons against himself, made it a criminal offence to put someone else's name to such products (Suetonius, *Augustus* 55). It was not censorship that controlled the writer, but social pressure. The forces of the market in literature were the individuals who both commissioned and acted as patrons for writers and who were at the same time involved in the battle for political primacy with their peers [142–9]. This rather limited the writer's apparent freedom to 'do his own thing'.

425. The poet Ovid (43 BC – AD 17) is a good example of what could happen to a writer who got on the wrong side of authority. He wrote much frivolous verse and was exiled to Tomis on the Black Sea in AD 8 for, as he tells us himself, 'a poem and a mistake' (*Tristia* 2.207). The 'mistake' may have been some error of judgement in referring to the sexual habits of the emperor Augustus' granddaughter Julia. The 'poem' was the mock-didactic *Ars Amatoria* ('Techniques of Love'), which openly advocated adultery in the face of Augustus' legislation of 18 BC. In *Tristia* 2 ('Poems from exile'), Ovid complains bitterly of punishment for what he sees as something others have got away with: 'Such things [i.e. writing about sex] form part of the output of learned men, and, thanks to our rulers, have become common knowledge [because of public libraries sponsored by the élite]' (419–20). Later Ovid refers to saucy Roman merchandise (fig. 9.7), points out that there have been other ironical 'Techniques of . . .' before, which he was following, and then turns to examples of obscene mimes by Roman writers, put on at *ludi* before 'girls ready to marry, matrons, men and boys – and most of the Senate' (501–2).

At the climax, he daringly addresses the emperor himself:

Augustus, . . . you have watched such things often in person, often put on the show yourself (so affable is your greatness in every sphere); with those eyes that are at the service of the world you have viewed adultery on the stage – without getting upset. If it

9.7 Ovidian eroticism? Cf. [297].

is all right to compose mimes that represent obscenities, my subject surely deserves a smaller penalty. (*Tristia* 2. 509–16)

Perhaps it did. But it made no difference when Augustus himself was the judge and he considered Ovid to have crossed him.

426. Consequently, a patron's wishes had an important influence upon a writer's choice of material, genre (see below) and aesthetic and political stance. It is no accident that the patron of Ennius the author of the *Annales* ('Annals') was the Cato who wrote *Origines* ('Roots'), and that Statius should wax loud in eulogy of the emperor Domitian (*Siluae* 4.2.1ff.), since he gave him a villa near Alba. But although, for example, the work of Virgil and Horace is awash with direct ideological support for Augustus' regime (cf. [84–5]), it was not inevitable that only 'political' poetry would be produced.

427. None of this should prejudice us against Roman literature. A writer, like any *cliens*, was in an *amicitia* relationship with his patron, and such relationships were at the heart of Roman society [10, 216, 329]. It is easy enough to label Horace or Statius 'insincere', because they say things which we feel they had to say in praise of their patrons or regimes. But that is no reason to believe that they necessarily were insincere either about their patrons or the causes they espoused. Besides, they lived in a society where it was expected that benefactors should be given their due. And if the writer gained immortality for himself, how could he refuse it to those who had helped him to attain it?

Attitudes to writing and reading

428.

Much was said against the commander-in-chief himself [Scipio] – his dress and bearing were un-Roman, and not even soldierly; he strolled about the gymnasium in a Greek cloak and sandals, and wasted his time over books and physical exercise. (Livy 29.19)

I promised you in an earlier letter that there would be work to show for this spell away from home, but I am no longer very positive on the point. I have taken so kindly to idleness (*otium*) that I can't tear myself away from it. So I either amuse myself with books, of which I have a goodly store at Antium, or I count the waves (the weather is unsuitable for mackerel fishing). To writing I feel a downright repugnance. (Cicero, *Letters to Atticus* 2.6; at the time, Cicero was engaged on a 'Geography')

Despite the fact that many Romans read books, mere reading seems to have made them feel guilty. We can see this attitude very clearly from the two texts cited above. Scipio was supposed to be conducting a *war*, not allowing himself and his men to be drawn into *luxuria*. Reading books is an integral part of that opposition between fruitful *negotium* and fruitless *otium* [373]. In Cicero, the guilt emerges from his misuse of *otium*; reading turns out to be the equivalent of 'counting waves', a proverbially useless activity. What he *should* be doing is *writing*.

429. The implication is that a real Roman will be an active man, fighting, administrating, or generally *producing*. If he puts leisure before duty, then he lets the side down. If he does have leisure, it ought not to be wasted. So reading *is* justifiable, but only if it results in writing. This attitude can be seen everywhere. For example, Quintilian in his *Institutio Oratoria* ('An Orator's Education') recommends a reading-list in Greek and Latin literature. However, its purpose is not to give pleasure in its own right, but to provide ideas for the orator's own products (10.1). This explains why Romans believed that literature was not basically for pleasure (*uoluptas*), but for usefulness (*utilitas*)[277].

430. This doctrine of *utilitas* of course, fits technical writing, a field in which the Romans were productive, easily enough. For example, Varro (M. Terentius Varro) writes in the introduction to his *Rerum Rusticarum Libri* ('On Agriculture'):

I cannot allow the Sibyl to have uttered prophecies which benefited mankind not only while she lived, but even after she had passed away, and that too to people whom she never knew . . . and not *do* something, even while I am alive, to help my friends and kinsfolk. Therefore I shall write for you three handbooks, to which you may turn whenever you wish to know, in a given case, how you ought to proceed in farming (1.3–4)

431. But Romans expected usefulness eveywhere else too. The result was that, if a work could not be technically useful, it must be made *morally* useful. Horace, for example, argues that his sometimes rather raunchy *Satires* have a moral purpose, because they show people how to behave by offering up good and bad examples for inspection: did not his father, Horace goes on, point out to him when a child individuals whose conduct should be avoided or imitated (*Satires* 1.4.105–29)? This motive underlies also the collections of wise sayings so loved by Romans, e.g. 'The Sayings of Cato' (*Dicta Catonis*) and the anecdotes of Valerius Maximus (*Facta et Dicta Memorabilia* 'Memorable Words and Deeds') which were studied everywhere in the schools of the Roman empire.

432. Poetry caused the Romans a particular problem. On the one hand, it was an undeniably superior achievement of earlier Greek culture (Romans generally considered the Greeks over whom they now ruled vastly inferior). On the other, it was hard not to see it as rather frivolous. Eratosthenes (*c.* 275–194 BC), for example, a Greek scholar from Alexandria, had argued strongly that poetry aimed at entertainment (Strabo 1.2.3) and it was a commonplace of criticism that 'poets tell many lies' (Plutarch, *Moralia* 16A).

433. Horace got out of the problem by arguing both sides of the coin: 'Poets either want to be of use or to give pleasure, or to say things which are both pleasing and useful for life at the same time . . . The poet who has mixed the useful (*utile*) with the pleasurable (*dulce*) wins every vote, by delighting and advising the reader at one and the same moment' (*Epistle to the Pisos* 333–4, 343–4). In other words, giving pleasure was an acceptable motive for a writer (so that for example love poetry, which could hardly be said to *teach* anything, was tolerated), but it was much more acceptable if pleasure and utility could be combined. Lucretius, attempting to describe the nature of the world in his 'On the Nature of the Universe' (*De Rerum Natura*) and save men from fear of death, made the same point: his delightful poetry was like sugar round the rim of a cup of medicine. On the whole, Romans were pretty much in favour of the Stoic view that poetry aimed at instruction (Strabo 1.2.3–9; *c.* AD 17).

434. The Romans helped this argument along by claiming, as the Greeks did, that the poet was possessed by a kind of prophetic inspiration. For example, they called their poets *uates*, a term which meant both 'poet' and 'prophet'. This shifted responsibility for the 'frivolous' onto the Greek god Apollo and other inspirers of poetry.

9.8 Scene from New Comedy: mosaic panel by Dioscurides of Samos ('street musicians') showing an episode from Menander's *Theophoroumene*.

The challenge of Greek literature

435.

Their race is quite worthless and unteachable, and I speak as a prophet that when it gives us its literature, it will ruin everything. (Cato the Elder writing to his son: Pliny, *Natural History* 29.13)

Conquered Greece took her uncultivated conqueror captive and invaded rustic Latium with the arts. (Horace, *Epistles* 2.1.156–7)

These two quotations neatly set out the paradox. For Cato, Greek literature was dangerous. It was foreign. It undermined the Roman ideals set out in the preceding section (cf. [43]). So, we are told, when the future general Agricola enthused over philosophy 'beyond what was allowed a Roman and a senator', his sensible mother took him in hand (Tacitus, *Agricola* 4) and he ended up as the doyen of Roman military aristocrats.

Yet the quotation from Horace shows that the Greeks won a cultural war to match the Romans' military conquest. Romans accepted Greek literature's historical primacy (and often enough paid lip-service to its aesthetic superiority [378]) and were open about their enjoyment of Greek material. Plautus and Terence, for example, recycled Greek 'New Comedy' (late fourth–third century BC) in Latin: fig. 9.8). Since it retained its Greek setting, Greek names and *mores*, and the characters got into terrible scrapes, it gave Romans a chance to feel superior to Greeks: but they still recognised brilliant comedy when they saw it. Indeed, elsewhere in the letter quoted above, Cato remarks: 'it is a good idea to dip into their [Greek] literature, but not to learn it thoroughly'. Even Cato was not totally opposed to it. So, in time, Greek literature was incorporated into *Romanitas*, the sense of what it meant to be Roman.

436. As a result, it quickly became the standard practice for those Romans who had completed their education in Rome to go to Athens to study. But Roman acceptance of Greek literature was never uncritical. Their passion for *utilitas* saw to that. Consequently they took Greek literature and used it for their own, Roman purposes. The story of Roman literature is at one level the vast enterprise of naturalising, or 'Romanising', this impressive Greek heritage. Much later St Augustine adopted the same principle in recommending that Christians should regard pagan literature as the Jews had regarded the riches of Egypt – take what is good and put it to your own uses.

437. Romans went about this naturalising process in any number of ways. Ennius, for instance, took Homer, composer of the great epic *Iliad*, as his model for a great epic history of Rome in the same style and form. Plautus staged comedies which look at first sight to be merely translations of Greek originals, but in fact fed all sorts of Roman elements into them. For example, in the prologue of *Amphitryon* (line 72: see *Reading Latin: Text*, Section 3) the god Mercury mentions the *aediles*, the Roman magistrates in charge of the *ludi* at which the play would be performed. Virgil, on the other hand, in his *Aeneid*, took characters from Greek myth (e.g. Trojan Aeneas) and suffused them with the Roman ethos, turning them into heroes who would found Rome (fig. 9.9); as we have seen, he even drew on events of personal significance to the emperor Augustus himself. Catullus, in his poem describing how he travelled 'through many peoples and over many seas' to bury his brother in the Troad (i.e. where Troy was) in Asia Minor (poem 101), alludes to the opening of Homer's *Odyssey*, which describes how Odysseus on his travels 'wandered very far after he had sacked Troy . . . and saw the cities of many men' (1.1–3). In this way, Catullus seeks to elevate his personal sorrow by connecting it with a higher literary plane.

438. The Roman attitude to Greek literature can be compared with the way Romans successfully managed to control a diverse empire over such a long period – i.e. they acknowledged and used the strengths of the people they had subdued. The Greeks, powerful and unconquerable as a cultural force, were accepted for what they were and made to work for Rome. Roman writers both acknowledged the Greek inspiration for their work and struggled to outdo it,

9.9 Aeneas wounded: painting from Pompeii closely based on an episode in the *Aeneid* (12.383–416).

even while ostensibly accepting Greek superiority. For example, Horace explicitly states (*Odes* 4.2.1–4): 'Whoever is eager to emulate Pindar, Iulus, is venturing on wings waxed with Daedalus' art and is destined [like Icarus] to give his name to a glassy sea.' But both here and in *Odes* 4.4 (celebrating the victory of Drusus in Germany in 15 BC), Horace is trying to do just that. Very occasionally, a writer even makes a claim for Roman superiority. For example, Propertius writes of the as yet unfinished *Aeneid* of Virgil: 'Make way, Roman writers, make way you Greeks! Something greater than the *Iliad* is being born' (2.34b.65–6).

439. In one sense, the Romans won, even though Greek literature retained its independence right to the end of the Empire (and beyond – see Epilogue). Greek literature had in a political sense become 'Roman' as early as the histories of Polybius and Appian in the second century BC. But in the time of the Greek cultural revival of the second and third centuries AD ('The Second Sophistic' [111ff.]), there was a movement towards writing Greek only in the purest style ('Atticism', i.e. writing like Plato and Demosthenes, seven hundred years earlier). Yet even then a writer such as the Greek satirist Lucian of Samosata (second century AD), who deliberately avoids admitting a knowledge of Latin, uses the term 'us' when he is speaking of the fantasy of an attack by barbarians upon the power of Rome.

Principles of composition

Imitatio *and* uariatio

440.

The Geography which I had purposed is really a big undertaking. Eratosthenes, whom I had meant to follow, is sharply censured by Serapio and Hipparchus ... And really the material is hard to set out, monotonous, and not so easy to embellish as it looked ... (Cicero, *Letters to Atticus* 2.6)

The main genres of literature had already been established by the Greeks – epic, history, comedy, philosophy, tragedy, pastoral, lyric, oratory, didactic. They ascribed an 'inventor' to and made up 'rules' for each genre (thus Thespis was said to have invented tragedy). The Romans did the same, claiming only one new invention – hexameter verse satire – and ascribing it to Lucilius. In the passage above, Cicero takes the genre of 'geography', a subset of didactic, and realises it stylistically by embellishing it in various ways. That is, he brings to bear on it all the resources of vocabulary (*lexis*), figures of speech (e.g. metaphor) and arrangement which his rhetorical training had taught him. So he is doing two things. He is imitating the genre (*imitatio*), and he is presenting the material culled from other sources in as varied a way as possible (*uariatio*). Such stylistic games-playing was of very great importance to Roman authors because style had to be suited to the material presented if its moral effects were to be felt. Consequently, writers speak of specfic styles, for example 'elevated' (suitable for tragedy) and 'low' (suitable for comedy or verse satire). Such styles should be kept strictly separate.

441. Some modern scholars detect an equally rigorous set of rules defining the permissible *content* of specific types of poem. They have noticed that much of the content is the same as that which was gathered in textbooks for successful speech-writing by people like, for example, Menander Rhetor (third century AD). These rules for content may be divided into two classes: primary elements (by which the type of the poem is recognised) and secondary elements (commonplaces, or *topoi*). For example, in the *propemptikon*, 'poem of farewell' (such as Propertius 1.6), the primary elements involve (i) a person departing (ii) a person bidding him farewell (iii) a relationship of affection between the two and (iv) a setting appropriate to the farewell. The *topoi* of the *propemptikon* include, for example, reasons why the poet cannot go with his friend (e.g. illness, or the orders of a superior). The point of this style of composition is to challenge an audience to admire the artistry involved in another type of *uariatio*. Given the emphasis on rhetorical education at Rome, some such interaction between rhetorical schemes and poems is certainly probable.

Originality, trustworthiness and rhetoric

442.

Imitation by itself is not enough. It is the sign of a lazy mentality to be content with what has been discovered by others. (Quintilian, *An Orator's Education* 10.2)

History has one function and one goal – utility; and this is achieved only by truth. (Lucian, *How to Write History* 9)

A writer was not expected merely to recycle earlier material. He would be criticised for so doing. Juvenal in Satire 1 [419] complains that he is bored by *recitationes* because of his over-familiarity with the material presented to him: 'I know all the mythical landscapes like my own back-room: the grove of Mars, that cave near Aeolus' island belonging to Vulcan. The stale themes are bellowed daily in rich patrons' colonnades, till their marble columns crack with a surfeit of rhetoric' (lines 7–13: translated by Peter Green, Penguin). Consequently, the writer was expected to bring in material from his own experience. So, for example, in his first Eclogue, Virgil introduces Greek shepherds in imitation of his third-century BC Greek model Theocritus (the 'inventor' of pastoral) (fig. 9.10), but portrays them grappling with problems of property confiscation which were occurring at the time of composition (*c.* 41 BC). Technical writers often claim that personal experience lies at the heart of their work. So Varro, writing about farming, says (*On Agriculture* 1.1.11): 'My remarks will be derived from three sources: what I have myself observed by practice on my own land, what I have read, and what I have heard from experts.' The point is that *fides*, 'trustworthiness', was crucial to all types of Roman literature, and describing one's own experience was the best way to claim it. The precedent was set by the Greeks. Homer, for example, appealed to the Muse to tell him the 'facts' about the story he was telling from so long ago: the Muse, after all, would know. The Greek historian Thucydides put tremendous importance on the veracity of eyewitness accounts (preferably his own). So the Roman historian Tacitus announced at the start of his *Annals* that he intended to write *sine ira et studio*, 'without anger or bias'.

443. Yet no student of Tacitus thinks that he succeeded. The problem was that rhetoric was at the very heart of Roman education, and its purpose was to

prepare students both to use and to recognise plausible (not true) arguments in every situation. Any orator, for example, was out to persuade the audience of the truth of his case, whatever the actual truth of the matter. This did not worry Romans. They were trained in rhetoric and could spot a rhetorical device a long way off. And writers knew this. Caesar, for example, had no difficulty in composing accounts of his campaigns in Gaul (*The Gallic War*) and against Pompey (*The Civil War*) with a heavy bias towards his own interest. It would seem true not only because it was rhetorically persuasive, but also because he himself had witnessed the events. It was, in other words, real. But the 'sincerity gap' could upset a later generation of readers for whom 'reality', 'truth' and 'the writer's life' were indissociable from each other. Petrarch, a central figure in the Italian Renaissance of the fourteenth century, rediscovered the lost *Letters* of Cicero. When he compared these with the lofty thoughts of Cicero's well-known rhetorical and philosophical works, he wrote a letter of his own to his dead ex-hero, bidding him farewell for ever (*Letters to Friends* 24.3)!

444. It is in poetry, though, that the effects of rhetorical training and the striving for originality and style are most strongly felt. Even our Pompeian graffito [415] is worth looking at more closely in this respect. The writer personifies the wall and likens the scrawlings upon it to items of baggage (such as might be carried by a mule or a slave). This is an amusing image: but the real

9.10 Sacro-idyllic painting from Pompeii reflecting the mood of Virgil's *Eclogues*.

joke lies in the fact that the writer distances himself from other people's graffiti not by rejecting the 'genre', but by adding one of his own. Graffito it may be, but this is a very self-conscious piece of work. We can see here in miniature the scope and the effect of Roman schooling. Once a student progressed beyond the basics, the formation given by the *grammaticus* and then the *rhetor* focused on language, style and persuasive presentation [368–71]. These then were the essential rhetorical foundations of Roman literature and major focuses of Roman literary criticism [371, 448–53].

445. It is important here to re-emphasise also the point made in [371] about 'sincerity'. If we ask of our graffito 'did the writer really mean it?' or construct from the words a scenario in which a good man is driven by the idiocy of others to stand up and be counted, we have missed the point. This was a trap Romans too fell into, especially when they had a bone to pick with a writer (as Augustus did with Ovid – see [425]). This point, and the more sophisticated view that the poet creates a 'persona' which is not to be identified with the poet himself, are woven together by Catullus amusingly in poem 16:

> *Pedicabo ego uos et irrumabo,*
> *Aureli pathice et cinaede Furi,*
> *qui me ex uersiculis meis putastis,*
> *quod sunt molliculi, parum pudicum.*
> *nam castum esse decet pium poetam*
> *ipsum, uersiculos nihil necesse est;*
> *qui tum denique habent salem ac leporem,*
> *si sunt molliculi ac parum pudici,*
> *et quod pruriat incitare possunt,*
> *non dico pueris, sed his pilosis*
> *qui duros nequeunt mouere lumbos.*
> *uos, quod milia multa basiorum*
> *legistis, male me marem putatis?*
> *pedicabo ego uos et irrumabo.*

I'll bugger the pair of you, bum-boy Aurelius and queer Furius. You've judged me indecent from my poetry, because it's a bit off the straight and narrow. Look, the pious poet must be decent himself. There's no need for his poems to be. They are witty and charming if they're a bit unstraight and indecent, and have the power to titillate, well, I don't mean youngsters, but those shaggy guys who can't arouse their obstinate organs. Just because you've read my piece about 'a thousand kisses' [poem 7], do you think I'm not quite all man? I'll bugger the pair of you.

Aurelius and Furius have accused Catullus of writing 'soft' verse (the word *molliculi* is used of catamites, passive homosexuals). Catullus is adopting an amusing *persona* – that of the active homosexual threatening to bugger anyone who accuses him of being a passive one. The poem is full of irony. Catullus argues that he is personally respectable – and will prove it by buggering anyone who disagrees. The voice of a poem, then, might be taken to represent that of the author. But equally, it was possible for an author to claim distance from what his poems said, by arguing that he was only adopting the literary conventions of the day.

Learning and allusion

446. Since the late second century BC, some Roman love-poets had been tentatively experimenting with the work of Greek love-poets of the third century and after. These were the so-called 'Hellenistic' poets, sometimes called 'Alexandrians', because Alexandria in Egypt was a hotbed of Hellenistic poetic experiment (at any rate, the terms distinguish them from the 'Classical' Greek poets of the fifth–fourth century BC). One of the main features of Hellenistic poetry was *doctrina* – its commitment to poetry full of learning and allusions to other poets and poetry. In 73 BC the Hellenistic poet Parthenius, a Greek from Nicaea (in what is now Turkey), arrived as a prisoner -of-war in Rome. He was freed, and it was thanks largely to him that the ideal of poetic *doctrina* caught on in Rome too, being taken up seriously by the *neoteroi* (a name given by Cicero), the trendy younger poets like Catullus, before becoming characteristic of all subsequent poetry.

447. Sometimes this feature can seem like mere learning for learning's sake. At other times, it seriously elevates the poetry. Catullus, wondering how many of his mistress Lesbia's kisses will satisfy him, answers: 'as many as the grains of Libyan sand that lie in silphium-bearing Cyrene between the oracle of sweating Jove and the holy tomb of ancient Battus' (7.4–6). He takes us to a far country (North Africa), and mentions some details associated with it: an important and expensive medicinal herb (silphium), a desert shrine (Jove's oracle at Siwa in the south-east, famous all over the world, consulted by Alexander the Great) and the ancient King Battus, who had founded Cyrene in the north-west, home of Callimachus, most famous of the Alexandrian poets whom Catullus was imitating. This site and these names do poetic work, flattering Lesbia by associating her kisses with a romantic, distant country which has a lush and suggestive past, in which she too, thanks to Catullus, now has a share.

Interpretation

448. It is not possible for us to know how the average Roman read and interpreted texts. But there is bound to be a strong correlation between the ways in which people are educated and the ways they read literature. So we may judge the main interests of Roman readers by examining what the ancient literary critics say, since these individuals were directly involved in the education of readers and writers.

When Roman critics talked about literature, they tended to ask three questions. What is the content? Does it have an effect on me? How does it produce that effect? Here we can see the result of rhetorical training on the Roman mind: for rhetoric (invented as a systematic technique of persuasion by fifth century BC Greeks) was all about selection of material and the use of technical devices to produce effects on the audience [371].

449. How different our own approach is can be illustrated with the help of the following extract from the introduction to a popular school edition of George Eliot's *Middlemarch*:

Thus one particular aspect of the novel's narrative structure may lead us close to its *thematic* heart. Once we accept the interweaving of concurrent stories, the advantages of this technique become obvious. By means of it George Eliot can refract her *meanings* into the individual colours of different characters and settings, can create a network of parallels and contrasts which expresses her vision of life while at the same time paying homage to the variegated qualities and plenitude of the human race. (W.J. Harvey, Penguin edn 1965, p. 12: our italics)

The italicised phrases focus attention on a central question we tend to ask of literary texts ('what is it about?') and one of the ways we have of finding the answer (locating its 'themes'). The underlying assumption is that the surface of a text will not give us the answer to the question of what it 'means'. On this assumption, we have built a sophisticated system of reading which allows examiners to test whether a student can deal with the 'deeper' aspects of a text, and resist the 'natural' tendency simply to retell the story.

450. Roman readers do not make this assumption. So, for example, when the poet Propertius describes Virgil's (fig. 9.11) work, he does not talk about 'themes' or 'structures' or 'meanings'. He says what it contains. Propertius, for instance, speaks (with elegant *uariatio*) of Virgil's *Aeneid*, *Eclogues* and *Georgics* thus (2.34B.61ff.):

Let Virgil tell of Actium's shore, which Phoebus guards and Caesar's sturdy vessels: now he raises the arms of Trojan Aeneas and the walls founded beside Lavinium's shores [*Aeneid* 8 and 1] . . . You sing beneath Galaesus' shady pine-groves of Thyrsus and of Daphnis with the worn reed-pipes, or how ten apples and a kid that's just let go pressed udders are able to seduce a girl. You're lucky to buy your love so cheap with fruit! [*Eclogues*] . . . You sing the precepts of Ascra's ancient poet [Hesiod], in which field corn, on which slope vines grow green . . . These words will be welcomed by every reader they find . . . [*Georgics*].

9.11 Virgil: portrait of the poet holding a scroll of the *Aeneid*, accompanied by the Muses of Tragedy and History.

451. In the following passage, we can see in more detail how the critic responded to literature. Here the second century AD Greek sophist Favorinus from Arles in Gaul, quoted by Aulus Gellius, compares two poetic passages which deal with the same thing, namely the Sicilian volcano, Mt Etna:

The friends and intimates of Virgil . . . remark that . . . the products of his genius, while still new, were inchoate and imperfect, but by cultivating and working over them he gave them lines and features. For what he left perfect and polished . . . blooms with every excellence of poetic beauty. What he left for revision . . . is quite unworthy of the name of this most elegant and tasteful of poets . . .

'Among the places that one thinks should have been revised and corrected is in particular the passage about Etna (*Aeneid* 3.570ff.). Wanting to rival old Pindar's poem on the nature and the burning of the mountain, he amassed material and language of such a kind that, at least here, he is more unnatural and turgid than even Pindar, whose eloquence has been judged too rich and gross.

'To show you what I mean, I will recite Pindar's poem on Mount Etna, as far as I remember it (*Pythians* 1.21ff.):

From its depths belches forth fire untouchable,
in pure fountains: by day rivers roll forth a flood of smoke,

blazing: but at night rocks are borne
by the red rolling flame to the deep sea-plain, crashing;
that monster sends up dreadful fountains
of fire: a fantastic sight to see,
a wonder for men there to hear.

'Listen now', Favorinus went on, 'to Virgil's lines, which I should be right in saying that he started rather than completed:

The harbour itself lies wide, untouched by the winds'
approach: but hard by thunders Etna with dreadful crash;
sometimes bursting a dark cloud into the sky,
smoking with pitchy whirl, and incandescent ash.
It raises fire-balls, licking the stars.
Sometimes rocks, torn mountain entrails,
it lifts, belches out, groaningly rolls into daylight
liquefied stones, seethes up from lowest depths.

'First of all,' he said, 'Pindar kept to the facts, and tells us the truth about what happened there, what the eye actually saw – namely that by day Etna smoked, by night it flamed. Virgil, however, anxious to look for words that resound and crash, makes no distinction, and mixes day and night up. Again, the Greek poet brilliantly described the fountains of fire belching forth from the depths, rivers of smoke aflow, dark whirling wreaths of flame carrying (as it were) fiery snakes down to the sea-coasts. [*Note how Favorinus is himself using the technique of 'uariatio' in relaying Pindar's words.*] But our poet, wanting to translate "a flood of smoke blazing", grossly and tastelessly piled up "a dark cloud smoking with pitchy whirl and ashes". Again "fire-balls" for "fountains" is a harsh and improper metaphor. "Licking the stars" is another empty and pointless addition. Further, to speak of "a dark cloud smoking with pitchy whirl and incandescent ash" is something hardly interpretable or even intelligible. Things that are incandescent do not normally smoke nor are they dark. Or else he used "incandescent" in a vulgar and illicit way for "hot" – not "fiery" or "shining". Of course, in fact, "incandescent" (Latin *candens*) is connected with whiteness (Latin *candor*), not heat (Latin *calor*). As to causing stones and rocks to be belched forth and lifted up and then immediately liquefy and groan and roll into daylight – none of this is in Pindar. No one ever heard such a thing; it is the most monstrous of monsters.' (Aulus Gellius, *Attic Nights* 17.10.2–19: tr. M. Winterbottom, *Ancient Literary Criticism*, ed. D.A. Russell and M. Winterbottom, Oxford 1972, 550–1)

452. Favorinus is interested in the process of composition. How did Virgil actually make his verses? With infinite care, except that he had not finished the polishing process when he died. He is also interested in the source. Where did Virgil get his description from, and how does he compare with the original? Unfavourably, as it turns out. He criticises Virgil's logic ('Pindar keeps to the facts . . . what he actually saw; Virgil mixes up day and night'). Here there is a lapse in the poet's *fides*, 'trustworthiness'. He criticises Virgil's taste ('"fire-balls" for "fountains" is a harsh and improper metaphor'); his intelligibility ('"a dark cloud smoking with pitchy whirl and incandescent ash" is hardly interpretable or even intelligible'); and his improper use of words ('things that are incandescent do not normally smoke nor are they dark'). Quite simply, the poet had not yet put enough effort into these lines. Interestingly, Virgil might well have agreed with these criticisms. We know that he was unsatisfied with the *Aeneid*, and asked on his deathbed for it to be burnt.

453. Source, logic (or 'being true to the facts'), taste, intelligibility, word-usage, effort – these are the typical criteria of the aesthete in the Roman world. Other things Roman critics were especially interested in were: clarity, pace of narrative, convincing character, morally improving sentiments, 'dignity' – the use of the appropriate style for the material – and consistency. Again, we can sense rhetorical education behind all this: a jury will be persuaded, for example, by clear, consistent arguments, convincing motives, intelligible reconstructions, elegant language, original formulations, logic and reason – but not by the reverse. And it all requires hard work. The following passage, where Quintilian compares Greek and Roman historians, exemplifies well some of these points.

But in history we do not need to yield to the Greeks. I should not be afraid to match Sallust with Thucydides; and Herodotus should not be angry to find Livy put on a par with him. For Livy shows extraordinary grace and brilliant lucidity in narration, while in his speeches he is indescribably eloquent, so nicely is everything that is said adapted to circumstances and character; and to put it mildly, no historian has better judged his use of emotions, particularly the gentler ones. Hence, by quite different qualities, he equalled the wonderful speed that we associate with Sallust. It was, I think, an excellent dictum of Servilius Nonianus that these two are on the same level rather than alike. Nonianus himself I have heard recite; he was a man of splendid talents, full of pointed reflection, but more diffuse than the dignity of history demands. That dignity was excellently maintained, especially in the books on the German war, by a slightly earlier writer, Aufidius Bassus, thanks to his style. He is deserving of approval in all respects, though in some points he falls short of his own powers. (*An Orator's Education*, 10.1.101–3: tr. M. Winterbottom, *Ancient Literary Criticism*, ed. D.A. Russell and M. Winterbottom, Oxford 1972, 395–6)

Literary history

454. This chapter has been broadly concerned with Roman views of what literature was for and how they read it. The Romans, though, saw their litera-ture as developing, from something more crude to something more sophisti-

cated. Modern scholars also tend to classify in terms of development, but it is usually towards a peak ('The Golden Age') and then away into decadence ('The Silver Age') and the mechanical or merely odd ('Later Latin Literature'). While it is not necessary to import such broad aesthetic judgements, it is in fact possible to use these categories to express development in terms of taste and political and educational change.

455. The initial period ('The Early Republic', third to second century BC) is characterised by the imitation of Greek models, especially in drama (Plautus and Terence). But it also sees the construction of a native genre of historical writing (Cato's *Origines*), the presentation of Roman material in Greek poetic form (Ennius' *Annales*) and, slightly later, the invention by Lucilius of the only non-Greek literary genre, satire. This period coincides politically with the expansion and consolidation of the Roman empire. Writers of the 'Golden Age' (such as Horace) and later tended to regard much of this material as rather roughly produced.

456. The late Republic and early Empire (c. 100 BC to AD 14) is known as the 'Golden Age'. It was a period of political turmoil followed by a political change which developed into the rule of one man, Augustus [50–90]. In the earlier part of the period (Lucretius, Catullus, Gallus etc.), we can see poets joining coteries with opposing aesthetic and, often, political views. But increasingly, from the 30s BC onwards, the successful writers (Virgil, Horace) have thrown in their lot with Octavian/Augustus, and literature begins to propagate the new ideology. Aesthetically, the late Republic was distinguished from the early Republic by a strong influence from Hellenistic Greek poetry (third century – first century BC). This was effected especially by the presence at Rome of the Hellenistic writer Parthenius of Nicaea (in Asia Minor: [446]).

457. The post-Augustan early Empire (AD 14–180) is usually known as the 'Silver Age'. Here we have poets such as Lucan, Persius, Juvenal, Martial and Statius, and historians such as Tacitus. But in the later part of this period, we also see a strong revival of Greek writing within the empire (the so-called 'Second Sophistic'), with authors such as Plutarch and Lucian. Politically, the period is characterised by a deepening autocracy which appears to limit literary expression severely. The poet Lucan, writing in the 50s or 60s AD, was forced to commit suicide for writing the 'Civil War' (*De Bello Ciuili*), an epic on the Civil War of the 40s BC, in which Caesar was successful. The problem was the apparent praise of the defeated, Republican, Pompey. The atmosphere altered somewhat in the period following the death of Domitian (AD 96), when Juvenal and Tacitus published their works. It is usual to see the increasingly wooden poetry of this period as an index of the greater hold rhetoric now has on the educational process.

458. The period from *c.* AD 180 to the end of the empire (AD 476) has a great diversity of material to offer, including Apuleius' novel *Metamorphoses.* The chief characteristic of this time, however, is the emergence of a Christian literature in competition with the pagan. It culminates in the writings of the Church Fathers St Jerome, St Ambrose and St Augustine in the late fourth century. See the Epilogue for a brief account of later developments.

Details of the dates and writings of the main Latin authors can be found in Appendix 2.

FURTHER READING

F. Cairns, *Generic Composition in Greek and Roman Poetry* (Edinburgh, 1972)

R. M. Ogilvie, *Roman Literature and Society* (Harmondsworth, Penguin, 1980)

D. A. West and A. J. Woodman (edd.), *Creative Imitation and Latin Literature* (Cambridge, 1979)

D. A. West and A. J. Woodman (edd.), *Poetry and Politics in the Age of Augustus* (Cambridge 1984)

Sourcebook:

D.A. Russell and M. Winterbottom, *Ancient Literary Criticism* (Oxford, 1972)

10
Roman art and architecture

The Republican period

Introduction

459. In his *Satyricon* the author Petronius makes his narrator Encolpius visit an art exhibition.

I came into a picture gallery with a marvellous collection of paintings of all sorts. I saw the work of Zeuxis not yet overcome by the ravages of time, and I studied with a kind of thrill the sketches of Protogenes, rivalling the truth of Nature herself. But when I came to the picture of Apelles which the Greeks call the One-Legged I positively worshipped it. For the outlines of the figures were defined with such subtlety and such fidelity, that you would think that the painting captured their souls as well. (*Satyricon* 83)

Leaving aside the satirical aims of the author, who may be poking fun both at the pretensions of Encolpius and at the language used by contemporary art-critics, this passage reveals two basic truths about art in Roman times. Even in the first century AD the works which people 'of taste' most admired were the Greek masterpieces of the fifth and fourth centuries BC (the period to which Zeuxis, Protogenes and Apelles all belonged); and the quality which they revered above all others was truth to nature, 'naturalism'. Greek naturalism remained a dominant strand in art till late antiquity; and to some extent the history of Roman art is a story of its gradual emancipation from Greek influence.

The beginnings

460. At the beginning Rome had no strong native tradition of artistic production. The city developed in the shadow of the Etruscans and in the early period her art and architecture were very much under the influence of

Etruscan art, which was itself under the influence of the art of the Greeks [8ff.]. Indeed, when Rome wanted a cult-statue and sculptural ornaments for the temple of Jupiter on the Capitol, built around 500 BC, she sent for an Etruscan artist from nearby Veii. The resulting works were carried out in the media favoured by Etruscan artists, bronze and terracotta. Etrusco-Italic influence remained dominant until the fourth century, but from this period onwards the Romans came increasingly into contact with the Greek tradition. Already in the early fifth century it seems that two Greek artists from southern Italy had received a commission to decorate the temple of Ceres in Rome. Later, as Roman power expanded over central and southern Italy, and ultimately extended overseas, the Romans became directly exposed to the mainstream of Greek art and architecture. The resulting wave of Greek influence was the catalyst which triggered the emergence of Roman art [40–3].

The plunder of Greek art

461. One of the first symptoms of a Roman admiration for Greek art was the plunder of statues and paintings from captured cities. The plunder of statues had already characterised the conquest of Etruria: cult-statues had been taken from the temples of Veii [20] and Praeneste, and in 264 a Roman general took 2,000 statues from Volsinii. Such depredations were partly inspired by religious motives: the spoils were deposited as thank-offerings in temples. But, with the conquest of Greek cities, other motives began to prevail: a desire to beautify the city, a concern for self-advertisement on the part of the victorious generals, ultimately a genuine passion for Greek art. A turning-point was the capture, in 212 and 209 BC, of Syracuse and Tarentum, the artistic capitals of Sicily and Magna Graecia, which started a huge flow of art-treasures to Rome. Further acquisitions followed the defeat of the Aetolians in 188, that of the Macedonians in 167, and, most spectacularly, the sack of Corinth by L. Mummius in 146 [34–9].

Greek artists working for Roman patrons

462. The influx of Greek art-works promoted a fashion for them: people did not merely want to look at them in temples and public places, they wanted to acquire them for their houses and villas. But while generals and provincial governors could get statues, silver plate, paintings and so forth by plunder, others had to buy them on the art-market. Greek artists were not slow to appreciate the advantages of the situation; they rapidly adapted to producing

10.1 Portrait-statue of a Roman (so-called Pseudo-Athlete) from Delos. Early first century BC.

works for sale to Roman collectors. Among the most successful were the so-called Neo-Attic workshops which emerged in Athens and elsewhere during the second century BC to create a nice line in up-market garden furniture decorated with conventional reliefs of Greek mythological subjects broadly based on models of the fifth and fourth centuries. In some cases the Roman and Italian patrons for whom they worked were resident in the eastern Mediterranean: the business colony established on Delos, for example, commissioned many portraits and statues from Athenian artists (fig. 10.1). In other cases works were shipped to Italy; specimens of Neo-Attic reliefs have emerged from the wrecks of ships which foundered on the way, for example one which went down off Mahdia in Tunisia round 80 BC. Soon, however, Greek artists began to move to the new centre of patronage. The first came back in the baggage trains of Roman generals; thus after the defeat of the Macedonians in 168 BC Aemilius Paullus brought back the Athenian painter and philosopher Metrodoros, partly to act as a tutor to his children, and partly to carry out paintings celebrating his campaigns. Others apparently came under their own steam. We hear of an Alexandrian Greek named Demetrios living in Rome in the 160s who is described as a *topographos*, probably a painter of illustrated maps. A prominent family of Athenian sculptors which is attested as working in Olympia, Delos and elsewhere also made at

10.2 Round temple by the Tiber in Rome, probably the temple of Hercules Victor. Late second century BC.

least four cult-statues for late-second-century temples in Rome, and there can be little doubt that they migrated to Italy for these lucrative commissions.

Greek-style buildings in second-century Rome

463. What Greek artists had to offer was a mastery of working in fine materials – precious metals, bronze, and especially marble – and a brilliant tradition of producing works on a monumental scale and in a fluent, natural-istic style. Some of the same features characterised their architecture, and it is not surprising to find that the importation of Greek materials and workman-ship under the patronage of Roman grandees led to an increasing 'Hellenisation' of Roman buildings. This tendency was most pronounced in the second half of the second century, after the final annexation of Greece, when one or two almost purely Greek buildings were erected in Rome. The temple of Jupiter Stator in the Portico of Metellus, completed between 146 and 121 BC, was the city's first all-marble building; it was designed by a Greek architect from Cyprus, used Pentelic marble imported from the neighbour-hood of Athens, and was apparently Greek in both plan and ornament. The little round temple by the Tiber (fig. 10.2), built probably towards the end of the century, again employs Pentelic marble and a Greek decorative vocabulary, including Corinthian capitals and ornament which is closely related to work produced in Asia Minor during the Hellenistic period.

The Italian current in architecture

464. But direct importation of this sort was the exception rather than the rule. It tended to be confined to temple architecture, and even in temple architecture there were important elements in the Roman–Italian tradition which could not be easily suppressed. The result was a fusion of ideas. As early as the third century the typical old Etruscan or Roman temple, squarish with broad, spreading eaves and built of limestone or volcanic stone with a superstructure of timber protected by painted terracotta revetments, had begun to move towards the Greek style, with high columns, a stone superstructure and a compact roof; and by the second century it had evolved into a new Roman type which represented a thorough intermingling of the two cultural strands. This new type, though using the materials and ornamental forms of Greek architecture, retained a distinctive shape (partly dictated by religious factors). Whereas Greek temples were constructed on low, stepped platforms and were more or less symmetrical, with colonnades enclosing the central building (*cella*) on all four sides, Roman temples were raised on high podia (fig. 10.3)

10.3 Frontal temple of Roman type: the Maison Carrée in Nîmes (AD 2–3).

and approached only from the front, generally by a monumental stairway. The emphasis was thus on the frontal aspect of the building, and the columns were often confined to the front and sides, with a plain wall at the back. A favourite setting for such temples was against the rear wall of a square surrounded by porticoes, which again emphasised the front. One particular type of temple peculiar to Rome and its sphere of influence has three *cellae* side by side; it may have been designed initially for the cult of the Capitoline triad, with Jupiter, Juno and Minerva each presiding over one of the chambers.

Concrete architecture

465. While religious architecture, by its very nature, remained more conservative, other types of building, especially utilitarian buildings, developed in directions for which there was no real precedent in the Greek world. A crucial contribution of Italy and the Romans was the invention of concrete. This happened towards the end of the third century, probably as the outcome of experiments with a *pisé* (rammed clay) technique of the type familiar in North Africa, knowledge of which may have reached Italy at the time of the Hannibalic Wars [29ff.]. It was found that a mixture of lime, water and a gritty substance, such as sand, produces on setting a strongly cohesive and durable material which can be used either to bond masonry or in its own right as a building material. Once discovered, concrete construction was gradually perfected during the following three centuries as, by trial and error, builders came to appreciate its potential. Greek architecture had depended essentially upon carefully shaped stonework assembled without mortar and upon 'trabeated' (post and lintel) construction, techniques which were prodigal of material, which required a high degree of skill at all stages, and which severely restricted the size of interiors. The concrete used by builders in Roman Italy was far less wasteful (the debris of stone-cutters was absorbed as an aggregate), it was much more effective for the construction of vaults, and once properly set it created a homogeneous mass which was less vulnerable to collapse than dry stone construction. Moreover it required less skilled labour: most of the skill came in the planning stage, and the actual execution was a mechanical process, so could be carried out by the slaves who were available in abundance after Rome's Eastern conquests. This opened the way to large-scale building projects. Among the earliest examples was a massive vaulted warehouse near the river-port in Rome, the Porticus Aemilia (193 BC), needed for the imports of grain required to feed the new metropolis ([219, 234]; fig. 5.6). Another was the quay at Puteoli, where it was discovered that an admixture of the local volcanic sand (*puluis puteolanus*, or pozzolana) gave the concrete 'hydraulic' properties, which enabled it to set even under water.

10.4 Substructures of a sanctuary on Monte Sant'Angelo at Terracina, the so-called Temple of Jupiter Anxur. Early first century BC.

Blending of Italian materials and techniques with the Greek decorative vocabulary

466. In the late second and early first century BC, increasing confidence in the handling of concrete led to the production of a number of great architectural complexes which show a precocious mastery of the new techniques. The sanctuary of Fortune at Palestrina, the so-called temple of Jupiter Anxur at Terracina (fig. 10.4), the temple of Hercules Victor at Tivoli – all were ambitious civic enterprises funded by central Italian cities which had acquired great wealth from the commercial opportunities offered by Rome's expansion to the East. Each used concrete vaulting in the substructures of terraces which shaped hillsides; and they favoured principles of planning (e.g. axial symmetry) and certain basic forms, such as a square enclosed by porticoes on three sides (introduced already in Asian cities of the Hellenistic period), which were to enjoy enduring popularity in Roman architecture. Particularly important for the future were features which resulted from a tension between the old Greek and the new Roman–Italian styles of building: vaulted passages supported on one side by a colonnade, concrete vaults decorated with sunken coffers inspired by Greek panelled ceilings, or arched façades on which the traditional columns and entablature were imposed as a decorative screen. This blending of Italian structural techniques with the Greek decorative vocabulary was to be one of the most fruitful contributions of the Roman age to the history of architecture.

The emergence of Roman portraiture

467. Just as Roman architecture developed from a fusion of Greek and indigenous elements, Roman sculpture emerged from the harnessing of Greek materials and expertise to the demands of Roman and Italian patrons. Nowhere is this more apparent than in portrait-sculpture. Greek portraits had become more realistic and matter-of-fact in Hellenistic times, with greater emphasis placed upon the depiction of age and experience; but for royal portraits in particular this was always tempered with idealisation. The image of Alexander the Great served as a model for all his successors: thus even a seventy-year-old king tended to be represented with romantically flowing hair and an upward tilt of the head suggestive of divine inspiration. The grandees of the Roman Republic took over this image. Among the first was T. Quinctius Flamininus, who was depicted on a gold coinage issued by the Greeks in honour of his symbolic proclamation of the liberation of Greece in 196 BC ([36]; fig. 1.6). The very idea of portraying a living individual on coins put Flamininus on a par with Hellenistic monarchs, and the style of the portrait, which shows the Roman general with the far-away gaze and agitated hair of a Hellenistic king, reinforced the message. Nothing so blatant was attempted in Italy itself till the last years of the Republic. But Pompey, significantly another general who had campaigned in the East, was commemorated by portrait-statues and heads in the style of Hellenistic monarchs (fig. 1.10); there is a conscious borrowing of traits from the portraits of Alexander, such as the king's sideburns, rising forelock, and the tilt of the head to one side.

Private portraits

468. Private portraits developed along very different lines, and here Italian social conventions were the determining factor. There had always been a strong interest in creating images of individuals in Italy, particularly in connection with the rituals of death. In Etruscan contexts we find them associated with funerary monuments; portraits of the dead appear, for example, on the ash-urns of Volterra and on the lids of Etruscan sarcophagi. In every case the head was the focus of attention, the body being ignored or simplified. In Rome there was a tradition among patrician families of keeping wax masks of

one's ancestors (*imagines maiorum*), which were worn by living members of the family in funeral processions. These in due course gave way to bronze or stone busts ([304ff.], fig. 3.5). There also grew up a tradition both in Rome and in other Italian cities (here matched by developments in the Hellenistic East) of setting up honorary statues of magistrates (usually after death) in public places. So many of these statues accumulated in the Roman Forum that the censors of 158 BC had to order a clear-out. All these strands contributed to the development of Roman private portraiture. They help in different measure to explain its salient features – an emphasis upon the head at the expense of the body, and an apparent predilection for the portrayal of old age. This last feature was symptomatic also of the structure of Roman public life, which imposed minimum ages for the holding of offices and generally placed a premium on long years of service and experience [168].

Verism

469. One of the most striking manifestations of Roman private portraiture was the so-called 'veristic' style, which emerged at the beginning of the first century BC and remained in currency till Augustan times and beyond. Verism meant the uncompromising depiction of the external features of the sitter: faces were represented with sharply cut creases, even with wrinkles and warts. To some extent this type of portraiture developed out of the realism of Hellenistic portraiture (indeed many of the artists were clearly Greeks); but it went much further than any Greek antecedents, and there must have been external factors which dictated the development. One was probably the practice of taking death-masks. There is evidence for a connection between death-masks and Roman funerary portraits; several death-masks have been discovered in tombs (including, from a later period, three half-masks from a tomb in Rome, one of which was a model for the stucco head of a boy found there). It is possible that the *imagines* too may have been worked with the aid of such masks [304–6]. Certainly some portrait-heads of the mid first century BC closely resemble death-masks (fig. 10.5). A further factor was the increasing demand for portraits, especially among the *nouveaux riches*. Whereas the upper classes, both in Rome and the Italian municipalities, had the money and taste to engage the best Greek portrait-sculptors, the freedmen and well-to-do members of the *plebs* who had no tradition of commissioning portraits and were unaware of the possibilities of subtle character analysis and dramatic enhancement available in Hellenistic art seem to have patronised second-rank workshops whose members lacked experience in the field and tended to concentrate on outward appearances, even to the point of exaggeration. In some

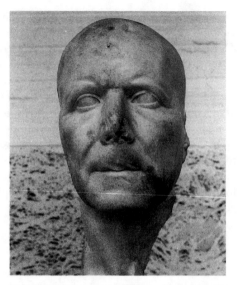

10.5 Veristic portrait resembling a death-mask. First century BC.

cases the linear style of these portraits, even when executed in marble, betrays the chisel technique of sculptors trained in the native tradition of working softer stones – even perhaps the modelling technique of workers in terracotta. Increased demand led also to an ever greater production of busts in preference to full-length statues; busts were quicker and cheaper to carve and took up less space, which made them better suited to display in domestic and funerary contexts.

Classicising statuary

470. Just as domestic and funerary portraits proliferated during the late Republic, so did the practice of collecting classical or classicising statues. There were not enough original Greek works to meet the demand, and many who wished to own a Greek statue could not afford the real thing. It was therefore necessary to produce copies (fig. 8.5). Copying became a flourishing industry, especially after the introduction of improvements in the methods of mechanical reproduction around the beginning of the first century BC. Along with faithful copies came deliberate variations upon the classical types. Some artists, notably Pasiteles and his pupil Stephanos, Greeks from southern Italy, produced pastiches: statues which combined a head from one work with the proportions of another and the posture of a third, or improbable pairs of statues from different sources engaged in conspiratorial conversation. Others endowed old types with new meanings: the best-known example is the cult-statue created by Arcesilaus for Julius Caesar's temple of Venus Genetrix, which was based upon a late-fifth-century Aphrodite. The passion for collecting, copying and adapting led to new forms of display. Many public buildings, such as theatres, fountains and baths, came to be designed to show off sculptures or other works of art; and certain architectural motifs, such as the niche, were developed specifically as settings for statues. Quite frequently an architectural façade contained a series of statues set in niches or intercolumniations; their arrangement would be dictated as much by a desire for formal balance as by any thematic links, and well-known types were sometimes reproduced in mirror image to provide balancing pairs. Many of the same principles governed the display of statues in private houses or gardens. One of the finest known collections comes from the so-called Villa of the Papyri at Herculaneum, where a vast assemblage of statues and busts in both bronze and marble, including portraits of philosophers, orators and kings, and representations of deities, athletes, dancers and animals, was distributed round courtyards, gardens and closed rooms. These works were arranged partly according to type and partly to secure a pleasing balance of forms; despite modern attempts to argue otherwise, there seems to have been no consistent and thoroughly worked out ideological programme.

The emergence of 'luxuria' in interior decoration

471. Private statue-collections are one aspect of the taste for a luxurious life-style which developed in Italy during the second and first centuries BC. Another, and far more widespread, was the introduction of Hellenistic forms of interior decoration, notably mosaic pavements and coloured wall-plaster. Both are widely attested already by the second century. In this period mosaics were often very fine, with figured panels carried out in minute chips of stone so arranged as to produce remarkable pictorial effects. Many of the best pieces were clearly imported from the Hellenistic East. Such are the two panels with scenes from plays by Menander found in the so-called Villa of Cicero at Pompeii; they carry the signature of the Samian Dioscurides and are set in marble trays for ease of transport. Even the famous Alexander mosaic, a battle-scene measuring over 5 metres by nearly 3 metres, is now thought to have been an import. The wall-decorations associated with such mosaics belonged to the so-called First Pompeian Style in which plaster was raised in relief to simulate slabs of brightly coloured stone. This form of stuccowork was ultimately inspired by monumental masonry or by patterns of marble veneer applied in Hellenistic palaces. Surrounded by such decorations, the wealthy burghers of Rome and the Italian municipalities could feel that they lived like kings. Indeed, the House of the Faun at Pompeii, 3,500 square metres in area, and decorated with numerous mosaics and fine stucco wall-decorations, was truly comparable to the dwellings of Eastern potentates.

The Second Style of wall-decoration

472. In the first century BC stucco relief gave way to a purely pictorial form of wall-decoration, the Second Style. This began as a fairly straightforward rendering of coloured blockwork behind screens of columns which are made to appear to project through the use of shading and perspective. But the illusion was soon elaborated by the introduction of further planes of depth and by ever new and more adventurous combinations of motifs. Pavements in compensation gradually lost their pictorial elements, and tended to become abstract and monochrome. We can follow the development through excellent examples in Rome and the villas outside Pompeii – the House of the Griffins in Rome, the Villa of the Mysteries at Pompeii, the Villa of the Poppaei at Oplontis (fig. 10.6). In its grandest manifestations, the Second Style is extraordinarily rich and imaginative; though based loosely on real architecture, it is not a literal transcription of anything that was ever built but a series of marvellous variations on architectural themes. With its brightly coloured stones and gilded enrichment, it probably evoked for the householder vague ideas of oriental luxury. This kind of decoration was clearly expensive to produce and was reserved for an élite of well-to-do patrons. Where it occurs in the houses of Pompeii, it tends to be limited to the best rooms of the house and was carefully preserved (or imitated) when re-decorations took place later.

Art as propaganda

473. A final aspect of Republican art to be considered, and one of great significance for the future, is the use of art for propaganda. A tradition of art celebrating military and political events was long established at Rome. Paintings were carried in triumphal processions or set up by victorious generals in public places: we hear of one as early as 264 BC exhibited by M'. Valerius Maximus Messalla on the side of the Senate-house to illustrate a victory of his in Sicily [429]. From the second century onwards this practice

10.6 Architectural decoration of the Second Style. Mid first century BC.

was increasingly exploited for personal aggrandisement. After the capture of Carthage in 146 BC [39], L. Hostilius Mancinus displayed a painting of his role in the successful assault and gave lectures on it to bystanders, thereby securing election to the consulship. Later generals, such as Lucullus, Pompey and Caesar, used emotional paintings in the Hellenistic manner to heighten the drama of their military achievements. Another sort of propaganda was the use of coins by mint officials to illustrate the deeds of their ancestors: G. Serveilius, for instance, moneyer about 127 BC, issued a coin showing his ancestor M. Serveilius, the consul of 202 BC, engaged in a famous single-handed combat. But these aspirations achieved more permanent form in the so-called 'historical reliefs'. The first examples are very much in the Greek style and were certainly executed by Greek artists. But the frieze of the monument of Aemilius Paullus at Delphi (fig. 1.7), which illustrates the Roman general's victory at Pydna in 168 BC [38], shows an unusual concern for factual detail, with the shield-types of the two armies carefully distinguished and the inclusion of a reference to the specific event which sparked off the battle – a skirmish caused by a runaway pack-horse. In Rome itself the reliefs from the base of a monument set up to commemorate Sulla's victory in the Jugurthan War are more traditional [51–2]. Evidently the work of Neo-Attic artists established in Rome, they employ an allegorical method in which depictions of captured armour and pairs of Victories standing on either side of a garlanded shield symbolise the success. The statue-group which stood on the base, however, is thought to have represented a real event, Jugurtha being handed over to Sulla as a prisoner by Bocchus, king of Mauretania; the composition is known from a coin minted by Sulla's son a generation later.

Roman messages in relief sculpture

474. The alliance of Greek workmanship and Roman propagandist subject-matter can be traced through the first century into the reign of Augustus. Particularly interesting are the reliefs from the so-called Altar of Domitius Ahenobarbus, actually a statue-base. On three faces this shows a marine cortège of sea-nymphs and Tritons celebrating the nuptials of Neptune and Amphitrite, a typical mythological subject rendered in a confident, full-blown Neo-Attic style; but the fourth face depicts a Roman census ceremony rendered with considerably less assurance (fig. 3.4). Recent examination has suggested that this fourth face is in a different kind of marble from the rest, and it is now believed that the marine reliefs were imported, possibly reused, from a Greek source, while the census relief was specially commissioned; the artist was no doubt Greek, but the subject was an unfamiliar one for which he had to create a new iconography. The census clearly refers to a specific ceremony associated with the individual benefactor, or an ancestor of the benefactor, who had the statue-base erected. In a frieze from the Basilica Aemilia in the Roman Forum, probably carved during a restoration of the building between 55 and 34 BC, the propaganda is less personalised in that the subject-matter seems to have been the legends associated with the foundation of the city and especially with the career of Romulus: the rape of the Sabine women, the death of Tarpeia and so forth. But the Aemilian family, which gave its name to the building and financed the restoration, claimed descent from Romulus, so there was once again an element of self-glorification. In the surviving reliefs the modelling of the bodies, the way in which the composition spreads figure by figure along the surface, and the sparing use of landscape details – all attest the continuing prevalence of the Hellenistic style.

The Augustan age

Augustus' use of imagery

(i) Roman legends

475. The coming to power of Augustus ushered in an age when the propaganda of the individual became synonymous with the propaganda of the state [85ff.]. The emperor, learning from the example set by the power-brokers of the late Republic, made visual propaganda one of the bulwarks of his régime. There were various aspects to this propaganda. One was the emphasis on Roman legends. Augustus' efforts to affirm a Roman historical identity and specifically to stress the links between the Julian family and the legendary founders of the city automatically promoted the popularity of artistic representations of the foundation legends. That such representations were not wholly new is attested by the Basilica Aemilia frieze and the painted frieze of a small late-Republican tomb on the Esquiline; but they received an extra boost from the publication of Virgil's *Aeneid* in 19 BC. The importance of Roman legend to Augustus' political programme was clearly demonstrated in the emperor's *Forum Augustum*, dedicated in 2 BC, which contained a gallery of statues of the heroes of Rome's past (fig. 2.4). The types of Romulus with the spoils won in single-handed combat with the king of Caenina and of Aeneas saving his father and son from the ruins of Troy became famous symbols (fig. 7.1; cf. [7, 301]): they were reproduced, for example, in statues and paintings of the following years at Pompeii.

(ii) Allegory

476. A second aspect of Augustan visual propaganda was the skilful and controlled use of allegorical messages. These are most obviously represented on the coinage, the one vehicle of artistic imagery which reached almost every inhabitant of the empire, however humble. Personifications of Peace or Victory, trophies of captured armour symbolising military successes, cornstalks promising peace and prosperity, a capricorn (Augustus' birth-sign) carrying a *cornucopia* and framed by the laurel-wreath of Apollo (Augustus' patron deity) – the variety of motifs on coin-reverses is never-ending. Similar messages appear in relief sculpture. The breastplate of the marble portrait-statue of Augustus from Prima Porta (fig. 2.6), which is almost certainly a copy of a prominent statue in bronze, depicts a historical event (the restoration in 20 BC of the standards captured by the Parthians at the battle of

Carrhae [70]) elevated to a higher plane by symbolic representations of the world order, peace and plenty, under the patronage of Apollo and Diana. The imagery has often been compared to that of Horace's *Carmen Saeculare* ('Secular Hymn'), composed for the Secular Games of 17 BC. Still more potent are the images on the Altar of Augustan Peace (*Ara Pacis Augustae*), begun in 13 BC and completed in 9 BC. Here the depiction of a precise event, the sacrifice in honour of Augustus' homecoming from a tour of the provinces, is enhanced by being juxtaposed with scenes from Roman legend (Aeneas sacrificing, the wolf and twins) and allegory (personifications of Rome seated on a pile of weapons and of Mother Earth amid symbols of peace and plenty)[6–7]. The whole ensemble forms a tightly knit programme stressing Augustus' links with the first founding of Rome and the new Golden Age that was being inaugurated. At the same time the representation of the imperial family, children and all, in a processional relief on the enclosure wall (fig. 2.5) both illustrates the importance of the family-unit in the emperor's social agenda and subtly aims to habituate the viewer to the idea of a dynastic succession.

(iii) Portraiture

477. A third aspect of Augustus' visual persuasion is his use of portraiture: he and his advisers introduced the ruler portrait to Rome. In this he picked up the baton from his adoptive father, Caesar, who (for all his reluctance to take the title 'king') had been the first Roman to emulate the Hellenistic monarchs in having his head represented on official coinage in his lifetime and had also allowed his statue to be set up in temples with those of the gods and made of materials, such as gold and ivory, previously reserved for the gods. Augustus was ostensibly more cautious, but no less deliberate in the use of his image as a focus of loyalty. His head appeared on the obverse of coins throughout his reign, setting an example which was followed by all his successors; and his sculptured portrait was promulgated according to official types which changed from period to period according to the *persona* that he wished to project. In his early years, before the battle of Actium, he appeared very much like a Hellenistic ruler, youthful, Apollo-like, with wind-tossed hair and a slight upturn of the head, features probably established by some famous statue or statues now lost (fig. 1.11). But after the settlement of 27 BC [79], he adopted a sterner, more dignified image suitable to his new title 'Augustus' – the so-called Prima Porta type, distinguished by its oval face, large ears and characteristic pincer-and-fork hairstyle (frontispiece). This type remained canonical for the rest of his reign, apart from some slight concessions to the

onset of old age. Though there was clearly an element of fidelity to the emperor's real physiognomy, it seems that by any normal yardstick the portraits were idealised; they certainly do not conform very well to the description given by Suetonius, which suggests a man of rather ordinary, if not unprepossessing, appearance. His artists clearly played down the defects and brought out the good points. Once established, the types were disseminated by means of plaster casts to the far-flung corners of the empire, ensuring that the imperial image was as familiar in Spain or Syria as it was in Italy.

Propagandist architecture

478. In addition to his use of visual imagery for propaganda purposes, Augustus and his advisers also exploited architecture to win support. This meant constructing buildings that were not only impressive (and provided employment) but also popular and useful. Here again he followed the examples set by his predecessors. The Forum of Augustus, a colonnaded piazza dominated by the temple of Mars Ultor, emulated (and surpassed) the Forum of Caesar. The theatre of Marcellus, completed in 11 BC, emulated and surpassed the theatre of Pompey. The portico of Octavia, a monumental square enclosing the temples of Juno Regina and Jupiter Stator, was a successor to similar buildings of Republican times, one of which (that of Caecilius Metellus) it actually replaced. Ambitious aqueducts constructed by the emperor's friend and chief minister Agrippa supplemented Republican aqueducts such as the Aqua Marcia. The Baths of Agrippa introduced a new building type of mass appeal. The pre-eminent factors in this programme are clear: a concern for the water-supply, an interest in keeping the public entertained, a desire to provide open spaces in an overcrowded city. In many of the new buildings, especially those of mass circulation, such as theatres and baths, concrete played a major role. Where Greek theatres were dependent on hillsides to support their auditoria, Roman ones could stand on flat ground and exploit concrete substructures to obtain corridors and staircases to the seating. For baths, concrete vaults, capable of achieving much greater spans than trabeated architecture, offered the possibility of creating vast internal spaces.

Augustan classicism

479. If Augustus' reign promoted further progress in the development of concrete architecture, in religious building and especially in architectural ornament it was more conservative. In many respects there was a deliberate harking back to the ideals of fifth-century Greece. This classicising tendency applies not just to architecture but to the other arts as well, including sculpture. It is possible to regard the Augustan era as the first true neo-classical age in history. The Prima Porta statue, for example, has a dignity and aloofness which appear consciously classicising, while its pose and proportions recall the work of the great Greek sculptor Polyclitus. The extensive use of marble for sculpture and architecture, aided by the opening a few decades earlier of the quarries at Luna, north-west of Pisa, placed Rome on a par with fifth-century Athens. Architectural ornament revived classical models, if sometimes in new guises and with new emphases (and often applied as a veneer to structures which were actually of concrete). Sometimes there was specific copying of Athenian prototypes. Carved elements from the Erechtheum in Athens, notably the caryatids (supporting members in the form of female figures) and some of the column-capitals, were precisely replicated in the porticoes of the *Forum Augustum*, apparently by means of casts brought from Greece. Exactly the same kind of copying was fostered by Lord Elgin in a later neo-classical phase.

Private art

480. In private art, some of the main fashions of the time were inspired perhaps by developments associated with the court of Augustus. It was during his reign that wealthy householders were swept by a passion for a new style of wall-painting, the Third Pompeian Style, which replaced the fictive architecture of the Second Style with effects based upon bright colours, two-dimensional schemes, and miniaturist polychrome ornament, all serving as a frame for central pictures (fig. 10.7). The Third Style represents a revolution in taste, but that it emerged from the latest phase of the Second Style is illustrated by the decorations of that phase in Augustus' own house on the Palatine. Here the painted columns were already becoming unrealistically slender, and plant-forms and arabesques were beginning to intrude – trends which were to harden in the following period. There was also a strong vein of Egyptianising ornament, a fashion evidently inspired by the conquest of Egypt in 30 BC. One of the earliest complexes of decorations which can be classified as Third Style comes from a villa at Boscotrecase, just north of Pompeii, identified with good reason as a property of the imperial family. Here the only architectural elements were pencil-thin columns and entablatures forming the pavilions which contained the central pictures; and they were little more than frames from which all sense of depth had disappeared. The pictures of the Third Style seem often to have taken their inspiration from Greek 'old masters' (well-known panel-paintings, many of which had been brought to Rome to be displayed in

10.7 Third Style wall-decoration in Pompeii. First half of first century AD.

the public buildings of Caesar and Augustus), but the wall-painters generally adapted them to the immediate context, changing the number of figures, the colour-schemes and the background settings. A favourite device was to put familiar mythological compositions in vast idyllic landscapes. No doubt an educated householder would be reminded of the poems of Theocritus, Virgil or Ovid. A less educated one – somebody like Encolpius [459] – might simply take pleasure in the snob-value of decorating his walls to look like the picture-galleries of the nobility.

The imperial period

The Julio-Claudian image

481. Augustus' successors followed his lead in exploiting art for visual per-suasion. Significantly, though few of them were blood-relations of Augustus, their portraits tended to be very similar to his; they were almost all represented with boyish faces and tousled hair. Indeed, some of the princes of the dynasty cannot be distinguished from one another. Artists working in the service of the imperial family had clearly settled on an iconographic model to which their portraits should conform. Claudius [96ff.], a shambling, slobbering figure according to Suetonius, appears in less flattering guise, with a weak chin and strongly protruding ears, but even his portraits are coloured by the Julio-Claudian image, and the gigantic scale and divine attributes of the best-known statues (those in the Vatican and at Lepcis Magna in Tripolitania) stress his majesty. Perhaps the most radical departure from the model comes with Nero [98ff.], who adopted a more romantic image, complete with waving hair and sideburns in the Hellenistic manner. As a philhellene with a passion for Greek poetry, a penchant for chariot-racing and grand dreams of Eastern conquests, he may consciously have chosen to model his image upon that of the Hellenistic kings.

Dynastic propaganda

482. The nature of their portraits indicates the concern of the Julio-Claudians to legitimise the dynastic principle of rule by stressing their links with Augustus. Another aspect of the development of the dynastic idea was the formation of galleries of statues of the emperors in the temples of Roma and Augustus founded throughout the empire: in many cases, as at Veii in Italy and at Lepcis Magna, these statues were on a colossal scale, indicating an equation between rulers and gods. It became normal to deify emperors after death (provided that they had not blotted their copybooks), and there was a tendency to regard even the living emperor as divine. The idea of a divine or quasi-divine ruling house appears even more clearly in some smaller works. A relief in Ravenna shows an array of members of the imperial family posing in divine guise: Augustus with the oak-wreath and sceptre of Jupiter, his consort Livia as Juno, and two of the princes, perhaps Livia's sons Drusus and Tiberius [89]. All are barefoot, as gods were customarily shown. A similar kind of glorification appears not just in publicly displayed works but in those that were in private possession. Various large sardonyx cameos, probably carved by artists attached to the imperial court as gifts to favoured friends and foreign dignitaries, combine dynastic propaganda with allegory. The finest is the *Gemma Augustea* in Vienna (fig. 10.8), which commemorates a military campaign conducted in Germany by Tiberius and his nephew Germanicus on Augustus' behalf in AD 12; they are shown in the presence of Roma and Augustus himself, who is being crowned by a personification of the Civilised World, while further allegorical figures (Earth and Ocean) look on. The Great

Cameo of France is a similar piece, though larger and with more figures; it dates to the time of Tiberius and apparently represents the emperor and his family taking leave of the dead Germanicus, who is being transported to the realm of the gods (including, of course, Augustus) by a winged horse. A further token of the desire of the Julio-Claudians to emphasise the unity of the ruling dynasty was the building of the Altar of Piety (*Ara Pietatis*) in honour of Livia. Begun by Tiberius and completed by Claudius, this seems to have imitated the *Ara Pacis Augustae* [476], with similar ornamental detail and similar processional reliefs.

Nero's Golden House: a new imperial luxuria in Rome

483. The Julio-Claudian dynasty foundered upon the egotism and megalomania of Nero, whose excesses ultimately alienated the senatorial class. But one of the major sources of his unpopularity was also the greatest artistic and architectural achievement of his reign. Taking advantage of the destruction caused by a disastrous fire in AD 64, Nero turned a large area of central Rome

10.8 Gemma Augustea: sardonyx cameo (19×23 cm) with reliefs commemorating Tiberius' German campaigns of AD 10–11.

into a private park, complete with a lake, a colossal bronze statue of the sun-god carrying the emperor's features, and a palatial residence noted for its revolving domes and decorations inlaid with gems and encrusted with gold [99]. Part of this villa, the Golden House, still survives, buried beneath the later Baths of Trajan (fig. 2.10). It is decorated throughout in the new Fourth Style, which is based upon perspectival architecture of a fantastic kind, but which in this particular context is more remarkable for its extraordinarily rich and delicate half-plant, half-animal forms – the 'grotesques' (so named because the remains of the villa were like *grotte*, 'caves') which inspired the painters of the Italian Renaissance. Architecturally its importance lies in a new confidence in the handling of concrete, now brick-faced, and a determination to experiment with new shapes of room (e.g. octagonal) and new structural forms (e.g. groined cross-vaults). The experimentation is still not entirely successful, because it results in several awkward transitions and redundant spaces. But it breaks important ground; and within a generation the new flexibility was to be brought to mastery by the architect Rabirius in Domitian's palace on the Palatine (fig. 2.12).

A change of image: the Flavians

484. After the débâcle of Nero's reign and the bloody wars between senatorial claimants which followed his death, a change of emphasis was almost inevitable [102ff.]. It was supplied by Vespasian, the first of the Flavian emperors, who came not from the urban nobility but from the local aristocracy of central Italy. His new image is clearly signposted by his portraits, which break with the idealisation of the Julio-Claudians and employ a type of verism; the emperor is depicted, no doubt realistically, as square-headed, wrinkled and balding (fig. 2.11). The choice is deliberate; Vespasian wished to emphasise the difference between himself and his predecessors, especially Nero, and that meant expressing qualities like experience and common sense, the virtues that had been prized in earlier days. For the same reason he cultivated a simple life-style and gave practical assistance in the rebuilding of the Capitoline temple in Rome, which had been destroyed in the civil wars. His popularist approach is epitomised by the symbolic filling of Nero's lake and its replacement by the first concrete amphitheatre in Rome, the Colosseum (fig. 10.9), a building designed to house the gladiatorial games and wild beast hunts which were the favourite entertainment of the masses (figs. 5.1, 5.2). The Colosseum, with its great elliptical auditorium supported entirely on a network of passages and stairways of circulation, could house crowds in the region of 50,000 and was the most ambitious of all ancient spectator buildings; it served as a model for

10.9 The Colosseum, Rome: the Flavian amphitheatre begun by Vespasian (after AD 70) and symbolically placed on the site of the lake of Nero's Golden House.

numerous further amphitheatres in Italy and the provinces. Further popularist buildings were put up by Vespasian's successors. His elder son Titus, for instance, built a new set of public baths, the first known example of the symmetrically planned bathing establishments of the so-called 'Imperial' type, including not only bath-chambers and exercise-yards but also meeting-rooms, lecture-halls and libraries, which were produced in ever grander versions over the next two and a half centuries.

Historical art

485. The practice of celebrating political and military events by means of relief sculptures gained strength during the Imperial period. A continuous series of monuments with such reliefs documents the progress. An interesting novelty of the early Empire was the introduction of background elements to provide specific settings; the earliest known examples are the temples of *Mars Ultor* and *Magna Mater* represented in sacrificial scenes on the *Ara Pietatis* [482]. At the same time sculptors grappled with the problem of suggesting large numbers of people. An important milestone is represented by the Arch of

Titus, erected after the emperor's death in AD 81 [104]. Here, in addition to a relief at the centre of the vault showing Titus being conveyed heavenwards on an eagle, there are relief-panels high on the side-walls which illustrate his triumphal procession after the sack of Jerusalem (figs. 3.1, 8.7; cf. [122, 380]). One shows the emperor himself in his chariot, being led by Roma and crowned by Victory (the inclusion of allegorical figures is a standard feature of the historical reliefs), the other a section of the procession carrying booty, including the menorah (ceremonial seven-branched candelabrum) and table taken from the Temple in Jerusalem. In each case the impression of a crowd is effectively conveyed. This is achieved partly by the way in which the procession is made to appear to come out of the background at one end and then turn back into it at the other, partly by the representation of spears and spoils in low relief against the 'sky' so as to suggest that they are held by hidden figures, and partly by the inclusion of background heads, again in low relief, between those of the foreground.

The Column of Trajan

486. The panels of the Arch of Titus were followed, barely 30 years later, by one of the masterpieces of historical relief, the spiral frieze of the Column of Trajan ([106]; figs. 4.2, 4.3, 4.4). This combines the use of precise landscape settings with a continuous narrative technique (i.e. successive episodes represented against an uninterrupted background) to tell the story of the emperor's two campaigns in Dacia. In addition, in order to accommodate the maximum number of figures while working in shallow relief, the artists have used a combination of horizontal and bird's-eye perspective, which results in the background figures being set above the foreground. The reliefs thus form an even network of detail covering the whole surface. In terms of content, the frieze has taken some liberties with the historical record (at least with the chronological order of events), but much of the detail is careful and precise, evidently based on sketches made in the field. A remarkable feature is the emphasis placed on the routine activities of the army; speeches, sacrifices, the building of camps, the receiving of envoys – all play a much greater part than actual scenes of combat. But the oddest feature of all is the very idea of wrapping the frieze round a column. It is an effective way of compressing a lengthy frieze into a narrow space, but the reliefs are difficult to follow from ground-level, and even if there had been upstairs galleries on the adjacent buildings this would not have helped much, because the viewer would have seen only one side at a time. Honorary columns supporting statues (as Trajan's did) were a familiar form of monument, going back to the early Republic, and decorative columns with spiralling vine-scrolls and the like are not unknown; but there is no known precedent for a column encircled by a narrative frieze. The project was probably the brainchild of an anonymous Trajanic architect or designer, who borrowed ideas from various sources (including possibly illustrated papyrus scrolls). It was to be copied, albeit with significant changes in style and emphasis, by the designer of the column of Marcus Aurelius, erected 70 to 80 years later.

A change of image: Hadrian

487. The accession of Hadrian saw another change in the imperial image. The new emperor was a man of culture, a lover of things Greek (his detractors called him *Graeculus* – 'Greekling'), and an inveterate traveller who made a point of going to see famous monuments and works of art. More than any previous emperor, apart perhaps from Nero, he had a personal interest in art and architecture; indeed, his architectural activities led to a quarrel with Trajan's chief architect Apollodorus which resulted in the latter being put to death. One of the keynotes of the new reign was a classical revival. The emperor himself revived the wearing of a beard in the classical Greek style (fig. 2.13), setting a trend that was followed by most of his successors; sculptors produced statues of a classicising type, notably the portraits of Hadrian's favourite courtier Antinous; architects turned back to classical models for the design and decoration of temples (notably the temple of Venus and Rome, designed by Hadrian himself). But at the same time Hadrian's reign ushered in an ever bolder and more assured use of concrete. His villa at Tivoli (fig. 5.3), a landscaped complex, which, like many Republican villas, adopted the names of famous monuments of the Greek East for its different component parts, was positively *avant garde* in its employment of curvilinear planning; it also introduced new types of dome, such as 'melon' or 'pumpkin' domes, including specimens with alternate flat and concave segments. One of the most radical changes saw a complete inversion of the pre-existing canons of architectural form. For the first time a building was designed (the vestibule of the Piazza d'Oro) in which interior space dictated the form of the exterior. A supreme example of the triumph of the interior is the Pantheon in Rome (fig. Ep.2), which is a plain drum externally, but internally offers a rich play of advancing and receding forms decorated with coloured marbles and columnar pavilions and spanned by a vast hemispherical dome – the widest ever built before the present century. The measures taken to address the problems created by the weight of this dome are remarkable: the materials incorporated in the concrete are graded so that the heavier come at the bottom and the lighter towards the crown, the thickness of the dome is reduced as it rises, the outward thrust is buttressed by the thickness of the enclosing drum, the downward pressures are carefully distributed by a system of relieving arches in the walls. Nothing is left to chance.

Wall-paintings and mosaics

488. Social changes which took place during the first century AD, notably a rise in the strength of the commercial classes and a more even distribution of wealth across the social spectrum, led to an increased demand for painted wall-decoration. This resulted in quicker and more careless work, as illustrated by much of the Fourth Style painting produced in Pompeii between 62 and 79. It seems that more and more people felt the social necessity of decorating their houses with murals, even where they lacked the spending power to employ first-rank painters. The same is true of Rome and Ostia in the second century: alongside careful and creative work, there is a much higher proportion of work which is slapdash and uninventive. What is true of Italy is true also of the provinces. Wall-paintings were disseminated ever more widely: even in a new frontier province like Britain there was hardly a town which could not have sustained at least one or two full-time firms of decorators. Much of the work produced tended to be a tired reworking of earlier formulae; architectural forms were often reduced to meaningless patterns; and colour-schemes were dominated by red and yellow ochres, pigments which were available relatively cheaply and in abundance. It comes as a pleasant relief to encounter more careful and skilful work such as a red and black scheme with candelabra peopled by animals and mythical creatures at Cologne, or a wall with architectural fantasies on a ground of yellow and vermilion at Southwark in London. As wall-paintings became increasingly accessible to all classes of clients, there was a tendency for their prestige as status-symbols to be transferred to the more expensive and time-consuming art of mosaic. During the second century mosaics became more widespread, and figured schemes enjoyed a revival. Different types prevailed in different parts of the Roman world: all-over figure-compositions in black silhouette on a white ground (fig. 10.10) in Italy and the Balkans; polychrome 'carpet' mosaics with figures and motifs within a geometric pattern in Africa and the north-western provinces; centralised schemes surrounding Greek-style central pictures in the East (e.g. at Antioch in Syria).

10.10 Detail of a black and white silhouette mosaic showing the adventures of Odysseus, here his encounter with the Sirens.

New residential and commercial architecture

489. The same social changes which led to the 'vulgarisation' of domestic wall-painting also contributed to improvements in urban housing. Here the experience gained in concrete construction over the previous three centuries was put to use in a programme of urban renewal which primarily affected the great commercial cities of central Italy, notably Rome itself and its port at Ostia, but which also influenced other major cities of the Mediterranean. The dangers and discomforts of life in the overcrowded capital are vividly recorded by writers such as Juvenal: the old ramshackle tenement blocks, built too quickly by speculators, often using inferior or inflammable materials, were all too prone to collapse and conflagration (cf. [210–11]). One of the consequences of the great fire of AD 64 was that Nero launched a rebuilding programme that took precautions against the possibility of further such disasters by laying down minimum spaces between buildings, restricting their height, and insisting on the use of fireproof materials. This is where brick-faced concrete came into its own. At Ostia, which expanded rapidly after the building of Trajan's new harbour in the early second century, it became the standard technique of construction, employed for high-rise blocks and warehouses alike (fig. 7.11). In Rome the evidence is much less well preserved, but a fine example of the new urban architecture survives in Trajan's 'markets', an aggregation of

shops and offices which climbed the hill above the emperor's new forum (fig. 6.12). This complex, in which the basic unit is the simple wide-doored and barrel-vaulted shop, achieves an astonishing flexibility of planning, moulding itself to the various levels and various angles of a site of the most unpromising configuration. At the same time it illustrates how even a workaday technique could acquire its own aesthetic. The brick surfaces are shaped into a delicate play of shallow pilasters and pediments which framed the openings in much the same way as the applied orders of monumental stone façades. In terms of design, the residential and commercial blocks of the Imperial city were one of Rome's legacies to the modern world; many of their features reappear in Italian cities of the Renaissance and may well be part of a continuing tradition which survived the Dark Ages.

The Antonines: changing modes of expression

490. During the Antonine period the language of classical art began subtly to change. This can best be seen in state reliefs. A traditional style continues in set-pieces, such as the front of the base of a column erected in honour of Antoninus Pius [106], which is carved with a cold and academic depiction of the emperor's apotheosis, modelled on a relief of Hadrian, and a series of eleven panels from an arch of M. Aurelius, which show stereotypes of imperial propaganda – the emperor distributing largesse (*largitio*), showing clemency (*clementia*), arriving in Rome (*aduentus*), setting out on an expedition (*profectio*), delivering an address (*adlocutio*). But a totally new style appears on the side-panels of Pius's column-base (fig. 10.11), which depicts a parade of cavalry. Here the figures are rendered with stumpy proportions, and appear one above another in a curious combination of 'normal' with bird's-eye view – a device which was prefigured to some extent on Trajan's column, but which was there softened by the presence of a landscape setting whereas here it is thrown into sharp prominence by the use of a completely neutral background. The best precedents for this style are to be found in certain funerary and religious reliefs commissioned by middle-class patrons of the first century AD, for example in a relief from Amiternum (central Italy) which shows a funeral procession. It had previously lacked the prestige associated with the naturalistic Graeco-Roman style, but from now on it begins to appear not just in private but also in official art. The reliefs of Marcus' column and, early in the third century, the Arch of Septimius Severus in the Roman Forum both employ it. There is probably no single explanation for the change from a more 'sophisticated' to a more 'naïve' kind of art, but one important purpose must have been to make the message *clearer*. If the language of imagery is reduced to simple,

10.11 Side-panel of the base of the column of Antoninus Pius: parade of cavalry. Soon after AD 161.

more easily readable symbols, it will become more accessible to the viewer. Illusionism, which is concerned primarily with its own internal logic, gives way to exposition, which prioritises the needs of the outside observer.

Frontality

491. Another aspect of the same trend was the increasing preference for the frontal position in the rendering of figures. This motif was used in the reliefs of Marcus' column, partly to emphasise the emperor (who was also shown on a slightly larger scale than the other figures), partly again for clarity of presentation, now a more important objective than achieving a narrative flow. Frontality was nothing new. It had appeared in official reliefs, especially those which placed emphasis on the nature rather than the actions of the figures, as early as Julio-Claudian times, for instance in the relief at Ravenna; and it had always been a characteristic of portrait statues, especially those that were designed to stand in niches. But the motif had previously been accompanied by a degree of relaxation (the torso was turned slightly to the side, or one leg was relaxed). It now became rigid and hieratic. Accompanied by an ever-increasing simplification of the bodily form, it turned into the dominant mode of early Christian and Byzantine art. Under Constantine, in the fourth century, it was even used for the emperor's head on coinage. It was well suited to the ethos of a society in which the emperor became godlike, or was regarded as the god's intermediary; his artistic image would make him appear to stare straight at or over the viewer, thus demanding either a direct response or respect. The result is an almost complete reversal of the classical tradition of art, which tended to show the gods as aloof and uninterested in mortal affairs: Roman art has finally emancipated itself from its Hellenistic roots.

FURTHER READING

J. J. Pollitt, *The Art of Rome c. 753 BC – 337 AD. Sources and Documents* (Englewood Cliffs, NJ, 1966; reprinted Cambridge, 1983)

A. Boethius, *Etruscan and Early Roman Architecture* (Pelican History of Art), 2nd edn, revised by R. Ling and T. Rasmussen (Harmondsworth, 1978)

J. B. Ward-Perkins, *Roman Architecture* (New York, 1977)

J. B. Ward-Perkins, *Roman Imperial Architecture* (Pelican History of Art), 2nd edn (Harmondsworth, 1981)

D. E. Strong, *Roman Art* (Pelican History of Art), 2nd edn, edited by R. Ling (Harmondsworth, 1988)

Epilogue: The ghosts of Rome

Rome refuses to die

492. Some entities seem too powerful to die. They leave not just their physical traces behind them, but their ghosts too. The world of Rome is like that. Its body is, of course, the city of Rome itself, the *urbs aeterna*, which still lives on, a modern city and once again the capital of Italy. Its ancient buildings jostle at every point with the clutter of another 1,500 years of development. Its ghost, however, wanders.

The idea of Rome

493.

You can see what remains of Rome, the very place which once seemed to be mistress of the world. She has been so worn down by a succession of immense sorrows, deserted by her citizens, under pressure from her enemies, her buildings in ruins, that we can see fulfilled in her the words uttered by the prophet Ezekiel against the city of Samaria . . . Where is the Senate? Where is the people now? Their bones have turned to dust, their flesh has rotted, and their whole range of secular offices has been blotted out . . . Since the Senate is no more and the people has perished, and yet among the few who are left sorrows and groans increase daily, Rome is empty and burning . . . (Gregory the Great, *Homily on Ezekiel* II.6.22)

By the time of the end of the empire in the West in the fifth century AD, Rome had already become a backwater. Procopius (*History* 3.2.25–6) even tells us of an emperor at Ravenna who confused 'Rome' with the name of a pet chicken. When Rome was being besieged by the Lombards in 593, Pope Gregory I (590–644) spoke of its greatness as long past (see the passage above). Yet the idea of Rome, as opposed to the real city, continued to be important from then right up until the Italian Risorgimento ('Rebirth') in 1870, when Rome again became

317

Ep.1 Roman temple turned into a Christian church. Temple of Antoninus and Faustina in the Roman Forum, now the church of S. Lorenzo in Miranda.

the capital of Italy. The idea continued, and in a sense the reality did too, in the use made of Rome by the Christian Church. Gradually, over its first few centuries, the Bishop of Rome began to seem to have some greater influence than others of his peers. We are all familiar nowadays with the result. The Vatican City in Rome is the centre of the Roman Catholic Church and the Pope is its head. In a way, the 'universal empire' of Rome was replaced by the universal Church, and Augustus' 'city of marble' was taken over as the centrepiece and symbol of the city of God – and its marble plundered to create it (fig. Ep.1).

The new Roman empire

494.

My powers of expression are overwhelmed by King Charlemagne, in his acts most just, the world's head, the people's love and pride, Europe's venerable peak, best of fathers, hero, Augustus; but also the power in a city [Aachen] where a second Rome in a new blossoming rises to great heights in massive bulk, touching the stars with its high-walled domes. (Einhard (?), *c.* AD 800)

The Eastern Roman empire became a separate entity soon after the foundation of Constantinople in 324 by the emperor Constantine. It was built on the site of the city of Byzantium. Hence the name 'Byzantine empire', which is used for the period after 629 AD. Its language was Greek. This Roman empire lasted until the Turks captured Constantinople in AD 1453.

But the idea of a Western empire refused to die. By 563, the emperor Justinian (527–65) had reconquered much of the Roman territory taken by invaders in the fifth century. This was a temporary revival. What paved the way for the continuation of the idea of a Western Roman empire was a collusion between the Church and the rulers of the Franks. In 496, the Frankish King Clovis (481–511) had been converted to catholic Christianity. In 800, Charlemagne was crowned emperor by Pope Leo III. It was a fundamental tenet of his propagandists that his regime was a new Roman empire. From 1254, this new Church-backed entity was known as the 'Holy Roman Empire' and lasted until the abdication of Francis II in 1806 (he became merely emperor of Austria as Franz II). A startling witness to this perception of continuity is the 'Kaisarsaal' or 'Hall of the Caesars' at Schwarzburg Castle. In the mid-eighteenth century, this room was decorated with seventy-six medallions containing portraits of all the 'emperors' from Caesar to Charles VI (d. 1720).

495. Rome's achievements have inspired many empire-builders. The idea of Rome was one of the spurs to the movement to reunite Italy in the nineteenth century. It prompted the tragi-comic attempts of Mussolini to build a new empire in the twentieth century. It is frequently invoked by those who plan a new united Europe today.

The Latin language

496.

The Latin language has been accepted by almost everyone as though by public consent as the common tongue of all the Christian peoples. I recall that at times there have been some who wrote to our king even in their own language and that it was in turn proposed that they should receive a reply in our Slavonic tongue, so that when they seemed too conscious of their own position and importance, we should not seem altogether negligent of our own. But in this, as in other matters, one should look to the agreement of the majority of the Christian rulers and peoples and use Latin . . . (Rainold Heidenstein, 1553–1620)

The main reason why Rome's ghosts have been able to walk so freely since the end of the ancient world is because Latin became the medium through which the world was educated, at least in Western Europe, and then beyond that in those areas colonised from it (the Americas, Africa etc.). This tradition was due to the fact that the universal Church adopted the universal language as its own. In the monasteries of the medieval world, the worship of God through the liturgy went on in Latin. Latin texts (Christian and pagan) were studied (though a poem like Virgil's *Aeneid* was read both for style and as an allegory of the journey of the human soul, rather than for its Roman content). All commentaries, hymns, poems, dramas, annals, letters, laws and saints' lives were written in Latin. As a result, Latin remained the language of education, and it was not until the late seventeenth century that scholarly and theological works were normally produced in vernacular languages. Newton's epoch-making *Philosophiae Naturalis Principia Mathematica* ('Mathematical Principles of Natural Philosophy') appeared in 1687. The parliaments of Croatia and Hungary used Latin until 1847 and 1848 respectively. Latin remains an important subject in the secondary-school curriculum in the last decade of the twentieth century. It is the history of Latin, then, which explains both the occurrence of Roman ghosts and the survival of interest in the language and Roman culture. Let us look finally at some of the rich results of this continued familiarity.

Roman ghosts

Visual ghosts

497. In the Italian Renaissance (late thirteenth to sixteenth centuries) a major change of taste and educational focus led not only to renewed interest in Rome's pagan literature, but also to the rediscovery of its architectural and artistic heritage. The recycling of Roman architecture and sculpture dates from this time. As a result, there is no city in the Western world which does not bear the visual imprint of Rome. And since the fashion belonged among the leisured classes, this visual legacy is particularly notable in the great country houses of the Renaissance and post-Renaissance period. The illustrations show a drawing of the Pantheon and Lord Burlington's imitation of the temple, built in the garden at Chiswick House in the early eighteenth century (figs. Ep. 2 and Ep. 3). New archaeological discoveries encouraged further imitations. The excavations at Pompeii in the early nineteenth century for instance, explain Alfred Norman's recreation of a Pompeian house for Prince Jérôme Napoléon in Paris in 1854–9.

498. The images of Rome's virtuous heroes were also used from the Renaissance on to make ethical or ideological points. The *studiolo* of Federico da Montefeltro at Urbino (1470s) was decorated with such images and the *Cambio* in Perugia likewise (1452–7). A school of painters in France in the

Ep.2 Section through the dome of the Pantheon drawn by Andrea Palladio, published as an engraving in *I quattro libri dell'architettura* (1570). Isaac Hare's translation into English (1738) was dedicated to Richard, Earl of Burlington. Cf. [487].

eighteenth century produced massive canvases of scenes from Rome's history, encouraged by government representatives intent on using the ideas of frugality and patriotism associated with the early Roman Republic as a model for France. But literary texts might of themselves inspire pictorial images. Ovid's *Metamorphoses* was particularly productive. The picture (fig. Ep. 4) shows Juno confiding Io, a woman loved by Jupiter, but now transformed into a cow, to the care of the monster Argus, and reflects *Metamorphoses* 1.624–5.

The ghosts of Roman ideas

499. There are two major ideas apart from empire itself which the modern world owes to Rome. These are Law and Republicanism.

(i) Law

Roman Law has been able to exert its influence because of the survival of the
Emperor Justinian's code of AD 533–4 [407ff.], which we know as the *Corpus
Iuris Ciuilis* ('Body of Civil Law'). It contains four parts, the *Digest* (or
Pandects), the *Code*, the *Institutes* (a textbook) and the *Nouellae*. Its impact
was limited in the period after the break-up of the Roman empire. But from
around 1070, when it was rediscovered, it became a text central to the development of legal practice and theory in the Middle Ages. It was studied and commented on continuously and these 'glosses' formed the curriculum in the
newly burgeoning schools of law which spread outwards from Bologna. The
use of the lawyers trained in these institutions first by the Roman Catholic
Church, and then by kings, princes and cities (except in England), ensured a
practical role for Roman Law. Even in the seventeenth, eighteenth and nineteenth centuries, the notion that Roman Law had been *usu receptum*
('accepted by usage') continued to allow it to influence academic study. This in
turn contributed to a process known as *usus modernus Pandectarum* ('the
modern use of the *Digest*'), because of the growth of a system of consulting

Ep.3 Lord Burlington's version of the Pantheon, Chiswick House.

Ep.4 Painting by Claude Gêlée, called Le Lorrain. Juno entrusts Io to the care of Argus.

learned experts. In Holland this trend produced the so-called 'Roman–Dutch law' which was exported to South Africa and was left in force by the English after their seizure of the Cape Colony in 1806. It is still the basis of law in the Republic of South Africa. Texts of Roman Law can even today be referred to in court because they have been 'accepted by use'.

(ii) Republicanism

500. Study of the Roman Republican political system suggested the whole idea of *representative democracy* as incorporated in the constitutions of the republics which began to appear from the eighteenth century onwards. In the United States of America, the House of Representatives and the Senate are two elected bodies which balance one another and share powers between them under the President. In Rome, the magistrates were elected by the popular assemblies, but policy was decided by the Senate, and implemented by the magistrates with *imperium* (see chapters 3 and 4). Direct democracy, which

has scarcely any modern imitators, was a Greek invention. One might multiply very easily examples of the reapplication of Roman constitutional ideas. One will suffice. In 1347, Cola di Rienzo initiated a populist revolution in Rome designed to re-establish the Roman Republic and free the government of the city from the control of the papacy. He used to this end a bronze tablet (actually dating from AD 70, the principate of Vespasian) to argue for the right of his contemporary citizens of Rome to be heirs to the privileges in administration of their ancient forebears.

Verbal ghosts

501.

> If you could hear, at every jolt, the blood
> Come gargling from the froth-corrupted lungs . . .
> My friend, you would not tell with such high zest
> To children ardent for some desperate glory,
> The old lie: *Dulce et decorum est*
>   *Pro patria mori.*   (Wilfred Owen)

There are four levels at which Latin words still command our attention. Most visibly, there are the Latin technical terms which crowd our languages. It is no accident that in everyday use it is the sexual vocabulary which contains most. A sense of *decorum* still governs the public expression – where that is deemed essential – of such things as *ejaculatio praecox* and *coitus interruptus*. Secondly, there are Latin expressions. Many have been naturalised into the language, for instance *e.g. exempli gratia*, 'for the sake of an example'. Some have historical roots in the period when Latin was generally employed as the official language. Such is the British monarch's title *Fidei Defensor*, 'Defender of the Faith'. It was originally conferred by Pope Leo X on Henry VIII in 1521 for a (Latin) book he wrote in defence of Catholicism. Unfortunately, Henry then divorced Catherine of Aragon and appointed himself head of the Church in England! Third there are quotations, some at one time so familiar to an educated public, that they could be used as shorthand. An example is the employment by Wilfred Owen in 1917 of a motto derived from Horace, *Odes* 3.2.13 (which few now believe was intended seriously by Horace), 'it is sweet and proper to die for one's fatherland', to undercut the jingoism of the patriotic children's writer and poet Jessie Pope (her 'Who's for the trench, / are you my laddie?' had been published in the *Daily Mail* in 1914). Finally, of course, there is the creation of a Latinate intellectual vocabulary in the European vernaculars (Latin: *creare, Latinus, intellectus, uocabulum, Europa, uernaculus*).

Literary ghosts

502.

Of man's first disobedience and the fruit
Of that forbidden tree, whose mortal taste
Brought sin into the world, and all our woe,
With loss of Eden, till one greater Man
Restore us, and regain the blissful seat,
Sing, Heavenly Muse . . . (Milton, *Paradise Lost*, 1.1ff.)

Next, and perhaps most prolifically of all, there are the literary ghosts, spawned by fifteen hundred years of close familiarity with the Roman classics by writers first of Latin, then of vernacular languages. Until the early nineteenth century, the classical doctrine of *imitatio* (see chapter 9) held sway. Hence, we readily find examples of close use of classical models, as is shown by the following two instances from Renaissance English drama. Shakespeare used Ovid's *Metamorphoses* (in the translation of Golding – Shakespeare had 'small Latin and less Greek') for the play within a play of 'Pyramus and Thisbe' in *A Midsummer Night's Dream*. Ben Jonson made very detailed use of a number of classical sources, including Sallust's *Catiline*, for his *Catiline* of 1611.

503. One might take as an example of continuing influence the history of the epic. Virgil's *Aeneid* served as the basis for Einhard's glorification of Charlemagne in the (Latin) poem quoted above [494]. Petrarch (1304–74), founder of the Italian Renaissance, really thought his Latin epic *Africa* would be the guarantee of his fame. Much later, in the seventeenth century, we have Milton's vernacular epic, *Paradise Lost*. It shows a remarkable affinity to Virgil's masterpiece in four respects (besides its *twelve* books): (i) its form ('blank verse', rhyme being 'the invention of a barbarous age'); (ii) its use of a divine 'apparatus' (the Devil is a major character); (iii) its highly mannered and Latinate syntax. For example, 'Me miserable!'=*Me miserum* (4.73); 'To whom the great Creator thus replied' (the italicised words form a *connecting relative*: 3.167); 'Forthwith on all sides *to his aid was run*' (the italicised words are a direct translation of an *impersonal passive* in Latin: 6.335); (iv) its Latinate vocabulary. For example, 'intend'='consider' (*intendere*); 'conjured'='conspired' (*coniurare*); 'adust'='dried' (*adustus*); 'impediment'= 'baggage' (*impedimentum*); 'omnific'='all-creating' (*omnis*+*facio*); 'gurge'='whirlpool' (*gurges*); 'pravity'='wickedness' (*prauitas*).

Ep.5 Roman legionaries as portrayed in the Asterix cartoons.

Roman bric-à-brac

504. In the twentieth century, Greek material has been rather more fashionable, perhaps, for recycling. But Roman subjects have had a continuing appeal for cinema audiences. One thinks of *Ben-Hur* and *Spartacus*, for example, which established our view of galleys and chariot-races indelibly. Fellini's *Satyricon*, among many others, has done the same for our image of Roman decadence. There have been many novels devoted to Roman subjects. The best-known in English, perhaps, are Robert Graves' *I, Claudius* and *Claudius the God*, adapted for TV in the 1960s. But it is worth mentioning the Swiss dramatist Dürrenmatt's *Romulus der Grosse* ('Romulus the Great'), which is an amusing investigation of the last Western emperor.

505. But it is not only the large-scale which shows the deep penetration of our consciousness by Roman images (even if these are merely images of images). All around, we can see trivial examples of this impact. There are Roman-style porticoes on fast-food stores and statue niches on minute houses on large estates. There are togas and gladiators in Bugs Bunny cartoons. There are Roman soldiers in Asterix books (fig. Ep.5). There are Latin tags on British pound coins. There is a laurel wreath on the Whitehall cenotaph.

For all this, the world of Rome is ultimately responsible.

FURTHER READING

R. Jenkyns (ed.), *The Legacy of Rome* (Oxford, 1992)

R.R. Bolgar, *The Classical Heritage and Its Beneficiaries* (2nd edition, Cambridge, 1958)

APPENDIX 1: ROMAN EMPERORS

The emperors are listed in chronological order from Augustus (*not* Julius Caesar). Unmarked dates are AD.

Augustus	27 BC – AD 14	
Tiberius	14–37	
Gaius (Caligula)	37–41	Julio-Claudian
Claudius	41–54	dynasty
Nero	54–68	
Galba	68–9	
Otho	69	
Vitellius	69	
Vespasian	69–79	
Titus	79–81	Flavian dynasty
Domitian	81–96	
Nerva	96–8	
Trajan	98–117	
Hadrian	117–38	
Antoninus Pius	138–61	Emperors adopted by predecessor

From this time, it was common for emperors to share the Principate. Brackets show the most important of these 'collegial' reigns (see further note after Probus 276–82).

Marcus Aurelius	161–80	
Lucius Verus	161–9	
Commodus	180–92	
Pertinax	193	
Didius Julianus	193	
Pescennius Niger	193–4	
Clodius Albinus	193–7	

Septimius Severus	193–211 ⎫	
⎧ Caracalla	198–217 ⎬	Severan dynasty
⎩ Geta	211 ⎭	
Macrinus	217–18	
Diadumenianus	218 ⎫	Severan dynasty
Elagabalus	218–22 ⎬	
Severus Alexander	222–35 ⎭	
Maximinus (the Thracian)	235–8	
⎧ Gordian I	238	
⎩ Gordian II	238	
⎧ Pupienus	238	
⎩ Balbinus	238	
Maximus	238	
Gordian III	239–44	
Philip (the Arab)	244–9	
Decius	249–51	
Trebonianus Gallus	251–3	
Volusianus	251–3	
Aemilianus	253	
⎧ Valerian	253–60	
⎩ Gallienus	253–68	
Claudius II (Gothicus)	268–70	
Quintillus	270	
Aurelian	270–5	
Tacitus	275–6	
Florianus	276	
Probus	276–82	

From this time, we see the beginning of a formal system of four emperors, two senior (called Augustus) and two junior (called Caesar). But its complexities are too great to be shown by bracketing names. For further information on this period, see A.H.M. Jones, *The Later Roman Empire 284–602* (Oxford, 1964).

Carus	282–3
Numerianus	283–4
Carinus	282–5
Diocletian	284–305
Maximian	283–305
Constantius	293–306
Galerius	293–311
Severus	305–7
Maximinus Daia (or Daza)	305–13
Maxentius	306–12
Constantine I	306–37

Licinius	308–24
Constantine II	337–40
Constans	337–50
Constantius II	337–61
Gallus	351–4
Julian (the Apostate)	355–63
Jovian	363–4
Valentinian I	364–75
Valens	364–8
Gratian	367–83
Valentinian II	375–92
Theodosius I	378–95

In 392, the empire was partitioned between West and East. The following is a list of emperors up to the end of the empire in the West.

Western emperors		Eastern emperors	
Honorius	392–423	Arcadius	392–408
Constantius III	421	Theodosius II	408–50
Valentinian III	425–55	Marcian	450–7
Petronius Maximus	455	Leo I	457–74
Avitus	455–6	Leo II	474
Majorian	457–61	Zeno	474–91
Libius Severus	461–5		
Anthemius	467–72		
Olybrius	472		
Glycerius	473–4		
Julius Nepos	474–5		
Romulus Augustus (Augustulus)	475–6		

APPENDIX 2: LATIN AND
GREEK WRITERS

The following is an alphabetical list of the writers quoted or mentioned in this book (including ancient Greek writers and Greek writers who belong to the Roman world and Medieval and later Greek and Latin writers); writers of individual letters in Cicero's collections are not listed here (e.g. Q. Metellus Celer), nor are writers known only from fragmentary quotations (e.g. Scipio Aemilianus); however, some important works without a known author are listed (e.g. the *Periplus Maris Erythraei*).

In all cases, the writer's name and dates are followed by the names of their work(s). In some cases, a brief account is given of their main work(s). Greek writers are indicated by (G) after their name. If you cannot find information here on the author you are interested in, or need more, you might try *The Oxford Classical Dictionary*, 3rd edn 1996, ed. S. Hornblower and A. Spawforth.

Acts of the Apostles (G) (late first century AD). An account of St. Paul's journeys up to his arrival in Rome.

Ambrose, St (AD 340–97), bishop of Milan. He is most famous for his hymns (the Medieval Latin for one of which is *ambrosianum*).

Appian (G) (b. *c.* AD 81), from Alexandria. He became a Roman citizen and *procurator Augusti*. Under Antoninus Pius he wrote his *Roman History*, in 24 books, of which 6–7 and 18–21 are complete, 1–5 and 8–9 are fragmentary and 10 and 18–24 are lost.

Apuleius (b. *c.* AD 123), from Madaura in Africa. He studied at Carthage, Athens and Rome. His marriage to Pudentilla, wealthy widowed mother of a friend, brought a prosecution from her family before the governor at Sabrata in 158/9 for having used magic to procure her fortune. His defence speech (*Apologia*) survives. He was acquitted and became a leading orator (his eloquence can be tasted in the *Florida*) and chief priest in the province. In 160, he wrote the *Metamorphoses*, usually known as 'The Golden Ass', a long Milesian tale about a young man called Lucius who is transformed into an ass while dabbling in magic. However, the final book (11) shows a philosophico-religious purpose behind the stories of magic, as Lucius is released from his animal state by the goddess Isis, into whose cult he is initiated.

Archilochus (G) (*fl.* either second half of eighth or second half of seventh century BC), from Paros. Writer of personal epigrams, iambic poems of attack and abuse, and fables, among many other types of verse.

Aristides, Aelius (G) (AD 117 or 129–181 or later), from Mysia. A sophist who studied at Athens, spent much time at the temple of Asclepius at Pergamum trying to cure a chronic illness, and lived out his life in Smyrna. Most famous for the *Sacred Discourses* (in six books, the last unfinished), which record revelations made to him by Asclepius, he was an 'Atticist' who also wrote speeches of various kinds (e.g. *On Rome*, a eulogy of the city, and *Panathenaicus*, a potted history of Athens), treatises (e.g. *On Rhetoric*) and prose hymns.

Aristotle (G) (384–322 BC), from Stagira in Chalcidice. A pupil of Plato (q.v.), tutor to Alexander the Great, and later founder of his own school, the Lyceum. A voluminous writer, whose surviving works are not the dialogues so prized for their literary qualities, but treatises apparently reflecting the courses given at the Lyceum. These include *Nicomachean Ethics*, *Politics*, *Poetics*, *Rhetoric*, *Prior and Posterior Analytics*, *Physics*, *Metaphysics*, *History of Animals* among many others.

Augustine, St (AD 354–430), from Thagaste in North Africa. His most influential works were the *Confessions* and *The City of God*.

Augustus (63 BC–AD 14), the first Roman emperor. An account of his positions (*honores*), of the monies he disbursed from his private funds for public purposes and of his military conquests, was set up outside his Mausoleum on bronze tablets and in copies on stone elsewhere (including Ancyra, where the most complete text has survived). Properly called *Index Rerum Gestarum*, it is now usually known as *Res Gestae* ('Achievements'). It is a major source for the Principate of Augustus.

Aurelius, Marcus (G) (AD 121–80), emperor from 161–80. He wrote some letters in Latin to his tutor Fronto, but his major achievement is the *Meditations*, written in Greek while on campaign. They are a series of aphorisms and reflections which follow the Stoic doctrines as outlined by Posidonius (q.v.).

Caesar (=C. Julius Caesar) (100–44 BC); see chapter 1; he wrote *Commentaries*, seven books on the campaign in Gaul (58–2 BC) and three on the Civil War (49–8 BC). A final book was added to each of these later by his lieutenants. The style is plain, but elegant, with dramatic and effective narrative. Cicero commented that only a fool would try to improve on his accounts (*Brutus* 262). Caesar's aims were (i) to record his own achievements (cf. Augustus), (ii) to give technical advice to military commanders (cf. *Gallic War* 4.17 for an account of the bridging of the Rhine), (iii) to justify his own political actions (e.g. *Civil War* 1.7, where he says he was forced into the war to maintain his 'standing' *dignitas*).

Callimachus (G) (third century BC), from Cyrene. A bibliographer and poet who spent much of his life attached to the great library at Alexandria. Little survives from over 800 volumes attested by a Byzantine writer. We have several *Hymns* and a book of *Epigrams*. But his influential *Aetia* (imitated among others by Ovid (q.v.) in the *Fasti*) is almost completely lost, as is his *Tables*, a catalogue of the library. His learned style was adopted by poets from Catullus (q.v.) on [446–7].

Cassiodorus (=Flavius **Magnus Aurelius Cassiodorus**, senator) (*c.* 490–583), founder of the monastery of Vivarium, for which he wrote the *Institutiones* ('Instructions'), a guide for the education of his monks. He also wrote the *Chronica*, a summary of

Roman history to AD 519. His lost history of the Goths is summarised in the *Getica* by Jordanes. The *Variae* ('Miscellany', *c.* AD 538) contain the most important letters and edicts he had written on behalf of the Gothic kings while prefect of the praetorium.

Cato (=**M. Porcius Cato**) ('The Elder') (234–149 BC), consul 195, censor 184. He wrote speeches, the *Origines* ('Roots': the early history of Rome, and the period from the Punic Wars to his own day, in seven books) and (the only survivor, though altered and adapted by later writers) *Rerum Rusticarum Libri* ('On Agriculture'). The *Dicta Catonis* ('Sayings of Cato') are a later, pseudonymous compilation.

Catullus (=**C. Valerius Catullus**) (*c.* 85–*c.* 54 BC) from Cisalpine Gaul, of a well-off family, served in Bithynia on the staff of a provincial governor for one year; we have his small collection of poems. They include some longer pieces (such as no. 63, about the youth Attis, who sailed to Phrygia, and, after castrating himself in a moment of frenzy, led the worship of the mother-goddess Cybele, only to regret his action when restored to sanity, and the minor epic or 'epyllion' no. 64, which tells of the wedding of Peleus and Thetis). But he is best known for his shorter personal poems, especially the love poems addressed to 'Lesbia' (generally identified with Clodia, the wife of the Metellus who was consul in 60 BC). Many of these analyse with compelling directness and a minimum of ornament the dilemma of the lover whose affair has turned sour. The series of poems addressed to a single woman had no Greek antecedents, but was the start of the Roman love-elegy (see Propertius, Tibullus, and Ovid). Catullus and his circle (which included the political orator and poet Calvus and the poet Cinna) were inspired by the third and second century Greek poetry of Alexandria, whose chief characteristics were erudition and polish.

Cicero (=**M. Tullius Cicero**) (106–43 BC), from an equestrian family from Arpinum in south Latium, consul 63 BC; (i) writer of oratory and treatises on rhetoric. We have 58 speeches delivered to Senate, law-courts or popular assemblies; among the most well known are the six speeches against Verres, the four against Catiline, and the sixteen *Philippics* against Mark Anthony; these are revised and polished versions and some of them (such as the five 'second action' speeches against Verres) were never delivered. *On the Orator* focuses on the general principles and practice of oratory, *The Orator* on the ideal orator and his education (including science, philosophy and rhetoric), *Brutus* lists eminent Roman orators and describes their qualities. (ii) Writer of letters. We have over 800 letters in four collections (*To his Friends, To Atticus, To Brutus, To his Brother Quintus*). Most were not designed for publication and are informal in style, with ellipses, colloquialisms and playful use of Greek words. (iii) Writer of philosophical works. These include: epistemology (*Academics*), political philosophy (*On the Republic, On the Laws*), theology (*On the Nature of the Gods, On Fate, On Divination*), ethics (*On Ends, Tusculan Disputations, On Friendship, On Old Age, On Duties*). Most are written in the form of the Aristotelian dialogue, with participants making long speeches in turn. The settings are Roman, but often in the past; e.g. *On Old Age* is set in 150 BC with Cato (q.v.), Scipio Aemilianus and Laelius (q.v.) as speakers.

Cicero, Quintus Tullius (102–43 BC), brother of M. Tullius Cicero and supposed author of the surviving *Commentariolum Petitionis* ('Pamphlet on electioneering') as well as four letters to his brother, was also a writer of (now lost) tragedies.

Columella (=**Lucius Iunius Columella**) (*fl.* AD 60), from Gades in Spain. In AD 60–5 he wrote *De Re Rustica*, 'On Agriculture', a treatise in twelve books, which relies much on his personal experience of estate management.

Demosthenes (G) (384–322 BC), an Athenian politician. His surviving orations include political speeches (for example the *Philippics*, which attacked Philip of Macedon – the title was given later to Cicero's speeches against Mark Antony) and private law-court speeches.

Digest (*Digesta*), the name given by Justinian to the main part of his codification of the law, which came into force on 30 December 530. It is also know as *Pandectae*.

Dio Cassius (G) (=**Cassius Dio Cocceianus**) (*fl.* 194), from Nicaea in Bithynia. He wrote a history of Rome from the beginnings to AD 229, of which books 36–54 (68–10 BC) survive in full, 55–60 (9 BC–AD 46) in epitome, and 17 and 79–80 in part.

Einhard (*c.* 770–840), educated at the monastery of Fulda and later an important advisor in the court of Charlemagne. He wrote a treatise on the Cross, and about sixty letters, but is most famous for his biography of Charlemagne (*Vita Karoli Magni*). He may also have written an epic about Charlemagne which is known as *Karolus Magnus et Leo Papa* ('Charlemagne and Pope Leo').

Ennius (=**Q. Ennius**) (*c.* 239–169 BC), from Calabria in South Italy (a part Greek, part Oscan, part Latin area); brought to Rome by Cato (q.v.) after fighting for Rome in the second Punic War, where he became tutor to the noble Fulvii. He was a leading writer of Roman tragedy, adapting classical Athenian drama (especially Euripides). He also wrote comedies and a verse miscellany called *Saturae* ('Satires'). His most important work was *Annales* ('Annals': now fragmentary), a history of Rome from earliest times to his own day, using Homer as a model and written in hexameters.

Epictetus (G) (*c.* AD 55–*c.* 135), from Hierapolis in Phrygia. Originally a slave of Epaphroditus, Nero's freedman and secretary, he was allowed to attend philosophy lectures by Musonius Rufus, and later freed. Flavius Arrianus (Arrian) collected his lectures, which survive in four books. He also published a summary of his Stoicism in the *Encheiridion* ('Manual').

Epicurus (G) (341–270 BC), from Samos, founder of the philosophical school which bears his name. Of his voluminous writings (e.g. 37 books *On Nature*) very little survives (three letters and two collections of maxims). He was a fundamental influence upon Lucretius (q.v.).

Eratosthenes (G) (*c.* 275–194 BC), from Cyrene. A pupil of Callimachus (q.v.), he succeeded Apollonius of Rhodes as the librarian at Alexandria. He wrote on literary matters (*On Ancient Comedy* was in *c.* 12 books), on chronology, mathematics, astronomy and geography (where his was the first systematic treatment). His works survive only in fragments.

Fabius Pictor (G) (=**Quintus Fabius Pictor**) (*fl.* 218 BC), a Roman senator who wrote a history of Rome in Greek, as a way of selling Roman institutions and policy to the Greeks. The work (which is lost) began from Aeneas, dated the foundation of Rome at 748/7 BC and went down to Fabius' own times.

Festus (=**Sextus Pompeius Festus**) (fl. second century AD), a grammarian whose epitome of the lexicographical work of Verrius Flaccus survives.

Florus (=**Lucius Annaeus Florus**?) (*fl.* AD 100), from Africa. Author of the *Epitome Bellorum Omnium Annorum DCC* ('Conspectus of all the Wars Fought in the Previous 700 Years'), a two-book panegyric of the Roman people. A fragment of a dialogue and some of his poetry survive.

Frontinus (=**Sextus Julius Frontinus**) (*c.* AD 30–104), probably suffect consul in AD 74. Excerpts survive of his two-book treatise on land-surveying. The *De Re Militari* ('On Military Science') is lost, but the four books of the *Strategemata* ('Stratagems') survive. As *curator aquarum* ('Water supremo') under Nerva in AD 96, he started a work on Rome's water-supply (*De Aquis Urbis Romae*), whose two books were completed under Trajan.

Fronto (=**Marcus Cornelius Fronto**) (*c.* AD 100– *c.* 166), from Cirta in Numidia, tutor in rhetoric to future emperors Marcus Aurelius and Lucius Verus. He was suffect consul in 143. His letters to Marcus Aurelius and others survive.

Gaius (second century AD), one of the most famous Roman jurists. His *Institutionum Commentarii Quattuor* ('Institutes') were the basis for the 'Institutes' of Justinian, and given legislative validity from the same day as the *Digest* (q.v.).

Galen (G) (AD 129– *c.* 199), from Pergamum in Asia Minor. He became court-physician to Marcus Aurelius. A voluminous writer of philosophical and medical books, which fill twenty volumes in the only complete modern edition.

Gallus (=**Gaius Cornelius Gallus**) (*c.* 69–26 BC), from Forum Iulii. He was a poet and a general and a friend of Augustus, who lost the emperor's goodwill and committed suicide as moves were made to prosecute him. His four books of love-elegies (*Amores*) are lost (except for one line). Parts of some poems were recently discovered on a papyrus from Qasr Ibrim, in Egypt (see fig. 9.6).

Gellius, Aulus (*c.* AD 130–*c.* 180). His *Noctes Atticae* ('Attic Nights') in twenty books (of which book 8 is lost, along with the beginning and the end) is a haphazard collection of short discussions of various topics of philosophy, history, law, grammar etc. written in a style tending towards the archaic. It is mainly used for its information on early Latin writers, especially the many passages it quotes from them.

Gregory the Great (*c.* AD 540–604), from Rome, pope from 590 until 604. His writings include fourteen books of letters, homilies, dialogues, the *Moralia* ('Ethical Teachings'), and the *Regula Pastoralis* ('Pastoral Rule').

Heidenstein, Rainold (1553–1620), from Koenigsberg. He was a civil servant and royal historiographer of King Stephen Bathory. He composed important works in Latin on Polish and Russian history and a tract on the chancellorship of Poland, *Cancellarius* *sive de Dignitate et Officio Cancellarii Regni Poloniae* ('The Chancellor or On the Position and Office of the Chancellor of the Kingdom of Poland').

Henry VIII (1491–1547), king of England 1509–47. He won the title *Fidei Defensor*, 'Defender of the Faith', for a book written by him in 1521 entitled *Assertio Septem Sacramentorum contra Martinum Lutherum* ('Assertion of the Seven Sacraments Against Martin Luther'), in defence of the Catholic Church.

Hesiod (G) (seventh century BC), from Ascra in Boeotia. His surviving works include the two didactic poems *Works and Days* and *Theogony*. He was regarded as the 'inventor' of the didactic genre.

Hipparchus (G) (*c.* 190–after 126 BC), from Nicaea in Bithynia. Mainly known as an astronomer (his *Commentary on the Phaenomena of Eudoxus and Aratus* in three books survives), he also wrote a geography critical of that of Eratosthenes (q.v.) and important in the development of mathematical geography.

Homer (G) (eighth/seventh century BC?), to whom are traditionally ascribed the great epic poems *Iliad* and *Odyssey*, which were imitated by Virgil in the *Aeneid* (q.v.).

Horace (=Q. **Horatius Flaccus**) (65–8 BC), from Venusia in the south-east of Italy, son of a freedman (an auctioneer's agent or debt-collector); educated at Rome and Athens, where he joined the Republican cause under Brutus and Cassius. He fought on the defeated side at Philippi (42 BC). His father's land was confiscated, but he was pardoned and employed as a secretary in the public service. In 38 BC, Virgil introduced him to Maecenas, who became his patron and established him on an estate at Tivoli (Tibur). His first two works, *Epodes* and *Satires* (two books), published in 30 BC, were dedicated to Maecenas. The *Epodes* is a collection of miscellaneous personal poems on love, politics and war in the metres of the seventh-century BC Greek poet Archilochus. The *Satires* follow the lead of Lucilius (q.v.), the inventor of this peculiarly Roman genre. They have a strong ethical agenda, wrapped up in their tongue-in-cheek tone ('what's to stop me telling the truth with a smile?', *Satires* 1.1. 24–5). But their subject-matter is not confined to themes such as human failings like lust, greed and ambition. The poems also deal with the nature of satire itself (1.4 and 10; 2.1), Horace's own life (1.6; 2.6), amusing incidents (the statue of Priapus 1.8; the social climber 1.9; the pretentious dinner-party 2.8), and philosophy (2.3 and 7). It has been suggested that Book 1 is highly political in its portrayal of the good sense, humanity, self-irony and humour of the Maecenas circle (which extends, of course, to Octavian – see 1.5). Some years later came two books of *Epistles*, which may be seen as a direct continuation of the *Satires*. The second book contains a letter to Augustus about literature (2.2). A third book contains the famous *Epistle to the Pisos*, usually known as the *Ars Poetica* ('Art of Poetry'). Horace's major work is the *Carmina*, the four books of *Odes*. The first three, dedicated to Maecenas, were published in 23 BC and the fourth, requested by Augustus, in 13. They are a mixture of personal and political poems. The first deal with such things as the pleasures of wine, love, friendship, poetry and the countryside, mingled with urbane and ironic philosophical reflections offered to the friend to whom his remarks are in each case addressed. The second reflect the shifting moods of the political situation over a period of great uncertainty: (i) guilt over the civil war (1.2) and the neglect of religion and morality (3.6.1–4, 16–48); (ii) fear that Octavian might use his victory harshly (3.4.41–2, 65–8): (iii) worry that illness or misfortune would carry him off before he achieved his aims (1.35.29–40): (iv) gratitude at Augustus' restoration of peace and prosperity to Italy (4.5, 15). His models are the sixth-century BC Greek poets Sappho and Alcaeus, among others, and he boasts of his achievement as the transfer to Latin of complex Greek metres (*Odes* 3.30.13–14). However, he was well aware of the Romanness and originality of his political poems, such as the so-called 'Roman Odes' which begin book 3. There (3.1.2–3) he describes himself as 'a priest of the Muses, uttering songs not heard before'.

Isidore (Bishop of Seville *c.* AD 602–36), a writer on history and natural philosophy, as well as a commentator on the Old Testament. His most influential work, crucial in the transmission of knowledge from the ancient world to the Middle Ages, was the *Etymologiae* ('Etymologies'), an encyclopaedia dealing with the seven liberal arts and a large variety of additional material.

Javolenus Priscus (=**Gaius** (or **Lucius**) **Octavius Tidius Tossianus Javolenus Priscus**) (*c.* AD 60– after 120), a prominent jurist whose *Epistulae* ('Epistles') were excerpted by Justinian's (q.v.) compilers for the *Corpus Iuris Civilis*.

Jerome, St (*c.* AD 331–420) was translator and editor of the version of the Bible known as the *Vulgate* and a prolific commentator on the Bible. He also wrote a large number of letters which have survived.

Justinian (=**Flavius Petrus Sabbatius Justinianus**) (*c.* AD 482–565), Roman emperor from 527–65. In February 528 he established a commission to codify imperial laws from Hadrian's time onwards. This was published as the *Codex Justinianus*. It was followed shortly by the *Digest* (q.v.) and the *Institutiones* (see **Gaius**).

Juvenal (=**D. Iunius Iuvenalis**) (*c.* AD 55–*c.* 130). There is hardly any reliable external evidence about Juvenal, except that Martial (q.v.) knew him. His sixteen *Satires* in the tradition of Lucilius (q.v.) were published in five books in the reigns of Trajan and Hadrian. The persona of the satirist moves from the angry and indignant in books 1 and 2, to the more detached and philosophical in later books. Juvenal's technique is to assault the reader with a barrage of examples, leading up to a pointed and memorable epigram. Famous examples are *probitas laudatur et alget* ('honesty is praised and freezes': 1.74), and *mens sana in corpore sano* ('(you should pray for) a healthy mind in a healthy body': 10.356). The themes of his pieces include the homosexuality of pseudo-philosophers (Satire 2), the unequal treatment of a client invited to dine with his patron (5), the iniquity of women and the inadvisability of marriage (6) and the necessity of showing a good example to one's children (14).

Laelius (=**C. Laelius**) (second century BC), orator and philosopher, member of the circle of Scipio Aemilianus and central figure in Cicero's dialogue 'On Friendship' (*De Amicitia*); see also Lucilius, Polybius, Panaetius.

Livius Andronicus (*c.* 284–204 BC), a war-captive from Tarentum in South Italy. He translated the *Odyssey* and produced the first drama at Rome (240 BC). He wrote tragedies and comedies, adapted from Greek sources.

Livy (=T. **Livius**) (59 BC–AD 17), born near Padua, but came to Rome soon after Actium (31 BC). Never formally under Maecenas' patronage, he none the less attracted the attention and encouragement of Augustus for his history of Rome. This covered the period from the foundation to 9 BC and was in 142 books. Only 1–10 (covering 753–293 BC) and 21–45 (covering 219–167 BC) survive. Livy probably planned to continue the work to the end of Augustus' reign (AD 14), but died before its completion. His history belongs to the annalistic tradition (contrast Caesar and Sallust), based ultimately on the annual records of magistrates and significant religious events called *tabulae pontificum*. Livy's stance was aristocratic and Republican. According to a speaker in Tacitus (*Annals* 4.34), he praised Pompey so much that Augustus called him 'the Pompeian'. But his Roman patriotism and ethos must have endeared him to Augustus none the less. In his *Preface* (3), he claims to be 'preserving the record of the greatest nation in the world' and his accounts of the various legends of the monarchy and early Republic show enthusiasm for the standard Roman virtues. On the other side is a Sallust-like pessimism about 'recent times in which the might of a long powerful people is beginning to destroy itself' (*Preface* 4). Livy invites the reader to trace the moral decline of Rome to 'the present day when we can endure neither our vices nor the remedies needed to cure them' (*Preface* 9). These parts also recall some of the early *Odes* of Horace (q.v.) and may belong to the period before the positive side of the Augustan achievement began to assert itself.

Lucan (=M. **Annaeus Lucanus**) (AD 39–65), nephew of Seneca. He joined the Pisonian conspiracy against Nero and was forced to commit suicide. His incomplete poem (ten books) *Bellum Ciuile* ('The Civil War') describes the Civil War between Caesar and Pompey, but blatantly takes the side of Pompey and criticises Caesar's victory at Pharsalus as spelling the end of liberty for generations to come (7.632–46).

Lucian (G) (*c*. 120–after AD 180), from Samosata in Syria. A sophist who travelled around the Roman world giving displays of his work, he was a satirical writer who invented the comic dialogue (a cross between the philosophical dialogue and Old Comedy) and most famously wrote a spoof travel narrative (the *True History*). A large body of his writings is extant.

Lucilius (=C. **Lucilius**) (d. 102 BC), a wealthy knight from Suessa Aurunca in Latium. He was a member of the circle of Scipio Aemilianus (*c*. 185–129 BC). He was the first writer of the hexameter satire, though his earlier works used trochaic metres. Only fragments survive of his 30 books of *Satires*, which covered a vast range of topics and were notable for their open attacks upon political enemies.

Lucretius (=T. **Lucretius Carus**) (*c*. 98–*c*. 55 BC), a noble; we have his six books *On the Nature of Things*, a hexameter didactic poem, based on the philosophy of Epicurus (q.v., and see chapter 8), who had taught that the object of life was pleasure (not the gratification of desires, but rather the absence of pain: Greek *ataraxia*). The human soul was, like everything else, a collection of atoms which would one day be dissolved. So the soul was mortal and there was no need to fear death or the afterlife. The gods exist, but do not concern themselves with humans. His philosophy is argued with almost religious fervour. He follows the precedent set by Greek philosophers like Empedocles (*c.* 495– *c.* 435 BC) in writing in verse.

Martial (=**M. Valerius Martialis**) (*c.* AD 40–*c.* 104), born and educated in Spain. He came to Rome *c.* 64 and enjoyed the patronage of Seneca and Lucan (q.v.) until their disgrace. His later patrons included the emperor Domitian, under whom he wrote eleven of his twelve books of *Epigrams.* For eulogies of the emperor, see 7.5 and 8.21. Martial's reward was an honorary tribunate and membership of the equestrian order (3.95.5–10). His poems are satirical, presenting a vivid picture of sexual perverts, legacy-hunters, spendthrifts, domineering wives, would-be poets, incompetent doctors, the vain, the ugly, the rich and the poor.

Menander (G) (*c.* 342–292 BC), from Athens. A comic poet, the acknowledged master of Greek 'New Comedy', a genre based on situation and character, whose plays were among those 'imitated' by Plautus (q.v.) and Terence (q.v.).

Menander Rhetor (G) (third century AD), from Laodicea. He wrote a surviving treatise on epideictic ('show') oratory, in which he articulates the rules of hymns, prayers, encomia etc.

Nepos, Cornelius (*c.* 100–25 BC), from Cisalpine Gaul. He wrote a universal history (*Chronica*) which is lost and love-poems and anecdotes (no longer extant). Of his 16 books *De Viris Illustribus* ('Famous Men'), one has survived on foreign generals (mostly Greek). We also have a life of the elder Cato and of his contemporary Atticus.

Newton, Sir Isaac (1642–1727), physicist, author of *Principia Mathematica Philosophiae Naturalis*, published in 1687. In this work the famous Newtonian laws of motion were first articulated.

Obsequens, Julius (fourth century AD?). He composed tables of prodigies from 249 to 12 BC (of which those for 190–12 BC survive).

Ovid (=**P. Ovidius Naso**) (43 BC–AD 17), born at Sulmona (90 miles north-east of Rome), of an established middle-class family. Studied in Rome and Athens. Though directed towards a legal and political career, by the age of twenty-five he had chosen poetry instead. His first work was the *Amores* ('Loves'), a collection of love-elegies (that is, written in elegiac couplets) centred around a woman called Corinna. His approach is detached, amused, even cynical, enjoying love as a game and parodying the earnestness of his older contemporaries in the same genre Propertius and Tibullus (qq.v.). Next came the *Heroides*, a series of verse-epistles (also in elegiac couplets), written in the personas of deserted heroines of mythology to their lovers. There followed the *Ars Amatoria* ('Technique of Love'), a mock-didactic treatise on the art of seduction. Its lessons are countermanded by the *Remedia Amoris* ('How to fall out of love'). Ovid was in dangerous waters here, given Augustus' programme of moral reform. He essayed political correctness in his *Fasti*, six books (of a projected twelve) of elegiacs on the twelve months of the Roman calendar, explaining the origins of Roman rites and customs. This was followed by his *Metamorphoses*, a compendium of Greek, Roman and Near Eastern myths involving transformations of shape, in which Ovid led up to the apotheosis of Julius Caesar as the culminating transformation and referred to the future divinity of Augustus. But his attempts at ingratiation failed and in 8 AD, after being implicated somehow in a scandal connected with Augustus' family, he was exiled to Tomis on the Black Sea. The scandal (he calls it an *error*) was half of the reason. The other was a *carmen* (the *Ars Amatoria* – see [425]). His last works are two collections of verse-epistles (again in his favourite elegiac couplets), the *Tristia* ('Sad poems') and *Ex Ponto* ('Letters from Pontus'), addressed to friends, mostly complaining of his lot and pleading (in vain) for his recall. Ovid had loose connections with Messalla, Tibullus' patron, but was in fact independent. He wrote poetry as a path to immortality (*Amores* 1.15.1–8), to entertain, not to instruct or move. His greatest merit is his wit, with which he combines a great narrative skill.

Palladius (=**Rutilius Taurus Aemilianus Palladius**) (fourth century AD), composer of fourteen books on agriculture and an elegiac verse poem on grafting.

Panaetius (G) (*c*. 185–109 BC), from Rhodes. He was a Stoic philosopher (head of the Stoa from 129) and member of the circle of Scipio Aemilianus (see also Polybius, Laelius, Lucilius). Cicero used one of his works in *De Officiis* ('On Duties').

Parthenius (G) (*fl.* 73 BC), from Nicaea, a poet whose presence in Rome was a crucial factor in the influence of the 'Alexandrian' style. He wrote mainly elegiac verse, little of which has survived. His *Love's Labours* (*Erotika Pathemata*), prose outlines of love stories from Greek literature for the use of his poet friend Gallus (q.v.), have survived.

Paul, St (G) (first century AD), writer of many *Epistles* to the newly formed Christian churches collected together in the New Testament. See also Acts of the Apostles.

Periplus Maris Erythraei ('Circumnavigation of the Erythraean Sea') (first century AD), a manual for navigators and traders describing the coastal routes from Egypt to India and along East Africa.

Persius (=**A. Persius Flaccus**) (AD 34–62), from a well-to-do Etruscan family, wrote one book of six *Satires*, and died young, apparently of natural causes. He was much influenced by Horace (q.v.), but is more opaque and takes a resolutely Stoic line.

Petrarch (=**Francesco Petrarca**) (1304–74), from Arezzo. The founder of the Italian Renaissance, with its emphasis on the study of the classical writers for their ethical teachings. He was a voluminous writer of Latin prose (e.g. *On the Solitary Life*, *The Remedies for Both Types of Fortune*) and verse. He wrote poetry in Italian, but regarded Latin as the primary literary language. His verse epic *Africa* was published after his death, in 1396.

Petronius (=**T. Petronius**), probably identical with Nero's *arbiter elegantiae* ('arbiter of elegance'), who was consul in AD 61 and died in 66. Tacitus (*Annals* 16.18) records that Nero 'regarded nothing as enjoyable or refined unless Petronius gave his approval to it'. His *Satyricon*, originally a twenty- or even twenty-four-book work in a mixture of prose and verse, told with many digressions the story of Encolpius. The only section to survive substantially is centred on the dinner-party given by the vulgar *nouveau riche* Trimalchio. As for the rest, it seems that sexual escapades are a predominant feature of the narrative, but so is discussion of literature.

Philo Judaeus (G) ('Philo the Jew') (*c.* 30 BC–*c.* AD 45), from Alexandria. He was a writer of philosophy and biblical exegesis, strongly influential on later Greek Christian thought. Much of this work is extant. For his trip to Rome, see [94].

Philostratus (G) (=**Flavius Philostratus**), a member of the intellectual circle of the emperor Septimius Severus and Julia Domna. He wrote, among other works, the *Life of Apollonius of Tyana* and *Lives of the Sophists*. The latter gives lively accounts of many contemporary practitioners of the rhetorical arts.

Pindar (G) (518–after 446 BC), from Cynoscephale near Thebes in Boeotia. He wrote lyric poetry for wealthy patrons. Four books of his *Epinician* ('Victory') *Odes* survive, celebrating victories at the great panhellenic festivals.

Plato (G) (*c.* 429–347 BC), from Athens. The writer of 25 philosophical dialogues, in many of which Socrates is an interlocutor, and the *Apology*, a version of Socrates' defence speech. In the *Republic*, he sketched the ideal society and developed the notion that reality is secondary to the 'Ideas' or 'Forms' upon which it is based. In *Laws*, he outlined legislation for the management of a society such as existed in actuality. In around 385 BC, he established the Academy, a school near the grove of Academus outside the city walls.

Plautus (=**T. Maccius Plautus**) (*c.* 254–184 BC), 20 of whose comedies survive, adapted from Greek 'New Comedy' (Menander (q.v.) and others). The plays are all *palliatae*, that is, in Greek dress, with Greek settings, names, costumes and masks. However, the musical element is now much greater and the plays are more like musical comedy than spoken drama. Plautus' plays are characterised by bold character-drawing (e.g. tricky slaves, mercenary pimps, swaggering soldiers), exuberant language and less realism than in Menander.

Pliny (the Younger) (=**C. Plinius Caecilius Secundus**) (*c.* AD 61–112), nephew of **Pliny the Elder** (=**C. Plinius Secundus**, AD *c.* 23–79), who wrote the encyclopaedic *Natural History*, and died studying the eruption of Vesuvius which buried Pompeii and Herculaneum. Pliny the Younger had a successful political career, becoming praetor under Domitian in 93, consul in 100, and governor of Bithynia in 110–12. He later represents himself (*Letters* 3.11) as having been in the same danger as his Stoic friends, executed in the year of his praetorship (see *Letters* 9.13). It seems unlikely. His *Letters* were written and (with the possible exception of book 10) published under Trajan. The first nine books contain personal letters, highly polished, self-contained pieces, each dealing with a single theme (for example, 6.20, on the eruption of Vesuvius, addressed to Tacitus (q.v.)). The tenth book contains his correspondence with Trajan concerning the official business of his governorship of Bithynia, which included the problem of how to proceed with Christians (10.96 and 97). There is also one speech surviving, the *Panegyric*, which contrasts the misdeeds of Domitian with the actions of Trajan.

Plutarch (G) (=**L. (?) Mestrius Plutarchus**) (*c.* AD 45–*c.* 120), from Chaeronea. Among his voluminous works are the *Moralia*, a series of ethical essays, and the *Parallel Lives*, which set side by side the lives of famous Roman and Greek statesmen.

Polybius (G) (*c.* 200–after 118 BC), from Megalopolis. He was a member of Scipio Aemilianus' circle (see also Panaetius, Laelius, Lucilius). Books 1–5 and some excerpts of his forty-book *Histories* are extant. It treated Roman history down to 146 BC.

Posidonius (G) (or **Poseidonius**) (*c.* 135–*c.* 51/50 BC), from Apamea on the Orontes. A philosopher who had studied under Panaetius (q.v.), he founded a school at Rhodes which was attended by Cicero. A strong supporter of Pompey, he composed fifty-two books of *Histories* (lost), which continued the story of Rome from the end of Polybius (q.v.) to the dictatorship of Sulla. His interests covered a wide area, but he was especially influential in meteorology. His work is lost, but it formed the basis of Seneca's *Natural Questions.*

Procopius (G) (b. *c.* AD 500), from Caesarea in Palestine. His main works are the *History of the Wars of Justinian* in eight books and *The Secret History.*

Propertius (=**Sextus Propertius**) (b. *c.* 50 BC), from a landowning family near Assisi. He composed four books of elegiacs, the first published in 29, the fourth in 16. The range of the poems, both in theme and tone, is large. Book 1 (the *Monobiblos*), is largely concerned with his mistress Cynthia. She was identified by the ancients with a real person, Hostia, as were also the Lesbia of Catullus (Clodia) and the Delia of Tibullus (Plania). Book 3, however, attempts to imitate the *Aetia* of Callimachus (q.v.) and in Book 4 we find some 'official' pieces, dealing with Augustus and his relatives (4.6, 4.11). See also Tibullus and Ovid for love-elegy, which grew from the combination of two Greek genres, the elegiac love-epigram and the longer elegiac poem on the loves of gods and heroes.

Quintilian (=**Marcus Fabius Quintilianus**) (b. *c.* AD 35), from Calagurris in Spain. He was a well-known teacher of rhetoric at Rome, given a public appointment by Vespasian. His 'An Orator's Education' (*Institutio Oratoria*) was published in 12 books in AD 95. It covers the training of an orator from childhood on. The central idea was that rhetoric should produce a cultivated man of good character. The work was very influential in the Italian Renaissance.

Revelation (G) (first century A.D). The final book of the New Testament, sometimes known as the *Apocalypse.*

Sallust (=**C. Sallustius Crispus**) (86–35 BC) from Aminternum, in Sabine territory north-east of Rome, served in Caesar's army, reached the praetorship and was governor of Numidia (46), was prosecuted for extortion and retired to write history. We have *Catiline* and *Jugurtha* (see chapter 1 for the historical context). He also wrote *Histories* of the period 78–67 BC, which survive in fragments. He was strongly moralistic, emphasising issues which illustrated the decline and corruption of the Roman state, ascribable to the wealth created by the wars of the second century BC (*Catiline* 6–13). His style is epigrammatic and colourful.

Scriptores Historiae Augustae ('Writers of Imperial History'). A collection of biographies of emperors from AD 117–284 (with 244–59 missing). The work is modelled on that of Suetonius (q.v.). There is disagreement as to the date, authorship and purpose of the work(s), though the MS. tradition claims that six different authors wrote them during the period of Diocletian and Constantine.

Seneca (=**Lucius Annaeus Seneca**) (*c.* 4 BC–AD 65), from Cordoba in Spain, son of the rhetoric teacher **Annaeus Seneca** (whose *Controuersiae* and *Suasoriae* survive). He held the quaestorship under Tiberius, gained a reputation in the Senate under Gaius, and was exiled by Claudius. Recalled as tutor to Nero, he played an important part in the imperial administration as Nero's political adviser. By AD 62 he had fallen from favour and retired from politics. In 65, he was forced to suicide on suspicion of complicity in the conspiracy against Nero led by the Stoic Piso. The central paradox of his life was that he combined immense wealth with preaching Stoic philosophy, in which worldly goods were not to be valued. His writings include twelve philosophical treatises in the Ciceronian manner (e.g. *On Anger*) and a collection of *Letters to Lucilius*, essays on ethics in an epistolary style, modelled (though not doctrinally) on the letters of Epicurus. Seneca also wrote nine tragedies, mostly based on Sophoclean and Euripidean originals, but designed for recitation rather than performance, and with exaggerated rhetorical effects.

Serapio (G) (second or first century BC), from Antiocheia. A mathematical geographer, later than Hipparchus and Panaetius (q.v.), who thought the sun was eighteen times the size of the earth.

Silius Italicus (=**Tiberius Catius Asconius Silius Italicus**) (*c.* AD 26–*c.* 101), consul 68, wrote the *Punica*, an epic poem on the Second Punic War in seventeen books, the first six of which were published under Domitian, whose military exploits of 92–3 he praises.

Statius (=**P. Papinius Statius**) (*c.* AD 45–96), son of a schoolmaster of Greek ancestry from Naples, whose success as a professional poet began at the accession of Domitian (AD 81). In 91, he completed his twelve-book epic, the *Thebaid*, which treats the quarrel of Oedipus' sons Eteocles and Polynices and owes much to Virgil's *Aeneid*. Its popularity is attested by Juvenal (*Satires* 7.82–6). A second epic, the *Achilleid*, was unfinished at his death. He also wrote five books of short poems, the *Siluae* (lit. 'Woods', but signifying 'new material'), between 92 and his death. These graceful occasional poems for various patrons were composed in various metres and include congratulations, consolations, birthday-poems, wedding-poems and some fulsome eulogies of Domitian (1.1; 1.6; 4.1–3).

Strabo (G) (64/3 BC–*c.* AD 21), from Amasea in Pontus. His *Historical Sketches* in forty-seven books are lost. The seventeen books of his *Geography* are extant. He is critical of Eratosthenes (q.v.) and uses Posidonius (q.v.).

Suetonius (=**Gaius Suetonius Tranquillus**) (b. *c.* AD 69), perhaps from Pisaurum, perhaps from Hippo Regius in Numidia. His *De Viris Illustribus* ('Famous Men') survives only in abbreviated and fragmented form. His biographies of the first twelve emperors (including Julius Caesar) survive complete, except for the beginning of *Julius*.

Tacitus (=P. **Cornelius Tacitus**) (AD *c. 56–c.* 117), praetor 88, consul 97, governor of Asia 112–13. His major works (neither survives complete) are the *Histories* and the *Annals*. But we also have three shorter monographs: *Agricola*, a biography of his father-in-law (governor of Britain 78–85), written in 98, *Germania*, an ethnographic treatise (*c.* 98), and the *Dialogue on Oratory* (*c.* 106). The *Histories*, of which we have the first four and a half books of a probable twelve, were written *c.* 100–9 and covered the period AD 69–96. The *Annals*, written *c.* 110 onwards, of whose original eighteen books we have large parts of 1–6 and all of 11–16, covered the period from Tiberius' accession to the death of Nero. Tacitus makes the usual claim that history must publicise virtue and deter from vice (*Annals* 3.65), but more specifically he is intent on tracing the decline of liberty in the face of despotism and deploring the accompanying decline in morals. His account of the period is deeply pessimistic and it has proved hard for readers to accept his claim to be writing 'without rancour or prejudice' (*Annals* 1.1).

Terence (=P. **Terentius Afer**) (184–159 BC), an ex-slave from Carthage. He wrote six comedies adapted from Greek New Comedy originals, including the *Woman from Andros* (*Andria*) and *The Self-Tormentor* (*Heauton Tomoroumenos*). Less flamboyant than Plautus, he achieved his greatest success as the major inspiration for later European comic drama.

Theocritus (G) (*c.* 300–*c.* 260 BC?), from Syracuse. His surviving poems include epigrams, brief epic narratives and mimes. But he is most famous as the inventor of bucolic or pastoral poetry, which was imitated by Virgil (q.v.) in the *Eclogues*.

Thucydides (G) (*c.* 460–*c.* 399 BC), from Athens. He wrote a history of the Peloponnesian War in 8 books (incomplete at his death).

Tibullus (=**Albius Tibullus**) (*c.* 55–19 BC), from Latium, who wrote under the patronage of M. Valerius Messalla Corvinus (an opponent of Octavian at Philippi who changed sides and became consul with him in 31). He composed sixteen poems, published in two books, the first (with ten poems) in 27, the second (containing six) perhaps postumously. The pieces are written in elegiac metre and mostly concern his love for Delia, Nemesis and Marathus. But, like Propertius, he also turns his hand to other themes, as in the pious commemoration of his patron's triumph in 27 (2.1). See also Propertius and Ovid for Roman love-elegy.

Twelve Tables (451–50 BC). The earliest codification of Roman Law, established by a commission of *decemuiri* and originally set up on wooden or bronze tablets in the Forum.

Ulpian (=**Domitius Vlpianus**) (d. AD 223). One of the last of the leading Roman jurists, he wrote around 280 books. He was cited in the compilations of Justinian (q.v.) more than any other writer.

Valerius Flaccus (=**Gaius Valerius Flaccus**) (d. *c.* AD 93), wrote eight books of an unfinished epic *Argonautica*.

Valerius Maximus (*fl.* 14 AD), writer of nine books of *Memorable Deeds and Words*, dedicated to the emperor Tiberius, possibly published after AD 31.

Varro (=Marcus Terentius Varro) (116–27 BC), probably from Reate, was Rome's most outstanding philologist and antiquarian. He is said to have edited 490 works by the age of 77. We have the titles of 55 works, but only two survive in more than fragments. We have Books 5–10 of his *On the Latin Language* (originally 25) and all three books of his *On Agriculture*.

Velleius Paterculus (*c.* 19 BC–after AD 30). from Campania. His two books of *Roman Histories* (of which a part of Book 1 is missing) cover the period from Romulus to AD 30.

Virgil (=P. Vergilius Maro) (70–19 BC), born in Mantua in the Po valley, from a landowning family whose estates were confiscated after Philippi (42 BC); educated at Cremona, Milan and Rome, he joined Catullus' circle, then moved to Naples to study philosophy under the Epicurean Siro. Here, under the influence of Alexandrianism, he wrote the *Eclogues* (*c.* 42–*c.* 37 BC). They are modelled on the *Idylls* of the Greek pastoral poet Theocritus (q.v.) and are a work of highly polished poetry in the Alexandrian manner. Two of them (1, 9) reflect the confiscations of land for the resettlement of war veterans after Philippi. At this time Virgil was under the patronage of Asinius Pollio, a former lieutenant of Caesar's who had gone on to fight for Antony. But Maecenas won Virgil over and at his instigation Virgil wrote the *Georgics* (*c.* 36–*c.* 29 BC), a didactic poem on farming. In some of its technical details (e.g. astronomy, beekeeping) it displays an Alexandrian love of erudition. But it also sounds a note of patriotic pride, in the cities, rivers, and heroes of Italy as well as its climate and crops (2.136–76), and in the old traditional Italian way of life which made Rome great (2.532–4). It represents Octavian as the potential restorer of peace and morality to a land physically and morally devastated by the wars (1.498–514). Virgil's great epic, the *Aeneid*, promised in the *Georgics* (3.46–8) and written (*c.* 29–19 BC) with the encouragement of Maecenas and Augustus, was almost complete when he died on his way back from Greece. Virgil had ordered his executors to destroy the work if unfinished at his death. Augustus countermanded the instruction. The poem tells Aeneas' story in a narrative shape borrowed from Homer (q.v.). Beginning with a storm and shipwreck off Carthage (book 1; cf. *Odyssey* 5), Virgil contrives to include a narrative of the fall of Troy in Aeneas' own words to the Carthaginian queen, Dido (books 2–3: cf. *Odyssey* 9–12). Aeneas' journey onwards towards his fated foundation of Lavinium (first step on the chain towards 'the high walls of Rome', via Alba Longa) involves a visit to the Underworld (book 6: cf. *Odyssey* 11). His arrival prompts stiff resistance from the Italians, under Turnus, whose chosen bride Lavinia is now promised to Aeneas (cf. the wrath of Achilles in the *Iliad*). Aeneas is given immortal armour by Vulcan. The shield is described in detail, with its scenes of future Roman history (book 8: cf. *Iliad* 18). At the end, after a lengthy single combat, Aeneas sends Turnus' soul complaining to the Underworld (book 12: cf. *Iliad* 22). But Virgil has other literary debts. His accounts of the fall of Troy (book 2) and (even more) of the fate of Dido (who falls in love with Aeneas, book 4) make much use of the techniques of Greek tragedy. And he has by no means abandoned his Alexandrian past. In addition to the polish, craftsmanship, and compression of the poem (12 books to do the *Odyssey* and *Iliad*'s 48!), he has used the portrayal of the abandoned Medea in Apollonius' *Argonautica* in his evocation of Dido. There are also passages of extended description whose origins are Alexandrian (e.g. the personification of Rumour, 4.173–88, or the alteration of Aeneas' fleet into nymphs, 10.215–59). Into this narrative, Virgil infuses a patriotic vision of the future of Rome under Augustus, which owes something to the native tradition of Roman epic, and specifically to Ennius (q.v.), whose rhythms and phrases – sometimes whole lines – are recalled in the parts which deal with this material. Much of it is contained in four passages: the speech of Jupiter to Venus in book 1 (257–96), the revelations of Anchises to Aeneas in book 6 (756–853), the scenes on the shield in book 8 (626–731), and the final agreement between Jupiter and Juno in book 12 (791–842). These passages emphasise that it has been Rome's destiny from the beginning to conquer the world (1.278–82) and to impose peace and civilisation (6.851–3). They portray Augustus as the culmination of that destiny (1.286–8), as a man fated to be a god (1.289–80), as the restorer of peace and morality (1.291–6), and as the bringer of a new golden age (6.791–3); he is also the conqueror of distant peoples and places (6.793–800) and the victor of Actium (8.675–713). They show a pride in the small towns of Italy (6.771–6) as well as in the site of Rome (8.337–69) and they emphasise that the new race will be based on the traditional qualities, customs and religion of the Italian people (12.807–42).

Vitruvius (= **Vitruvius Pollio** (or **Mamurra?**)) (*fl.* 50 BC), an architect and military engineer, was the writer of ten books *On Architecture*.

Writers of Imperial History see *Scriptores Historiae Augustae*

Zeno (G) (*c.* 333–262 BC), from Citium in Cyprus. He founded the Stoic school of philosophy.

APPENDIX 3: CROSS-REFERENCES WITH THE TEXT OF *READING LATIN*

This list of topics, names and Latin words is broken down by section of *Reading Latin: Text*. Paragraph references are not given, since these can readily be found in the other indexes and Appendices. Items relate to (i) the categories of the General Index, (ii) the Topographical Index and Index of Personal Names, (iii) the Index and Glossary of Latin Words, (iv) in the case of writers, also to Appendix 2.

Reading Latin (Text) 1 Intro.
comedy
familia, family
houses
slaves

1A

marriage

1B

Lares

1C

praetors (*praetores*)

1D

children
taverns
dowry
patria potestas , paternal authority

1E

property-groupings, census, knights, senators, *proletarii*

1F

retailers

1G

fides
temples, shrines
gods (*see also Index of Personal Names under Fortune, Peace, Victory*)

2A

prostitution
nummi, cash
weapons
writing
biclinium see *triclinium*
slaves
generals (*imperatores*), commanders

2B

Greek literature

2C

soldiers, Roman army, veterans
gods
Minerva

2D

Troy
triumphs

2E

omens and portents

3A

legions, Roman army, soldiers, veterans
Jupiter
Mercury

3B

legati, legates
cavalry

3C

fishermen/fishing (*for* fish-vendors, *see*
retailers)
dress

3D

emotional relationships

4 Intro.

Sicily
provincial government
Roman empire
de repetundis, extortion

4A(i)

forum, forum
statues

4A(ii)

Magna Mater, Cybele
Scipio

4A(iii)

Ceres
rituals
women
provincials

4A(iv)

amici, friends

4B(i)

women

4B(ii)

consuls, praetors

4B(iii)

meals

4B(iv)

Roman citizens
governors

4C(i)

silver-plate
art, Greek

4C(ii)

prouincia, provinces
patronus, patrons

4D(i)

ships
pirates
staff (of a governor), *comites*

4D(ii)

Sertorius
execution of Roman citizens

4E(i)

praefectus, prefects
wine

4E(ii)

ships, navy, naval power
pirates

4E(iii)

pirates

Syracuse
war, Hannibal, Sicily

4F(i)

punishment of Roman citizens
forum, *forum, Forum Augustum*
lictors
Venus

4F(ii)

eques, knights
Roman citizens
Sertorius
crucifixion

4G(i)

libertas, freedom
Roman Law

4G(ii)

eques, knights
execution of Roman citizens
crucifixion
Roman Law
parricide
libertas, freedom

5 Intro.

Caesar
senators
equites, knights
magistrates – quaestors, praetors,
consuls, tribunes of the plebs, aediles
cursus honorum
Senate
imperium, power
dignitas, dignity
amicitia, friendship
clientes, clients
patronus, patrons
nobilis, nobility
Cicero
Catiline

nouus homo, 'new man'
Sallust
Virgil
names
Sulla

5A(i)

censors
Senate
women
consulship
Cicero
Catiline
nobility, *nobilis*
nouus homo, 'new man'
comitia, assemblies of the people
Manlius

5A(ii)

women
debt
Sempronia
Greek literature, Roman literature, literature
poetry
matronae, wives

5A(iii)

consulship
Cicero
women
courts (of law)
Catiline
Manlius, C.
eques, knights
senators
Etruria
senatus consultum ultimum
Metellus Celer, Q.
Picenum
money-lenders
nexum, debt-bondage

5B(i)

Gaul, Gauls
forum, forum

5B(ii)

patronus, patrons

5B(iii)

public meetings (*contiones*)
nobility, *nobilis*
Gabinius

5C(i)

slaves

5C(ii)

praetors
bridges

5C(iii)

Senate procedure
consuls, praetors
execution of Roman citizens
temples
Sibyl, prophecy
Caesar
Cato the Younger

5D(i)

Vestal Virgins
paterfamilias, paternal authority

5D(ii)

forum, forum
temples

5D(iii)

equites, knights
census, property-groupings, *proletarii*,
senators, knights

5D(iv)

census, property-groupings, *proletarii*,

senators, knights
Penates
Vestal Virgins
temples
libertas, freedom

5E(i)

Senate
prison
gens, tribes

5E(ii)

legions, Roman army
Gallia Transalpina

5F(i)

uirtus, Roman virtues
Roman army
battles, oratory
gloria, fame
libertas, freedom
patria, fatherland

5F(ii)

conspiracy
exile
uirtus, Roman virtues
Fortune
Victory

5G(i)

battles
standards
legatus, legates
veterans

5G(ii)

weapons

5G(iii)

civil war
Victory

6A(i)

poetry
Catullus
Alexandria
Venus

6A(ii)

Pollio, Asinius
metre
Spain

6A(iii)

homosexuality

6A(iv)

Metellus Celer, Q.
Lesbia, Clodia
as, cash
Catullus

6A(v)

Cyrene
plants
Battus
adultery
Catullus

6A(vi)

women, love

6A(vii)

India
comites
Arabia
Parthians, Parthia
Nile
Alps
Caesar
Rhine
Britain

6B Intro.

provincial government
Cilicia

Pompey
Caesar
Illyricum
Gaul
Spain
Crassus
triumvirate
Parthia
Carrhae

6B(i)

senatus consultum, decrees of the Senate
books

6B(ii)

Pompey
Caesar
Gaul
Gauls

6B(iii)

proconsuls
gladiators
aediles, curule
wild-beast hunts (*uenationes*)
games

6B(iv)

panthers
negotiatores, entrepreneurs

6B(v)

imperator, generals, commanders
imperium, power

6B(vi)

consulship
Roman army
Parthia
Rubicon

6B(vii)

Spain
Cicero
Pompey

6B(viii)

civil war
Pharsalus

6C Intro.

Pharsalus
Caesar
civil war

6C(i)

oratory
battles
dignitas, dignity
libertas, freedom

6C(ii)

weapons
cavalry
centurions
tribunes, military
silver-plate
luxury

6C(iii)

forts
senators

6C(iv)

Caesar
Egypt
Ptolemy
Cleopatra
Alexandria
Pompey
tribunes, military

6D Intro.

Greek literature
Roman literature
Catullus
Alexandria

Callimachus
metre
genre
imitatio, imitation
Lucretius
Virgil
Horace
Ovid

6D(i)

Lucretius
didactic
Hesiod
Epicurus, Epicureans
pietas, Roman virtues
sacrifice
gods

6D(ii)

Virgil
Sibyl
sculpture
astronomy
oratory
imperium, power

6D(iii)

Horace
Maecenas
clients, *clientes*
landowners/landed estates
Augustus
pietas, Roman virtues

6D(iv)

Menander
epigrams
Gallus
Propertius
Tibullus

ACKNOWLEDGEMENTS
FOR ILLUSTRATIONS

BMCCRR=H.A. Grueber, *Coins of the Roman Republic in the British Museum* (1910)
BMCCRE= H. Mattingly and R.A.G. Carson, *Coins of the Roman Empire in the British Museum* (1923–64)
DAIR=Deutsches Archäologisches Institut Rom
ICCD=Istituto Centrale per il Catalogo e la Documentazione, Rome

Frontispiece Rome, Vatican Museums (Museo Chiaramonti, Braccio Nuovo) 2290. R.J. Ling 97/13.

Chapter 1

1.1   ICCD E/33227.
1.2   British School at Rome. R.J. Ling 99/30.
1.3   Relief on a marble altar in Arezzo. Cast in Museo della Civiltà Romana, Rome. R.J. Ling 98/26.
1.4   Vasari, Rome, 11574.
1.5   Cast in Museo della Civiltà Romana, Rome. R.J. Ling 98/14 .
1.6   British Museum.
1.7   Wim Swaan.
1.8   Roger Wilson.
1.9   British School at Rome.
1.10   Copenhagen, Ny Carlsberg Glyptotek 597. Jo Selsing (courtesy Ny Carlsberg Glyptotek).
1.11   British Museum (*BMCCRR* Rome 4340).

Chapter 2

2.1   R.J. Ling 99/1.
2.2   DAIR 82.3640.
2.3   Photo R.J. Ling 85/4.
2.4   Drawing after P. Zanker, *Power of Images*, fig. 149.

2.5   R.J. Ling 83/5A-6A.
2.6   Cast in Museo della Civiltà Romana, Rome. R.J. Ling 98/17.
2.7   Paris, Louvre MA 1234. R.J. Ling 86/3.
2.8   British Museum (*BMCCRE* Claudius 32).
2.9   Funerary relief in Vatican, Museo Gregoriano Profano (9556). R.J. Ling 54/7A.
2.10   Drawing after W.J.T. Peters and P.G.P. Meyboom (British Archaeological Reports International Series 140, fig. 2.1).
2.11   Rome, National Museum of the Terme 330. DAIR 54.797.
2.12   R.J. Ling 95/28.
2.13   Paris, Louvre. R.J. Ling 86/4.
2.14   From the Roman fort at South Shields. Museum of Antiquities, University of Newcastle upon Tyne. Photo: Lindsay Allason-Jones.

Chapter 3

3.1   DAIR 79.2491.
3.2   Coin (*denarius*) minted by L. Vinicius (17–15 BC). British Museum (*BMCCRR* Rome 4477).
3.3   R.J. Ling 82/17.
3.4   Relief from the so-called Altar of Cn. Domitius Ahenobarbus (actually a statue-base), found in the area of the Temple of Neptune. Late second or first century BC. Paris, Louvre. Caisse Nationale des Monuments Historiques.
3.5   Rome, Palazzo dei Conservatori. DAIR 37.378.

Chapter 4

4.1   Coin (*denarius*) minted by P. Nerva (113 or 112 BC). British Museum (*BMCCRR* Italy 526).
4.2   Reliefs on Trajan's Column, Rome (scenes VIII-IX). AD 112–13. DAIR 73.1799.
4.3   Reliefs on Trajan's Column, Rome (scenes X-XI). AD 112–13. DAIR 91.154.
4.4   Reliefs on Trajan's Column, Rome (scene XXI). AD 112–13. DAIR 91.95.
4.5   First century BC. Rome, National Museum of the Terme. DAIR 32.412.
4.6   Rome, National Museum of the Terme 5623. R.J. Ling 100/33.

Chapter 5

5.1   Detail of a mosaic pavement in a villa at Bad Kreuznach (Rheinpfalz). Third century AD. R.J. Ling 72/31A.
5.2   Detail of a mosaic pavement in a villa at Nennig (Mosel). Third century AD. R.J. Ling 76/16.
5.3   R.J. Ling 98/3.

5.4   Painting in Pompeii VI 10,1 (room B). DAIR 31.1751.
5.5   DAIR 34.207.
5.6   Museo della Civiltà Romana, Rome. DAIR 73.1095.
5.7   R.J. Ling 99/4.
5.8   ICCD N/54129.
5.9   Mosaic pavement in the Piazzale delle Corporazioni, Ostia. R.J. Ling 96/17.
5.10   Mithraeum under the church of Santa Prisca in Rome. Early third century AD. Fototeca Unione 5284 F.
5.11   Painting from Herculaneum. Third quarter of first century AD. Naples, National Museum 8924. Katholieke Universiteit, Nijmegen (P. Bersch and H. van de Sluis).

Chapter 6

6.1   DAIR 58.3010.
6.2   Mosaic in the Piazzale delle Corporazioni, Ostia. R.J. Ling 96/5.
6.3   Fototeca Unione 3045.
6.4   Mosaic from Carthage, now in Tunis, Bardo Museum. Late fourth century AD. R.J. Ling 90/7.
6.5   Mosaic at Cherchel (Algeria). Early third century AD. DAIR 64.737.
6.6   Painting from the property of Julia Felix at Pompeii. Third quarter of first century AD. Naples, Archaeological Museum 9069. Soprintendenza Archeologica, Naples C 364.
6.7   Drawing after *Phoenix* 24 (1970), 340, fig. 2.
6.8   By permission of Vindolanda Trust and University of Newcastle upon Tyne.
6.9   Relief from a funerary monument at Neumagen (Mosel). Trier, Landesmuseum NM 739. R.J. Ling 71/20.
6.10   Rome, formerly Palazzo Massimo alle Colonne. DAIR 4656.
6.11   First century BC. CNRS (A. Chéné), Centre Camille Jullian.
6.12   R.J. Ling 94/30A.
6.13   Second half of the first century BC R.J. Ling 99/24.

Chapter 7

7.1   British Museum (*BMCCRR* East 34).
7.2   Vatican Museum, Sala dei Busti (592). DAIR 76.600.
7.3   DAIR 77.2132.
7.4   Drawing after E. La Rocca and M. and A. De Vos, *Guida archeologica di Pompei* (1976).
7.5   Pompeii, House of the Small Fountain. R.J. Ling 100/2.
7.6   House of the Menander, Pompeii. R.J. Ling (Pompeii Research Committee 93–4/33).
7.7   Rome, Torlonia Museum. DAIR 35.246.

7.8   Pompeii, House of the Lovers. R.J. Ling 100/11.
7.9   Pompeii (IX 1, 3). R.J. Ling 100/7.
7.10   Pompeii, Villa of the Mysteries. R.J. Ling 100/20.
7.11   Drawing after A. Boethius and J.B. Ward-Perkins, *Etruscan and Roman Architecture* (1970), fig. 111.

Chapter 8

8.1   Villa at Lullingstone, Kent. Mid fourth century AD. Photo M.B. Cookson (courtesy of National Monuments Record).
8.2   Relief from a funerary monument at Neumagen (Mosel). Trier, Landesmuseum NM 180. R.J. Ling 71/15.
8.3   Oxford, Ashmolean Museum 1962.37. Ashmolean Museum, Oxford K1176.
8.4   Inscribed bronze tablet in Lyon, Musée de la Civilisation Gallo-Romaine. C. Thioc, Musée de la Civilisation Gallo-Romaine de Lyon, Conseil Général du Rhône.
8.5   From Gabii (central Italy). Paris, Louvre Museum. R.J. Ling 86/18.
8.6   Ruth Westgate.
8.7   Triumphal relief on the Arch of Titus, Rome (soon after AD 81). DAIR 79.2494.
8.8   From the Villa of the Papyri at Herculaneum. Naples, National Museum 5465. DAIR 85.1476.
8.9   Rome, Palazzo del Senato. Mansell Collections.

Chapter 9

9.1   Naples, Archaeological Museum 9058. Soprintendenza Archeologica, Naples A 2819.
9.2   Roman Baths Museum. The size is 5.9×8.5 cm. Photo R.L. Wilkins (Institute of Archaeology, Oxford).
9.3   R.J. Ling 99/17.
9.4   Museo della Civiltà Romana, Rome. DAIR 73.998.
9.5   R.J. Ling 95/22.
9.6   Photo C.J. Eyre (courtesy of Egypt Exploration Society).
9.7   Scene of love-making on an Arretine bowl. Late first century BC. Oxford, Ashmolean Museum 1966.250. Ashmolean Museum, Oxford K1037.
9.8   From Pompeii. Naples, Archaeological Museum 9985. Soprintendenza Archeologica, Naples 5027, ex 1195.
9.9   Naples, National Museum 9009. Photo Anderson 23430.
9.10   Naples, National Museum 9488. Third quarter of first century AD. DAIR 59.2003.
9.11   Mosaic from Sousse, now in Tunis, Bardo Museum. Early third century AD. DAIR 61.548.

Chapter 10

10.1   Athens, National Museum 1828. Wim Swaan.
10.2   DAIR 59.128.
10.3   R.J. Ling 80/3A.
10.4   Roger Wilson.
10.5   Rome, National Museum of the Terme 1184. R.J. Ling 100/37.
10.6   Villa of the Poppaei at Oplontis, room 15. E. Hyman and P. Chorley.
10.7   House of the Anchor. After F. and F. Niccolini, *Le case ed i monumenti di Pompei* (1854–96).
10.8   Vienna, Kunsthistorisches Museum IX A 79.
10.9   R.J. Ling 94/33A.
10.10   From a villa outside Rome. Vatican Museum, Braccio Nuovo. R.J. Ling 97/10.
10.11   Vatican Museum. R.J. Ling 99/28.

Epilogue

Ep.1   R.J. Ling 82/5.
Ep.2   After A. Palladio, *I quattro libri dell'architettura* (1570).
Ep.3   Warburg Institute.
Ep.4   National Gallery of Ireland, Dublin 763.
Ep.5   After Gorcinny and Uderzo, *Astérix chez les Bretons* (1966).

INDEX AND GLOSSARY
OF LATIN TERMS

This index contains all the Latin (and Greek) words and short phrases used in the text and Appendix 2, together with a literal translation and references to each occurrence by paragraph number for text and by App. 2 (author) for Appendix 2. Longer quotations and titles of works are translated in the text and Appendix 2 where they occur, and are not repeated here. For information about Latin textbooks, the formation of plurals, and consonantal -*u*-, see Notes 3 and 4 (p. xvii).

de facto: 'actual'   138
defixio/-nes: 'curse'   415
dendrophori (G): lit. 'tree-bearers'   268
deliciae: 'favourite'   351
denarius/-i: 'denarius' (unit of coinage)   420
de repetundis: 'about getting back (sc. money wrongfully obtained)'   184
dictator (=*dictator rei gerundae causa*)
    'dictator' ('dictator for the purpose of governing the state')   15, 73, 134–5, 136
dictator perpetuus: 'perpetual dictator'   73
dignitas: 'dignity', 'status'   411, App. 2 (Caesar)
dignitas sumptuosa: 'costly status'   279
diuisores: 'distributors'   142
doctrina: 'learning'   445
domi: 'at home'   327
dominus/-e: 'master'   329, 352
domus: 'house'   338, 352
domus aurea: 'Golden House'   99
dulce: 'sweet', 'pleasant'   433
dulcissima: 'sweetest'   344
duouir: 'duovir' (local magistrate)   268

ejaculatio praecox: 'premature ejaculation'   501
Epistulae: 'letters', 'epistles'   406, 407
error: 'mistake'   App. 2 (Ovid)
eques/equites: 'knight', 'cavalryman'   93, 140, 159, 161, 191, 192
Europa: 'Europe'   501
exempli gratia: 'for (the sake of an) example'   501

facio: 'I make/do'   503
factio: 'faction'   69
familia: 'household'   302
familiaris/-es: 'intimate friend'   329
fasces: 'bundle of rods'   130, 131, 134, 158
fauces: lit. 'throat' ('entrance passage to a house')   327
feriae Latinae: 'Latin holidays'   204. 205
Fidei Defensor: 'Defender of the Faith'   501
fideicommissum: 'trust'   320
fides: 'oath'   279
    'trustworthiness'   442
filiusfamilias: 'son-of-the-household', 'son-in-power'   310
fores: 'doors'   327
foris: 'out of doors'   327
formula: 'formula'   403
forum: 'market-place'   138
Forum Augustum: 'Forum of Augustus'   475, 479
forum piscatorium: 'fish market-place'   294
forum uinarium: 'wine market-place'   294

GENERAL INDEX

This index is an index of topics, except that it includes names of tribes/peoples, some wars and festivals.

For names of places and buildings, consult the Topographical Index and for names of individuals and gods, consult the Index of Personal Names. References are to paragraph numbers.

191, 238

praetors (*praetores*)/praetorship, 15, 30, 32, 52, 69, 97, 130, 132–3, 135, 137, 138, 140, 142, 145, 147, 148, 150, 152, 158, 164, 165, 168, 169, 170, 178, 180, 187, 403, App. 2 (Pliny, Sallust, Tacitus)

prayers, 81, 85, 243, 246, 258, App. 2 (Menander Rhetor)

prefects (*praefectus*), 107, App. 2 (Cassiodorus)

price: control, 48, 138; inflation, 283; variation, 283

priesthoods, 16, 19, 366

priests (*pontifex/pontifices*), 46, 86, 255, 360, 365, 406, App. 2 (Apuleius)

principate, *see* emperors

prison, 91, 210, 211

prisoners (of war), 125

privilege, 207–18

processional reliefs, *see* reliefs

processions, 124, 304, 468, 473, 476, 482, 485; *see also* parades, triumphs

proconsuls/proconsular power, 52, 79, 147, 150, 154, 169, 183, 187

procurator (*procurator*), 268

production and consumption, 268–300, 462

profit(ability), 240, 277, 279, 280, 287, 292, 299, 300, 333, 404

pro-magistrates, 123, 145, 150, 151, 152, 154, 155, 169, 171, 172, 173, 185, 187, 189, 285

propaganda , 86, 91; visual, 473, 474, 475–8, 481–2, 484–7, 490–1

property, 58, 59, 91, 132, 140, 147, 160, 173, 192, 214, 276, 279, 280, 292, 310, 312, 314, 317, 320, 321, 322, 324, 406, 413

property-groupings (*classes*), 52, 140, 160, 173, 175, 176, 278

prophecy / prophetic inspiration, 107, 434

pro-praetors, *see* pro-magistrates

prorogation, 150, 151

proscriptions, 58, 59, 74, 76, 184

prosecutors/prosecutions, 46, 49, 51, 71, 91, 93, 100, 137, 222, 279, 324, 404, App. 2 (Apuleius, Gallus, Sallust); *see also* majesty, trials

prostitution, 227

provinces, 19, 30, 32, 39, 44, 46, 48, 70, 71, 72, 75, 79, 81, 82, 84, 88, 101, 108, 109, 113,

128, 133, 141, 147, 150, 151, 152, 172, 178–84, 185, 186, 189, 191, 192, 194, 238, 241, 285, 374–7, 380, 409, 411, 414, 415, 462, 476, 484, 488, App. 2 (Apuleius); *see also* governors, staff

provincials, 48, 73, 74, 109, 110, 184, 376, 383, 409

provincial government, 44, 68, 73, 179–84, 407

public buildings, 5, 8, 42, 73, 106, 112, 141, 217, 466, 470, 478, 480, 493; *see also* architecture

public finance(s)/financing, 15, 140, 141, 181, 192, 193, 222, 223, 241, 244, 322, 361, 466; *see also* finance

public meetings, 200, 280

public works, 8, 141

publicans *see* tax-collectors

Punic Wars, 132, 133, 135, 178, 292

punishment of Roman citizens, 1, 130; *see also* execution

purification, 139, 259

pyramids, 107

Pythia, 244

quaestors (*quaestores*)/quaestorship, 15, 59, 136, 138, 141, 142, 145, 164, 165, 167, 168, 178, 181, 189, 192, 268, App. 2 (Seneca)

queens, App. 2 (Virgil)

race, 235

reading and writing, 43, 369, 416, 422, 428–34

rebellion, *see* uprisings *and* conspiracy

re-election, *see* election(s)

Register of Triumphs (*Fasti triumphales*), 11, 27

relationships, *see* emotional relationships, marriage

reliefs, 86, 378, 462, 473, 474, 476, 482, 485, 486, 490, 491

religion, 9, 16, 24, 69, 116, 120, 122, 123, 126, 137, 139, 197, 224, 254–67, 282, 318, 359, 360–6, 375, 380–4, 389, 391, 392, 461, 464, 465, 490, App. 2 (Apuleius, Catullus, Horace, Livy, Virgil); *see also* auspices, cult, myth, prayers, priests, shrines, temples

Renaissance, 270, 300, 371, 443, 483, 489, 497,

TOPOGRAPHICAL INDEX

This list contains the place-names and the names of buildings and monuments mentioned in the text and Appendix 2. Names of individuals and gods are to be found in the Index of Personal Names and those of tribes/peoples in the General Index. The majority of the places mentioned here can be found on maps 1–5. For further geographical information about the Roman world, *see* N.G.L. Hammond, *Atlas of the Greek and Roman World in Antiquity*, Park Ridge, NJ, 1981. References are to paragraph numbers.

INDEX OF PERSONAL NAMES

This index contains only the names of individuals, familes and gods. For names of tribes, philosophical schools, wines etc., *see* General Index. For buildings or monuments, see Topographical Index. Where a Latin name appears in brackets, see also Index and Glossary of Latin Terms. Names of emperors in Appendix 1 do not appear here unless they are in the text. Reference to Appendix 2 (Latin and Greek writers) is not given unless it is to another name under their entry. The abbreviation (E) signifies an Emperor, (K) a king, (Q) a queen. References are to paragraph numbers.

Roman names are listed under the *nomen* (see Notes, p. xvi, 2), unless the person is generally referred to by one of the other names. In these cases (e.g. Caesar, Cicero, Gaius (E)), the name is listed under the most familar form.

INDEX OF PASSAGES

This list includes all general references (e.g. Apuleius *Metamorphoses*) to works in the main text and all specific references (e.g. Martial 1.103.10) in text, Appendix 2, and captions to illustrations. All references are located by paragraph number in the text, by App. 2 (author) in Appendix 2, and by fig. (no.) for illustrations. For more information about writers and their works, consult Appendix 2.